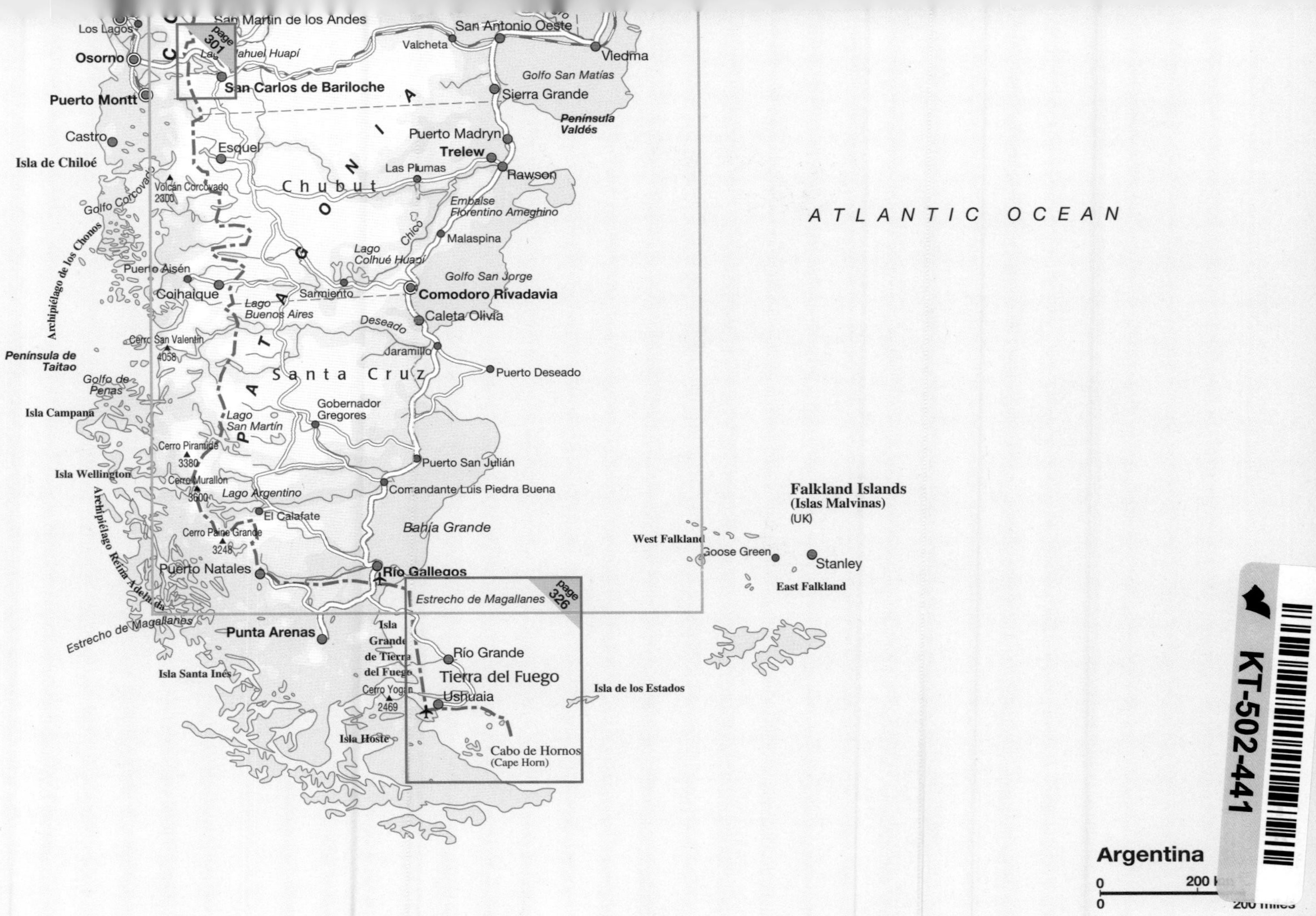

Argentina

200 miles

200 km

0

0

ATLANTIC OCEAN

Falkland Islands
(Islas Malvinas)
(UK)

Stanley

East Falkland

Goose Green

West Falkland

Isla de los Estados

Viedma

San Antonio Oeste

Golfo San Matías

Sierra Grande

Península Valdés

Valcheta

Puerto Madryn

Rawson

Trelew

Embalse Florentino Ameghino

Las Plumas

Chico

Las Plumas

Malaspina

Golfo San Jorge

Comodoro Rivadavia

Caleta Olivia

Puerto Deseado

San Martín de los Andes

Nahuel Huapi

Lago

San Carlos de Bariloche

page 301

Esquel

Volcán Onichdao 2800

Lago Colhué Huapi

Sarmiento

Sarmiento

Deseado

Jaramillo

Santa Cruz

Puerto San Julián

Comandante Luis Piedra Buena

Bahía Grande

Estrecho de Magallanes

page 326

Río Gallegos

Río Grande

Tierra del Fuego

Ushuaia

Cabo de Hornos
(Cape Horn)

Isla Hoste

Cerro Yogán 2469

Isla Grande de Tierra del Fuego

Punta Arenas

Puerto Natales

El Calafate

Lago Argentino

Lago San Martín

Cerro Piramide 3380

Lago Buenos Aires

Gobernador Gregores

Cerro Murallón 3600

Cerro Pique Grande 3248

Coihaique

Puerto Aisén

Cerro San Valentín 4058

Golfo de Penas

Isla Wellington

Isla Campana

Península de Taitao

Archipiélago de los Chonos

Estrecho de Magallanes

Archipiélago Reina Adelaida

Isla Santa Inés

Los Lagos

Osorno

Puerto Montt

Castro

Isla de Chiloé

Golfo Corcovado

CHUBUT

Chubut

INSIGHT GUIDES

ARGENTINA

DISCOVERY CHANNEL

APA PUBLICATIONS

Part of the Langenscheidt Publishing Group

L

INSIGHT GUIDE
argentina

ABOUT THIS BOOK

Editorial
Project Editor
Rachel Lawrence
Editorial Director
Brian Bell

Distribution

United States
Langenscheidt Publishers, Inc.
36–36 33rd Street 4th Floor
Long Island City, NY 11106
Fax: 1 (718) 784 0640

UK & Ireland
GeoCenter International Ltd
Meridian House, Churchill Way West
Basingstoke, Hampshire RG21 6YR
Fax: (44) 1256 817988

Australia
Universal Publishers
1 Waterloo Road
Macquarie Park, NSW 2113
Fax: (61) 2 9888 9074

New Zealand
Hema Maps New Zealand Ltd (HNZ)
Unit D, 24 Ra ORA Drive
East Tamaki, Auckland
Fax: (64) 9 273 6479

Worldwide
**Apa Publications GmbH & Co.
Verlag KG (Singapore branch)**
38 Joo Koon Road, Singapore 628990
Tel: (65) 6865 1600. Fax: (65) 6861 6438

Printing

Insight Print Services (Pte) Ltd
38 Joo Koon Road, Singapore 628990
Tel: (65) 6865 1600. Fax: (65) 6861 6438

©2007 Apa Publications GmbH & Co.
Verlag KG (Singapore branch)
All Rights Reserved
First Edition 1988
Fourth Edition (updated) 2007

The first Insight Guide pioneered the use of creative full-color photography in travel guides in 1970. Since then, we have expanded our range to cater for our readers' need not only for reliable information about their chosen destination but also for a real understanding of the culture and workings of that destination. Now, when the internet can supply inexhaustible (but not always reliable) facts, our books marry text and pictures to provide those much more elusive qualities: knowledge and discernment. To achieve this, they rely heavily on the authority of locally based writers and photographers.

How to use this book

Insight Guide: Argentina is struc-
tured to convey an understanding of
the country and its culture and to
guide readers through its sights
and activities.

◆ The **Features** section, indicated
by a yellow bar at the top of each
page, covers the country's
history, culture, and
people in a series of
informative essays.

◆ The main **Places**
section, indicated by
a blue bar, is a

complete guide to all the sights and areas worth visiting. Places of special interest are coordinated by number with the maps.

◆ The **Travel Tips** listings section, with an orange bar, at the back of the book, provides a handy point of reference for information on travel, hotels, shops, restaurants, and more.

The contributors

This edition was supervised by **Huw Hennessy**, building on material written in the previous edition by writers **Deirdre Ball**, **Elena Decima**, **Philip Benson**, **Tony Perrottet**, **Federico Kirbus**, and **Parry Jones**. The history arti-

cles were revised and updated by **Nick Caistor**, journalist and former Latin America Editor at the BBC World Service. The majority of the Places section was updated by **Jill Hedges**, with information on Tierra del Fuego supplied by **Caroline Mouzo**, who lives in Ushuaia. **Fiona Anderson**, a writer who lived for six years in Bariloche, updated the Patagonia chapter and also wrote new features on The National Identity, Food and Wine, and Outdoor Adventure.

Latin dance expert **Shannon Shiell** updated the Tango article and also wrote about other music and dance in Argentina. Natural history writer **David Burnie** revised the feature on Wild Argentina, as well as writing the color feature on Patagonian wildlife.

For this new and updated version of *Insight Guide: Argentina*, **Nick Caistor** further revised and updated the History, Features, and Places sections, building on the work he did on previous versions of the book. He also wrote the features on Argentine Writers, New Argentine Cinema, and A Tango Tour of Buenos Aires. **Ana Caistor-Arendar**, a freelance editor and journalist based in Buenos Aires, updated the Travel Tips section and wrote the box feature on Latin Beats.

Many of the photographs were taken by **Eduardo Gil**, with others by **Volkmar Janicke** and **Mireille Vautier**. The book was indexed by **Malcolm Henley** and proofread by **Sylvia Suddes**.

This version was commissioned by **Alyse Dar** and edited by **Rachel Lawrence**.

Map Legend

▬ ▪ ▪	International Boundary
– – – –	Province Boundary
⊖	Border Crossing
▬ ▪ ▬	National Park/Reserve
– – – –	Ferry Route
Ⓜ	Metro
✈ ✈	Airport: International/Regional
🚌	Bus Station
🅿	Parking
❶	Tourist Information
✉	Post Office
✝ ✝ ✝	Church/Ruins
✝	Monastery
☾	Mosque
✡	Synagogue
🏰 🏯	Castle/Ruins
∴	Archeological Site
∩	Cave
⌶	Statue/Monument
★	Place of Interest

The main places of interest in the Places section are coordinated by number with a full-color map (e.g. ❶), and a symbol at the top of every right-hand page tells you where to find the map.

INSIGHT GUIDE
argentina

CONTENTS

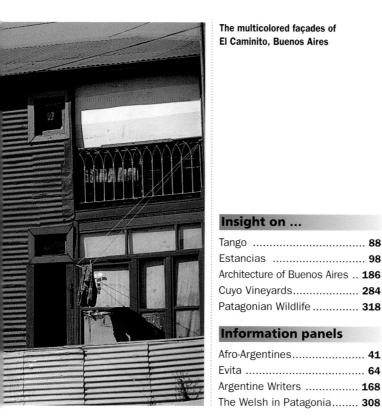

The multicolored façades of
El Caminito, Buenos Aires

THE BEST OF ARGENTINA

From natural wonders to estancias, and adventure sports to art galleries...

here, at a glance, are our recommendations, plus some tips

that even Argentines won't always know

BEST ADVENTURE TOURISM

- **White-water rafting** in the Atuel Canyon near Mendoza.
- **Trekking** near El Chaltén, around the lakes and glaciers of Parque Nacional Los Glaciares.
- **Snowboarding** at Las Leñas in Mendoza province, South America's top winter sports resort.
- **Off-road exploration** around the Salinas Grandes salt flats in Jujuy province.
- **Whale watching** off Península Valdés, Argentina's number-one wildlife spot.
- **Horseback riding** in the hills of the Lake District, Patagonia.
- **Climbing** Cerro Catedral or Monte Tronador in Parque Nacional Nahuel Huapi near Bariloche.
- **Cross-country skiing** in the mountains around Ushuaia.

ONLY IN ARGENTINA

- **Iguazú Falls** Situated on the border between Argentina and Brazil, these are some of the most spectacular waterfalls in the world, with 275 cascades spanning over 2.5 km (1½ miles). *Page 235*
- **Quebrada de Humahuaca** The beautiful valley of rock in Northwest Argentina which was once part of the Camino Inca and is now a UNESCO World Heritage Site. *Page 261*
- **Mount Aconcagua** The tallest peak in the Andes, and the second-highest mountain outside the Himalayas. *Page 277*
- **Perito Moreno glacier** in the southern Lake District. Seeing huge lumps of ice break off this enormous glacier is an unforgettable experience. *Page 315*
- **Ushuaia** The world's southernmost city and the jumping-off point for trips to Antarctica. *Page 329*
- **La Boca** The lively Buenos Aires neighborhood settled by Italian immigrants in the 19th century, which is famous for its brightly colored buildings. *Page 161*

ABOVE: the magnificent Iguazú Falls.
LEFT: hiking up to Mount Fitz Roy.

ARGENTINA'S MELTING POT

Here are some of the places where the different communities and nationalities that make up modern-day Argentina have made their mark.

- **Tilcara** This village in the Quebrada de Humahuaca offers visitors a good insight into traditional indigenous life.
Page 261
- **El Bolsón** A little corner of Alpine Europe nestled in the mountains of Río Negro province.
Page 303

- **Formosa** Capital of Argentina's northeast region, the town of Formosa is close in spirit to Paraguay and Brazil.
- **Trelew** In Chubut province, this is the only place outside Wales to hold an annual Eisteddfod.
Page 306
- **The Hurlingham Club** A prestigious country club in Buenos Aires, named after one in London, and a center for BA's Anglo-Argentine community.

BEST ESTANCIAS

Here is a selection of some of the most picturesque estancias in Argentina. *(See also page 346.)*
- **Estancia Villa María** Luxury estancia designed by Alejandro Bustillo, located just 50 km (30 miles) from Buenos Aires.
- **El Ombú de Areco** Historical estancia set in beautiful grounds near San Antonio de Areco in Buenos Aires province.

- **El Rincón de Cobo** Coastal estancia near Pinamar, Buenos Aires province, offering horseback riding and fishing.
- **La Demasiada** Working estancia with Aberdeen Angus cattle, near Balcarce in Buenos Aires province.
- **Finca la Falda** Charming estancia on the way to the Valles Calchaquíes in Salta province.

BEST OF BEEF

Here are some of the best cuts of Argentine beef. Order yours *jugoso* (rare), *a punto* (medium), or *bien hecho* (well done).
- *Bife de lomo* Tenderloin, the most expensive and tenderest cut of all.
- *Bife de chorizo* Not, as the name might suggest, a type of sausage, but a sirloin or porterhouse steak.

- *Bife de Costilla* T-bone steak. You'll need a good appetite to finish one of these enormous steaks.
- *Tira de asado* Juicy, flavorful rib roast.

TOP: rustic luxury at Estancia La Demasiada.
ABOVE: the finest steak you'll ever taste.
LEFT: catching up on the local gossip in Trelew.

BEST FESTIVALS

Here are some of Argentina's most exciting festivals. *(See also Calendar of Festivals and Events, page 353.)*

● **Fiesta de la Vendimia** Wine festival held in Mendoza at the end of February.

● **World Tango Festival** Held every two years in October in Buenos Aires.

● **Festival Internacional de Ushuaia** Festival of music, dance, and theater, every April.

● **Festival de Cosquín** Argentina's most traditional folk music festival, held every January.

● **International Guitars Festival** Month-long guitar festival in Buenos Aires during October.

BEST FOOD AND DRINK

● **Empanadas** Tasty pasties with many different fillings.

● **Locro** The filling meat and corn soup of the northern regions.

● **Matambre** A meat roll or "hunger-killer."

● **Dulce de leche** The ubiquitous super-sweet spread.

● **Alfajores** Cookies sandwiched together with *dulce de leche* and smothered in chocolate or sugar.

● **Maté** The refreshing, but bitter herbal drink that is very much an acquired taste.

BEST NATIONAL PARKS

● **Parque Nacional Mburucuyá** in Corrientes province with *quebracho* forests and an abundance of wildlife. *Page 232*

● **Parque Nacional Los Cardones** in Salta province. Protects endangered cacti. *Page 254*

● **Parque Nacional Talampaya** A UNESCO World Heritage site in La Rioja province. Includes important archeological and paleontological sites. *Page 283*

● **Parque Nacional Lanín**, near San Martín de los Andes. Named for the Lanín volcano; great fishing. *Page 297*

● **Parque Nacional Los Alerces** near Esquel, Patagonia and home to Fitzroya trees. *Page 304*

● **Parque Nacional Los Glaciares**, southern Patagonia. Home of the Perito Moreno glacier and the Fitz Roy mountain range. *Page 314*

● **Parque Nacional Tierra del Fuego** Coastal reserve near Ushuaia with southern beech forests; great for birdwatching. *Page 331*

ABOVE: celebrating the grape harvest in Mendoza. **LEFT:** maté gourds. **BELOW:** the majestic Perito Moreno glacier.

ARGENTINA FOR FAMILIES

- **La República de los Niños**, La Plata. Argentina's answer to Disneyworld. *Page 193*
- **Parque de la Costa** Take the Tren de la Costa to this amusement park in Tigre. *Page 190*
- **Museo de los Niños** Interactive museum for children aged 3–12, in the Mercado de Abasto shopping center in Buenos Aires. *Page 356*
- **Wildlife watching on Península Valdés** A wonderful opportunity to see penguins, seals, sea lions, and thousands of different birds along the shore or go on a whale watching boat trip. *Page 307*
- **Outdoor Activities in the Lake District** Watersports, cycling, and horseback riding in the summer, and snowboarding and skiing in the winter. *Pages 357–359*
- **Tren del Fin del Mundo** Train that travels from just outside Ushuaia into the Tierra del Fuego National Park. *Page 330*

BEST MUSEUMS AND GALLERIES

- **Museo Nacional de Bellas Artes**, Buenos Aires. Argentina's most impressive fine art museum, which includes paintings by Renoir, Monet, and Rembrandt. *Page 180*
- **Museo de Arte Latinoamericano de Buenos Aires** (MALBA) This stylish, purpose-built gallery in Palermo houses an impressive collection from the early 20th century to the present day. *Page 181*
- **Museo Evita**, Buenos Aires. Details the life of Eva Perón through artifacts, photographs, and film, as well as exquisite items from her wardrobe. *Page 65*
- **Museo Mundo Yamana**, Ushuaia. Interesting scale models depict the way of life of the Yamana people who once inhabited Tierra del Fuego. *Page 331*
- **Museo Casa Ernesto Che Guevara**, Alta Gracia. A small but interesting museum containing artifacts relating to the life of "El Che." *Page 224*
- **Museo Arqueología de Alta Montaña**, Salta. Houses the remains of three Inca children found frozen at the peak of Mount Llullaillaco in 1999. *Page 257*

TOP TIPS FOR TRAVELERS

Check, check, and check again: Always check whether you need to reconfirm your coach/plane/boat ticket before departure. Bus companies, especially in more remote areas, may allocate your seat to someone else unless you confirm your return journey and it is always advisable to reconfirm domestic and international flights 24 hours before departure.

Enjoy the view: If flying south from Bariloche to El Calafate or from El Calafate to Ushuaia, request a seat on the right-hand side of the airplane in order to catch a glimpse of the Patagonian Andes poking up through the clouds.

Get your tax back: Look out for the "Global Refund" stickers in shop windows, particularly in large cities. This scheme allows foreign tourists to claim back most of the tax on products costing more than US$70. *(For more information, see page 356.)*

Stay up late: Don't even think about going out to eat before 9pm, unless you want to be sat in an empty restaurant. Argentines tend to dine late and party even later, with most bars open until the early hours.

Learn Spanish: While you're likely to meet a lot of Argentines who speak impressively good English (or indeed Italian, German, or French), it pays to at least learn the basics. Argentines enjoy a chat and you won't have much difficulty finding people to test your language skills on.

BIENVENIDOS

Argentina, South America's second-largest country, is opening up to foreign tourists

The welcome in Argentina is as big and warm as the country itself. Its landscapes range from the subtropical north inside the Tropic of Capricorn, with the spectacular waterfalls of Iguazú on the border with Brazil and Paraguay, to the dry uplands of the Andean mountains, where Argentina is most like its northerly neighbors of Bolivia and Peru.

Then there are the vast flat grasslands of the pampas, where thousands of cattle still roam almost at will, and mile upon mile of fertile crops, and where the horse is often still the best way to get around. To the west lie the Andes and Aconcagua, the tallest peak on the American continent. Further south, there are the unspoilt lakes and glaciers of Patagonia, as well as the penguin colonies and whale-watching spots around Península Valdés. At the tip of the mainland lies the island of Tierra del Fuego, which has its own bleak charms, and Ushuaia, the world's southernmost town and the departure point for Antarctica.

Wherever you travel in Argentina, it is the people you meet who will make you feel most welcome. In the north and in Patagonia, many of the locals remain close to the original inhabitants. In Patagonia you might also meet descendants of Welsh, German, or other European immigrants, while all over the country there are people of Spanish and Italian origin, often living in small, whitewashed towns around a central Spanish-style square. The provincial capitals too, from modern Mendoza in the west to colonial Salta and Córdoba in the north, each have their own distinctive character.

But nowhere is the welcome warmer than in the Argentine capital, Buenos Aires. An extraordinary sight from the airplane as it rises from the flat expanse of sea and pampas, it is even more fascinating once you have landed. The 12 million inhabitants of this cosmopolitan city have created a culture all of their own. Whether you want to dance tango, watch a soccer match, or go to the opera, or simply enjoy some sightseeing, eating in a fine restaurant, or chatting in a cafe, Buenos Aires has everything to offer. Make sure that you meet some of the *porteños* (inhabitants of the port) along the way: they will make you feel truly welcome in this proud and often surprising land. ❏

PRECEDING PAGES: the Perito Moreno Glacier, southern Patagonia; riding up to the south face of Aconcagua.
LEFT: a gaucho in the making.

FROM JUNGLES TO GLACIERS

Its enormous latitude span gives Argentina a dramatically varied landscape, from windswept southern steppe to the subtropical north

Argentina is a land of many riches, but silver is not one of them. This is something that the early Spanish explorers did not know when they gave the country its name (*argentum* is the Latin name for silver). Although great quantities of the precious ore were discovered in Bolivia and Peru to the north, it was here that the name stuck.

Present-day Argentina is an enormous country, the eighth largest in the world and the second largest (in population and area) in South America, after Brazil. It is made up of 23 provinces, one of which includes part of Tierra del Fuego, several South Atlantic islands and a 49-degree wedge of Antarctica which ends at the South Pole. However, the Antarctic sector overlaps with claims by Chile and Great Britain, and the South Atlantic islands in question (Falklands/Malvinas) are currently under British control.

Disputed territories aside, Argentina covers an area of nearly 2.8 million sq. km (1.1 million sq. miles). The islands and Antarctic land together cover an additional 1.2 million sq. km (480,000 sq. miles). The country is 3,500 km (2,170 miles) long and 1,400 km (868 miles) across at its widest point.

As one might expect, a country covering this much terrain has a great diversity of topography and climate. While most of Argentina lies within the temperate zone of the Southern Hemisphere, the climate ranges from tropical in the north to subantarctic in the south. In general, Argentina's climate is moderated by the proximity of the oceans on either side of the continental landmass, and the towering barrier of the Andes to the west also plays an important part. This diversity of environments has endowed Argentina with a broad spectrum of plant and animal life.

The country can be divided roughly into six

PRECEDING PAGES: sunset over Mount Aconcagua, South America's highest peak (6,980 meters/23,034 ft).
LEFT: husband and wife in the Northwest.
RIGHT: the high-flying Andean condor.

geographical zones: the fertile central pampas, the marshy Mesopotamia in the Northeast, the forested Chaco region of the central north, the high plateau of the Northwest, the mountainous west, and the windy steppe of Patagonia. These areas include everything from steamy subtropical jungles to glaciers and snow-capped mountains.

Grassy heartland

The pampas are, perhaps, the terrain for which Argentina is best known. These fertile alluvial plains were once the home of the legendary gaucho (cowboy), and today they are the base for a large percentage of the nation's wealth.

These grasslands cover much of central Argentina, stretching south, west, and north in a radius of 970 km (600 miles) from the city of Buenos Aires. Argentines boast of the richness of the pampean earth – some saying the topsoil reaches a depth of 2 meters (6 ft), others that it is as deep as 5 meters (16 ft).

The pampas have two subdivisions: the

humid pampa *(pampa húmeda)* and the dry pampa *(pampa seca)*. The humid pampa lies in the easterly part of the country, mostly in the province of Buenos Aires. This wetter area supports much of the nation's agriculture: grains, primarily wheat and soya, are grown here. The humid pampa is also the heart of the cattle industry. The grass-feeding of cattle gives Argentine beef its celebrated flavor. The pampas' development took a large leap with the British building of a railroad system during the late 19th century and the importing of British cattle breeds.

Virtually all the *pampa húmeda* has been carved up and cultivated. Many of Argentina's landowners have their estancias here, properties which often run to hundreds of thousands of hectares. The dry pampa lies further to the west, where the Andes help bring about a less humid environment.

Sierras and rivers

The smoothness of the pampas is broken up at several points by low-lying sierras. The major ranges are the Sierra de Tandil and the Sierra de la Ventana in the east, and several parallel ranges in the central provinces of Córdoba and San Luis.

A BARREN LAND

There is little vegetation that is native to the pampas. In some areas there is a fine grass that grows low, while in other places there are tall, coarse grasses mixed with low scrub. The only tree that grew here as a native, the ombú, is not even really a tree; it's a weed. Although it grows to a substantial size, its moist fibers are useless as fuel for burning. Historically, its most useful function was to provide shade for tired gauchos as they rested beneath its branches to sip their maté tea. Over the years, many non-indigenous plants have been brought in. Tall rows of trees serving as windbreaks are everywhere and break the monotony of the landscape.

The Río de la Plata (River Plate) basin has as its tributaries more than six major rivers, among them the Paraná, the Uruguay, and the Paraguay. It drains a huge area of South America, including eastern Bolivia, most of Paraguay and Uruguay, and a large part of southern Brazil.

The Río de la Plata basin finds its outlet in the Río de la Plata estuary, the mouth of which lies just northwest of Buenos Aires. The delta area of the river is laced with countless small waterways which have created a unique marshy ecosystem. The major port of Buenos Aires was developed along the marshy banks of the estuary, but constant dredging is needed to keep the channels free from silt deposits.

Subtropical forests

The isolated northeast area of Argentina is referred to as Mesopotamia, as most of it lies between the Paraná and Uruguay rivers. The whole area is crosscut by rivers and streams, and much of the land is marshy and low, receiving a lot of rainfall.

The southern sector, with its swamps and low, rolling hills, has an economy supported by sheep farming, horse breeding, and cattle raising. This is one of the major wool-producing areas of the country.

Toward the north, the climate becomes subtropical and very humid. The economy in the north is based on agriculture, with the principal crops being a form of tea, yerba maté *(see page 130),* and various types of fruit. Enormous tracts of virgin forest have been lost to a lumber business that has become increasingly important to the Argentine economy.

Toward the northern tip of Misiones province in the Northeast, a plateau of sandstone and basalt rises from the lowlands. The landscape here is characterized by a rough relief combined with fast-running rivers. Straddling the northern border with Brazil are the magnificent Iguazú Falls *(see pages 235–236),* which have more than 275 separate cascades, falling more than 60 meters (200 ft) through the lush subtropical forest.

The hunting ground

North-central Argentina is called the Chaco. It is the southern sector of the Gran Chaco, which extends into Bolivia, Paraguay, and Brazil, and which borders on the north with Brazil's Mato Grosso region. In the local dialect, *chaco* means "hunting ground," and across this wide, empty region there are many animals to justify the name.

The area is covered by flat jungle plains, marshland, and palm groves in the east, and

> ### THE TREE OF LIFE
>
> One of the Chaco's main economic activities is the harvesting of the *quebracho* tree, which has a resin used in the tanning of leather. Fine leathers are a major by-product of the cattle industry in Argentina.

by drier savanna to the west; the climate ranges from the tropical to the subtropical. The Chaco lies within the Río de la Plata river basin, and although it is dry throughout most of the year, the torrential summer rains cause extensive flooding.

Forests in this area contain high-quality hardwoods, and lumbering is a major industry. Most of the cleared areas of the forest are used for cattle ranching, but cotton and other crops, such as sunflowers, maize, and soya are also planted.

High desert and mountains

Going west from the Chaco, you reach the plateau region of the Northwest, where the bordering Andes create an arid or semi-arid environment over much of the terrain. Here the elevation rises steadily until it reaches the Altiplano (high plateau) on Argentina's northern border with Bolivia. Along this stretch, the Andes are divided into two parallel *cordilleras* (ranges), the Salta-Jujeña to the west and the Sierra Subandina to the east.

The Puna is a dry, cold desert that stretches over the Andes north from the province of Catamarca toward Bolivia and covers part of

LEFT: Lago Argentino, Santa Cruz province.
RIGHT: toco toucan, from the subtropical Northeast.

northern Chile as well. Here the population, largely of mestizo (Amerindian-Hispanic) descent, raises goats, sheep, and llamas.

Further to the east, the barometer swings dramatically once more as the climate across much of the provinces of Tucumán, Salta, and Jujuy becomes mountain tropical, with mild winters. Along with cattle ranching, there are vineyards, olive and citrus groves, and tobacco and sugar-cane plantations. Vegetable farms lie in the valleys and piedmonts.

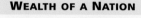

WEALTH OF A NATION

The Cuyo area is blessed with mineral wealth. Copper, lead, and uranium are mined, and oil discovered here and in Patagonia has made Argentina nearly self-sufficient in that vital resource.

eroded, and dotted with scrub vegetation. Rivers nourished by the melting snows of the Andes cut through the desert.

It is these same rivers which, with the help of an extensive irrigation system, allow for large-scale agriculture in the region. The Cuyo is the heart of Argentina's wine country; the arid climate, sandy soil, and year-round sunshine provide the ideal conditions for viticulture (see page 131). Citrus fruits are also grown here.

Open steppe

South of the Río Colorado, covering more than a quarter of Argentina, is Patagonia, where a series of dry plateaus drop from the Andes toward the rugged cliffs of the Atlantic coast.

The Patagonian Andes are lower than those to the north, and are scattered with lakes, meadows, and glaciers. Many of the slopes are forested. The central steppes are battered by sharp winds, and toward the south these winds become nearly constant. The terrain has been eroded by these winds as well as by rivers and glaciers.

In the low, wide river valleys of northern Patagonia, fruit and vegetable farming is made possible with irrigation. Toward the south, the rivers run through deep, flat-bottomed canyons. But although there is rainfall throughout most of the year, the climate is cold and doesn't lend itself to successful vegetation. The plains are covered by grasses, shrubs, and a few hardy trees. The harshness of the land means that sheep raising is the major economic activity.

To the south, between the Strait of Magellan and the Beagle Channel, lies Tierra del Fuego. The climate here is subantarctic, and although that sounds rather intimidating, it could be worse, given the latitude. The nearness of the Atlantic and the Pacific waters helps to moderate the temperatures somewhat, and some parts of the island are quite green, also providing grazing for sheep. ❑

Grapes and citrus fruit

The central-western section of Argentina, comprising the provinces of San Juan, Mendoza, and San Luis, is known as the Cuyo. The Andes here become a single towering range, with many peaks reaching over 6,600 meters (21,780 ft). West of Mendoza lies Aconcagua, at 6,980 meters (23,030 ft) the highest peak in the Western Hemisphere. Just south of Aconcagua is the Uspallata Pass (a former Inca road), which at its highest point of 3,800 meters (12,540 ft), crosses into Chile.

Fingers of desert extend eastward from the glacial mountains and down into the plains. A great deal of the land here is dry and wind-

LEFT: giant *cardon* cactuses of the Northwest.
RIGHT: Cerro Torre in Parque Nacional Los Glaciares, southern Patagonia.

Decisive Dates

PRE-COLUMBIAN PERIOD: 10,000 BC–AD 1480

c. 10,000 BC Nomadic tribes reach Argentina from the north, and settle in the Andes and along the coast.
500 BC–AD 600 Ceramic cultures emerge in Jujuy and San Juan. Tafi culture flourishes in present-day Tucumán, in the Northwest.
600–1480 Growth of urban centers in the Northwest and west; development of skills in fine metalwork.
1480 The Incas conquer northwestern Argentina, building roads and fortresses and forming trade links.

THE SPANISH EMPIRE: 1516–1809

1516 Spaniard Juan Díaz de Solis discovers Río de la Plata (River of Silver) and claims it for Spain.
1536 Pedro de Mendoza founds the settlement of Nuestra Señora de Santa María del Buen Aire (Buenos Aires). It is wiped out by disease and attacks from local indigenous tribes.
1551 Santiago del Estero, in the foothills of the Andes, is founded by colonists from Peru. It is the oldest permanent Spanish settlement in Argentina.
1580 Buenos Aires is founded a second time by the conquistador Juan de Garay.
1594 Decree by King of Spain that no trade should go through Buenos Aires, but instead has to leave South America via Lima, Peru.

1776 Buenos Aires is made capital of the fourth Spanish viceroyalty in the Americas, covering present-day Argentina, Uruguay, Paraguay, and Bolivia.
1806–07 British troops invade and occupy Buenos Aires, but are twice expelled.

THE INDEPENDENT REPUBLIC: 1810–1900

1810 With Spain occupied by Napoleon's troops, an independent junta of government is named in Buenos Aires on May 25. (This date is later celebrated as the birthday of independence).
1816 Argentine Congress formally declares itself a state on July 9.
1817 Argentine independence hero José de San Martín leads Argentine troops across Andes mountains to fight Spanish loyalists in Chile. Battles of Chacabuco and Maipú.
1820 Battles break out between the caudillos (landowners) representing interior provinces and forces of Buenos Aires for dominance of newly emerging state.
1826–27 Bernardo Rivadavia is elected president and curbs the power of the Catholic church.
1829–52 Argentina is dominated by the caudillo Juan Manuel de Rosas, who gradually assumes dictatorial powers, and rules continuously from 1835–52.
1852 Rosas' army is defeated by Urquiza. Rosas flees to England, where he dies in exile in 1877.
1853 Argentina's constitution is adopted on May 1. Buenos Aires province is separated from the rest of the country; Paraná is the national capital until 1861.
1862 The capital is moved back to Buenos Aires.
1864–69 Argentina joins Uruguay and Brazil to fight against Paraguay in the War of the Triple Alliance.
1869 The total population of Argentina is around 1.8 million with 178,000 living in Buenos Aires.
1879 The "War of the Desert" – General Julio A. Roca defeats remaining indigenous tribes and pushes back southern frontiers. Roca elected president.
1890 Radical Party (Radical Civic Union) is formed.
1898 General Roca's second term in office.

INTO THE TWENTIETH CENTURY: 1900–45

1910 First century of independence is celebrated. Argentina is one of the richest nations in the world.
1916–30 Radical Party comes to power. Hipólito Irigoyen is president from 1916–22 and 1928–30.
1930 Military step into politics for the first time in 20th century, under General José F. Uríburu.
1932 General Agustín P. Justo is elected president, representing the military-conservative alliance.
1943 Government is overthrown by the military GOU (Group of United Officers), one of whom is Colonel Juan Domingo Perón.

PERONISM AND AFTER: 1945–82

1945 Juan Perón, now Minister of War, is arrested in October after the formation of the General Confederation of Labor (CGT), then released after huge rally.

1946 Perón, now married to Eva Duarte (Evita), is elected Argentine president on February 24.

1949 Peronista Party is formed.

1951 Perón is re-elected with 67 percent of vote. A year later Evita dies from cancer.

1955 Protests from Catholic church and unrest among armed forces leads to coup. Perón flees into exile.

1958 Arturo Frondizi (Radical Party) becomes president.

1962–63 Military government returns to power.

1963–66 Government of moderate Arturo Illía, but unions and electorate are still dominated by Peronism.

1966 Armed forces intervene again; General Juan Carlos Onganía is made president.

1970 Growing unrest among politicians and workforce leads military to oust Onganía. General Alejandro Lanusse eventually comes to power, and announces presidential elections for March 1973. Perón declares intention of returning to Argentina.

1973 Peronists win elections, with Héctor Cámpora as candidate. Violence breaks out among opposing left- and right-wing factions within Peronism.

1974 Perón takes over as president. Isabel, Perón's third wife, is made vice president amid social tension and violence. Perón dies on July 1; Isabel is declared president of an increasingly divided nation.

1976 Military junta overthrows Isabel Perón on March 24. "Process of National Reorganization" begun under leadership of General Jorge Videla, the army commander in chief. "Dirty war" is launched to suppress opposition. Between 9,000 and 30,000 Argentines are abducted, tortured, and killed by security forces.

1978 Argentina wins its first World Cup as host nation.

1980–81 General Videla steps down and is replaced by General Viola, but is removed by General Galtieri.

1982 General Galtieri sends troops to occupy the Falkland Islands/Malvinas, claimed by Argentina since independence from Spain. Argentina surrenders with the loss of 600 soldiers to Great Britain.

ARGENTINE DEMOCRACY: POST-1983

1983 In the wake of defeat in the South Atlantic, military government collapses. Radical Party candidate

PRECEDING PAGES: the prehistoric Cueva de las Manos, in Santa Cruz province.
LEFT: early depiction of Patagonian Amerindians.
RIGHT: the Malvinas War Memorial in Buenos Aires, commemorating the 652 Argentine soldiers who lost their lives in the conflict.

Raúl Alfonsín is elected president on December 10.

1985 Report on disappearances during military dictatorship is published: *Nunca Más* documents almost 9,000 cases of people secretly abducted.

1985–87 Trial and conviction of military junta leaders held responsible for disappearances.

1986 Argentina wins its second World Cup, in Mexico.

1989 Unable to control inflation or offer coherent economic policy, Radical Party loses election. Peronist candidate Carlos Saúl Menem is elected president.

1991 The peso is pegged to the US dollar. Economic stability is restored for the first time in three decades.

1992 Restoration of diplomatic relations with Great Britain for the first time since 1982.

1993 National constitution is changed to allow re-election of president.

1995 President Menem is re-elected.

1999 Fernando de la Rúa, of the Radical Party, wins the election.

2001 President de la Rúa resigns after protests at rising poverty in which 27 protesters are killed. Argentina has four presidents in a two-week period.

2003 Nestor Kirchner, governor of Santa Cruz province, takes office as president.

2004 On New Year's Eve, a fire in a Buenos Aires nightclub kills 188 people and injures 700.

2005 President Kirchner announces that the restructuring of the country's debt has been a success, and repays the IMF early.　❑

PRE-COLUMBIAN PERIOD

Though less well documented than their counterparts elsewhere in South America, Argentina's early inhabitants were self-sufficient peoples with basic artistic skills

According to a theory accepted by most archeologists, the first inhabitants of the Americas originally came from Asia. During one of the many ice ages, the Bering Strait between Asia and Alaska became a land bridge, which human beings crossed in their search for new lands and sources of food.

The first arrival of humans in the American continent is placed somewhere between 30,000–25,000 BC. These Asiatic people, the theory goes, gradually spread southwards through the American landmass, making Argentina and Chile the last places to be inhabited by humans. It is possible that these early inhabitants reached the southern tip of South America by about 11,000 BC. The Los Toldos site in Santa Cruz province seems to support this theory.

In recent years, other archeologists have suggested that the first people to have arrived in South America may have traveled across the Pacific from Australia, and have settled the Amazon and other areas before North America was first colonized. As yet, there is little conclusive evidence as to which theory may be correct.

Different climate

The last advance of the ice sheet in South America occurred between 9,000 and 8,000 BC, provoking different effects from those in North America. No ice sheets covered the pampas of Argentina or the jungles of Brazil. The principal manifestation was that the Andes, the great chain of mountains that forms the spine of South America, had more ice covering it then than it does today.

The environment was also different, since many more lakes existed than is the case today, and the sea level was lower, rendering many areas, now under water, very tempting campsites. The Atlantic side of the continent,

which today has a large and not very deep submarine platform, was very likely much wider, extending outward from today's pampas and Patagonia to form a still larger plain. The rainfall pattern was also different and areas such as now-arid Patagonia were then covered with grass.

For many thousands of years the natives of this area developed separately from the inhabitants of other continental landmasses. Furthermore, it seems, they had relatively little contact with the great civilizations of the Central Andes.

When the first Spaniards finally entered Argentina during the 16th century (*see page 37)* they did not find the great cities and pyramids of Meso-America or a splendid empire such as the one the Peruvian Incas had built in only 100 years; they found a country sparsely populated from the northwestern Puna to the tip of Tierra del Fuego. Nor was this population homogeneous in its development.

LEFT: petroglyph, thought to depict the devil, from Talampaya, La Rioja province.
RIGHT: pre-Columbian ceramic figure, from Córdoba.

Forts and farming

What is now Argentina's Northwest was definitely the most culturally developed area. Throughout the centuries this area received the influences that diffused from Bolivia (during the peak of the Tiahuanaco Empire, about 1,000 years ago) and Peru (especially during the expansion of the Inca Empire, which incorporated northwestern Argentina within its great realm).

The early 16th century found the natives of the Northwest living in architecturally simple stone houses, in towns with populations that might have reached 3,000 people in some cases, making this area the most densely inhabited.

The Central Mountains and the region around Santiago del Estero were less developed. Small villages existed in this region, in some cases with semi-subterranean houses. Although agriculture was practiced, hunting and gathering still played an important role. Ceramics were made but were rather crude, and little or no metal was worked in the area. Many of the metal pieces were imported from the Northwest.

Fish and nomads

Life in the northeastern region of Argentina had many of the characteristics of that in the Central Mountains, except that the presence of two

Many of the towns were walled, located on hill tops for defense purposes, and had their own ceremonial buildings. Intensive agriculture and irrigation were practiced everywhere and domestic animals, mostly camelids such as the llama and alpaca, were widely used for transportation, wool, and meat.

Most of the arts had reached a high level of development by the 16th century; good ceramics, woodcarvings, excellent metalworking (mostly consisting of copper and bronze pieces), and stone sculptures have been found, relics of the different groups living in the area. Tribes and confederations of tribes were the units of political organization.

major rivers, the Paraná and the Uruguay, added a new dimension to the region's economies: fishing. Although pottery was known, metallurgy seems to have been absent. Unfortunately, to date this is one of the less archeologically studied areas of the country.

The region which encompasses the southern half of the country from Santa Fe and Córdoba to the southernmost islands, had very little permanent architecture. Many of the groups here were nomadic and erected temporary settlements with simple houses of branches or hides. Almost no agriculture was practiced, with hunting (both on land and at sea) and gathering playing important roles. Pottery was either not known or, when made, very crude. Metalworking was unknown until the migration of Araucanian tribes from Chile. Most of the tools were of stone or bone. In Patagonia it is estimated that some of these roaming bands had up to 150 members.

Hunter-gatherers

Although there are many archeological sites throughout Argentina, the dating of many of them has still not been satisfactorily settled, and only a few can be ascribed to the end of the Pleistocene and beginning of the Holocene Period, about 10,000 to 9,000 BC.

Many archeologists call the earliest-known cultural tradition the "hunting tradition" or the "hunting and gathering tradition." As the names suggest, these early groups roamed the country, living from the hunting of big game and the collection of plants, seeds, and fruits. Many of the animals hunted and eaten are now extinct. The early sites occupied are often either rock shelters or caves.

The Los Toldos caves, in Santa Cruz province, have walls and ceilings covered with paintings, mostly of hands, done in what is called "negative technique" (the hand is placed on the wall and the paint applied around it). Because some of the stone artifacts from the early levels have paint remains, it is thought that the cave paintings also correspond to the early levels, that is circa 9,000 BC.

Stone points

The hunting tradition survived for several thousand years, even until European contact in some areas. The related archeological sites have certain common characteristics: the absence of ceramics and metal, no clear sign of the practice of agriculture (although by 2,500 BC, some milling stones are present in some of the places), and the presence of stone and bone tools and objects for personal decoration.

Sea hunters

Development was uneven throughout the country and certain areas within the Patagonia and Tierra del Fuego zones never moved beyond the hunting tradition stage. The Tunel site, on

the Beagle Channel, on the southern coast of Tierra del Fuego, testifies to that. After a first occupation, oriented on guanaco (a relative of the llama) hunting, the inhabitants gradually converted to a sea-oriented economy.

For 6,000 years – until their full contact with the Europeans in the late 1800s – their economy and way of life remained mostly within a sea-based hunting and gathering pattern, complemented by hunting and seed and fruit collection. The lack of revolutionary changes does not reflect primitiveness or cultural backwardness but a successful and, with time, comfortable adaptation to the local

CAVES OF KNOWLEDGE

Bones and other items found in caves have yielded much information about Argentina's early history.

The Fells and Pailli Aike caves, located on the southern tip of the continent, contain horse, guanaco (llama family), and ground-sloth bones, together with those of humans. In southern Chile, the Eberhardt cave has remains of the Mylodon (giant sloth) and Onohippidon (early horse). The Los Toldos site is a group of caves containing horse bones. All these sites have stone tools; some of them have bone tools and Eberhardt has worked hides. The sites represent a pattern of seasonal nomadic occupation that followed the food resources.

LEFT: finely worked ancient stone tools.
RIGHT: carved obelisk from the Parque de los Menhires, Tucumán province.

environment by people who knew their resources and how to exploit them.

Agriculture arrives

In other areas the hunting tradition gave way eventually to agriculture. The transformation was from a pattern of collecting fruits, seeds, and leaves when and where they could be found (nomadism being a consequence of this regime) to an organized pattern of planting, tending, and collecting the fruits within a more restricted area, and this usually led to more fixed settlements.

Within the New World, Mexico and the

Andean area were the centers of domestication of wild plants. The vegetables and fruits that with time became the main staples of all the pre-Columbian societies and later of the European settlements – maize, potatoes, squash, beans, peppers – appear in either Meso-America or the Andean area by approximately 5,000 BC.

Ceramics and standing stones

The advent of agriculture is often closely followed by the development of ceramic skills. It is possible that the harvesting of crops and the new phenomenon of surplus food was an incentive for the making of containers which could hold and store seeds and fruits. Although pottery appeared in the New World during the 4th millennium BC, it is not seen in Argentina's archeological record until circa 500 BC. Most ceramic cultures occurred in the northern half of what is now Argentina.

To the Early Ceramic Period, which extended from about 500 BC to AD 600, belong several cultures which occupied an arch extending from the center of Jujuy to the eastern part of San Juan province. One of the early complexes is the Tafí culture of Tucumán, which is noted for its stone sculptures. Some of these beautiful carved monoliths (which reach 3 meters/10 ft in height) have stylized human faces.

The people of the area lived in settlements formed by groups of houses arranged around a central square. Their diet included *quinoa* (an Andean cereal), potatoes, and possibly maize, and they practiced llama herding. Mounds have been found which were used either for burials or as platforms for special structures.

Another extraordinary example of excellent stone sculpture is found at the site of the Alamito culture, on the Tucumán–Catamarca border. The statues here (both of women and men) reached an unusual level of development, with an almost abstract style both powerful and expressive.

In contrast to these stone-oriented cultures there is Condorhuasi, a culture in which ceramic art reached levels of expression not known in any other groups. Strange figures, often with both animal and human characteristics, are shown sitting and crawling, usually with globular bodies and legs, painted in a variety of white and red, cream and red, or black and red combinations.

Defensible settlements

The Middle Ceramic Period, dating from AD 650 to 850, witnessed the development and continuation of the advances made by preceding cultures, the existence of full agricultural communities living in permanent settlements, and the herding of llama and alpaca.

Architecture was still not impressive – at times just clay walls, probably with straw or wood roofs. Ceramic art continued to be developed, but stonework declined. Metalworking was by then highly developed, with the making of bronze and copper axes, needles, tweezers, bracelets, and disks with complicated designs.

The distinct differences in the quantity of artifacts found in graves is a clear indication that by now social stratification existed. The lack of monumental works or clear examples of organized labor points to a still simple political organization. The Aguada complex (mostly from Catamarca and La Rioja) is a good representative of this period.

The Late Ceramic Period, AD 850–1480, witnessed some changes. Settlements became larger, some in defensible locations, and thick walls made of round stones are found in many sites. Roads, cemeteries, irrigation works, and what were probably ceremonial centers gradually began to appear.

The ceramic urn (used for the burial of children) is one of the markers of the period. These vessels (40–60 cm/16–24 inches in height) often have painted human faces showing what could be tear marks. Other markers are beautiful metal disks or breastplates lavishly decorated with human head and snake motifs.

Inca invasion

Finally, in AD 1480, the invading forces of the Incas arrived, led by Topa Inca. This period saw the peak expansion of the vast Inca Empire, as they conquered what was to become the northwest region of Argentina. Remains of Inca roads, *tambos* (places of rest, supply, and storage), and *pucarás* (forts) can be found in the region. The Incas introduced their well-formed styles and artistic values and many of the pieces of this period are little more than local reproductions of original Inca pieces.

Encounter with Europe

When the first Spaniards arrived in Argentina in the early 16th century, it is thought that there were perhaps 500,000 indigenous people, living in numerous scattered groups. Two-thirds of them were estimated to live in the Northwest of the country, or in the central highlands of Córdoba and San Luis, which is where the Comechingones lived. Further south were the Tehuelche tribes, referred to by the Spaniards as "Pampa Indians," and the Patagones of Patagonia, and in Tierra del Fuego, where the Selk'nam and

Mannekenk groups lived. It is thought that the bonfires the Selk'nam lit on their boats inspired the name Tierra del Fuego.

The first native inhabitants to encounter the Spaniards were probably the nomadic Querandí of the pampas, who lived in temporary shelters and hunted with bolas, weighted balls on leather thongs. In common with all the other indigenous groups, they had no horses, did not use the wheel for transport, and had no gunpowder or firearms. This meant that though they resisted the Europeans for several decades, their technology was no match for the invaders. ❏

LEFT: stone face of unknown significance, from the Parque de los Menhires, Tucumán province.
RIGHT: the ruins of Quilmes. Tucumán province.

MER

DE

SUD. ou

PACI:

Mer

FICQUE.

DE

CHILI.

MER

LANIC.

Tropicque du Capricorne.

PARTIE

DU

PE=

Los

Char

CAS.

ROU

P

A

TU

CO.

PAR

CHA=

Tama

coa

GVA=

CV=

G=

MAN.

Iuries.

TERRE MA=

GELLA=

NIC=

QUE=

Patagons.

TERRE DE

FEU ou Isles Maire

FROM CONQUEST TO INDEPENDENCE

The Spanish invasion brought European civilization to Argentina, but by the
19th century the people were keen to break free from their distant rulers

The first half of the 16th century was a period of intense exploration on behalf of the Portuguese and Spanish crowns. Not quite 10 years after Columbus's first voyage to the New World, Amerigo Vespucci was probing the eastern shores of South America. Today, many credit him with the European discovery of the Río de la Plata, although standard Argentine accounts cite Juan de Solís as the first European to sail these waters.

Solís reached the Río de la Plata estuary in 1516 and named the river Mar Dulce or Sweet Sea. Not long after, while Solís was leading a small party ashore, he was killed by Charrúa tribesmen, along with all but one of the sailors accompanying him. After killing the Spaniards, the natives proceeded to eat them in full view of the rest of the crew still on board ship.

In 1520, Ferdinand Magellan, on his voyage to the Pacific, was the next explorer to reach what is now Argentina. Then came Sebastian Cabot. Sailing under the Spanish flag, and drawn by rumors of a mountain of silver, he was the next to venture into the Río de la Plata region in 1526. He reached modern-day Paraguay, where the Guaraní Amerindians gave him some metal trinkets. Thus inspired, Cabot named the muddy stretch of water, the "River of Silver."

Also drawn by reports of great wealth in the region, the Spanish nobleman Pedro de Mendoza led a large expedition to the area. On February 3, 1536, he founded Santa María de los Buenos Aires. The natives were at first helpful, but then they turned furiously against the Spaniards. As one of Mendoza's soldiers wrote: "The indians attacked our city of Buenos Aires with great force… There were around 23,000 of them… While some of them were attacking us, others were shooting burning arrows at our houses…" The natives finally

PRECEDING PAGES: 17th-century map of Argentina.
LEFT: a satirical view of the conflicts between the Spanish conquistadors and the Amerindians.
RIGHT: mural of the resettlement of Buenos Aires.

retreated under the fire of Spanish artillery.

Mendoza and his men never did locate any great mineral wealth and left Buenos Aires to eventually found Asunción in Paraguay.

A second group of Spaniards, this time approaching overland from Chile, Peru, and Upper Peru (today's Bolivia), was more suc-

cessful in founding lasting settlements. The Northwest towns of Santiago del Estero, Catamarca, Mendoza, Tucumán, Córdoba, Salta, La Rioja, and Jujuy were all founded in the second half of the 16th century, with Santiago del Estero being Argentina's oldest outpost (founded in 1551).

Northwest and central supremacy

Throughout the 17th century and during most of the 18th, the Northwest was the center of activity in Argentina. This was mostly due to protectionism on the part of the King of Spain, who in 1554 prohibited traffic on the Río de la Plata. Manufactured goods from Spain and enslaved Africans were shipped in a South American triangular trade via Panama and then Peru. The king's ruling was of great benefit to the Spanish colonial cities of Lima (the capital of the Viceroyalty of Peru) and Mexico City but meant that the Río de la Plata estuary remained isolated and commercially backward.

While Argentina was part of the Peruvian viceroyalty until 1776, two areas of the colony became important centers. Tucumán developed into a

SEAT OF LEARNING

The University of Córdoba is Argentina's oldest university (and the second oldest in South America). It was founded by the Jesuits in 1613 to instruct pupils in philosophy and theology.

successful agricultural region, supplying wheat, corn, cotton, tobacco, and livestock to neighboring Upper Peru. Somewhat later, Córdoba attained status as a center of learning, with the establishment of the Jesuit university in 1613.

Córdoba also prospered economically, owing to its central location and fertile lands. By contrast, Buenos Aires, which had been refounded in 1580 by Juan de Garay, was a small town that relied on smuggling for its income. Because all manufactured goods had to come the long route from Spain via Panama, prices were very high, and this led to flourishing contraband traffic.

Shift in power

The decline of the Andean mining industries, coupled with growing calls for direct transatlantic trade, finally persuaded the Spanish Crown to establish the new viceroyalty of Río de la Plata, with its administrative center at Buenos Aires.

With a new viceroyalty, which included Argentina, Uruguay, Paraguay, and parts of Upper Peru, Spain hoped to exert greater control over a region which was growing in importance. Buenos Aires experienced an explosion in population, increasing its numbers from 2,200 in 1726 to more than 33,000 by 1778. Upwards of a quarter of this rapidly growing population was Afro-Argentine and still held in bondage. Many others were of mixed Amerindian and Spanish parentage, a consequence of the fact that the Spanish population in the viceroyalty was predominantly male.

Some of these mixed-race Argentines settled on the pampas, where they lived off the many thousands of cattle that ran wild, becoming superb horsemen thanks to the huge numbers of horses that had also escaped. In time, these horsemen became the famous gauchos, whose free, nomadic lifestyle was in strong contrast to the niceties of Buenos Aires.

The growing importance of the viceroyalty of the Río de la Plata did not go unnoticed in Europe. The Franco-Hispanic alliance during the Napoleonic Wars (1804–15) resulted in a loosening of Argentina's ties with the motherland when Spain's fleet was destroyed by the British Navy. This meant that the Spanish colonies in Latin America were open for British attention.

The British invasion

In 1806, and again the following year, the British invaded Buenos Aires. During the first invasion, the inept Spanish viceroy fled to Montevideo, across the Río de la Plata, taking with him many of his troops. The retaking of the city was left to Santiago de Liniers, a French officer serving in the Spanish Army, who organized the remaining Spanish troops and the local inhabitants. The British were quickly routed but were to return soon afterwards.

After seizing Montevideo in spring 1807, the British tried to recapture Buenos Aires with an army of 10,000. They were met by Liniers and his men, and by women pelting them with roof tiles and pouring boiling oil on them from above. The English commander of the expedition, promptly evacuated his troops.

Beyond the immediate consequences of repelling the invaders, a number of important effects stemmed from the confrontations with the British. Pride in the colony was a nat-

DEATH ON THE STREETS

When British troops invaded Buenos Aires for the second time in 1807, the city's streets were turned into what they later called "pathways of death" and the British were forced to surrender.

relations; a *cabildo abierto* (open town council) in Buenos Aires deposed the Spanish viceroy and created a revolutionary junta to rule in his stead.

Bernardino Rivadavia, Manuel Belgrano, and Mariano Moreno were three criollo intellectuals who, inspired by European liberal thought, channeled their energies toward the creation of a new nation based on a re-ordering of colonial society. Naturally enough, the old order – rich merchants, *estancieros* (large landowners), mem-

ural outcome of having defeated a large and well-trained army with a mostly local militia. In addition, tensions arose between the criollos (Argentine-born colonists) and the Spanish administration. Thoughts of developing an economy without the strictures and regulations of a distant Crown in Spain began to enter the minds of leading criollos.

Independence steps

Napoleon Bonaparte's invasion of Spain in 1808 provided the final push for a rupture in

LEFT: rampant Spaniards on the hunt in 1586.
ABOVE: the first British invasion, 1806.

bers of the clergy and, indeed, the whole colonial administration – was violently opposed to anything that might compromise its status in the country.

A house divided

This lack of unity made the realization of an independent nation much more of a tortured process than the criollo intellectuals could have imagined. Indeed, a civil war was in the making following what the Argentines call the May Revolution. On May 25, 1810, an autonomous government was set up in Buenos Aires. This date is still celebrated in Argentina as the birthday of independence, although a formal declaration was not made until six years later.

These early years were not easy; the people of the viceroyalty were split along political, class, and regional lines, setting a Buenos Aires elite against the loyalists from the interior provinces. The *Unitarios* (Unitarians) were intent on having a strong central government, to be based entirely in offices in the capital, Buenos Aires. Meanwhile, the *Federales* (Federalists) campaigned for a loose confederation of autonomous provinces.

A confusing series of juntas, triumvirates, and assemblies rose and fell, as one group

gained the upper hand for a brief period only to lose the advantage to another. The eight original jurisdictions of the viceroyalty dwindled to three, and these then fragmented into seven provinces.

A congress was called to maintain whatever unity was left. On July 9, 1816, the congress at Tucumán formally declared independence under the blue and white banner of the United Provinces of South America.

Enter José de San Martín

The task of ridding the continent of Spanish armies remained. José de San Martín was to execute one of the boldest moves of the South American wars of independence. Gathering a large army, San Martín crossed the icy Andes at Mendoza in 21 days and met and defeated Spanish soldiers at Chacabuco in Chile (1817). He again engaged the Spaniards, this time at Maipú (1818), where he ended Spanish rule in Chile once and for all.

San Martín then amassed a fleet of mostly British and US ships to convoy his army the 2,400 km (1,500 miles) to Lima in Peru. The Spanish Army evacuated the city without fighting, wishing to keep their forces intact. It was at this time, in 1822, that San Martín met the other great liberator of South America, Simón Bolívar, at Guayaquil. What was discussed at this meeting is not known and has kept historians speculating ever since. The upshot, though, was San Martín's retirement from battle, leaving the remaining honors to be garnered by Bolívar.

From obscurity to sainthood

San Martín was posthumously elevated to a position of sainthood by the Argentines. Today, every town in Argentina has a street named after him and every classroom a portrait of the general crossing the Andes on a gallant white horse.

It was a different story, however, when he returned to Buenos Aires in 1823 from his campaigns on behalf of Argentina. He received no acknowledgment for the services he had rendered his country. Soon afterwards San Martín left for France, where he was to die in obscurity in Boulogne. ❏

A CHARISMATIC LEADER

Basil Hall, a contemporary of José de San Martín's, described him thus: "There was little, at first sight, in his appearance to engage attention; but when he rose up and began to speak, his great superiority over every other person… was sufficiently apparent… a tall, erect, well-proportioned, handsome man, with a large aquiline nose, thick black hair, and immense bushy whiskers… his complexion is deep olive, and his eye, which is large, prominent and piercing, jet black; his whole appearance being highly military… The contest in Peru, he said, was a war of new and liberal principles against prejudice, bigotry and tyranny."

LEFT: the formal declaration of independence on July 9, 1816, in Tucumán.

The case of the Afro-Argentines

Argentina's greatest puzzle is the vanished Afro-Argentines. Historians throughout the years have offered diverse explanations. Ordinary citizens are ready with stories that range from the plausible to the ludicrous.

Argentines of African heritage existed in large numbers – comprising 30 percent of the Buenos Aires population for almost 40 years (1778–1815). Slaves were first brought to Argentina in the 16th century by their Spanish owners. Due to the peculiar trading arrangements with the Spanish Crown, most slaves were imported to Buenos Aires via Panama and Peru and then overland from Chile, thereby greatly increasing their price. Others were brought in illegally, directly to Buenos Aires or from Brazil.

Argentine slaves were generally domestic servants but also filled the growing need for artisans in the labor-short colony. While the degree of their labor differed greatly from that of plantation workers in Brazil and the United States, they suffered similarly. Families were torn apart, gruesome punishments awaited runaways, and the status of black people in society was kept low, even after emancipation.

Black Argentines are recorded as having fought bravely in the struggle for independence and in San Martín's armies. Partly as a result of this, black and mixed-race slaves were declared free in 1813, although formal legislation was only passed in 1853. One early-1800s law stipulated that the children of slaves would be free upon birth, though their mothers would remain slaves. However, it was not unusual for slave owners to spirit their pregnant slaves to Uruguay, where slavery was still legal, and then bring both mother and child back to Argentina as slaves.

The North American professor George Reid Andrews has done much research to uncover the fate of the black population in his important work, *The Afro-Argentines of Buenos Aires, 1800–1900*. He offers no definitive conclusions, but he has explored in depth some of the more likely theories.

Reid Andrews offers four possible explanations for the disappearance of the Afro-Argentines. The first is that many of the men were killed fighting

in the wars of independence, and in the War of the Triple Alliance against Paraguay in 1865. Another reason could be their gradual absorption into the general population with the arrival of hundreds of thousands of European immigrants from the 1860s onwards. The great yellow-fever epidemic of 1871 and the general ill health and horrendous living conditions of the black population is also cited as a possible factor. Finally, Reid Andrews explores the decline of the slave trade (outlawed in 1813) and its impact on a community that would not have its numbers refreshed with new shipments of human chattel.

Census figures for the city of Buenos Aires from

1836 to 1887 point to a steep decline in the numbers and percentages of black people, from a figure of 14,906 or 26 percent of the total population to 8,005 or 1.8 percent.

The contributions black people made to Argentine society have, for the most part, been written out of the records. After the early 19th century, Afro-Argentines to all intents and purposes disappeared or were intentionally made to vanish. One must sift through prints and photographs of the late 1800s to discover that this group, although in decline, remained a part of the greater community. In these representations we can see Afro-Argentines working as gauchos or as street vendors or artisans in Buenos Aires. ❏

RIGHT: an Afro-Argentine street vendor, a common sight in mid-19th century Buenos Aires.

INMORTALIDAD

DON

EL DIA

UIJOTE

EL JUICIO

Lit. J. Ribas y Hno

TRAVELERS' TALES

Travelers in the 18th and 19th centuries painted a colorful picture of Argentina as a country where wild-west violence was a part of daily life

Today's traveler to Argentina follows in the wake of a tremendously diverse group of people who have roamed across the country, explored its mountains and coasts, and witnessed the major events in its history.

While Magellan and the early Spanish discoverers left vivid records of their voyages, it was in the 19th century that scientists such as Alexander von Humboldt and Charles Darwin began to take a closer scientific interest in the land, its inhabitants, its flora and fauna. As trade and industry developed, a wide range of visitors from Europe and the United States visited Argentina, and many published their travel diaries.

The reader of travel literature, especially of the 18th- and 19th-century vintage, discovers many of the wonders of Argentina that no longer exist. These fabulous tales need to be approached somewhat cautiously because many of the travelers neither spoke the language nor necessarily understood the events unfolding before them. Nonetheless, these accounts provide the color and flavor that is sometimes missing from published scientific diaries.

As one might expect, the early traveler faced a broad spectrum of perils that, in the case of Argentina, included robbery, Amerindian attacks, diseases such as yellow fever and syphilis, lack of adequate food and shelter, and often painful modes of transportation.

In the 18th century, Argentina and its capital were still very much a provincial outpost of the Spanish Empire. Many visitors were priests, such as the German Jesuit Miguel Herre, who wrote rather dismissively: "Buenos Aires is called a city, but in Germany many villages are larger... in itself, Buenos Aires is ugly; it has only three churches, with ours, the worst, found near the center by the fort. On one side is the Franciscan convent, on the other the attractive

cathedral built in lime and bricks and covered in tiles; all the buildings are built with sticks and mud, like swallows' nests."

The dangers, though, seemed to be far outweighed by the joys the voyager experienced. Unexpected hospitality in the most out-of-the-way places, chance encounters along the road,

the sight of Tehuelche natives and gauchos displaying their equestrian skills, and the exhilaration of visiting places few had seen before were some of the high points the foreigner might come across.

The city of good air

The 19th-century traveler would often commence his or her itinerary in Buenos Aires. Charles Darwin, in 1833, described the city as "large and I should think one of the most regular in the world. Every street is at right angles to the one it crosses, and the parallel ones being equidistant, the houses are collected into solid squares of equal dimensions, which are called *quadras*."

PRECEDING PAGES: a caricature of Argentine political life, 1893, from the magazine *Don Quijote*.
LEFT: morning maté in an upper-class salon.
RIGHT: 19th-century watercolor of a colonial church.

Writing 10 years after Darwin, Colonel J. Anthony King commented that: "The market place of Buenos Ayres [*sic*] is… the center of all public rejoicings, public executions, and popular gatherings. It is in the market place that Rosas hung up the bodies of many of his victims, sometimes decorating them… with ribbons of the Unitarian color [blue], and attaching to the corpses labels, on which were inscribed the revolting words, 'Beef with the hide'."

J.P. and W.P. Robertson wrote a series of letters from South America which they published in 1843. What first impressed them were the methods of transportation in the city.

"Nothing strikes one more on a first arrival in Buenos Aires than the carts and carters. The former are vehicles with large wooden axles, and most enormous wheels, so high that the spokes are about 8 feet [2 meters] in diameter, towering above both horses and driver; he rides one of these animals… The first sight you have of these clumsy vehicles is on your landing. They drive off like so many bathing-machines to your hotel, a dozen carters, just like a dozen porters here, struggling… for the preference in carrying ashore passengers and their luggage."

Even in the mid-19th century, travelers to

Buenos Aires were impressed by how much of a melting pot the city was. Writing in 1853, Scottish traveler William MacCann expressed his amazement: "The varieties of complexion and costume, including specimens of the human race from almost every country of the world, and the Babel of tongues from all nations, so confound the senses that it is difficult to describe the effect. Surely no other city in the world could present such a motley assemblage; and the diversity of physiognomy is so great that one might doubt if mankind are all descended from a common stock." (*Two Thousand Mile Ride Through the Argentine Provinces.*)

Perils of the unknown

Dangers on the road were certainly plentiful for both traveler and native alike. Francis Bond Head, an English mining engineer who spent two tempestuous years, 1825–26, in the Argentine outback, and whose book *Rough Notes Taken During Some Rapid Journeys Across the Pampas and Among the Andes* is one of the best travelogues on Latin America, was well prepared for the violence he knew he would face.

A HAZARDOUS LAND

Darwin described the trials of the terrain. "Changing horses for the last time, we again began wading through the mud. My animal fell, and I was well soused in black mire – a very disagreeable accident."

ing double-barreled gun in my hand. I made it a rule never to be an instant without my arms, and to cock both barrels of my gun whenever I met any gauchos."

Head, aptly named "Galloping Head," describes the dangers Amerindians posed. "A person riding can use no precaution, but must just run the gauntlet, and take his chance, which, if calculated, is a good one. If he fall in with them, he may be tortured and killed, but it is very improbable that he should happen to find them on the

Head wrote that, "In crossing the pampas it is absolutely necessary to be armed, as there are many robbers or *saltadors*, particularly in the desolate province of Santa Fe. The object of these people is of course money, and I therefore always rode so badly dressed, and so well armed that although I once passed through them with no one but a child as a postilion, they thought it not worth their while to attack me. I always carried two brace of detonating pistols in a belt, and a short detonat-

LEFT: *boleadora*-wielding Amerindians on the pampas.
ABOVE: indigenous settlement on the Sierra de la Ventana pampas.

road; however, they are so cunning, and ride so quick, and the country is so uninhabited, that it is impossible to gain any information."

Tehuelche and Puelche

Meeting an Amerindian could be a high point of a journey, as Lady Florence Dixie related in her *Across Patagonia* (1881). "We had not gone far when we saw a rider coming slowly towards us, and in a few minutes we found ourselves in the presence of a real Patagonia Indian. We reined in our horses when he got close to us, to have a good look at him, and he doing the same, for a few minutes we stared at him to our hearts' content, receiving in return as minute and careful a scrutiny from him."

One of Galloping Head's fondest wishes was to be able to spend time with the native South American. "His profession is war, his food simple, and his body is in that state of health and vigor that he can rise naked from the plain on which he has slept, and proudly look upon his image which the white frost has marked out upon the grass without inconvenience. What can we 'men in buckram' say to this?"

Country life

The gauchos were often perceived as being as wild as the Amerindians, and just as inter-

esting. Additionally, the gauchos and others living in the countryside were noted for their hospitality. Colonel King writes that, "whether in health or sickness, the traveler is always welcome to their houses and boards, and they would as soon as think of charging for a cup of water, as for a meal of victual or a night's lodging."

Darwin, too, was greatly struck by their manners. "The gauchos, or countrymen, are very superior to those who reside in the towns. The gaucho is invariably most obliging, polite, and hospitable. I did not meet with even one instance of rudeness or inhospitality." And once, when Darwin inquired whether there was enough food for him to have a meal, he was told, "We have meat for the dogs in our country, and therefore do not grudge it to a Christian."

In the country, far from doctors and hospitals, the people often relied on an assortment of folk medicine. Darwin was appalled at the remedies: "One of the least nasty is to kill and cut open two puppies and bind them on each side of a broken limb. Little hairless dogs are in great request to sleep at the feet of invalids."

Travelers were greatly impressed by the skills gauchos showed as they worked their horses, threw bolas to fell cassowaries – the South American ostrich – or lassoed cattle. Darwin witnessed such a sight: "I was amused by the dexterity with which a gaucho forced a […] horse to swim a river. He stripped off his clothes, and jumping on its back rode into the river till it was out of its depth; then slipping off over the crupper, he caught hold of the tail, and as often as the horse turned around, the man frightened it back by splashing water in its face. As soon as the horse touched bottom on the other side, the man pulled himself on, and was firmly seated, bridle in hand, before the horse gained the bank. A naked man on a naked horse is a fine spectacle; I had no idea how well the two animals suited each other. The tail of a horse is a very useful appendage."

While some travelers enjoyed this wild side of Argentine life, others noted how far the outside world had made an impact on the country. The first official British representative in Buenos Aires, Sir Woodbine Parish, wrote home proudly of the Argentine gaucho in the mid-19th century: "Take his whole equipment, examine everything about him – and what is

A POSITIVE PEOPLE

Julius Beerbohm, who wrote *Wanderings in Patagonia or Life Among the Ostrich-Hunters* (1879), had high praise for the original inhabitants of Argentina. "The Tehuelches are rather good looking… and friendly. Their foreheads are rather low, their noses aquiline, their mouths large and coarse… in general intelligence, gentleness of temper, chastity of conduct, and conscientious behavior in their social and domestic relations, they are superior not only to the other South American indigenous tribes, but also, all their disadvantages being taken into consideration, to the general run of civilized white men."

there not made of hide that is not British? If his wife has a gown, ten to one it is from Manchester. The camp kettle on which he cooks his food – the common earthenware he eats from – his knife, spoons, bits, and the poncho that covers him – all are imported from England."

Earth and sky

The size of the country and the rough paths made the traveler's trip through Argentina a very long one indeed. E.E. Vidal, another early 19th-century traveler, quotes the

ARMS AT THE READY

Darwin wrote that, "A traveler has no protection besides his firearms, and the constant habit of carrying them is the main check to a more frequent occurrence of robbery."

very roots, and nothing was presented to the eye but barrenness and desolation...We had but one small jar of water left, our thirst seemed to increase every moment."

Some of the most poetic descriptions of Argentine rural life in the 19th century were written by W.H. Hudson. Born in Argentina of a family from New England, as an old man he recalled his childhood on the pampas in books such as *Far Away and Long Ago*: "We see all around us a flat land, its horizon a perfect ring of misty blue color where the

unnamed author of *Letters from Paraguay*, who describes his trip from Buenos Aires to Mendoza, at the foot of the Andes, as taking 22 days in a large cart drawn by oxen. "We set off every afternoon about two, and sometimes three hours before sunset, and did not halt till about an hour after sunrise."

Having a sufficient supply of water was one of the obstacles the writer faced in his journey. "We were obliged to halt in a spot, where even the grass seemed to have been burned to the

LEFT: mural of indigenous tribesmen from Ushuaia, Tierra del Fuego.
ABOVE: Darwin's research vessel, the HMS *Beagle*.

crystal-blue dome of the sky rests on the level green world. Green in late autumn, winter, and spring, or say from April to November, but not at all like a green lawn or field: there were smooth areas where sheep had pastured, but the surface varied greatly and was mostly more or less rough."

Many travelers commented on the seemingly endless flat pampas. W.J. Holland, a US scientist on an expedition to Argentina in 1912, described the scene from his train compartment. "I have crossed the prairies of Minnesota and the Dakotas, of Kansas and Nebraska, of Manitoba and Alberta; I have traveled over the steppes of Russia; but in none of them have I seen such absolutely level lands as those which lie between Rosario and Irigoyen. The horizon is that of the ocean; an upturned clod attracts attention; a hut looks like a house; a tree looms up like a hill."

City life

In 1870 the Scottish writer and cattle rancher Robert Cunninghame Graham wrote of a central hotel in Buenos Aires: "Just at the corner of the streets called Twenty-fifth of May and Calle de Cangallo stood Claraz's hotel... The life of Buenos Aires ran before the door. Only three squares away, the two great Plazas, with their

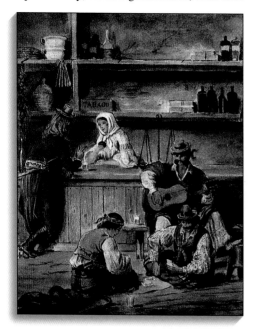

palaces and barracks, basked in the sun, or shivered in the wind, according as the Pampero whistled, or the hot north wind blew. The Stock Exchange was near, and up the deep-cut Calle de Cangallo, which looked more like a dry canal than a great thoroughfare, stood several of the principal hotels."

For female travelers, however, the capital was not always so welcoming. The North American Katherine S. Drier described what she had to contend with in Buenos Aires in 1918. "Before leaving for Buenos Aires everybody in New York told me that the Plaza Hotel was the only hotel in Buenos Aires, and that of course I would make it my headquarters during my sojourn there. But my information had been given me by men, and neither they nor I expected to find that the Plaza did not take women unaccompanied by their husbands or supposed husbands. Not even sisters accompanied by their brothers, or wives whose husbands have to travel, or widows, are made welcome. Much less respectable maiden ladies!"

Food and politics

Thomas Turner, describing one well-known and wealthy family at supper in the 1880s had this to say: "Of the domestic habits of the Argentines, their manners at table, *en famille*, it is impossible to give an attractive description. Their manners at table are ultra-Bohemian. They read the papers, shout vehemently at each other, sprawl their limbs under and over the table, half swallow their knives, spit with true Yankee freedom on the carpeted floor, gesticulate and bend across the table in the heat of argument, smoke cigarettes between the courses, and even while a course of which some of them do not partake is serving – a soothing habit which stimulates expectoration and provokes discussion – use the same knife and fork for every course – fish, entree, or joint, in a word, the studied deportment of the street is, in the house, exchanged for the coarse manners of the tap-room."

Turner was also shocked at the way politics dominated discussions, something that still is prevalent. "Although forbidden subjects are discussed by both sexes with zest and freedom, the staple topic of conversation is politics. Everybody talks politics... Even children talk politics, and discuss the merits of this, that or other statesmen with parrot-like freedom of opinion and soundness of judgment."

Argentina has always attracted travelers, drawn to its vast empty spaces and to the mix of people living there. Whether positive or critical, these wanderers and explorers have passed on the country's lore through their writing, which might otherwise have been lost to us. Taken together, they chart the rise of the nation from being an insignificant part of a vast empire to a modern, outward-looking country with a rich heritage. ❏

LEFT: a *pulpería* – multi-purpose saloon, general store, and community social center on the pampas.
RIGHT: a 19th-century gentleman farmer.

CAUDILLOS, TYRANTS, AND DEMAGOGUES

For most of the past two centuries Argentina has suffered under the political ambitions and misguided economic policies of dictators and military rulers

The years from independence to the start of the dictatorship of Juan Manuel de Rosas in 1829 were difficult for the United Provinces of the Río de la Plata (the earlier and grander name of the United Provinces of South America was dropped when the original grouping broke up). Bernardino Rivadavia, a man of great vision, valiantly but vainly attempted to shape the country's future.

Rivadavia was interested in establishing a constitution for the nation, forming a strong central government, dividing up the land into more equitable shares, and attracting immigrants to settle in the United Provinces. His plans were quickly sidetracked, however, by both caudillos in the interior, who were none too anxious to surrender any of their power, and by the draining Cisplatine War (1825–28) with Brazil over the status of Uruguay. When Rivadavia resigned from the presidency of the United Provinces in 1827 and went into exile, there remained little to show for his years of effort.

Caudillo and tyrant

Juan Manuel de Rosas, who ruled much of Argentina as his personal domain for more than 20 years, must be one of the most intriguing, if bloodthirsty figures in Latin American history. In his quest for power, Rosas forged a coalition of gauchos, wealthy landowners, and others.

Although born in Buenos Aires in 1793, Rosas was a product of the open pampas. It was here on his family's estancia that he learned to ride, fight, and toss the *boleadoras* (three stones attached to connected thongs, used to bring livestock down by tangling around their legs). Rosas became as skilled in these pursuits as any of the gauchos with whom he kept company, gaining their respect and later their support.

Rosas became wealthy in his own right at an early age. By his mid-twenties, he owned

thousands of acres of land and was a successful businessman, having helped to establish one of the first meat-salting plants in his province. He chose well when he married María de la Encarnación Escurra, the daughter of another rich family. She would later prove quite invaluable to Rosas' ascent to power, loyally plotting and organizing in a subtle but effective way on her husband's behalf.

To stem the rising tide of anarchy that followed the exile of Rivadavia, Rosas was asked to become the governor of the province of Buenos Aires in 1829. Rosas, a powerful caudillo and experienced military man, seemed the perfect individual to restore order and stability.

The problem with the Federalists was that there was little unity among the various factions. Those in the provinces demanded autonomy and an equal footing with Buenos Aires, while those espousing the Federalist cause in

LEFT: a colorful portrayal of the emerging new nation.
RIGHT: the tyrant Juan Manuel de Rosas.

Argentina's major city were not willing to surrender their premier position. As governor with extraordinary powers, Rosas signed in 1831 the Federal Pact which tied together the provinces of Buenos Aires, Entre Ríos, Santa Fe, and Corrientes.

The opposition to Rosas, the Unitarian League, was dealt a severe blow when its leader, José María Paz, was unhorsed by a Federalist soldier wielding *boleadoras*. Paz was jailed by Rosas. By 1832, the Unitarians had suffered a number of reverses on the battlefield and, for the moment, did not pose a great threat to the Federalists.

THE KILLING GAME

Under Juan Manuel de Rosas, horrific methods of silencing opponents became institutionalized.

The favored manner of despatching them was throat-cutting, reflecting the tradition of the gauchos. W.H. Hudson, naturalist and chronicler of the pampas, wrote that the Argentines "loved to kill a man not with a bullet but in a manner to make them know and feel that they were really and truly killing."

Another method employed was lancing: two executioners standing on either side of the prisoner would plunge lances into the body. Castration and tongue extraction were common means of torture.

When Rosas' first term as governor ended in 1832, he refused to accept another stint in office because the council of provincial representatives was unwilling to allow him to maintain his virtually unlimited authority.

Darwin and Rosas

Even out of power, Rosas continued to fight. He took command of the campaign against the native Argentine tribes in the south, and earned himself even more dubious glory by wiping out thousands of Amerindians.

During this Desert Campaign of 1833–34, the British naturalist Charles Darwin was entertained by Rosas. Of his meeting, Darwin wrote: "General Rosas is a man of extraordinary character; he has at present a most predominant influence in this country and may probably end up by being its ruler... He is moreover a perfect gaucho: his feats of horsemanship are very notorious. He will fall from a doorway upon an unbroken colt, as it rushes out of the Corral, and will defy the worst efforts of the animal. He wears the gaucho dress and is said to have called upon Lord Ponsonby in it, saying at the time he thought the costume of the country the proper and therefore the most respectful dress. By these means he obtained an unbounded popularity in the Camp, and in consequence despotic power... In conversation he is enthusiastic, sensible and very grave. His gravity is carried to a high pitch."

While Rosas was campaigning in the south, his wife waged a "dirty war" to have her husband reinstated as governor of Buenos Aires, forming the *Sociedad Popular Restauradora* and its terror wing, the *mazorca*. Doña Encarnación effectively hampered the efforts to rule of the three governors who followed Rosas.

The junta finally acquiesced to Rosas' demands and he assumed his post as Restorer of the Laws and governor in a regal ceremony on April 13, 1835. The red color of the Federalists became a distinguishing factor. Women wore scarlet dresses, while men wore red badges that proclaimed "Federation or Death." Decorating in blue, the color of the "savage Unitarians," could be cause for imprisonment or even execution.

Climate of fear

While Rosas did not create the brutal methods of repression that so characterized his regime, he did give a certain order and system to them in making himself supreme dictator. Generally speaking, Rosas' victims were not massacred wholesale but rather executed on an individual basis. Long lists of suspected Unitarians and the property they possessed were drawn up by Rosas' effective spy network, the police, the military, and justices of the peace. The actual numbers of those who perished remains unclear, but estimates range in the thousands. Whatever the number, Rosas created and maintained a climate of fear for more than 20 years.

With Rosas at the helm, Argentina did not prosper. He meddled in the affairs of neighbor-

noia, and widespread repression did nothing to help the growth of the nation.

In response to the atmosphere of terror and lack of freedom, Argentines organized in secret, and some in exile, to overthrow Rosas. These intellectuals, whose ranks included such luminaries as Bartolomé Mitre, Juan Bautista Alberdi, and Domingo Faustino Sarmiento, provided the rhetoric which galvanized the opposition.

A quick end

Justo José de Urquiza, a caudillo who had long supported Rosas, turned against the Restorer and organized an army that soon included thou-

ing Uruguay, but was never able to conquer its capital, Montevideo.

Extreme xenophobia on Rosas' part also kept the country from attracting much-needed immigrants and foreign capital. During two periods, the first from 1838 to 1840 when French troops occupied a customs house on the Río de la Plata, and then during the 1845–47 Anglo-French blockade of the river, the finances of Buenos Aires suffered severely. Rosas' treatment of European nationals, his extreme para-

sands of volunteers, and even many Uruguayans and Brazilians. On February 3, 1852, Urquiza's army engaged Rosas' demoralized and rebellion-weary troops at Caseros, near Buenos Aires. "The battle," as Mitre later wrote, "was won before it was fought." A new age in Argentina's history had begun, with Urquiza intent on consolidating the nation as one unit and not a collection of semi-independent provinces; progress in all areas came quickly.

State foundations

The period from Rosas' downfall to 1880 was a time of organizing the nation-state and establishing the institutions required to run it. The

LEFT: a Rosas soldier in Federalist colors.
ABOVE: Amerindians captured during the Desert Campaign.

major conflict of this period was an old one: the status of Buenos Aires in relation to the interior. This issue was finally settled in 1880 by federalizing the city and making it something like the District of Columbia in the United States.

Urquiza's first task was to draw up a constitution for Argentina. A constitutional convention was held in the city of Santa Fe and this meeting produced a document modeled on the Constitution of the United States. Among its provisos were the establishment of a bicameral legislature, an executive chosen by an electoral college, and an independent judiciary.

The Argentine constitution was accepted by the next president. Although the task of creating a national infrastructure was of great importance to Mitre, he found himself distracted by the Paraguayan War (1865–70). It took five years of bloody fighting for the triple alliance of Brazil, Uruguay, and Argentina to subdue the Paraguayan dictator Francisco Solano López.

Mitre was succeeded by Domingo Faustino Sarmiento whose role in promoting education in Argentina has taken on mythic proportions. It was during Sarmiento's administration (1868–74) that Argentina's progress soared. Hundreds of thousands of immigrants poured

the convention on May 1, 1853. Not surprisingly, Urquiza was chosen as the first president. During his tenure, he established a national bank, built schools, and improved transportation in the republic. But the role of Buenos Aires was still uncertain. There were, in fact, two Argentinas, one in wealthy Buenos Aires and the other in the interior with its capital at Paraná. A congress met in Buenos Aires in 1862 and decided that Buenos Aires would become the capital of both the republic and the province.

A succession of presidents

Bartolomé Mitre, an historian and former governor of the province of Buenos Aires, became

into the city of Buenos Aires, railroads were built, and the use of barbed-wire fencing spread, controlling the open range. Sarmiento continually stressed the need to push for a removal of the "barbaric" elements within Argentine society, namely the caudillos and the gauchos. He believed that groups such as these had kept Argentina from advancing at a faster rate.

Following Sarmiento came President Nicolás Avellaneda, whose inauguration in October 1874 almost didn't happen. Mitre, fearing a decline in Buenos Aires' prestige at the hands of such non-*porteños* as Sarmiento, Avellaneda, and Julio Roca (none of whom lived in the capital), led a revolt against the government. It took three months to crush this rebellion.

As Avellaneda's minister of war, Roca headed a series of expeditions against the natives of Patagonia in the infamous Conquest of the Desert which was concluded by 1879. Many thousands of square miles were opened up for settlement and exploration after this war, but the indigenous population never recovered.

Golden age

The next three decades saw a golden age in Argentina. New methods for chilling and then freezing meat, innovations in shipping, and the

The new meat and cereals economy required workers, and by the 1890s Argentina was receiving thousands of immigrants – mostly Italian and Spanish. The population grew from 1.8 million in 1869 to more than 4 million by 1895. These immigrants were attracted to Argentina because of the promise of "land, a house, and a job." Very often though, they arrived to find that the land was in the hands of great *estancieros*, or military men rewarded for their achievements in the War of the Desert. This meant the new arrivals were forced back into the growing cities and often they found that the second promise, that of

construction of rail networks all made possible intensive ranching and farming. The amount of cultivated land multiplied 15 times from 1872 to 1895, and cereal exports exploded between 1870 and 1900. Behind this accelerated economic growth lay the increased demand for foodstuffs in Europe. By the 1880s, the territory of Argentina had almost reached the boundaries of today, although it would be many more years before the exact borders with Chile in Patagonia and Tierra del Fuego were settled.

LEFT: the masses turn out for Loyalty Day, 1946.
ABOVE: Perón and Evita soak up their supporters' adulation from the balcony of the Casa Rosada.

having a good house to live in, was not met either. Families often had to live in crowded tenements known as *conventillos*, while the men went out to try to find the third thing promised: a job.

There was a corresponding growth in the intellectual field as well. Newspapers were founded, political parties sprang up, books were published, and a world-class opera house, the Teatro Colón, opened in Buenos Aires.

This is not to say that all was well in Argentina. Politics remained closed to most Argentines; a few had taken it upon themselves to run the country. The middle class, supporting the new political party, the Radical Civic Union, pressed for entry into what had been a government run by a small group of conservative families. Workers also became politicized and were attracted to the Socialist Party and the anarchists. Strikes hit Argentina at the turn of the 20th century and labor unrest grew. The workers found themselves expendable as the country struggled to pay back international loans and as imports began to exceed exports.

The effects of World War I

The war in Europe stimulated the Argentine economy in two ways. First, the belligerents' need for agricultural products skyrocketed;

working classes. These liberal policies were seen as a threat by the more conservative sectors of Argentine society, and in 1930 President Yrigoyen was toppled by a military coup. This military intervention set a sad precedent that was to be followed throughout the next half-century.

Weak civilian governments were allowed back after 1937, but by the time of the outbreak of the Second World War, Argentina was very divided politically and socially. The armed forces largely supported Italy and Germany, and in 1943 carried out another coup when it appeared that a pro-Allies president would be

second, the paralysis of European trade in manufactured goods encouraged local production. Impoverished urban artisans began to fill domestic demand as imports fell by 50 percent. This industrial boom revealed weaknesses in the Argentine economy – dependence on imported raw materials, lack of energy resource development, and a lack of capital – that would become crucial during the Great Depression, when the nation once more relied on local production.

The Radical Party came to power for the first time in 1916. Under Hipólito Yrigoyen, the Radicals introduced social security and other measures that benefited the middle and

elected. The new military government appointed a young colonel as Minister for War and Labor: he was Juan Domingo Perón.

A demagogue's demagogue

Perón's background certainly indicated no pro-labor tendencies. He attended a military college and rose through the ranks as a career officer. While stationed in Italy in 1939 as a military observer, he was impressed by the nationalism of the fascists. He also thought the state's intervention in Italy's economy to be logical. On his return to Argentina, Perón involved himself deeply in the secret military organization, the GOU (*Grupo Obra de Unifi-*

cación or Unification Task Force), which was composed of young agitators bent on remodeling Argentina's political system along the lines of those in Germany and Italy.

Perón used his position to build his power base. His labor reforms – job security, child labor laws, and pensions among them – were immensely popular with the working class. Furthermore, Perón tied union and non-union members together through the national welfare system, a move that assured him control over and allegiance from most workers.

The military became uneasy with Perón's growing power and arrested him. This led to a series of demonstrations, capped by a gigantic display in the Plaza de Mayo by the *descamisados* ("the shirtless ones"). Perón's consort, Eva Duarte, and labor leaders were behind these actions, rallying support for the imprisoned Perón. Within weeks he was free. He would soon marry Eva to legitimize their relationship in the eyes of the voters and the church. Perón sensed correctly that his moment on the national stage had arrived. In the presidential elections of 1946, Perón won with a majority of 54 percent. The clumsy US intervention in these elections, operating through its ambassador to Buenos Aires, ironically contributed to electing the man described by Washington as a "fascist."

In the years immediately following World War II, Argentina's agricultural exports were in great demand throughout Europe. Perón used the economic surplus to nationalize many industries – in 1948, he paid the largest check ever known to buy back the railway system from its British owners. Although storm clouds were gathering on the economic horizon, nobody seemed to notice: this was a golden age when every family could eat steak twice a day, and Perón was re-elected in 1951 with a massive 67 percent majority.

Severe droughts and a decrease in international prices of grain led to a 50 percent increase in Argentina's trade deficit. Eva Perón's death shortly after her husband's second inauguration left him without one of his most successful organizers and contributed to the malaise of the nation. Perón seemed to

---

LEFT: the revolution of September 6, 1930, in which General Uríburu ousted President Hipólito Yrigoyen.
RIGHT: President Onganía (*left*) and General Lanusse.

lose his willpower and left many decisions to his increasingly radical acolytes.

Middle-class revolt

Opposition to Perón grew. As inflation rose and other economic problems mounted, the middle classes became increasingly concerned. To many, he seemed like a dictator, imposing his views through class violence. The church hierarchy felt threatened by Perón's secular views on education, divorce, and prostitution. As in 1930, the armed forces responded by seizing power. In September 1955, a church-sponsored demonstration drew 100,000 to the center of

Buenos Aires. This was soon followed by the rebellious airforce's bombing of the Casa Rosada and the Plaza de Mayo. The army struck back against the dissident airforce while Peronist mobs burned churches.

Events were rolling out of control as the navy then rebelled, joined by some army units in the interior. Perón spared his country enormous bloodshed by not making good his promise to arm the workers, and instead fleeing to Paraguay.

Economically, Peronism left a contradictory heritage that was only dismantled under President Menem in the 1990s. Under strong protection from imports, local manufacturing grew but remained inefficient, costly, uncompetitive, and unable to provide sustained growth. At the same time, continued dependence on imported raw materials and capital goods, vulnerability to agricultural price cycles, and the burden of a state sector designed to provide high levels of employment and social welfare led to a series of balance of payment crises, beginning in the late 1950s.

For the next 18 years, the armed forces tried to rule Argentina without Perón and Peronism. Weak civilian governments were tolerated, but Peronists were not allowed to stand in any elections. The Peronist trade

unions were forced underground, and at the first sign of any social unrest, the armed forces intervened again.

Arturo Frondizi was the first president elected after Perón, in February 1958. His tenure was marked by a state of siege, an economic downturn, and some 35 coup attempts.

What brought Frondizi down was his decision to allow Peronists to participate in the congressional elections of 1962. Frondizi's attempts to accommodate the Peronists disturbed the Argentine military; they ordered him to annul the election results and when he refused to declare all Peronist wins illegal, the army stepped in.

Arturo Illia did not fare much better when he won the presidential elections in 1963. Although the economy was stronger than under Frondizi's administration, inflation remained oppressively high. Illia's minority government stood little chance of survival; the military was apprehensive over the president's inability to hold back the increasingly popular Peronist Party.

The next in line to try his hand at governing Argentina was General Juan Carlos Onganía, leader of the 1966 coup against Illia. Onganía ushered in a repressive era: political parties were banned; congress was dissolved; and demonstrations were outlawed.

The *Cordobazo* (Córdoba riots) of 1969 precipitated Onganía's departure from government. Argentina's second-largest city was the focus of anti-government activity among a new alliance of students, workers, and businessmen, all of whom had been badly hurt by Onganía's policies. Córdoba became a war zone, as soldiers battled with demonstrators. Over 100 were killed or wounded in the street fighting.

Onganía was ousted by General Lanusse and other military representatives. An obscure general assumed the presidency, lasting only nine months in office before Lanusse himself took charge. Yielding to the inevitable, he prepared the nation for a return to civilian elections, which were to be held in 1973.

Argentine society became increasingly divided. Lanusse introduced repressive measures to combat the activities of left-wing guerrillas groups, in particular the Peronist Montoneros and the Marxist People's Revolutionary Army (ERP). The struggle became increasingly violent, with more than 2,000 political and trade-union prisoners languishing in prison.

It was in this climate that the presidential election of 1973 took place. Perón chose Héctor Cámpora to run as his proxy as the head of the Peronist Justicialist Party. On a platform of national reconstruction, Cámpora won just less than half the vote. It was time for Perón to end his exile.

Round two for Perón

Perón's return to Argentina did not have auspicious beginnings. Two million were on hand at the international airport to greet the aging man they thought could restore order to the economy and dignity to the working classes. Riots among different groups of demonstrators and security police at the airport turned into pitched battles that left hundreds dead.

Cámpora resigned from office and in the new presidential elections Perón won with ease. Following past form, his third wife, Isabel, was given political power, as vice president.

The sudden death of Juan Domingo Perón on July 1, 1974 brought Isabel to the supreme position in the land, but her administration was an unmitigated disaster. She was no Evita and she had little to offer Argentina except her husband's name. Her government was marked by

Isabel Perón's inability to get a grip on Argentina's chronic economic problems, and her failure to curb rising terrorism, led the military to intervene yet again. In a move that was widely expected and hoped for by many, they removed the last Perón from the Casa Rosada on March 24, 1976.

The Proceso

Although the military had never proved itself any more able to solve the nation's problems, there seemed to be a different attitude with this band of uniformed men steering the nation. Each of the four successive juntas made a point

ultra-conservatism, corruption, and repression.

Additionally, Isabel came to rely for advice on one of Argentina's most bizarre and sinister figures, the ex-police corporal José López Rega. This Rasputin-like character wielded great power and founded the infamous right-wing terrorist group, the Alianza Argentina Anticomunista. Reportedly, under Lopéz Rega's influence, Isabel even took to employing astrological divination as a means to determine national policy.

LEFT: Perón's third wife, Isabel.
ABOVE: the Mothers of the Plaza de Mayo demonstrating over the "dirty war" of the 1970s.

PERÓN STILL AT LARGE

Although Juan Domingo Perón served as president for only 11 years, his shadow remains over Argentina. Even since his death in 1974, the man and his ideology have remained strongly influential. He elicits the most powerful and polarized of responses from the citizenry: complete adoration or utter revulsion. In his name, governments have fallen, terrorist acts have been committed, and workers organized. His greatest achievement was to harness the energy of the Argentine laborer. Through the workers Perón established a political party that is still a force to be reckoned with, and which abandoned its pro-labor stance only recently.

of co-ordinating efforts among the various branches of the armed forces. The first junta tried to lend legitimacy to its leadership by amending the constitution. This amendment, the Statute for the National Reorganization Process, called for the junta to shoulder responsibility of executive and legislative functions of the state. The period of military rule from 1977–83 has come to be known as the *Proceso*.

General Jorge Rafael Videla was chosen as the first president and he attacked the problem of left-wing guerrilla action through a campaign dubbed the "dirty war." The military had set about "cleansing" Argentine society of any

left-wing influence, whether real or imagined, by eliminating union leaders, intellectuals, and student radicals – even executing a group of high-school students who had staged a protest against rising bus fares. The whole campaign was conducted secretly, abductions often occurring at night. The rule of law was completely flouted. The authorities never admitted capturing anyone, and very few people were ever charged with any offence. Alongside this repression, the armed forces took control of the universities, schools, and the television, radio, and other media. Few people in Argentina realized at the time the scale of the human-rights violations being carried out in their name.

International condemnation, the pleas of human-rights groups, and the efforts of the mothers of the disappeared – the Madres de la Plaza de Mayo *(see page 151)* – did not alleviate state-sponsored terrorism.

The military dictatorship in Argentina was different from the one in Chile under General Pinochet during the same period, because none of its members sought to take all power for themselves. The original junta of the different branches of the armed forces made decisions together, and stepped down together in 1980.

Videla was succeeded by General Viola who was then forced from office and replaced by General Galtieri. In economic matters, the military fared no better. Foreign debt soared to US$45 billion while the inflation rate went from bad to worse, unemployment increased, and the peso was constantly devalued. It was in this climate that General Galtieri and his junta chose to try something new.

The Malvinas conflict

It was ironic that the Argentine military, having won its dirty war against its own people, was forced from power, through waging – and losing – a conventional conflict. Galtieri hoped to divert public attention from the growing domestic crisis by the traditional method of turning their attention to foreign matters, in this case the British-occupied Malvinas (Falkland) Islands.

The ensuing South Atlantic War was brief but bloody, beginning on April 2, 1982 with the Argentine invasion of the islands and ending with their surrender at the capital Port Stanley on June 14.

The disputed archipelago appeared the perfect target for Galtieri: the tiny and sparsely

THE DISAPPEARED

It was while General Videla held office that the majority of the *desaparecidos* (disappeared) vanished. Anyone who was suspected of anti-government activity, as broadly defined by the military, could be made to disappear.

Nuns, priests, schoolchildren, and whole families were kidnapped, raped, tortured, and then murdered by a nefarious coalition of the military, police, and right-wing death squads acting in the dubious name of Christianity and democracy. Estimates of the numbers of *desaparecidos* range from 10,000 to 30,000 people, of whom only the tiniest fraction had actually been involved in any kind of terrorist activities.

populated islands lay more than 13,000 km (8,000 miles) from the United Kingdom. However, Galtieri and the other military commanders did not consider the possibility that Britain would fight to retain its claim to the islands.

This major miscalculation was one of many that the Argentine junta was to make during the following weeks. Technically, tactically, and politically, Argentina's rulers blundered badly. The conscripted army was ill-prepared for battle against trained professionals and did not put up much of a fight, while the navy stayed in port after a British submarine sank the cruiser *General Belgrano* on May 2. Only the efforts of

Frequent demonstrations in the Plaza de Mayo and other city centers reminded him and the other military leaders that the only task left for them was to organize free and fair elections as quickly as possible.

End of military power

The military, knowing its days in power were numbered, sought to protect itself from anticipated criminal prosecution for human-rights abuses by issuing its own study, *The Final Document of the Military Junta on the War Against Subversion and Terrorism.* This white paper praised the efforts of the armed forces

the Argentine Air Force salvaged some military honor for the country.

Taught since school that the "Malvinas are Argentine," many people at first supported their armed forces' efforts to regain the islands. It soon became clear that the military claims about the conflict were untrue, and the eventual defeat dealt the whole nation a crushing blow.

General Galtieri resigned three days after the Argentine surrender and was replaced a week later by the retired general, Reynaldo Bignone.

LEFT: a pro-democracy rally of the 1980s.
ABOVE: the Mothers of the Plaza de Mayo campaigning for their "disappeared" loved ones.

in combating and defeating terrorism and denied any involvement by the administration in the barbaric actions undertaken during the "dirty war." As an extra protection, the government proclaimed a general amnesty for all those involved in the "extra-legal" efforts to crush the opposition.

The election campaign of 1983 was full of surprises. Many analysts expected a Peronist return to power or possibly a coalition government. A majority of voters, however, selected Raúl Alfonsín and his Radical Party to lead the nation out of repression. Alfonsín was sworn in as president on December 10, one day after the military junta dissolved itself. ❏

Evita

Although María Eva Duarte de Perón, known throughout the world as Evita, lived in the limelight only briefly, her impact on Argentine politics was enormous and continues today, more than five decades after her death. Her memory is zealously protected. The 1996 film of the stage musical *Evita*, starring Madonna, provoked outrage among many Argentines, who felt the sacrilegious pop star was sullying the name of their heroine.

Evita was venerated by the Argentine working class, mocked by the *grandes dames* of Buenos

Aires society, and misunderstood by the military establishment. Through all of this, she came to symbolize a wealthy Argentina, full of pride and with great expectations following World War II.

Her meteoric rise from her beginnings as a poor villager in the backwaters of the interior to a status as one of the most intriguing, engaging, and powerful figures in a male-dominated culture is a tale worth retelling.

Evita was born in the squalid village of Los Toldos in 1919, one of five illegitimate children her mother bore to Juan Duarte. After her father's death, the family moved to the provincial town of Junín, under the patronage of another of her mother's benefactors.

It was in Junín that Evita, at the age of 14, became determined to be an actress. In the company of a young tango singer, she ran off to Buenos Aires, the cultural mecca of Latin America, where she faced almost insurmountable odds in landing jobs in the theater. Her opportunities took a dramatic leap forward when a rich manufacturer fell for her and provided her with her own radio show. Shortly thereafter, Evita's voice became a regular feature on the airwaves of Radio Argentina and Radio El Mundo.

Evita's energy was boundless; her work pace became frenetic and she made powerful friends. Her lack of acting talent and sophistication did not seem to hinder her ability to attract important people to her cause. Among her admirers were the president of Argentina and, more importantly, the Minister of Communications, Colonel Imbert, who controlled all radio stations in the country.

Evita met Colonel Juan Domingo Perón, the reputed power behind the new military government, at a fund-raising event for victims of the devastating 1944 San Juan earthquake. She left the event on the widowed colonel's arm.

Despite being exactly half Perón's 48 years when they met, Evita assisted his rise to power in ways that were beyond the imagination of even the most astute politicians. When Perón became Minister of Labor and Welfare, Evita convinced him that his real power base should be the previously ignored masses of laborers living in the horrible *villas miserias* (slums) that still ring the capital city.

A stream of pronouncements issued forth from the ministry instituting minimum wages, better living conditions, salary increases, and protection from employers. Additionally, and most brilliantly, Perón won the support of the giant Confederación General del Trabajo (CGT or General Confederation of Labor), which embraced many of the trade unions. In the process, however, recalcitrant labor leaders were picked up by the police and sent to prisons in Patagonia.

It was not long before Evita called Perón's constituency to his aid. In 1945, an army coup was on the point of success when Evita called in all her chips. Upwards of 200,000 *descamisados* – the shirtless ones – entered the capital city and demanded that Perón be their president. The colonel accepted the mandate of the Argentine people.

Evita, now married to Perón, cemented her ties with the workers by establishing the Social Aid Foundation. Through this charity, scores of hospitals and hundreds of schools were built, nurses trained, and money dispensed to the poor. Evita also formed the first women's political party, the Perónista Feminist Party.

Although a cult was developing around her personality, she always told the people in her countless speeches that all credit should go to her husband and that she would gladly sacrifice her life for him, as they should sacrifice theirs. Perhaps Evita's finest hour came with her long tour of Europe, during which she met Franco, the dictator of Spain, Pope Pius XII, and the Italian and French foreign ministers. She dazzled postwar Europe with her jewels and elegant gowns. Her rags-to-riches story was told and retold in the press, and she was even on the cover of *Time* magazine.

to the *descamisados*. Evita's death on July 26, 1952 brought the whole of Argentina to a standstill. Her body was embalmed, and at her wake hundreds of thousands paid their last respects.

Death brought no respite however, and in 1955, Evita's corpse disappeared, stolen by the military after they had deposed Juan Perón. It was carried to Germany and then Italy, where it was interred for 16 years under another name. After negotiations, it was returned to her husband in Spain. Evita's long odyssey came to an end when Juan Perón died in Argentina in 1974. Her coffin was brought from Spain and lay in state next to that of the one she had said she would die for.

On the negative side, Evita would brook no criticism of her husband. Newspapers were closed, careers destroyed, and opponents jailed on trumped-up charges. She could be extremely vindictive, never forgetting an insult, even if it lay years in the past. Family and friends were placed in positions well above their levels of competence.

The people's heroine was dying by 1952, a victim of uterine cancer, but she kept up her intense work schedule. During her last speech, on May Day, her husband had to hold her up as she spoke

LEFT: Evita at her dazzling peak.
ABOVE: a personal portrait of the Peróns with their pet poodles.

Even though efforts to have her canonized in Rome have been met with polite refusal, Evita still holds near-saint status in Argentina. Graffiti proclaiming *¡Evita Vive!* (Evita lives!) can be seen everywhere. At the Duarte family crypt in the Recoleta Cemetery *(see pages 176–177)*, devotees still leave flowers and written tributes. In 2002, the Museo Evita opened in Palermo, housed in a former home for single mothers run by the Eva Perón Foundation.

Evita's epitaph, famously paraphrased in the Andrew Lloyd Webber–Tim Rice rock opera *Evita* and in Alan Parker's subsequent film of the musical, reads: "Don't cry for me Argentina, I remain quite near to you." It still rings true, more than half a century after her premature death. ❏

THE MODERN DEMOCRACY

*As Argentina fervently embraced free-market capitalism, inflation was defeated
and the future seemed bright. Then everything went horribly wrong*

For many Argentines, the collapse of the military government in 1983 marked the end of a cycle of armed forces' interference in political life which had begun in 1930. There was great enthusiasm for civilian rule, which brought new freedom in the press, in literature, and in general discussions. Many thousands of Argentines who had fled military rule to live in exile returned, helping to add to the sense of a fresh start in political and social life.

This was combined with an attempt to explain and come to terms with what had happened during the military dictatorship. In 1984 the Radical Party and its president, Raúl Alfonsín, set up a commission to report on the political violence and its victims. The result was *Nunca Más* (Never Again), which detailed how the military dictatorship had kidnapped, tortured, and killed at least 9,000 Argentines whom they had regarded as "subversive." The evidence gathered led to the public trial of the leaders of the military juntas, and the historic decision to condemn five of them to imprisonment for crimes against humanity.

The civilian government's determination to prosecute the military leaders caused great unease among the armed forces. There were several military uprisings against Alfonsín, which were put down only thanks to popular support for him, and the loyalty of the new military commanders. In response to this pressure, President Alfonsín brought in two laws, one which limited responsibility for the "disappeared" to the military high command, and the other which declared the time for prosecutions for human-rights abuses to have a definite end.

Inflation and debt

Another legacy from the military dictatorship which President Alfonsín found hard to cope with was its economic mismanagement. The

---

PRECEDING PAGES: a political meeting outside Buenos Aires' Cathedral in the historic Plaza de Mayo.
LEFT: Congreso Nacional, the political think-tank.
RIGHT: Peronist demonstrators, drumming up support.

juntas had borrowed money internationally to fund huge projects and to balance their budgets. Now inflation and debt, combined with the Radical Party's lack of experience in government, undermined President Alfonsín's popularity. To try to remedy matters, a new currency, the *austral*, was introduced but within months, inflation

of several hundred percent wiped out many people's savings, and restricted the government's ability to plan coherently.

This was the situation in 1989, when Argentines were called on to vote for a second time in their newly restored democracy. By now, many of the voters thought that the Radical Party had failed in its attempt to bring prosperity and good government to Argentina. So they turned once more to the Peronists, and voted for Carlos Saúl Menem. The flamboyant Menem was the governor of a small interior province who had been imprisoned by the military dictatorship; he appeared to represent traditional Peronist economic and social values: support for working people and national industry, and an "anti-imperialist" stance in foreign affairs.

The end of the Alfonsín administration was a sorry affair. During the period between Menem's election and the official handover, the Argentine economy collapsed to such an extent that the handover was brought forward by several months.

It soon became clear that Menemism was very different from traditional Peronism. From the start of his administration, Menem followed the recipes for success suggested by the International Monetary Fund. He began to sell off much of Argentine industry, from the nationalized oil concern to the telephones and railways. He

United Kingdom – although the question of sovereignty over the Falkland Islands remained unresolved. Argentina left the Non-Aligned Movement, and declared that its interests were the same as those of the developed Western world. At the same time, the president declared an amnesty for the military personnel and the guerrillas who had been involved in the political violence of the 1970s, thus attempting to draw a line under this tragic episode in the country's history.

The early 1990s were boom years for Argentina. Buenos Aires once again rivalled the cities of Europe and North America not only for the choice of goods in the huge new shopping

removed all tariff protection for Argentine industry, allowing cheaper foreign imports to start to flood Argentina. But his boldest and most controversial move was to pass a law which put the Argentine peso on a par with the US dollar. This was intended to solve all of Argentina's chronic inflation problems. The value of the Argentine currency was guaranteed by government reserves, which were boosted by strong exports and the revenues from privatization.

Prosperous interlude

President Menem attempted to change Argentina's relations with the rest of the world. Great efforts were made to heal the rift with the

malls, and its glitzy restaurants and elegant cafes but also in the quality and range of its films, plays, and books. The middle class often looked down on President Menem, with his love of fast cars and his taste for the celebrity lifestyle (memorably characterized as "pizza with champagne") but they enjoyed being consumers of the newly available goods, they traveled abroad again, and for the first time in many years rediscovered a pride in being Argentine.

This sense of satisfaction helped Menem to win a second period in office easily in 1995. However, problems soon began to mount. The fact that the Argentine peso was the same value as the US dollar made the country's exports overpriced compared to those of its regional rivals. The imported goods that middle-class Argentines enjoyed so much were also very costly, making it hard for the government to balance the books. Many thousands of Argentines had been put out of work by the sell-off of state concerns, and could find no other employment. All this put a great strain on social security and pension provisions, which in turn made it hard for the central government to achieve stability.

CHANGE OF FACE

Soon after his election as president, Menem's picturesque long hair and sideburns were shortened to more conventional lengths and his gaucho's poncho was left for special visits to the interior.

The discontent led to the creation of an anti-Peronist alliance of parties, including the Radical Party and the FREPASO (Front for a Country of Solidarity). This alliance was triumphant in the 1999 presidential elections, while the Peronists were divided by internal wrangling between supporters of President Menem and the candidate who eventually stood, Eduardo Duhalde, governor of the province of Buenos Aires.

The new president was Fernando de la Rúa of the Radical Party. Once again there was optimism

Scandals and discontent

The administration was increasingly mired in corruption. The press revealed all kinds of scandals, from the discovery that one of the congressmen voting for the government was a distant relative of the elected representative, brought in to support the Peronists, to accusations that the president and other high-ranking officials had been involved in multimillion dollar illegal arms sales. A lot of the money earned through privatization had ended up in the politicians' pockets.

LEFT: President Nestor Kirchner with wife Cristina – a federal senator.
ABOVE: a spirited display of support by *Menemistas*.

that things might change. In the event, De la Rúa and his allies failed to grasp the opportunity. His biggest mistake was to continue with the policy of parity between the Argentine peso and the US dollar. He also failed to create new employment opportunities, while Argentina increasingly struggled to keep up with its debt repayments.

Calamity

The crisis came to a head in December 2001. Exasperated unemployed workers and government employees, who had not been paid in many months, joined with Peronist trade unionists in violent street protests. As many as 30 people are thought to have died in the demonstrations, and the situation was so unstable that President de la Rúa resigned, fleeing the presidential palace in a helicopter to avoid the angry crowds.

At the end of 2001, Argentina had four presidents in two weeks. Eventually it was the head of congress, Eduardo Duhalde, who was appointed interim president and had sufficient authority to calm the situation. His government declared it would not meet the payments due on foreign debt, and, to re-activate exports and reduce debts, he ended the peso-dollar parity. This led to a huge devaluation, with the peso soon having only one third of its previous international value. Controversially, to avoid the complete collapse of the

economy, the government froze all the dollar deposits that Argentines had in their local banks, and the middle classes joined the demonstrations.

The emergency measures brought some financial stability but did not solve the underlying problems. The years of unemployment and underinvestment had led to unprecedented poverty and economic hardship and Argentines were shocked to see pictures of children dying of malnutrition. Many turned against all politicians: "*Que se vayan todos*" (Get rid of them all) was the rallying cry at the continuing street protests.

Many ordinary Argentines began looking for alternatives to the corrupt rule by career politicians. There was a huge growth in popular assemblies – local residents getting together in parks or street corners to press for solutions to their problems. Dozens of factories that had been forced to close were re-opened as co-operatives by workers who had been laid off. Because of the lack of cash, bartering centers mushroomed.

Presidential elections in 2003 saw Carlos Menem, who was seeking a third term in office, facing the governor of the remote Patagonian province of Santa Cruz, Nestor Kirchner. Menem won most votes in the first round but not enough to guarantee success; he pulled out of the second round, leaving Kirchner as president-elect, although he had polled only a little over 20 percent of the vote in the first round. A familiar South American scenario ensued: when judges tried to have him arrested over allegations of fraud, Menem fled to Chile, returning at the end of 2004 when the warrants were canceled.

Rebuilding confidence

Nestor Kirchner, sworn into office in May 2003, faced a daunting challenge in salvaging the country's economy and trying to reduce the poverty affecting almost half of all Argentines. Since then, the cheap peso has greatly boosted Argentina's exports. The surplus generated has been used to pay off the IMF loans; other huge foreign debts have also been settled.

In many ways, President Kirchner has returned to old-style Peronism. He has re-nationalized some of the privatized industries, and has brought in government programs designed to alleviate poverty. But opponents say his government also shows some of the bad aspects of earlier Peronism. Surrounded by a small clan of trusted associates, he prefers to issue decrees rather than have policies properly debated in congress. He is also accused of accumulating more power for the presidency, by controlling the judiciary and limiting the powers of the provinces. Remembering the difficulties President Perón had in the 1950s, observers worry what might happen when the economic situation is not so favorable.

Nevertheless, Argentina is very different from a generation ago. The armed forces play no political role and the rule of law is firmly established. Political debate thrives on every street corner, and, particularly in the capital and the large cities, there is renewed optimism about the future. ❏

LEFT: bleak news from the currency exchange market.
RIGHT: brightening up a quiet corner of Buenos Aires.

A PEOPLE OF PASSION

The country's large and varied immigrant populations
make for a colorful and diverse national identity and cultural life

Visit Bariloche in July and the Fiesta de las Colectividades ("Community Festival") will give you a taste of the different immigrant groups that make up Argentina. Spaniards, Italians, Germans, Swiss, Russians, Austrians, Slovaks, Danes, and Norwegians are there, amongst others, taking out and dusting off an often dormant sense of national identity, keeping alive the dance and song of a former life and entering a bustling mêlée around colorful stalls that sell typical food from pizzas to blinis. It's a vibrant celebration, with a characteristic indifference to time. And it's a curious revelation when friends who are indubitably Argentine unearth their cultural roots.

The original inhabitants of Argentina were divided into many distinct peoples, but their numbers were few. The first European settlers, in the 16th century, were almost all Spanish, as were those arriving over the next 300 years. A minority population of mestizos (people of Amerindian and Hispanic descent) developed early. A large number of enslaved Africans were brought in during the 17th and 18th centuries, and mulattos (people of black and Hispanic descent) and people of Amerindian/Afro-American descent formed a significant part of the population.

Yet the 19th century saw great changes in this ethnic make-up of Argentina. Through a concerted effort, the vast majority of the Amerindian population was wiped out by the Argentine Army. This freed the land for European settlers, though some say Patagonia is cursed because of the brutal manner of its liberation. After the abolition of slavery, the black population also faded from view *(see page 41)*.

A new frontier

At the end of the 19th century and turn of the 20th century, there was another wave of

PRECEDING PAGES: an annual religious pilgrimage in Northwest Argentina.
LEFT: lost in thought.
RIGHT: Russian immigrants in the 1930s.

immigration across the Atlantic from Europe. By 1914, the population of Argentina was about 30 percent foreign-born, and in some of the larger cities, the foreigners outnumbered the so-called natives. These new hands were put to work filling positions in the expanding agricultural industry, in cattle raising and processing, and in

the developing economies of the big cities.

Argentina's population increased fourfold between 1860 and the start of World War II. Most of the newcomers were agricultural workers, who had been promised "a job, a house, and land." They often found that none of these promises was fulfilled, and so were forced to live in Buenos Aires and the other cities, in crowded tenements or *conventillos*. The countryside remained in the hands of a few criollo landowners, which led to many of the political and social tensions between city and countryside throughout the 20th century.

Many of these newcomers came from Spain and Italy, but there were significant numbers from other nationalities. Many thousands of Jewish people fled persecution in Eastern Europe and Russia and came to Argentina. Some of them went to live on land bought for them by a Baron Hirsch, and became the famous "Jewish gauchos," while most of these pioneers ended up in the cities. As a result of this, Buenos Aires has the highest proportion of Jewish inhabitants (and psychiatrists) after New York.

Many thousands of Germans also came. Some of them headed south for the mountains and lakes that reminded them of home, and there are towns and villages in the Andes that look distinctly German still. Whereas the Germans

who came before World War II were most likely to be socialist or anarchist in their politics, after the war a fresh wave of Germans who had been Nazi party members or sympathizers arrived, among them the infamous Adolf Eichmann.

One of the most influential foreign communities in Argentina were the British. Although in Argentina they are known as the *ingleses*, most of these arrivals were in fact Welsh, Scottish, or Irish in origin.

Patagonia's Welsh

The Welsh, who left their native valleys to pursue this opportunity *(see page 308)*, must have had their doubts when the first arrivals in the 1860s walked for days across Patagonia's barren wastes in search of fresh water, until they reached the River Chubut.

The initial co-operation of the indigenous peoples, and their own tenacity, eventually yielded a string of prosperous settlements along the Chubut valley and so with legitimate pride, the Welsh cling to their national identity more fiercely than most. One of these Welsh towns, Gaiman, brings over someone from Wales each year to preserve and protect the native culture, and the annual *Eisteddfod* is as much a feature of life here as in Wales itself.

More English than the English

The first British settlers came to administer the building of the country's infrastructure, and their services helped to make Argentina one of the world's 10 richest countries by the beginning of the 20th century. To a large extent, it was British capital which built the Argentine railroad and banking systems in the 19th century. British money also helped develop the cattle industry, with modern methods of refrigeration, packaging, and transportation. Some Englishmen bought huge tracts of land in the south to raise sheep and, for a time, southern Patagonia seemed an extension of the British Empire.

The 1982 war over the Malvinas (Falkland) Islands was inevitably a tense time for Anglo-Argentines. Some left but for most, loyalty to Argentina triumphed. Argentines remain convinced of the legitimacy of their claim to the islands: even in the most remote and unlikely places stand large signs proclaiming *"Las Malvinas son Argentinas."*

Meanwhile, as with many immigrants, the Anglo-Argentines' recollections of home are

NATIVE SURVIVORS

Argentina has a huge immigrant population, each one maintaining parts of its culture. Indigenous populations survive in pockets, and while some native languages continue and traditional crafts enjoy a revival of interest, few tribes practice traditional lifestyles in more than a ceremonial sense. Quechua is still spoken in the North-west, where the Colla are the largest group. Chiriguan, Choroti, Wichi, Mocovi, and Toba are spoken in the Chaco; the Chiriguan are the principal tribe of Mesopotamia. The Araucano-Mapuches and the Tehuelche were the major groups in Patagonia and the pampas, but very few pure-blooded descendants survive today.

frozen in the past. There is a slightly archaic refinement, a quaint trust in "things British" which would, no doubt, be jolted by a brush with today's multicultural Britain.

British schools such as St. Andrew's and St. George's continue to thrive in Argentina, as does the British hospital. Polo and cricket continue to be played at weekends on the manicured lawns of the exclusive Hurlingham Club outside Buenos Aires. Rugby and football are other British imports, as evidenced by the English names of soccer clubs such as River Plate and Racing.

The British heritage, however, is fading as new

although he had to convert to Catholicism to become president.

Unlike many other Latin American countries, Argentina does not have a large Chinese community, but Buenos Aires can boast one Japanese neighborhood, while in recent years Koreans have been taking over many corner shops in the cities and towns.

Economic migrants

For many years, Argentina's standard of living was much higher than that of its neighbors. Its education system and universities were also much more developed. This has meant that

generations feel that US business English is more useful than the Queen's English, and pervasive cable TV reinforces the point. The trend now is to send children to US colleges rather than to more traditional English boarding schools.

Non-European arrivals

Many groups have also come to Argentina from outside Europe. From the former Turkish Empire there are many people of Syrian or Lebanese origin (popularly known as *turcos*). The best-known of these was former President Menem,

people from Bolivia, Paraguay, Uruguay, and Chile have frequently sought a better life in Argentina. These immigrants, as well as internal migrants from Argentina's poorer provinces in the north and west, tend to do the jobs most other Argentines shun: in the service sector, as laborers on building sites, or in agriculture. They are the first to suffer from any economic downturn.

The national identity

The fact that all these groups of incomers usually live alongside each other in harmony is a tribute above all to the Argentine education system. From the earliest years, schools insist that everyone is first and foremost Argentine –

LEFT: Araucanian woman. **ABOVE:** ephemeral masterpiece on a San Telmo sidewalk.

religions and languages other than Spanish are left for the individual to pursue. This has created a strong sense of national identity, although tensions remain.

For a start, there is the contrast between urban and rural life, all the more sharply drawn in a nation where suburbia scarcely exists. Of a total population of 39 million, some 12 million live in Buenos Aires.

The *porteño*, as the resident of Buenos Aires is known, thrives on the pace and bustle of life in the capital. Walk along Florida, Buenos

LED BY THE STARS

The increasing number of foreign stars such as Sylvester Stallone and Jane Fonda who have bought land in Patagonia has given locals a renewed interest in their land.

Aires' busiest shopping street, and the sleek sophistication is palpable, further accentuated by the inherent stylishness of the people. The latest trends may sometimes be slow to cross the Atlantic, but the Argentines don't need anyone to tell them how to look good, and elegant shopping malls continue to open in the capital.

Outside the capital, dress is generally more relaxed, though stylish nonetheless. Designer jeans are more commonplace than suits. Ties for men are not de rigueur.

City talk

In the coffee houses of Buenos Aires one thing is clear. The Argentines love to talk. People are articulate and lucid, confident in expressing their opinions. All matters, small or large, are worthy of comment. The most routine of meetings can erupt in animated discussion. Teenagers are rarely reticent. The problem is not getting people to talk, but rather to listen, with a rich and expressive vocabulary of gestures jostling with words for attention.

Soccer and politics are among the topics most likely to ignite conversation. Soccer is the big national sport, and team allegiances are strong. At a fairly early age most Argentines decide where those allegiances lie.

The political renaissance of the Alfonsín years, immediately following military rule, gradually slipped into disenchantment with politics and politicians during the Menem years. The economic crisis and rampant corruption which his successors have failed to resolve have further undermined faith in the political system and political parties, and disillusionment is widespread.

"In the camp"

Out on the estancias, or "in the camp" as the Anglo-Argentines say, it's a different story. The archetypal male is taciturn, especially in mixed company. He will still hold firm his opinions, often tinged with a wry melancholy, but he will waste fewer words on them.

Here the forum for discussion is not the coffee house but a maté *(see page 130)*. The thirst-quenching qualities of this home-brewed tea are of secondary importance to its social role. Passing the maté around is a decorous ritual. Traditionally the water is heated in a crude tin or kettle over an open fire, brewed in a small gourd, and sipped through a perforated metal straw called a *bombilla*. It's a convivial part of life, and not only in the camp.

So too is the *asado* (barbecue), where Argentines indulge their passion for meat to the full. Barbecues are usually communal affairs where everyone will be expected to put away about half a kilo (one pound) of meat. Salads are served nowadays as a concession to health fads, but real men stick to meat and dry bread washed down by beer and then a maté.

Nowhere more than at an *asado* is Argentine conservatism and chauvinism apparent.

Preparing the *asado* is a male preserve involving a certain way of positioning and timing of the meat to ensure it is cooked to perfection. Men stand around the fire cutting hunks of meat from the carcass with showy *asado* knives, while women sit at a rustic table and chat together. When all have eaten their fill the men continue their discussions over a maté, while the women depart to wash the dishes.

KISS ON THE CHEEK

In family, social, and even formal situations there is rarely any agonized uncertainty about the right greeting. People just kiss.

Nonetheless, Argentine family life has undergone a striking metamorphosis. Women now comprise nearly half of the workforce; 40 percent of Argentine households are supported by female breadwinners; and 50 percent of students at university are women. Argentina was the first country in Latin America to introduce quotas for women in elective congressional posts. As a result, women now hold 25 percent of seats compared to 6 percent in 1991, and Brazil, Bolivia, Venezuela, Peru, and Ecuador have followed this radical lead.

The extended family

Although old-fashioned chauvinism and its counterpart chivalry still exist, the overwhelming flavor of society, especially among the young, is of freedom and informality. This is in part a reaction, some say, to the years of military repression. Its also a reflection of the strength of the extended family.

Young people usually live at home until they get married, and even then may only move a few blocks away. Students do not often move out when they enter university, as they frequently attend schools in their home towns. The generation gap is far less apparent than in some countries. Young and old are used to each other's company, sharing news and ideas comfortably in contexts like family *asados*. Cousins are often best friends. The cool and studied indifference of adolescence exists, of course. But the overall impression is of people visibly enjoying life.

When a child reaches school-leaving age, most parents will put considerable effort into planning and preparing the class celebration. It's a milestone, a shared occasion among families and classmates, and just one telling demonstration

of how much the Argentines know about the art of celebration. Nightlife, for example, is vigorous. Many discotheques don't even get going until the early hours, and the music doesn't finish until daybreak.

Group mentality

Among young people, there is a keen sense of the individual, and yet there is also a very strong feeling of group identity. Children will pass through school with virtually the same classmates throughout. Usually all will share their birthday celebrations together.

All will take part in a week-long school trip to mark the end of their primary and secondary schooling and, by the time they emerge, the common bond of shared experience is enough to cement relationships for a lifetime. Besides, Argentines are by nature gregarious. Find an idyllic quiet picnic spot and, if a car should happen to pass, the occupants are as likely to join you as search for their own patch of solitude. Or witness the streets of Bariloche or Carlos Paz, popular destinations of these *viajes de egresados* (school-leaving trips), when students move in packs singing and chanting, crowding into group photographs, all sporting matching hats or jackets.

LEFT: a romantic evening in San Telmo.
RIGHT: a child of the Northwest.

Tactile behavior in Argentina is the norm. Not just a polite social peck, but touching, kissing, hugging, and linking arms, all with an easy, uninhibited warmth which no one in the country will misconstrue.

Taking their time

The relaxed social approach also applies to time frames. If it doesn't get done today it will surely get done tomorrow – the infamous Spanish "*mañana.*" When waiting for an Argentine to keep an appointment, whether for a cup of coffee or a

RED TAPE MAZE

Excessive bureaucracy is a part of daily life – buying a car or obtaining a passport involves an inordinate amount of paperwork.

Church and bureaucracy

The church is still a pervasive, if nominal influence. Constitutional reforms in 1994 continue to guarantee religious freedom, but Catholicism is no longer the state religion, nor does the president have to be a Catholic. About 90 percent of the Argentine population is Catholic, but less than 20 percent are practicing. Strict faith no longer seems to have a firm grip on the national psyche and only periodic observances remain, like catechism and first communion.

business meeting, allowance should be made for benign tardiness. It's a way of life. Beware of being asked to wait "*un momentito,*" literally a little moment – which might be considerably more; or of being assured that something is about to happen "*ya,*" or right away, which is similarly elastic. If you ask the mechanic when your car will be ready, the answer is usually "*última hora*" – closing time, whenever that might be.

This is partly due to a different work ethic. Here people are always ready to sacrifice a little efficiency for the sake of making work more enjoyable with a chat, a maté, and a few *facturas* (pastries).

However, it was only in 2002 that the government managed to pass a law to allow family-planning advice and free birth control. Until then the move was resisted strongly by Catholic groups in a country where abortion is still illegal and an imprisonable offense.

Argentina is a country which operates on a low level of trust. It may be because a chancer *(vivo)* who gets away with something is more likely to evoke grudging admiration here than moral indignation. As a result, bureaucracy has had to build in elaborate and often cumbersome systems of verification and security to reduce the scope for dishonesty. The public sector often lacks the resources to implement modern systems and is frequently unwieldy and inefficient. Obtaining a simple document may involve trips to the bank, the post office, and the police station, all in pursuit of the appropriate array of rubber stamps and validated papers. To open a business in Argentina demands 12 separate bureaucratic procedures and takes over three months. A paper chase which would drive many other nationalities wild is met with resigned acceptance by the otherwise volatile Argentines.

More than 80 percent of Argentines do not have faith in the legal system and do not use it, according to a national newspaper survey. Corruption has always been rife in the country but has increased owing to its economic woes.

Health matters

Visiting the doctor also requires this patience in abundance. Even children rise to the occasion, waiting passively, with neither toys nor books to distract them. But health matters are ready fuel for conversation. People exchange news of their ailments with remarkable openness. Virtual strangers will pat a pregnant woman's stomach as they make inquiries and pass judgment on the likely sex of the impending arrival.

Sophisticated medical care is available in Buenos Aires, less so in the provinces. There is also a growing interest in alternative medicines, and many traditional remedies are held dear.

Psychology, too, is something of a national hobby. A school may not have a photocopier or even stationery, but it will certainly have an educational psychologist. The study and practice of psychology was suppressed during the years of the Proceso (military rule from 1977–83). Military authorities viewed the field as subversive, and books on the subject were removed from public and private shelves. University departments were cut or closed down.

Living with the past

Ironically, repression in the Proceso era, together with the dirty war's legacy of harrowing memories, has contributed to the resurgence of interest in psychology. While the government's

LEFT: table football outside a bar in La Boca.
RIGHT: a butcher takes a breather.

OLD WIVES' REMEDIES

Anyone suffering from a stomach complaint, *empacho*, may be cured by a deft pull of the skin covering the lower vertebrae – *tirando el cuero*. It seems to work, whatever the logic.

policy has been to draw a line under the past and move forward, with an early amnesty for many military offenders of the period, public pressure has challenged this approach.

For many years, the mothers of the "disappeared" *(see page 151)* rallied in the Plaza de Mayo every Thursday, their white headscarves neatly embroidered in blue with the names of their lost children. Long years of steadfast campaigning have met with success that at times is bittersweet. Grandparents have been united

with grandchildren they never knew – children taken from women abducted while pregnant and placed for adoption with childless couples (some in the militia), whose natural mothers were then killed. Some of these children, brought up in loving homes, have been, and are being, torn apart by the truth.

Argentina is still trying to come to terms with the savage political repression of the 1970s. The truth about what happened to the thousands of "disappeared" is slowly becoming known, and more human-rights violators are facing trial. President Kirchner has made determined efforts to make sure that this dark period of Argentine history is cleared up once and for all. ❑

THE TANGO

*Out of the immigrants' melting pot that is Argentina, tango was born,
working its way out from the brothels and into the rest of society*

A music filled with nostalgia, sexiness, drama, and kitsch, tango is the soul of Argentina. Like the blues in the United States, it can express sadness and hard times, and yet it has survived triumphantly for more than a century. As a dance, it is enjoying a huge revival in Argentina and around the world, with tango world championships being held every year in Buenos Aires. But the music has also moved into the electronic era, with groups such as Gotan Project and Bajofondo Tango Club incorporating new sounds from rap to dub beats into its typical 5/8 rhythms.

But what are the origins of this sensual and melancholy music, so intimately identified with Argentina and its nerve center and capital, Buenos Aires? The story begins just as the 19th century was ending. At this time, the whole Río de la Plata region, in Uruguay as in Argentina, began to receive great waves of European immigrants. Most of them settled in and around the growing ports of Buenos Aires and Montevideo.

The mixture of Italian, Spanish, East European, and Jewish newcomers mingled with the local population, itself a combination of Hispanics, blacks, and indigenous Americans. Each of these groups had its own musical heritage.

In the rough-and-tumble world of the predominantly male immigrants and working poor, the pulsing rhythm known as the *candombe* that arrived with African slaves mixed with the haunting melodies of Andalusia and southern Italy and the locally popular *milongas* (traditional gaucho songs). Sometime during the 1880s, all these cultural elements fused to give rise to something completely new – the tango.

Music of the night

Exactly when and where is both a mystery and a hotly disputed controversy. The most important gathering place for the working classes in this period was the brothel. In the parlors, as customers waited their turn, musi-

cians played and sang suggestive and often obscene lyrics that gave the tango its early fame for ribaldry. Because of the context, only fragments of the earliest tango lyrics survived, and their authors remain anonymous or known only by colorful nicknames. It wasn't until 1896 that pianist Rosendo Mendizabal put his

name to *El Enterriano (The Man from Entre Ríos)*, the first signed tango.

But the men who spent their nights listening to tangos in the brothels lived by day in the overcrowded tenements that were concentrated in the older, southern areas of Buenos Aires. Inevitably, the tango began to spill out into the patios, there to be played by the local musicians, and to become part of other popular cultural forms, such as the much-attended theatricals known as *sainetes*.

A new audience

By the turn of the 20th century, the tango had increased its audience to include all but the still

---

LEFT: bringing a touch of style to the streets.
RIGHT: a tango duo on El Caminito, La Boca.

disapproving upper classes. During these early years, the configuration of a tango orchestra varied greatly. As many of the musicians were poor, they relied on whatever instruments could be hired. Guitars, violins, flutes, and the less transportable piano were joined by that most special of all tango instruments, the bandoneon, a close relative of the accordion.

In the 20th century's first decade, Buenos Aires, and with it the tango, underwent a transformation. Gradually the tango moved out of the poorest areas and

TANGO FOR TOURISTS

A number of clubs located in San Telmo feature tango music and professional dancers who provide tourists with the variety of tango flavors that made the dance a successful exotic export.

Sad Night). It was the end of one era and the beginning of another.

Carlos Gardel became tango's first international superstar. His career shows the most important developments of the genre in its first golden era. Despite the debate among aficionados, it seems likely that Gardel was born in Toulouse in France sometime around 1891. What transformed Gardel into a star and the tango into music with a far wider appeal, were recordings, radio, and cinema. Gardel went

into the salons of the rich. The dancing became more stylized, the lyrics less openly bawdy. But it was not until the music traveled back across the Atlantic and was taken up by the smart set in Paris that its fame became international. This international acceptance reinforced its success back in Argentina: what was good for Paris had to be good enough for Buenos Aires.

Carlos Gardel

Another source of change was the arrival of the recording industry. By 1913 a limited number of local recordings were being made, and in 1917 Victor Records captured the young voice of Carlos Gardel singing *Mi Noche Triste (My*

to France in 1929 and made films at Joinville, and in 1934 he signed a contract with Paramount in Hollywood, where he made five films.

By the time of his death in a plane crash in Colombia in 1935, Gardel had become the personification of the tango. When his body was taken to Buenos Aires, thousands gathered to say goodbye to the *"pibe de Abasto"* (kid from Abasto), the neighborhood around the old Central Market. In 1984 the local subway stop was renamed in his honor.

Highs and lows

Gardel's tragic early death seemed to many a confirmation that tango music and life were inextricably intertwined. Throughout the diffi-cult 1930s, songwriters like Enrique Santos Discépolo wrote poetic lyrics of loss, betrayed hope, and nostalgia for a golden age that had never really existed: "tango is a sadness to dance to," wrote Discépolo.

Thousands of world-weary *compadritos* adopted the Gardel uniform: a felt fedora hat, white scarf, and tuxedo, as they danced to increasingly sophisticated rhythms from ever-larger tango orchestras. This was the second golden age of tango, when the radio and dance

> **MUSIC MAKERS**
>
> Edmundo Rivero, one of the great tango singers of all time, said: "When all is said and done, the tango is no more than a reflection of our daily reality."

Tango renaissance

But tango music not only survived, it thrived. Musicians such as Astor Piazzolla, who spent most of his childhood in New York, brought in influences from jazz and classical music, creating what was called *nuevo tango* (new tango). This was tango to be listened to, like modern jazz, and although it had its followers, the old dancehalls fell into decay.

It was nostalgia that once again saved the tango. Many of the thousands forced into Euro-

bands in every city provided the backdrop for celebrations by every Argentine, and youngsters learnt the intricate dance steps almost as soon as they could walk.

In the late 1940s, tango became increasingly associated with Peronism and his kind of stri-dent nationalism. In consequence, it suffered when Perón was toppled and went into exile, giving way to more international styles such as pop and rock. In the 1960s, the last thing young Argentines wanted to be seen doing was dancing the old-fashioned, stale tango.

pean exile in the late 1970s listened to the music, crooned Gardel's *Mi Buenos Aires Querido* with tears in their eyes, and encour-aged a new generation of singers to revisit the 1930s classics. As the political scene opened up again in Argentina, tango made a triumphal return along with the exiles.

In Buenos Aires now there are several 24-hour tango radio stations. Argentines try to outdo each other by finding the most "authentic" *milonga* or ballroom where the music is played. Thousands of tourists come to see the tango shows and to learn the intricate dance steps. New groups have revitalized the music, and there are fans of its unmistakable rhythms from Japan to Finland. ❑

LEFT: painted plaque recalls a well-known melody.
ABOVE: it takes two – and a lot of passion.

A TANGO TOUR OF BUENOS AIRES

From the buskers and street dancers of La Boca to the glitzy dinner-shows of San Telmo, tango is as popular as ever in the Argentine capital.

The tango dance was born in the port of Buenos Aires more than a hundred years ago. Nobody is sure of its origins: its rhythms are a mixture of Spanish, African, Cuban, and indigenous Argentine dances. For many years it was banned from polite society in Argentina, because it was a product of the brothels and other low dives of the port area. Only when it became all the rage in France just before the World War I, was it taken up by everyone in Argentine society.

PURE PASSION

Close in spirit to jazz and the blues, tango has been in and out of fashion over the past ninety years, but has always survived and been taken up by another generation of young Argentines who recognize it as a true expression of their emotions. Argentines argue as passionately about their favorite tango orchestras and eras as they do about their football teams. Some say that tango should be danced to and not sung; others argue that tango reaches its highest expression when the nostalgia and longing of the music are put into words. One tango writer has called its rhythms "sadness you can dance to," but the intricate steps and subtle interplay between the two partners is exhilarating – and incredibly good exercise!

▷ **IT TAKES TWO...**
There are many styles of tango dancing, but Argentine tango is quite different from "ballroom" tango. The man leads the woman in a series of steps, often improvised, and the two hold their bodies in a continuous close embrace.

△ **DANCING THE NIGHT AWAY**
Several of the old dance-halls in downtown Buenos Aires from tango's 1940s heyday have been redecorated to cater for the new devotees of the dance. Some open morning, noon, and night for the *milongueros*, or dance fans.

△ **GARDEL'S LEGACY**
There are numerous organized tango tours of Buenos Aires and part of the trail is likely to focus on tango legend Carlos Gardel. One renowned venue, Esquina Carlos Gardel, is located on the site of the Chanta Cuatro restaurant where Gardel and friends once met to sing and while away the hours. Gardel died in 1935 but is still the idol of all Argentine tango devotees: "Gardel sings better every day" is a common expression.

THE LANGUAGE OF LOVE

△ EUROPEAN ROOTS

The bandoneon is the most important instrument of tango orchestras. A button accordion, it is thought to have been brought to Argentina by German sailors during the second half of the 19th century.

△ SIGN OF THE TIMES

The building at Corrientes 348 was immortalized in the tango classic "A Media Luz," a sad story of illicit love in the heart of Buenos Aires' smartest theater street. It is now a parking lot.

▽ BEHIND THE SCENES

Dressing for tango performances sees the men as "compadritos," a style copied from the immigrants who dressed up to dance in their finest fedoras, with a white scarf over a dark jacket.

△ BRIGHT LIGHTS

Tango is big business in Argentina today. There are numerous places in the center of Buenos Aires, including Señor Tango, to see slick and stylish performances. But as well as the glitzy shows for tourists, tango is still danced by Argentines in dance halls, bars, or patios whenever neighbors get together.

Many of the songs played by tango orchestras are written in the slang of the Buenos Aires port area known as *lunfardo*. This is thought to have originated in Genoa, where many of the Italian immigrants to Argentina came from, but in Buenos Aires words from Spanish, Portuguese, from the indigenous Indians of the pampas, as well as words of backslang (in which for example the word "tango" becomes "gotan"), have been added to the mix. As with the tango itself, *lunfardo* began in the poorest areas of the port on the margins of respectable society, but over the years, many new words and expressions have been added, and some of them, such as *mina* (a girl or woman) or *gil* (a stupid idiot), have passed into everyday language. The tangos of the 1930s and 1940s are full of *lunfardo* lines and images, which are often impenetrable to other Spanish-speaking Latin Americans. The ability to speak *lunfardo* (the word itself is thought to mean "outside the law") is proof that you are a genuine *porteño* (someone from the port of Buenos Aires), and it continues to thrive. Nowadays there are even *lunfardo* hip-hop artists proudly making up fresh *lunfardo* verses.

ORPHANS OF THE PAMPAS

Gauchos, once free-spirited individuals who lived off the land,
have been tamed and, through land privatization, driven to near extinction

The gaucho stands as one of the best-known cultural symbols of Argentina. This rough, tough, free-riding horseman of the pampas, a proud cousin of the North American cowboy, is maintained in Argentine culture as the perfect embodiment of *argentinidad*, the very essence of the national character. He has been elevated to the level of myth, celebrated in both song and prose, and well endowed with the virtues of strength, bravery, and honor.

Pampean orphans

As to the origin of the name gaucho, there are many theories which trace the word to everything from Arabic and Basque, to French and Portuguese. The most likely answer is that the word has joint roots in the indigenous dialects of Quechua and Araucanian, a derivation of their word for orphan.

The first gauchos were mostly mestizos, of mixed Spanish and native American descent. As with the North American cowboy, some also had varied amounts of African blood, a legacy of Argentina's slave trade.

Hides and tallow

Cattle and horses that had escaped from early Spanish settlements in the 16th century had, over the centuries, proliferated into enormous free-roaming herds, and it was this wild, un-claimed abundance that was the basis for the development of the gaucho subculture. The horses were first caught and tamed, and then used to capture the cattle.

Beef at that time did not have any great commercial value; there was more meat than the tiny population of Argentina could consume, and methods to export it had not yet been developed. This surplus led to waste on a grand scale; any excess meat was simply thrown away.

The primary value of the cattle was in the hides and tallow they provided, which were non-perishable exportable items. The first gauchos made their living by selling these in exchange for tobacco, rum, and maté; gauchos were said to be so addicted to this stimulating tea that they would rather have gone

without their beef. Their existence was fairly humble, with few needs. Most did not possess much beyond a horse, a saddle, a poncho, and a knife. The work was not terribly rigorous, and early travelers' accounts of the gauchos portray them as savage vagabonds who spent much of their free time drinking and gambling.

This combination of activities often led to a third favorite pastime: the knife fight. The violent lifestyle of the gaucho was looked upon with horror and disdain by city folk, but the animosity was mutual. The gauchos had nothing but scorn for what they saw as the fettered and refined ways of the city dwellers.

PRECEDING PAGES: a gaucho displays his wealth.
LEFT: gauchos from Salta with their stiff leather *guardamontes* (saddle guards).
RIGHT: gaucho from Estancia la Esocondida, Santa Fe.

Skilled horsemanship

The primary reputation of the gaucho, however, was that of a horseman, and this was well deserved. It was said that when a gaucho was without his horse he was without legs.

Almost all of the gaucho's daily chores, from bathing to hunting, were conducted from atop his steed. The first gauchos hunted with lassoes and *boleadoras*, both of which were inventions borrowed from the indigenous peoples. *Boleadoras* consisted of three stones or metal balls attached to the ends of connected thongs. Thrown with phenomenal accuracy by the gauchos, this weapon was designed to trip the legs of the fleeing prey.

The great emphasis placed on equestrian skills led to competition. Strength, speed, and courage were highly prized, and the chance to demonstrate these came often.

In one event, the *sortija*, a horseman would ride full tilt with a lance in his hand to catch a tiny ring dangling from a crossbar. Another test, the *maroma*, would call for a man to drop from a corral gate as a herd of wild horses was driven out beneath him. Tremendous strength was needed to land on a horse's bare back, bring it under control, and return with it to the gate.

FEARLESS COMPETITORS

Hair-raising competitions were commonplace, as gauchos took great pride in displaying their impressive equestrian skills. A good illustration of how these competitions were born of the necessity to develop skills in everyday survival is the practice of *pialar*. In this challenge, a man would ride through a gauntlet of his lasso-wielding comrades, who would try to trip up the feet of his mount. The object of the exercise was for the unseated man to land on his feet with reins firmly in hand. This kind of control was often necessary on the open plain, where hidden animal burrows presented a constant danger underfoot.

Ranch hands

Profound change came to the gauchos' way of life as increasing portions of the pampas came under private ownership. The gauchos, with their anarchistic and highly independent ways, were seen as a hindrance to the development of the land. Increasing restrictions were put on their lives, in order to bring them under authoritarian control and to put them at the service of the new landowners.

It was not only the land which came under private ownership, but the cattle and horses that were found on it, making them inaccessible to the free riders. The gauchos were suddenly put in the position of being trespassers and cattle thieves. This made their situation similar to that of the remaining tribes of plains Amerindians.

New order

With such an obvious conflict of interests, there had to be a resolution, and it was, predictably enough, in favor of the landowners. The open prairie lands were fenced off, and the disenfranchised gauchos were put to work at the service of the *estancieros*. Their skills were employed to round up, brand, and maintain the herds.

> **DISPLACED PEOPLE**
>
> With the privatization of land and cattle, when gauchos got into trouble in one area, they simply rode on to another, and, little by little, they were found further from the settled areas.

Informal armies

However, while the gaucho ceased to present an independent threat, he still had a role to play in the new social structure of the rural areas, and soon new bonds of loyalty were formed between the worker and his master. Powerful caudillos were gaining control over large parts of the interior, backed up by their gauchos, who served as irregular troops in private armies. This formation of regional powers was in direct contradiction to the goals of centralized government.

However, the gauchos maintained their pride. They refused to do any unmounted labor, which was seen as the ultimate degradation. Everyday chores such as the digging of ditches, mending of fences, and planting of trees were reserved for the immigrants who were arriving in increasing numbers from Europe. Yet when barbed-wire fencing was put up, fewer hands were needed to maintain the herds. Combined with the increase in agriculture, this led to even harder times.

LEFT: early gaucho, with distinctive toe-held stirrups.
ABOVE: round-up in Corrientes province, where the gauchos are renowned for working barefoot.

Gauchos were also, at various times, put to work in the defense of the central government. These skilled horsemen were first used in the armies that routed the British invasion forces in 1806 and 1807, and by all accounts, their services were invaluable. Gaucho squadrons were next employed in the war of independence from Spain, and again they displayed great valor. The last time that the gauchos fought as an organized force in the nation's army was during the Desert Campaign of the 1870s *(see page 54)*.

Stylish dressers

Although gaucho clothing was originally designed simply for comfort and practicality, the men of the pampas were born dandies, and their traditional outfits were always worn with a certain amount of flair.

The *chiripá*, a loose diaper-like cloth draped between the legs, was very suitable for riding. It was often worn with long, fringed leggings. These were later replaced by *bombachas*, pleated pants with buttoned ankles that fitted inside their boots.

Although store-bought boots with soles became popular with gauchos in later years,

the first boots were home-made, fashioned from a single piece of hide, slipped from the leg of a horse. Often the toe was left open. This had a practical function, as the early stirrups were nothing more than a knot in a hanging leather thong.

Around his waist the gaucho wore a *faja*, a woolen sash, and a *rastra*, a stiff leather belt adorned with coins. This leather belt provided support for the back during the long hours in the saddle. At the gaucho's back, between these two belts, was tucked the *facón*, a gaucho's most prized possession after his horse *(see page 99)*.

The outfit was completed with a kerchief, a hat, a set of spurs, and a vest, for more formal occasions. Over all this, a gaucho wore his poncho, which also served as a blanket at night and a shield during a knife fight.

The gaucho saddle was a layered set of pads, braces, and molded leather, on top of which sat a sheepskin that made the long rides more comfortable. In the region of the pampas where high thistles grew, a set of stiff, flared leather guards called *guardamontes* were used to protect the legs. The *rebenque*, a heavy, braided fine leather crop, was always carried in the riding gaucho's hand.

Martín Fierro

Just as the traditional gaucho way of life was fading in reality, it was being preserved in art. Poetry and music had always been popular with the gauchos, and the poet was usually a revered figure within the community.

The songs, stories, and poems of the *gauchesco* tradition, many of them composed in colorful dialect, often deal with the themes of love and nostalgia, but many of them are highly political in nature.

A masterpiece of Argentine literature is a two-part epic poem, *El Gaucho Martín Fierro*. Written by José Hernandez, and published in the 1870s, the work is a defense of the proud, independent ways of the gaucho, and a diatribe against the forces that conspired to bring him down, from greedy landowners to corrupt policemen and conscription officials.

Ironically, such works served to elevate the stature of the gaucho in the minds of the public, but not enough and not in time to save him. The

LIFE FOR *LAS CHINAS*

The family life of the gaucho was never a very settled one. Supposedly, the women of their early camps were captives from raids on nearby settlements. This primitive theft was perhaps one of the practices that made the gauchos so unpopular with city folk, But even when women later moved voluntarily out onto the pampas, the domestic arrangements were somewhat informal, with common-law marriages being the norm. These *chinas* (from the Spanish for servant or mistress), were rarely welcome on the estancias where the gauchos worked. The few that were allowed were employed as maids, wet nurses, laundresses, and cooks.

free-riding gaucho passed into the realm of myth, a folk hero who was the object of sentimentality and patriotic pride in a nation searching for cultural emblems.

Gaucho culture today

Although the historical line places the demise of the gaucho in the late 19th century, there is much that remains of gaucho culture in Argentina today. While the reduction of labor requirements in the countryside forced many gauchos into the cities, many remained on the estancias

GAUCHO-SPOTTING

Today, in small towns it is possible to stop for a drink in the *boliche* or *pulpería* (local bars), where gauchos gather for a gambling session after a hard day's work.

cho's pride is still his horse, and, as before, he usually does not own much beyond his mount besides his saddle, his poncho, and his knife.

The rodeo

Visitors can be rewarded after a little exploration along the back roads of Argentina, for that is where you can still find the gauchos at work. On a visit to an estancia, you might perhaps see a *domador* breaking horses, or men riding at breakneck speed with lassoes flying.

One of the biggest treats is to see a rodeo.

to work under the new established order.

Wherever cattle- and sheep-ranching is done in Argentina, you will find ranch hands working at the rough chores of herding and branding. Most are settled with a regular wage, but there are still itinerants who provide services such as fence mending and sheep shearing.

Despite the regional differences in nomenclature, dress, and bloodlines, these men share one tradition that makes them all gauchos in spirit, that of excellent horsemanship. A gau-

LEFT: a gaucho showing off his horseback skills, in a *sortija* competition.
ABOVE: a gaucho's grip is put to the test.

Some of these are large organized events, with an accompanying fiesta of eating, dancing, and singing. Bowlegged men gather at these celebrations, dressed up in hats, *bombachas*, and kerchiefs, with their *chinas* by their sides.

With some investigation and a little luck, it is possible to find more informal rodeos in the villages of the outback, where the gauchos will come from miles around to compete in rough tests of skill and bravery. Amid flying dust and spirited whooping you will see gauchos barrel racing and lassoing cattle with as much panache and pride as their ancestors ever had. ❏

A DAY IN THE COUNTRY – GAUCHO-STYLE

Argentina grew rich on its agricultural output, and a visit to a traditional ranch provides an insight into the gaucho's livelihood

One of the options for a day trip out of the city is a visit to an estancia (ranch). Many of these receive either day visitors or weekend guests, although most are also still active in their traditional livestock and agricultural work. There are a number of these establishments, particularly within a couple of hours' drive of Buenos Aires. Most were founded early in the 20th century and follow a similar layout: a tree-lined entry and main residential area (the trees forming a windbreak in the flat and often bare pampas), with a large main house in traditional criollo or imitation English, French, or Italian style, surrounded by gardens and lawns.

△ **IVY-COVERED ESTANCIA**
San Antonio de Areco, near Buenos Aires, has a number of beautiful old estancias, such as the ivy-covered Los Patricios.

WORKING UP AN APPETITE

Although agricultural methods have obviously changed since the 1920s heyday of the estancias, it is still possible to see traditional methods demonstrated for visitors. For those who can spare only one day for the outing, most estancias offer transport, and a traditional *asado* lunch composed of empanadas, grilled meat, sausage, and sweetbreads, usually accompanied by red wine. Thereafter, most offer a gaucho display of horsemanship and roping in the best rodeo style; in many cases, it is also possible to go horseback riding or take a ride in a sulky (open carriage). Estancias near the coast or one of Buenos Aires' many lakes may also provide fishing, and all offer fresh air, blue sky, green grass, and a glimpse of the endless pampas.

△ **LAS LANZAS, SALTA**
Traditional estancias can still be found, such as El Bordo de Las Lanzas in Salta province, with its cozy and elegant sitting room.

▽ **LA ESCONDIDA**
A parade of gauchos dressed to kill in their best clothes; and fine horses, also showing off their best tack and adornments.

◁ **GAUCHO GAMES**
Traditional horseback contests at estancias are a wonderful opportunity to witness the impressive riding skills of the gauchos.

TOOLS OF THE TRADE

Argentine gauchos have always been proud of the tools of their trade, and these have become a highly decorative part of their wardrobe.

The traditional gaucho knife *(facón)* is used for butchering, skinning, and even castrating animals, but also for self-defense and eating. The handle is usually of ornately carved silver. Spurs may also be made of silver and – like the ornamental silver belt buckles – are designed to stand out as well as to serve a practical purpose. The wide crops are made of braided leather with a loop at the end to make a sharp cracking noise.

The *boleadoras*, a set of three balls linked by rope, are used to capture and bring down livestock; the throwing of *boleadoras* was an indigenous art learned by the gaucho, and is a highly skilled task which requires infinite practice.

Also essential is the traditional maté gourd and *bombilla*, used to drink the tea-like maté, though nowadays these are often made of ornately carved silver or alpaca.

△ **ESTANCIA ALICE**
Enjoying a performance of traditional folk music over dinner at Estancia Alice, near El Calafate, which also offers sheep shearing displays and guided treks.

▷ **MARTIN FIERRO BOOK**
José Hernández's epic poem *Martín Fierro*, tells of the life and struggles of a hero, epitomizing the 19th-century gaucho and his betrayal.

WILD ARGENTINA

*From the humid subtropics to the windswept Patagonian steppe, Argentina's
diverse landscapes contain a dazzling array of exotic plants and animals*

If Argentina could be stretched out over
Europe, with its northwest corner positioned
over London, the country's easternmost
point would lie roughly over Budapest. Its
southernmost tip, Tierra del Fuego, would be
roughly over Timbuktu in Mali, about a third of
the way down the African continent.

Given this immense geographical spread, it is
not surprising that Argentina has such a great
diversity of plant and animal life. But biologi-
cally, size alone isn't everything. The country's
varied terrain – from the vast expanse of the flat
pampas in the east to the Andes mountains in the
west – ensures that Argentina has a huge variety
of wildlife habitats. There is also considerable
variation between the north, located inside the
Tropic of Capricorn, and the far south. These fac-
tors create the conditions for species as diverse as
jaguars, parrots, penguins, and whales to flourish.

Local species

For a long period in the Earth's distant history,
South America was an island continent. During this time, families of species evolved that
are found nowhere else. When the present land
bridge formed between North and South America, several million years ago, this isolation was
brought to an end. But even today, its effects
can still be seen. Many of Argentina's mammals and birds are "homegrown" South American specialties: first encounters with them
always leave a lasting impression.

Compared to many countries, Argentina's population, which numbers about 37 million, is small
and mainly urban, and its impact on wildlife has
been patchy. The pampas have been transformed
by farming, but in less fertile parts of the country
it is still possible to find places where signs of
human impact are few and far between. Although
there is pressure to increase agricultural production, Argentina has a well-developed system of

---

PRECEDING PAGES: a female elephant seal.
LEFT: a battle-scarred male elephant seal.
RIGHT: Magellanic penguins at Punta Tombo,
near the Península Valdés in Patagonia.

national parks and reserves. There is also a growing tendency to promote ecotourism, in an
attempt to preserve the country's natural riches.

Competition and survival

Argentina extends from the tropics to the subantarctic. It includes the highest point in the

Americas – Aconcagua, at 6,962 meters (22,840
ft) above sea level – and also one of the lowest,
the Salinas Depression on the Península Valdés,
which is about 55 meters (180 ft) below sea
level. The country has both very dry areas and
very wet ones, but it lacks the extreme winter
temperatures found in most continental
climates. This is due to the fact that, in the
south at least, the sea is never far away, and it
checks the worst of the winter cold.

Much of Argentina is either completely
open, or only lightly wooded. This kind of
terrain makes watching wildlife easy – if anything moves, you have a good chance of spot-
ting it. This is particularly true in the vast

expanses of Patagonia, and in Argentina's share of the Andean Altiplano. Some animals – such as Patagonian foxes – can be remarkably unfussed by the presence of humans, and will trot across dirt roads in broad daylight, giving cars a quick glance before moving on. Magellanic penguins, which are a highlight of any visit to Argentina, are even less concerned. They usually ignore people, until someone ventures within pecking distance of their nests.

NATIONAL PARKS

Argentina has almost 40 national parks and reserves, containing everything from astonishing waterfalls and glaciers to teeming bird life. They make a good place to explore wild Argentina.

point for a visit to Argentina. These huge, flat grasslands, where the soil is very fertile, have been almost completely fenced in, and most are either ploughed or grazed. The original wildlife of this area – described so evocatively by the writer W.H. Hudson *(see box)* – has struggled in the face of these changes. Many of the birds mentioned in Hudson's writings are still to be seen, but mammals have coped less well to the alterations produced by over a century of intense farming, and, as a

But after a long history of being hunted, other animals are more elusive. Despite being up to 1.5 meters (5 ft) tall, rheas – Argentina's equivalent of ostriches – can disappear among shrubs and bushes in less time than it takes to focus a pair of binoculars. Guanacos (relatives of the llama) also move off briskly at the first hint of disturbance, although at some parks and reserves, such as Cabo Dos Bahías in Patagonia, they are both so plentiful that they are almost impossible to miss.

In search of the pristine pampas

Buenos Aires province, which lies at the heart of the pampas, is the obvious stepping-off

FAR AWAY AND LONG AGO

In an age of rapid communications, it can be hard to imagine what life was like for the earliest European settlers on the pampas. One way to find out is to read *Far Away and Long Ago*, written by the novelist and naturalist William Henry Hudson. Hudson was born near Buenos Aires in 1841, and grew up on a sheep farm. In his book, he describes what often sounds like an idyllic childhood, with a vast natural playground full of wildlife at his doorstep, waiting to be explored. Hudson actually wrote the book in his seventies, when he was living in England, but his reminiscences of pampas life proved to be a lasting bestseller.

consequence, many of them are now scarce.

In this largely agricultural landscape, sporadic wooded areas and lakes act as magnets for wildlife. So does marshy ground, particularly where it backs onto the coast. Despite its notoriously hazardous traffic, RN 2, which runs from Buenos Aires to Mar del Plata, crosses this kind of country within its first 200 km (125 miles) outside the capital. Away from the main road, the region's lakes, rivers, and canals attract many different

BIRD-SPOTTING

The bird sanctuary for migrating birds at Punta Rasa is an ideal place to see seabirds and shorebirds, including migrants that use this area as a refuge from the North American winter.

province gives a flavor of a different kind of habitat, where the open pampas is replaced by palm-studded savannah. The park preserves only a few square kilometers of the palm-and-grassland landscape, but its wildlife makes the trip well worthwhile. Among its inhabitants are viscachas, nocturnal burrowing rodents that were once common throughout the pampas. They can weigh up to 9 kg (20 lbs), and their nighttime calls are loud, varied, and unnerving. The viscachas at El Palmar are unusually tame, but

fish-eating birds, including herons and snowy-white great egrets.

Perhaps the most representative pampas left today, largely because of the absence of ploughing, is the area surrounding General Lavalle and south to Madariaga. Between Lavalle and San Clemente there is a wildlife sanctuary, managed by Fundación Vida Silvestre Argentina, where some of the last surviving pampas deer can be seen in the wild.

Northwards from Buenos Aires, El Palmar National Park, near Concordia, in Entre Ríos

LEFT: flamingos along the Patagonian coast.
ABOVE: a group of alert vicuñas.

campers here must be tidy, as the animals may steal anything that is left out at night and cart it quickly off to their dens.

Subtropical east

In the Northeast, the Iguazú Falls are a highlight for any visitor to Argentina, but once the thrill of watching the water has worn off, the surrounding forest has much to offer: some 2,000 species of flowering plants, nearly the same number of butterflies and moths, 100 species of mammals including the elusive jaguar, and nearly 400 kinds of birds including hummingbirds and toucans. However, this kind of habitat is notorious for hiding its inhabitants.

Seeing its richness requires time and patience.

Elsewhere in Misiones province, Argentina's subtropical east, the future of the region's native hardwood forests looks uncertain. Many stretches have been felled, and the trees replaced by crops, such as soya, that give a more immediate yield, or in some cases by grazing land. Some areas are planted with pines for the paper-pulp industry: although these are technically still "forested," their value for wildlife is low.

> **MARSHLAND DELIGHTS**
>
> The Iberá Marshes, near Iguazú, are hard to get to and are virtually impenetrable. On the edges of the marsh, however, waterbirds provide a fascinating spectacle.

The Gran Chaco

The Gran Chaco is a vast low-lying region that straddles northern Argentina, as well as parts of Bolivia and Paraguay. The climate here becomes drier from east to west, splitting the Chaco into two merging parts. The Dry Chaco, in the west, is likely to appeal only to the most adventurous of travelers. Its wildlife is hugely diverse – reputedly including some exceptionally large snakes – but even for reptile-lovers, getting about in this region is a daunting task. The country is covered with dense thorn thickets crossed by very few roads, and there are no amenities for visitors.

The Wet Chaco to the east is easier to visit.

Although it has undergone some major clearance for agriculture over the past 25 years, it still contains some beautiful tracts of woodland interspersed with marshes, and is rich in wildlife. Traveling west from Corrientes or Resistencia, RN 16 is worth exploring at least as far as Chaco National Park.

The wet season in the summer (from December to March) is best avoided, for the heat is intense and the roads become impassable. Between April and November, conditions are more congenial, making it a good time to visit the national park. Here there are howler monkeys and many other mammals, but the main attraction for most visitors is the park's bird life, which includes guans, chachalacas, whistling herons, jabirú storks, jacanas, and ducks galore.

From Corrientes, both east and south, there are some very rich woodlands interspersed with wide-open grasslands and enormous marshes. RN 12 is paved in both directions, but the tougher earth roads which run northeast–southwest between the paved stretches, through places such as Mburucuyá and San Luis del Palmar, generally get into far more interesting wildlife habitats.

In Corrientes, in the region of the headwaters of the Iberá complex, where grass seas stretch from horizon to horizon, visitors sometimes catch a glimpse of the rare maned wolf. More closely related to foxes than to wolves, this slender member of the canine family has very long legs, making it look almost as if it is on stilts. Marsh deer also survive here – albeit in small numbers – and on larger estancias that are run with conservation in mind the endangered pampas deer can also be seen.

The Andean Northwest

The provinces of Jujuy, Salta, and Tucumán have a mixture of extraordinary scenery and fascinating wildlife, spread over a dizzying range of altitudes. All three have wet, subtropical regions, while Salta and Jujuy also contain much higher and drier areas as the land rises to the Andes mountains.

Calilegua National Park, for example, lies on the eastern slopes of the Andes, between 600 and 4,500 meters (2,000–15,000 ft), in the province of Jujuy. Visits are only practicable during the dry season (June through October or November) as the roads are frequently washed out the rest of the year. The road through the park rises steeply, crossing through a series of vegetation zones in rapid succession. The lowest is the Chaco vegetation, with its drunken or bottle trees *(Chorizia)*, known locally as *palos borrachos*. This zone also has jacarandas and tabebuias – trees that often burst into bloom while they are still leafless, toward the end of the dry season. Their spectacular lilac, yellow, or pink flowers are an impressive sight, attracting pollenating insects from afar. Higher up, the journey continues through a jungle dominated

approached slowly to avoid mountain sickness, or *soroche*, and an ideal way to do it is to travel up the Quebrada de Humahuaca in Jujuy *(see page 261)*. The journey begins in lush subtropical farmland, and ends in the thin and stunningly clear air of the Altiplano, more than 3,000 meters (10,000 ft) up. In this part of the Andes, water is often in short supply, and plants and animals have to cope with drought as well as intense sunlight by day and often chilling cold at night.

One animal – the vicuña – is quite at home in these conditions. Despite its dainty appearance, this smallest wild relative of the llama can sur-

by tipa trees *(Tipuaria)* and into the cloud forest of coniferous podocarp trees *(Podocarpus)* and moisture-loving alders *(Alnus)*.

The forest's animal life also changes with altitude, although many of the larger predators range throughout the park. Wildcats, including jaguars, pumas (cougars), ocelots, and jaguarundi all live here, although it takes skill and luck to spot them. They prey on deer, tapirs, peccaries, agoutis, and even capuchin monkeys, as well as many local birds.

The higher parts of Salta and Jujuy are best

LEFT: the chimango caracara, a widely seen hawk.
ABOVE: sea lions at the Península Valdés.

THE ARGENTINE OSTRICH

For the original inhabitants of the Argentine pampas, the rhea – or *ñandú* – was an important source of food, and of skin and feathers for clothing. Rheas were traditionally hunted with a bola – a collection of stones tied together with rope – which was thrown at the birds' necks or legs. During his extensive journeys in South America, the English naturalist Charles Darwin established that there are actually two species of these ostrich-like birds. The common rhea lives in the pampas, while the smaller species – known as the long-billed or Darwin's rhea – makes its home in Patagonia and in the foothills of the Andes.

vive at over 5,000 meters (16,400 ft), and it can run effortlessly in mountain air that leaves visitors gasping for breath. For a grazing animal, its hearing is not particularly good, but its large Bambi-like eyes give it superb long vision, allowing it to spot any kind of movement from a great distance.

The road up the *quebrada* gorge eventually leads to the dusty town of Abra Pampa, where the level landscape is ringed by distant mountains. At this altitude, the climate is too harsh for trees to thrive, but there is no shortage of wildlife. The region's woodpeckers and owls are particularly interesting, because they have had to adapt to a habitat without any cover. The owls dig burrows, while the woodpeckers peck nest holes into earth banks – both can often be seen in action from the road.

To the northwest of Abra Pampa, a vast natural bowl cradles Laguna de los Pozuelos, a protected lakeland reserve and home to thousands of flamingos *(see page 262)*. Three species live here, together with a host of water birds, including puna teal, avocets, and giant, and horned and Andean coots. At Lagunillas, on the western side of Pozuelos, there is a lake some distance from the road, giving a closer look at these birds.

HOME AND AWAY

Ask anyone where marsupial mammals come from, and the chances are that they will answer Australia. But, surprisingly, pouched mammals first evolved in the Americas. From here they reached Australia by spreading out across Gondwanaland, an ancient southern supercontinent. Marsupials still live in the Americas today, with several species in Argentina. Your chances of seeing any are very small, but if you are walking in wooded country after dark, look out for red eyes: the chances are that they belong to a mouse opposum. Another marsupial is the yapok, a large, semi-aquatic animal, which lives in and near rivers in the semitropical Northeast.

Dinosaur country

Roughly 800 km (500 miles) south of the Abra pampa region is an equally spectacular part of the Argentine Andes that sees far fewer visitors from abroad. In this stark landscape, erosion has carved out bizarre formations in sediments laid down millions of years ago. At Talampaya National Park in La Rioja province, deep-red cliffs flank a precipitous gorge – ideal country for the condors that soar overhead. In neighboring San Juan, the Ischigualasto Reserve contains a moonscape of eroded clay with rocky pillars and cliffs *(see pages 281–3)*.

Country like this has yielded a treasure-trove of fossilized animals over many decades.

Discoveries at Ischigualasto have included Herrerasaurus, an early meat-eating dinosaur that lived over 200 million years ago, and many other reptiles alive at that time. Further east on the pampas, Argentine paleontologists have unearthed fossils of what may be the largest flying bird ever to have existed. Named *Argentavis magnificens*, it had a wingspan of about 7.5 meters (25 ft), and measured over 3 meters (10 ft) from beak to tail. Like today's condors, this gigantic creature probably flew by soaring, a technique that works well in open, sunny landscapes that generate currents of rising air.

LAKE WITH A VIEW

The lakes fed by the Campo de Hielo glaciers are good places for visitors to catch a glimpse of waterfowl – including the region's famous black-necked swans.

Trees and ice

The Patagonian Andes, which stretch from Neuquén, through Río Negro, to Chubut and Santa Cruz, are one of the main playgrounds of Argentina, and also a stronghold of many of the country's native plants and animals. Among the animals visitors can expect to see are condors, geese, and parakeets, while native plants include southern beeches *(Nothofagus)*, an attractive broad-leaved tree that is covered with small scallop-edged leaves.

Southern beeches are a living legacy of South America's very distant past. At one time, South America formed part of Gondwanaland, a southern supercontinent that also included Antarctica and Australasia. The southern beech family evolved when Gondwanaland was still intact, but its member species became separated as Gondwanaland broke up, and the continents drifted apart. This explains the remarkable distribution of southern beeches today: as well as growing in South America, they also grow in Australia, New Zealand, and New Guinea – thousands of miles away on the other side of the Pacific.

The mountains here have a distinctly temperate feel. Rainfall increases toward the Chilean border, creating a landscape that contrasts vividly with the dry plains to the west.

The high regions are home to large flocks of upland geese in grassy valleys, ashy-headed geese in clearings in woods near lake

shores and rivers, and noisy buff-necked ibises nearly everywhere. The woods also contain rich and colorful flocks of austral parakeets and hummingbirds called greenbacked firecrowns. Both seem out of place in such surroundings, but they have successfully adapted to the region's cool conditions.

One of the most spectacular birds in the Patagonian Andes is the Magellanic woodpecker, the giant of its family. The male sports a bright scarlet head with a small crest,

while his all-black mate has a very long and floppy crest that curls forward.

This region is also the home of the torrent duck, which, as its name implies, is only seen in white-water rivers and streams. Torrent ducks dive and swim close to furious rapids as nonchalantly as if they were in a pond.

For many visitors, the highlight of a trip to this region is a chance to see Argentina's glaciers, which spill down from the Campo de Hielo – Patagonia's southern icecap, out of view on the crest of the Andes. Some of the most spectacular glaciers are contained within Los Glaciares National Park, near to El Calafate *(see page 314)*.

LEFT: the solitary puma ranges from the tropics down to the southernmost tip of the continent.
RIGHT: a Patagonian fox sits for a portrait.

Tierra del Fuego

When Charles Darwin sailed up the Beagle Channel in 1832, Tierra del Fuego was almost unknown to the outside world. Since then, European settlers have done much to transform the ecology of this remote and stormy region. Sheep and rabbits arrived in the 19th century, and beavers and muskrat were introduced in the 1940s, creating havoc in the island's woodlands by felling trees and damming streams.

More recently, unrestrained development has turned Tierra del Fuego's southernmost town, Ushuaia, into a busy, sprawling city, complete with the most southerly traffic jams in the world.

Where they are still intact, Tierra del Fuego's southern beech forests have a sombre and otherworldly feel. The winds this far south can be fierce and unrelenting, and growth is a slow business, with bleached branches showing where trees have lost their battle against the elements. But despite the hostile conditions, these forests are far from lifeless: austral parakeets fly among the trees, and condors often soar overhead. The Tierra del Fuego National Park is a good place not only to see these trees, but also glaciers and bare tundra. It offers many trails, such as the Senda Costera (Coast Trail) with the

Despite this, Tierra del Fuego is a fascinating destination for anyone interested in wildlife. The Beagle Channel is as beautiful as it was in Darwin's day, and its cormorants, sea lions, and fur seals can be seen at close quarters by taking a boat trip from Ushuaia. The Channel also has small colonies of Magellanic penguins, together with the occasional gentoo, a larger species with a bright-red beak. There's a good chance you might also come across kelp geese, as well as flightless steamer ducks. These remarkable birds get their name from the dramatic paddle-wheel-like spray they generate as they chase or escape from their rivals.

chance to get a glimpse of abundant wildlife, such as the famous giant woodpeckers.

The desert coast

Turning northward once more, the journey back to Buenos Aires crosses hundreds of miles of Patagonian steppe – a vast windswept plateau that rises gently from east to west. In this part of South America, the Andes intercept most of the moisture carried by the prevailing westerly winds, creating a rain shadow in their lee. As a result, Patagonia is unusually dry for somewhere so far south – the inland city of Sarmiento, for example, receives just 13 cm (5 inches) of rain a year.

The continental shelf in the South Atlantic east of Argentina is bathed by a nutrient-rich current flowing up from the south, and so inevitably attracts prodigious numbers of marine mammals, as well as sea birds. At one time many of these were ruthlessly hunted, but today the whales, seals, and penguins breed here largely unmolested.

In Chubut province, two reserves – Punta Tombo and Cabo Dos Bahías – are home to hundreds of thousands of Magellanic penguins during the

WILDLIFE EXCURSIONS

A range of overland safaris and whale-watching boat trips around the World Heritage Site, Península Valdés, are available, most of which are organized in nearby Puerto Madryn *(see page 359)*.

marauding orcas (killer whales), which create a threatening atmosphere between the months of March and May, as they lie in wait for young sea lions that venture innocently beyond the beach.

Moving inland

Away from the starkly beautiful coast, the protected status of Península Valdés benefits land animals as well. This is a very good place to see guanacos and rheas, and also maras – long-legged rodents that look something like a cross between a hare

summer breeding season. Further north, the Península Valdés is famous for its sightings of whales and seals. There is something to see on the coast throughout the year, with southern sea lions hauling out to breed between January and March, migrating southern right whales arriving in June, and elephant seals beginning to breed from September. By December they have given birth, and the adults can be seen lazing on the shingle, flicking flipper-loads of shells all over their bodies to help dislodge their molting fur.

In the shallows, a spectacular presence is the

LEFT: the mara, or Patagonian cavy.
ABOVE: the maned wolf.

and a small deer. The peninsula also teems with the well-known tinamous, dumpy ground-feeding birds that can often be seen on the side of the road. Despite their squat shape, biologists conclude that tinamous are probably more closely related to ostriches and rheas than to the game birds they resemble.

Heading north along the South Atlantic coast, the Patagonian plateau blends gradually with the pampas, and leads back to Buenos Aires. After the vast space and solitude of the far south of the country, the bustling crowds and hectic traffic can come as a shock. Nevertheless, even here you can be assured that the varied wildlife of Argentina is never far away. ❑

OUTDOOR ADVENTURE

The vast landscape of Argentina provides plenty of opportunity to enjoy the great outdoors, in either strenuous or leisurely activity

With snowcapped mountain ranges, dense forests, and more than 2,000 km (1,240 miles) of coastline, Argentina is a paradise for those in search of adventure and excitement and the opportunities are as immense as the country is vast.

One of the difficulties in tasting all that is on offer is the sheer distance that separates one place from another. Features which would be well-trodden tourist destinations in Europe often attract little attention, simply because they are literally hundreds of miles from anywhere, so that only the more intrepid traveler has the time to seek them out. From the lush rainforests of Misiones to windswept Tierra del Fuego, there is varied and abundant wilderness to experience and explore.

For the truly adventurous, the absence of commercial development on any significant scale in large tracts of Argentina is just an added attraction. There are, however, a string of developed and developing centers in the Andean foothills and also on the Atlantic coast, which offer a rich variety of adventure activities.

Climb and climb again

The Andes mountains, which run the length of Argentina's western border with Chile, have long attracted climbers from around the world. One of the main centers for climbing is in the province of Mendoza, about 1,300 km (800 miles) west of Buenos Aires, where the highest peak in the Western Hemisphere – Aconcagua (6,962 meters/22,840 ft) – is found. Scores of expeditions have scaled Aconcagua (the "Stone Sentinel") since Matias Zurbriggen of Switzerland first conquered it in 1897.

There are 10 recognized routes up the mountain, the northern approach being the most popular. It is possible to reach the top without any technical climbing expertise, although a

guide and appropriate acclimatization for the altitude are essential. A somber warning for those less prepared is the small cemetery at the foot of Aconcagua in Puente del Inca, the burial place of a number of climbers who have lost their lives in the attempt.

The main center for trekking and climbing

in this area is Villa Los Penitentes en route from Mendoza to the frontier. The Tupangato peak – a volcano reaching 6,650 meters (21,000 ft) – is also difficult, and can be reached only by riding mules part of the way. Less demanding peaks in the Andes include Catedral, Cuerno, Tolosa, Cúpula, Almacenes, and Pan de Azúcar, all between 5,300 meters and 5,700 meters (17,390 ft and 18,700 ft).

One popular range is the Cordón de Plata, just 80 km (50 miles) from the city of Mendoza. Here you can find fairly easy climbing. Such peaks as El Plata, Negro, Pico Bonito, Nevado Excelsior, Rincón, and finally Vallecitos (ranging from 5,000 meters to 6,300

PRECEDING PAGES: trekking in the Fitz Roy region.
LEFT: climbers dwarfed by the sheer granite face of Monte Fitz Roy, in southern Patagonia.
RIGHT: proud conqueror of the feisty *dorado*.

meters/16,500 ft to 21,000 ft) attract large numbers of hikers and climbers every year, both local and foreign.

For those without a head for heights, the whole area to the west of Mendoza also offers plenty of scope for mountain biking, trekking on foot or horseback across the Andes, and photographic safaris in off-road vehicles.

There are five key rivers in the area on which rafting is offered; the Mendoza, Tunuyán, Diamante, Atuel, and Grande. Kayaking and

ADVENTURE TOURS

There are local tour operators and organizations who specialize in many of the activities described here. *See the Travel Tips section, pages 335–373, for more details.*

from mountaineering to paragliding. Some 1,700 km (1,050 miles) from Buenos Aires, it is situated at the heart of Argentina's lake district, otherwise known as the "Switzerland of South America." The Club Andino in Bariloche is a good place to find out just what's on offer and to book up mountain lodges or *refugios*. The club can also arrange guides, who lead climbing and hiking expeditions. Most readily accessible are Cerro Otto for paragliding or the granite pinnacles of Cerro Catedral for climbers.

canoeing are also available, together with windsurfing, diving, water-skiing, and sailing. Malargüe, to the south of Mendoza, is a much smaller center but with special attractions. The nearby Caverna de las Brujas (Witches' Cavern) is so called because of the grotesque shapes of its stalactites and stalagmites. Also nearby is Lago Llancanelo, which has a great variety of bird life, including swans, flamingos, and ducks.

The Lake District

Farther south still, in Río Negro province, lies Bariloche, one of Argentina's most important centers for a whole range of outdoor pursuits,

A couple of hours' drive away lies the region's largest peak by far. Tronador, at 3,500 meters (11,500 ft), is 1,500 meters (5,000 ft) higher than any of the surrounding mountains. Its name, meaning "the thunderer," derives from the rumbling of its glaciers. There is a hostel in Pampa Linda at the foot of Tronador and a number of *refugios* for trekkers in the area. Although these tend to be crowded in December and January, the tourist trade in Bariloche is sharply seasonal, and outside these months (apart from the skiing months of July and August) is generally a much quieter time. It's an ideal area for horseback riding, with the option of crossing over to Chile.

One of the particular attractions of Bariloche is the sheer variety of vegetation within a radius of just 30 km (19 miles), by virtue of its position in the rain shadow of the Andes. Trek west and you soon enter temperate rainforest with dense thickets of bamboo and often impenetrable vegetation. Trek east and you find the magnificent sculptured landscape of the Valle Encantada, for example, and beyond it the vastness of the Patagonian Desert.

SNOWBOARDING

Snowboarding is as popular in Argentina as it is in Europe and the US and many of its most devoted fans travel to the Argentine mountains in order to enjoy the activity all year round.

Nacional Lanín, named after the volcano which is the same height as Mount Fuji (3,776 meters/ 12,389 ft), and to which it bears a striking similarity. Lanín offers a classic ascent for experienced climbers. To the south, the national parks of Lago Puelo and, nearer Esquel, Los Alerces, are beautiful areas for trekking and camping. Increasingly, tourists can go mountain-bike riding in the national parks, although this is often only during the summer months (December to April).

There is rafting on the relatively gentle Río Limay, which flows into Lago Nahuel Huapi, or on the Río Manso, whose name – "gentle" – belies the tougher challenge that its waters offer. Nahuel Huapi lake is part of the national park of the same name. Although the temperature of the waters and the treacherous winds which whisk down the arms of the lake have tended to discourage commercial development of water sports, plenty of opportunities do exist for windsurfing, scuba diving, canoeing, and sailing.

To the north of Nahuel Huapi is Parque

LEFT: top snowboarder Stefan Gimpl at Las Leñas.
ABOVE: cyclists take a break in Bariloche.

Take to the slopes

Skiing and snowboarding have grown steadily in popularity in Argentina, and facilities are being constantly upgraded. The two main centers are Bariloche, with its purpose-built resort of Cerro Catedral, and the newer Las Leñas resort (1,200 km/750 miles from Buenos Aires) in the province of Mendoza. Although the snowfall is notoriously unpredictable, the best season for snow is generally from June to October.

Bariloche is South America's biggest skiing resort, with more than 30 chairlifts and ski tows. There is a small ski run at Cerro Otto on the outskirts of the town, and it's also possible to do cross-country skiing in this area.

New locations such as Villa La Angostura, on the other side of Lago Nahuel Huapi, are being developed all the time. As in other areas of economic activity, experience from abroad has been brought in over the past few years, and given a dynamic boost to skiing, snowboarding, and other winter sports.

To the north, San Martín de los Andes is a picturesque and exclusive ski center, and is correspondingly more expensive. Further south, near Esquel, is the growing resort of La Hoya, where higher slopes usually guarantee a longer ski season.

THE TIP OF THE WORLD

Ushuaia is the world's southernmost town and the obvious center for exploring Tierra del Fuego. Various estancias near the town offer accommodation and opportunities for horseback riding, hiking, and participating in the day-to-day work of the ranch.

Much of Tierra del Fuego's swampy or forested terrain is more readily accessible on foot or on horseback than by vehicle. From Ushuaia itself there are daily boat trips to the outlying islands to see cormorants and sea lions. It is also possible, although not always easy, to charter yachts to Cape Horn or to see spectacular glaciers along the coast.

Santa Cruz province

El Calafate is the gateway to the Parque Nacional Los Glaciares, in Santa Cruz province. This is the main base for exploring the area, and in particular for visiting the Perito Moreno glacier, 80 km (50 miles) away at the far end of Lago Argentino. Trekking on the glacier is possible, both as a short trip and as part of a longer expedition taking in the Frias glacier and the ascent of Cerro Cervantes, over a period of two or three days.

The options for trekking in the area seem limitless. It is also ideal terrain for mountain bikes and four-wheel drive vehicles, both of which can be hired locally. Various estancias in the region offer horseback riding and trekking.

Some 230 km (140 miles) from Calafate – about four hours' journey – lie the spectacular Monte Fitz Roy (3,440 meters/11,000 ft) and Cerro Torre. Professional climbers regard Fitz Roy and the surrounding peaks as among the most difficult in the world to climb. It was scaled for the first time in 1952 by Lionel Terray and Guido Magnone. Cerro Torre (3,128 meters/9,500 ft) and its neighbors are right on the fringe of the Patagonian icecap, and as the westernmost peaks of the Fitz Roy chain they receive the full force of winds blowing in from the Pacific. The Italian Cesare Maestri and Austrian Tony Egger are credited with the conquest of the mountain in 1959, although Egger died in the descent, and there were serious doubts about the veracity of Maestri's claims.

Those keen to explore the area more fully would do better to stay in the rapidly developing settlement of El Chaltén. Facilities in this small town include several hostels, a gas station, and a few basic convenience stores. Although it lacks many of the tourist facilities of El Calafate, it obviously gives much readier access to the mountains. Buses leave El Calafate for El Chaltén early in the morning, giving an ideal opportunity to see rheas and guanaco en route.

Anglers' idyll

Argentina is crisscrossed by rivers and lakes (both natural and artificial) and includes more than 4,000 km (2,500 miles) of coastline along the Atlantic Ocean. Those features make it a fisherman's paradise, and species such as eel, catfish, trout, salmon, sea bass, shark, swordfish, sole, shad, and dorado are plentiful.

Year-round fishing is available at Argentina's coastal resorts, many of which are between 300–500 km (180–300 miles) from Buenos Aires. Mar del Plata is a prime fishing spot, as are the nearby resorts at Laguna Brava, where the local authorities regularly stock the waters and boats can be rented.

Quequén Grande, on the banks of the Río Necochea, is noted for its excellent trout fishing. Salmon and trout are also plentiful in the inland rivers and lakes to the south of Buenos Aires in the provinces of Neuquén and Río Negro. However, these regions are under the jurisdiction of the National Parks Board and a fishing license is required.

As well as being a ski resort, the attractive town of Bariloche on the shores of Lago Nahuel Huapi is also one of the best locations for trout fishing, and trout as heavy as 16 kg (36 lbs) are known to have been caught here. Some estancias in the surrounding area have lodges to cater for tourists and regularly draw dedicated fishermen from the United States to fish the superb rivers and lakes of the region. Carefully controlled hunting is allowed, too, subject to license.

In San Martín de los Andes, north of Bariloche, there are fly-fishing outfits that provide a comprehensive service, including lodging and equipment as well as skilled guides.

For those prepared to travel to the extreme south, Río Grande is the center for trout fishing on Tierra del Fuego. The winds are often fierce but the size of the trout offer due reward. Contact the Argentine Fishing Association (Asociación Argentina de Pesca) in Buenos Aires for more information (tel: 011-4383 6416).

Swing into action

Golf is another sport which has benefitted from the wide open spaces and the even climate of Argentina. The World Golf Championship was held in Buenos Aires in 2000 and there are numerous golf clubs all over the country, including the prestigious Jockey Club course in Buenos Aires, the picturesque Mar del Plata course on the Atlantic coast, and the course at the spectacular Hotel Llao Llao near Bariloche.

LEFT: canoeing on a lonely lake in northern Patagonia.
RIGHT: windsurfing on the open sea.

The wind in your sails

Argentina has some of the most ideal sailing conditions in the world, with a gentle climate, strong winds, and an abundance of lakes, rivers, and reservoirs. This potential is often still underdeveloped commercially in outlying regions.

However, there are yacht clubs along the banks of the fabled Río de la Plata, where members of the public can hire sailboats, sailboards, and yachts. There are also several rowing clubs clustered around the pleasant delta region of Tigre, on the outskirts of Buenos Aires. ❑

PENÍNSULA VALDÉS

One of Argentina's key attractions is its wildlife, with the World Heritage Site of Península Valdés renowned for its wildlife watching. Penguins and elephant seals can be seen along the coast, and it is possible to go by boat to observe southern right whales *(see page 309)*. Puerto Madryn, about 100 km (60 miles) from the peninsula, is the main tourist center offering scuba diving, mountain biking, and trekking. On Valdés itself, Puerto Pirámide lacks the facilities of its larger neighbor (accommodations are limited), but if camping by the shore you have ready access to the rugged coastline and can be woken by the sound of whales.

SPECTATOR SPORTS

The Argentine love of sport is clearly demonstrated by the stars now flooding the international soccer fields, tennis courts, and polo grounds

t should be an average enough day in Buenos Aires, yet the streets are strangely deserted. The banks are empty, the restaurants are quiet, and an eerie silence has settled over the entire city. The only people in sight are huddled around portable radios or television sets, their attention tightly focused on the latest news.

The outbreak of war? Some national disaster? No, this scenario occurs every time Argentina's national soccer team takes to the field, ample evidence of the sport's hold on the country. Every match commands the nation's rapt attention, and victories are cause for unrivaled celebration.

When Argentina won the 1986 World Cup tournament in Mexico, the highest honor in soccer, several hundreds of thousands of fans flooded the streets of Buenos Aires, Córdoba, Rosario, La Plata, and beyond. Makeshift parades materialized out of nowhere, thousands of cars jammed the avenues and side streets, and the nation found itself swathed in blue and white.

The world championship was the second for Argentina, having also captured the cup in 1978. But that tournament, hastily staged in Argentina by the ruling military government that had come to power not long before, fostered little of the pride and enthusiasm seen in 1986. The 1978 World Cup was perceived by many as a simple exercise in public relations designed to avert the world's eyes from Argentina's soaring inflation, mounting national debt, and human-rights violations. The national team has had more recent successes, reaching the final in 1990 and the quarterfinals in 1998 and 2006.

Soccer history

Soccer was introduced to Argentina in the 1860s by British sailors who passed the time in port playing "pick-up" games before the curious local onlookers. The large British community in Buenos Aires finally organized the game officially in 1891, and the balls, goalposts, and nets imported from Europe were checked through customs as "some silly things for the mad English."

But by the turn of the 20th century, Argentina had established its own soccer league. The Quilmes Athletic Club was formed in 1897, making it the country's oldest soccer team. Rosario Central (1899), River Plate (1901), Independiente (1904), and Boca Juniors (1905) quickly followed suit.

Argentina's national team also progressed rapidly, as proven by its performance in the inaugural World Cup held in Uruguay in 1930. Although still amateur and not highly regarded, Argentina defeated strong teams such as France and Chile en route to a place in the finals, before losing to Uruguay, 4–2.

Soccer became a professional sport in Argentina in 1931, and league games began to draw large, vociferous crowds. River Plate and Boca Juniors, which emerged from the middle-class Belgrano neighborhood and the working class Italian Boca district in Buenos Aires respectively *(see page 163–4)*, quickly became the two most popular teams in Argentina. Even today, around 50 percent of the nation's soccer fans support one of these two clubs. Such unbridled support is not necessarily a good thing – Argentine soccer has been increasingly troubled in recent years by crowd violence at its league matches, especially when rival fans such as River Plate and Boca Juniors meet.

Each club has its fanatical supporters, a group of hardcore and often violent fans called the "*barra brava*." As a result, many of the country's stadiums – including Boca's La Bombonera, are complete with moats, fences, and barbed wire designed to keep fans off the field and rival factions apart. But these measures have not stopped the violence. Critics blame soccer-club presidents for giving their *barra bravas* free tickets, paying for their journeys to away games, sponsoring their trips to World Cups, and even admitting them to board meetings.

Twenty teams compete annually in the Argentina First Division, playing a total of 38 matches between September and June. In addition, many of the top clubs compete in international tournaments such as the World Club Cup and the Libertadores Cup.

Argentines, like most South Americans, seem to have a special skill for soccer. Diego Maradona was a national hero long before he gained international prominence at the 1986 World Cup. When Maradona threatened to leave his club, Boca Juniors, for Europe in 1982, the government unsuccessfully tried to intervene by declaring him to be part of the "national patrimony."

Polo prowess

Of course, soccer is not the only sport in Argentina. Blessed with a climate that allows for a wide variety of sports year round, the country is also known for its polo, rugby, horse- and auto-racing, and tennis.

One of the first things many visitors ask is where can they see polo being played. Although it did not originate in Argentina, polo has evolved into an integral part of the national sporting heritage. Many of the world's best players and teams have come from this country. In addition, Argentina has top-flight breeding programs for ponies.

As with soccer, polo was introduced to Argentina by the English in the mid-19th century. The inherent riding skill of the Argentines, as proved by the gauchos, and the abundance of space, helped ensure that the sport flourished. At present, there are over 6,000 polo players registered in the country.

Polo tournaments are held all over Argentina throughout the year, but the bulk are played in spring and autumn. The top teams compete each November in the Argentine Open championship in the picturesque polo fields of Palermo, in central Buenos Aires, a competition which began in 1893. There is no distinction between ama-

PRECEDING PAGES: a pukka game of polo.
LEFT: *pato*, now played with a leather ball.
RIGHT: Argentine soccer fans at the 2006 World Cup.

teur and professional polo in Argentina. But many of the top players are regularly hired by foreign teams for huge sums. The favorite team in an international tournament is often the one with the most Argentine players, and there is big demand overseas for Argentine-trained polo ponies.

Passion for *pato*

The game of *pato* has been described by some observers as basketball on horseback, and it is one of the few sports indigenous to Argentina. The earli-

> **PONIES IN DEMAND**
>
> Specially trained by *petiseros* (trainers) at an estancia where polo is played, the short, stocky Argentine polo ponies are prized for their speed, strength, and ability to work with their riders.

pursuit of the prize. The sole rule of the sport was that the rider in possession of the *pato* had to keep it extended in his right hand, thus offering it to any opponent who caught up with him. Such skirmishes inevitably resulted in a fierce tug-of-war, and the unfortunate riders pulled from their saddles were sometimes trampled to death. The government banned *pato* in 1822, but a group of ardent supporters revived the game in 1937. They drew up a new set of rules, refined the sport, and established a

est references to the game can be dated back as far as 1610, but the game was probably played by the native inhabitants long before that time.

Pato is Spanish for "duck," and the unfortunate duck certainly got the worst of it in the game's formative stages. A duck was placed inside a leather basket with handles, the possession of which was then contested by two teams of horsemen – often farm workers or indigenous people – who attempted to grab the basket and return it to their estancia.

Any number of riders could participate in the game, and anything from lassoing an opponent to cutting free his saddle was permissible in

pato federation in 1938. Today, the game is played by teams of four riders, with a basket (like the type used in basketball) at each end of a regulation field.

The original duck has been replaced by a more acceptable leather ball with handles, and points are scored by passing the ball through the basket. This sport has steadily grown in popularity and is now as socially acceptable as polo. The annual national open championship is held in mid-December in Palermo, Buenos Aires.

Other equestrian sports

In a country where horses are plentiful and breeding is big business, horse racing and showjumping are also popular. There are race-tracks in most Argentine towns and plenty of opportunities for off-track betting, although the government oversees the official odds. The big races are held in Buenos Aires, often at the Jockey Club in the San Isidro suburb.

Horse shows are staged at numerous clubs in Buenos Aires and other major cities, taking place almost weekly from March to December. There is a fine tradition in this sport – as there is for dressage – and only the regular exportation of top horses has kept Argentina from gaining international stature.

Boom-time for tennis

Tennis has been played in Argentina since the 19th century, but it has always been a game largely for the middle and upper classes – until now. Fueled by the meteoric rise of Guillermo Vilas, an energetic and talented player who gained international prominence on the world's courts in the 1970s, tennis experienced an unprecedented boom.

The driven, dashing Vilas won the Masters in 1974 and the US Open in 1977, and soon became known as an international playboy. Linked romantically with such women as Princess Caroline of Monaco and countless Hollywood starlets, Vilas emerged as a national hero.

Virtually overnight, every young Argentine dreamed of being a professional tennis player. The number of players skyrocketed, as did the sales of rackets, balls, and shoes. Courts sprang up all over the suburbs of Buenos Aires – both municipal and privately owned – and Argentine players flooded the professional circuit.

One of the finest of that boom was Gabriela Sabatini, the teenage sensation who emerged as one of the top women players of the mid-1980s. Dubbed "Gorgeous Gabby" by the international press, Sabatini played her way into the top-10 rankings in 1986, quickly rising to the third seed. Sabatini retired from professional tennis in 1996. With 10 Argentine players in the world top 100, the sport is increasingly popular in Argentina, and the Buenos Aires River Plate Stadium

was enlarged in 2003 to hold 10,000 spectators, in time for the Davis Cup.

Rugby on the up and up

As with soccer and polo, rugby was introduced to Argentina by the British. But the sport inexplicably failed to catch on until the mid-1960s. That was when the Pumas, Argentina's national rugby team, rose to prominence with a string of international successes. Like tennis, the sport experienced a rapid growth of interest and a massive infusion of young talent.

Today, Argentine rugby ranks among the best in the world. Virtually every province

has its own federation, and international matches draw more than 50,000 fans.

Other growing sports

The fastest-growing sports for both spectators and players in Argentina are hockey and basketball. Although neither sports attract the mass following of soccer, the success of Argentine teams internationally has given both of them a huge boost at home. New basketball courts and hockey clubs have sprung up all over Buenos Aires and in the provinces. At the 2004 Olympics in Athens, the Argentine basketball team, led by Emanuel Ginobili, won gold. ❏

LEFT: rugby has become one of Argentina's most popular spectator sports.
RIGHT: at Palermo's racetrack in Buenos Aires.

FOOD AND WINE

Argentine cuisine is based on the best local produce, and no visitor should miss its home-grown beef, washed down with a glass of local red wine

Argentine cuisine is often seen as beef and more beef, but it has many more attractions. While the *parrillada* (grill) is the staple of the Argentine diet and restaurant fare, there are different regional dishes, and each of the immigrant communities has brought its own contribution to the table.

The Northwest has food that is closest to its Andean neighbors. This includes *choclo* (sweet corn), often made into *humita* (corn steamed in its leaves with meat), and potatoes, often used as part of the nourishing *locro* or stew. The meat in these stews will often be goat or even huanaco (a relative of the llama).

In Patagonia the meat is more likely to be lamb than beef, while the 2,000-km (1,200-mile) coastline offers many fresh fish that are increasingly being appreciated by Argentines and tourists alike.

A meat-eating nation

Beef is the Argentine's pleasure and joy, however, and there is a fierce pride in the quality of the meat. The best way of eating out here is to go native; often there is no choice. *Parrillas* or grills are ubiquitous and opting for a *parrillada mixta* (mixed grill) is an opportunity to try out the full range of the cow's anatomy without deference to personal scruples. The meal will usually begin with chorizo (spicy sausage), *morcilla* (blood sausage), or an empanada (meat pasty), before the real meat is served.

Cuts of meat aren't always comparable with those elsewhere, but some that are well worth trying are the *bife de lomo* (fillet steak), *bife de chorizo* (rump steak), and *tira de asado* (Argentine spareribs). For all the pride in their meat, the Argentines are not above eating offal: *riñones* (kidneys), *mollejas* (sweetbreads), *hígado* (liver), and *chinchulines* (the lower intestine, truly delicious when well crisped) are all eaten with relish.

Chicken is frequently included, but pork is

rather despised. A *parrillada mixta* will usually comfortably serve two Argentines or four to five uninitiated tourists.

Eating alfresco

The quintessential Argentine experience is the *asado*, or outdoor barbecue. At weekends you

will see people leaving the butcher with enough meat to last most cholesterol-conscious adults elsewhere in the world the best part of a month.

The preparation of the meat is elevated to an art form. Cuts of meat and sausages are spread over *parrillas* the size of bed frames. Whole lambs are staked and cooked slowly by adjusting their distance from the coals. Everyone eats their fill with appreciation and enthusiasm. *Chimichurri*, a delicious sauce of parsley, garlic, chili, and lemon, is used as a marinade and a condiment.

European variety

The European immigrants all brought their own foods to Argentina, which can often be found in

---

PRECEDING PAGES: perusing the menu in a cafe-bar.
LEFT: fresh beef at La Cabaña, Buenos Aires.
RIGHT: a quiet neighborhood cafe in San Telmo.

restaurants in Buenos Aires and other cities and towns. The Argentine cuisine of German origin includes *milanesas* – the Argentine equivalent of Wiener schnitzel, usually accompanied by local sauerkraut. In Bariloche in the south, the German, Swiss, and Austrian arrivals have ensured that climbers and skiers can enjoy all kinds of chocolate products.

The Spaniards, many of whom originated in the coastal region of Galicia, run the best fish and seafood restaurants, and the English introduced the "five o'clock tea" that is still on offer in many Buenos Aires' cafes.

But it is the Italian influence which is most apparent in Argentine food. Pizza and pasta of a high standard can be found everywhere and, until recently, were Argentina's only convenience food. Polenta is commonplace in the home, usually served with *tuco* or sauce, and so too *ravioles* which are bought fresh in boxes. *Noquis* – small potato dumplings similar to Italian gnocchi – are another regular feature of the diet.

Italian-style restaurants are the most common feature of Buenos Aires and the other cities, although the smarter restaurants in Puerto Madero and Palermo make a point of their "French" cooking, with more elaborate sauces and presentation. The great thing about

TIME FOR TEA

Given a distrust of vegetables and a weakness for sweet things, it is a miracle that the Argentines have any teeth at all. This miracle is perhaps attributable to maté, the tea brewed from yerba, a plant grown in the Northeast. Maté is not just a drink but a social ritual and a part of everyday life. This bitter green tea is made by adding hot water to leaves held in a seasoned gourd. The gourd is then passed to each participant in turn who drains it through a metal straw *(bombilla)*, before refilling it with hot water for the next participant. The maté may do several circuits before it is deemed washed out *(lavado)*. Occasionally, sugar and herbs are added to the yerba.

all Argentine food is that the meat and other produce are fresh and usually locally grown.

Although in the past it was very difficult for vegetarians to exist in Argentina, there are now restaurants serving salads and other dishes for those who cannot face the vast platefuls of meat.

Sweet fancies

Argentines have a notoriously sweet tooth and there are plenty of sweet things on offer, most of which feature *dulce de leche (see opposite)*. One of the simple pleasures of Argentine life are the *facturas*, which can be found in any *panadería* or bakery. These are small pastries such as *caras sucias*, literally "dirty faces," encrusted with brown sugar; *vigilantes*; or *media lunas*, which are usually sweet and rather doughy croissants. Others are topped with conserve, *dulce de leche*, chocolate, or ricotta cheese. *Facturas* are bought by the dozen and consumed as a snack at any time of the day from breakfast onwards.

Also popular to share at social gatherings are *masitas*, an infinite variety of tiny fancy confections. The bakery will make up trays of these delicacies by weight. *Churros*, Spanish-style fingers of deep-fried dough filled with *dulce de leche* and sprinkled with sugar are another delight, especially with hot chocolate. *Alfajores* are cookies filled with all manner of tasty sweet stuff and often coated in chocolate.

The ultimate Argentine confection is *mil hojas*, layers of fine pastry glued together with *dulce de leche* and then smothered in meringue. Even the Argentines eat this in only small quantities.

World-class wines

Argentina has been producing wine since the 16th century, when Jesuit priests brought the first vines to the country to produce sacramental wine for celebrating mass. It was in the second half of the 19th century, with mass immigration from Spain and Italy, that commercial wine production began. From the start, the region around Mendoza in the west was the center of the wine industry. Sheltered by the Andean mountains, with lots of sunshine, relatively mild winters, and deep, rich soil, the region proved ideal for vines. Vineyards are located all around the city, between 500 and 1,200 meters (1,600 and 4,000 ft) high.

For many years, wines from Mendoza and the neighboring provinces of San Juan, La Rioja, and the northern part of Salta, were aimed at the domestic market. Cheap red wine was produced in great quantities – occasionally so rough that it became an Argentine trait to add a splash or two of soda water to make it more palatable.

All this changed in the 1990s when President Menem opened up Argentina to foreign competition, which meant that many small Argentine firms were bought out. New technology and tech-

THE SWEETEST THING

Dulce de leche (literally "milk sweet") is made by boiling milk and sugar into a sticky conserve. It is spread on bread, used in cakes and pastries, or simply served on its own as a dessert.

niques have revolutionized the industry and it has begun to compete with Chile and other New World producers on the international market.

Only four or five of the traditional wineries still survive, the oldest among them being the González Videla vineyard, which has been producing red wines since 1840. More recent establishments such as Chandon, Norton, and Catena, are also keen to show off their vineyards – and sell a few bottles as well.

A lot of hope is being pinned on the devel-

opment of the Malbec grape, originally from France, but which seems perfectly suited to the soils of Mendoza. In many areas, this has replaced the Cabernet Sauvignon variety that used to be the favorite.

Further north, in Cafayate in Salta, the Torrontés grape is used to produce a fruity, aromatic white wine. Other whites being developed are from Sémillon and Chardonnay grapes.

Argentina is now the world's fifth largest exporter of wine, with over 2,000 producers. Tours of the wineries of Mendoza province have proved increasingly popular with tourists, with the spectacular backdrop of the Andes mountains adding an extra interest. ❏

LEFT: exquisite food from a top Buenos Aires restaurant.
RIGHT: waiter at La Biela, one of Buenos Aires' most famous traditional cafes.

PLACES

*A detailed guide to the whole of Argentina, with principal
sites clearly cross-referenced by number to the maps*

Argentina's landscapes are some of the most stunning in the
world. From the thundering waterfalls of Iguazú to Tierra del
Fuego with its soaring glaciers, the country's geographical
features delight. Roam the windswept grasslands of the pampas, ski
in sophisticated resorts arond Bariloche, or taste wine from the vineyards of Mendoza. Then there's the sophisticated city of Buenos
Aires with its rich cultural life, tree-lined boulevards, and bohemian
coffee houses. Visiting Argentina takes planning, for it is a huge
country and destinations often lie far apart. Getting from the deserts
of the Northwest to the coastal wildlife of Patagonia requires organization and time. Fortunately, Argentina has a solid infrastructure
geared for tourism. Comfortable hotels are available in all popular
spots, and in even the most remote reaches there are usually at least
campgrounds. Planes and buses run on convenient schedules and
cars can be rented. In some areas, one might even prefer to get around
on foot or horseback. An Aerolíneas Argentinas air pass enables one
to cover the larger distances at reduced rates.

In the following chapters the country has been divided up into
territories that one is likely to see as a whole: Buenos Aires, the
vacation coast, the central sierras, the northeast, the northwest, the
western wine country of the Cuyo, Patagonia, and Tierra del Fuego.
How much of an adventure you make of it is up to you.

Be mindful of the conditions dictated by the time of year when
you visit. During the regional high season (from December to
March), reservations may be hard to come by; winter rains may make
a park inaccessible; wildlife you will see in a particular spot depends
on migration patterns. These chapters will help you decide whether
you'd like to be sunbathing on the beaches of Mar del Plata in
January, gliding down the ski slopes of the Andes in August, or eating
a *bife de chorizo* in Buenos Aires any time of the year.   ❏

PRECEDING PAGES: the Fitz Roy range in Santa Cruz province; a gaucho surveys his
fertile land; Recoleta Cemetery, Buenos Aires.
LEFT: the prickly landscape of the Northwest.

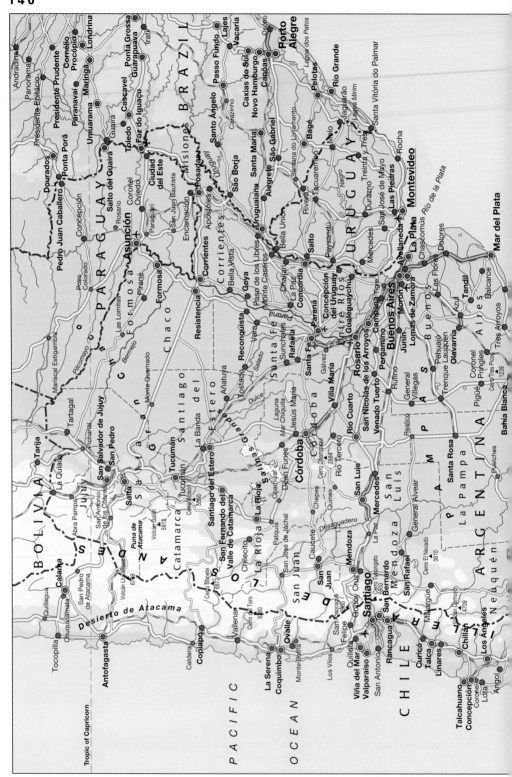

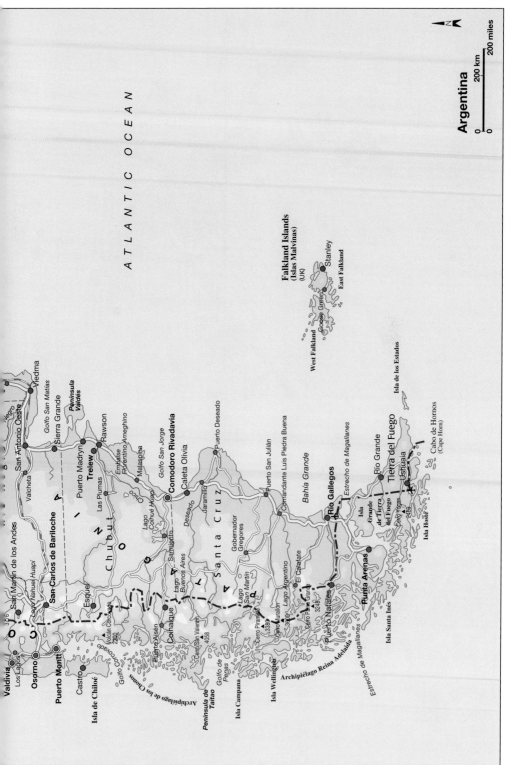

Argentina

N

200 km
200 miles

ATLANTIC OCEAN

Falkland Islands
(Islas Malvinas)
(UK)

Stanley
Goose Green
West Falkland
East Falkland

Isla de los Estados

Cabo de Hornos
(Cape Horn)

Viedma
Golfo San Matías
Península
Valdés
Sierra Grande
Rawson
Puerto Madryn
Trelew
Las Plumas
Embalse
Florentino Ameghino
Malaspina
Comodoro Rivadavia
Caleta Olivia
Golfo San Jorge
Puerto Deseado
Deseado
Jaramillo
Puerto San Julián
Comandante Luis Piedra Buena
Bahía Grande
Río Gallegos
Estrecho de Magallanes
Río Grande
Tierra del Fuego
Ushuaia
2469
Cerro Vega
Isla
Grande
de Tierra
del Fuego
Isla Hoste

San Antonio Oeste
Negro
Valcheta
Lago Colhué Huapi
Chico
San Carlos de Bariloche
Lago Nahuel Huapi
San Martín de los Andes
3776
Esquel
Volcán Corcovado
2300
Coihaique
Puerto Aisén
Cerro San Valentín
4058
Cerro Murallón
3380
Cerro Pirámide
3248
El Calafate
Lago
Buenos Aires
Lago
San Martín
Lago Argentino
San
Lago Viedma
3248
Puerto Natales
Punta Arenas
Isla Santa Inés
Estrecho de Magallanes
Archipiélago Reina Adelaida
Isla Santa Inés

Los Lagos
Valdivia
Osorno
Puerto Montt
Castro
Isla de Chiloé
Golfo Corcovado
Golfo de
Penas
Península de
Taitao
Archipiélago de los Chonos
Isla Wellington
Isla Campana

Gobernador
Gregores
Las Plumas
Samuento

C h u b u t
S a n t a   C r u z

Golfo San Matías

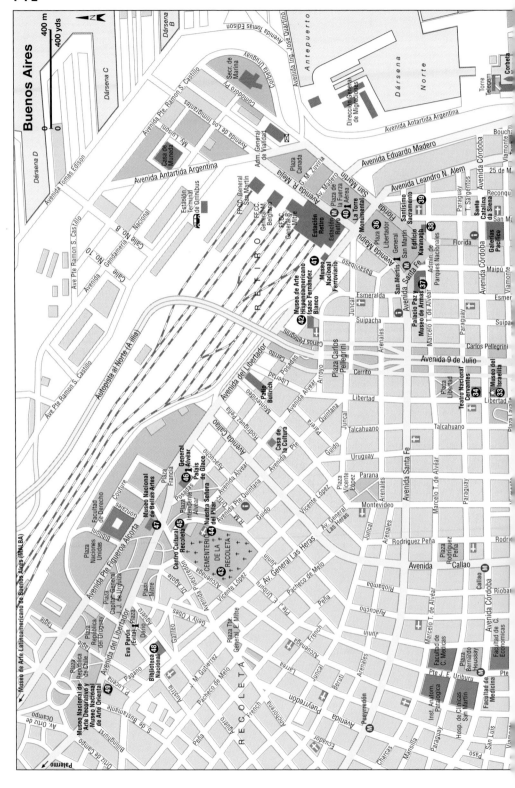

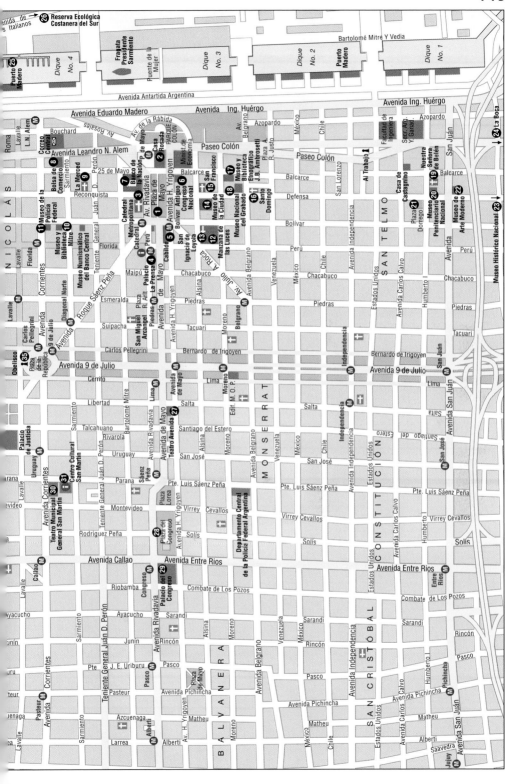

BUENOS AIRES

*Arguably the most cosmopolitan city in all South America,
Argentina's historic capital has breathtaking energy, spacious
grandeur, and self-confident style*

Map
on pages
142–3

Despite grand boulevards and hefty, ostentatious architecture, this is a city of villages, or more correctly barrios (districts) – 47 of them. It has been famously described as the Paris of South America, or as travel writer Paul Theroux put it, a "most civilized anthill." It is exuberant, stylish, and full of great pretense and hot gossip.

For visitors, the easternmost section of the city along the bank of the Río de la Plata (River Plate) will be the main area of interest. Hotels, museums, government buildings, shopping, and entertainments are located here in the districts of Palermo, Recoleta, Retiro, San Nicolás, Monserrat, San Telmo, and La Boca.

Many new shops and restaurants have opened over the past few years. The Puerto Madero opened in 1994 with exclusive eateries and apartments, and developments continue. Palermo Viejo is the latest area to have been dramatically revitalized and now boasts cultural centers, designer shops, and chic restaurants.

Buenos Aires, for all its enormity, is a very easy city to get around. Streets run on a logical grid pattern with regular numbering. The bus system is extensive and efficient. Taxi fares are currently low. But the nicest way to get around Buenos Aires is to walk. This is how you stumble upon the parks and interesting holes in the wall. The terrain is very flat, so it is easy on the walker. The only slopes are down to the old riverbank in the city center. But as you go, just be aware that pedestrians aren't accorded too many rights. Good luck, or as the locals say – *Suerte!*

LEFT: on guard duty at the Casa Rosada.
BELOW: street tango in San Telmo.

Founding and settlement

Historians still dispute the date of Buenos Aires' founding and the identity of its founder. What is certain is that in 1516, Juan de Solís disembarked here. Buenos Aires lies at the mouth of one of the world's largest rivers, which Solís named Mar Dulce (Sweet Sea). The western banks lead onto the pampas: flat, treeless land with extraordinarily rich black topsoil, ideal for agricultural planting. Solís also gave the river another name, the Lion's Sea, because of its brown tone and its vastness. This estuary later acquired the name Río de la Plata *(see page 37)*.

Pedro de Mendoza was the next European to arrive. In 1536, under Spanish royal auspices, he established the first settlement (some say in what is today Parque Lezama). He encountered the fertile pampas, as well as its inhabitants: hostile indigenous tribes.

After five years of continual attacks, the group moved upriver to found Asunción, Paraguay. Mendoza left two important legacies: the city's name,

Nuestra Señora de Santa María del Buen Aire, and hundreds of horses and cows that were to multiply and later become the foundation of the Argentine economy.

Finally, in 1586, Juan de Garay, a mestizo (of Spanish and indigenous blood) from Asunción, Paraguay, returned with 70 men and established a permanent settlement. A fortress was built facing the river, and the town square, Plaza de Mayo, was marked off to the west. At the far end of the plaza they built the Cabildo (the town council) and on the northern corner, a small chapel. Although new buildings have been constructed on the ruins, the plaza maintains this basic structure and is still the center of the city's official activities.

Buenos Aires was the last major city in Latin America to be founded. Not only was it geographically cut off from more developed trade routes, but, under Spanish law, the use of its ports for European imports and the export of precious metals from Potosí and Lima was prohibited. Logically, the English, Portuguese, and French took advantage of the lack of Spanish presence on the Río de la Plata, and illegal trade flourished. The settlement was able to survive in large part due to this contraband.

Manufactured goods were exchanged for silver brought from northern mining centers, and for cow hides and tallow. Construction materials also began to be imported, since the pampas had neither trees nor stones: homes were originally built of adobe and straw.

BELOW: booming trade in a 19th-century dockside warehouse.

Faced with competition in the region from other European nations, in 1776 Spain declared a viceroyalty upon what is now Argentina, Uruguay, Bolivia, Paraguay, and the northern section of Chile. Buenos Aires was made the site of central government. With its new judicial, financial, and military role, the city burgeoned as a regional power. Functionaries, lawyers, priests, military personnel, artisans, and slaves soon arrived, and the small village began its transformation into a major cosmopolitan city. In Latin America, only Lima and Mexico City exceeded its economic development at the time.

The *porteños* (inhabitants of the port) were accustomed to a certain economic and political independence from Spain. When, alone, they were able to repel two British invasions in 1806 and 1807, pride in the city's military prowess, and what later was to be called nationalism, ran high.

Independence and development

In 1810 the city's residents took advantage of Spain's preoccupation with Napoleon, and won more autonomy for themselves. However, it was not until 1816 that independence was declared for the whole country.

In the subsequent decades, the government of Buenos Aires was consumed with the struggle for control over the rest of the country. The Federalists, represented by Juan Manuel Rosas, the governor of Buenos Aires from 1829 to 1852, believed each province should maintain considerable power and independence. The Unitarians, who came to power when General Urquiza overthrew Rosas, sought the dominance of Buenos Aires over the rest of the country. The tension between residents of the interior and the *porteños* still exists.

Finally, in 1880, the dispute was resolved in a small street battle, and the city became a federal district, rather than simply the capital of the province of Buenos Aires. This was also to be a decade of intense change for the city. Under President Julio Roca, the mayor of the city looked to Europe and especially Paris as a model for change. Hundreds of buildings were constructed in imitation of the latest Parisian styles. New neighborhoods were created for the wealthy by filling in huge sections of the river, particularly in the northern parts of the city, where Retiro, Recoleta, and Palermo lie.

Map on pages 142–3

Boom and slump

It was also in the 1880s that mass immigration from Europe began, principally from Italy and Spain although also from Germany, Poland, and Britain, as well as Lebanon and Syria, and later Russia. By 1910, the city's population had risen to 1,300,000. Public services such as the tramway, running water, schools, and police protection were well under way. The city's literature, opera, theater, and other arts were spreading around the world. Suddenly, Buenos Aires was the Paris of Latin America for upper-class European and North American tourists.

Turkish immigrant with hookah pipe.

Throughout the 20th century, the architecture of Buenos Aires reflected its economic and political fortunes. Buildings from the Peronist 1940s and 1950s tend to show massive fascist-style grandeur, while skyscraper blocks of apartment buildings dot the landscape from the following decades.

With the return of political stability in recent years, and the election of a city mayor, there has been considerable restoration of the city center, while young professionals have returned to the old tenements or *conventillos* and made up with their imaginations what they have lacked in money.

BELOW: hanging out at the Galerías Pacífico shopping mall on Florida.

Like all great cities, Buenos Aires is constantly changing: from one season to the next, the most fashionable area can switch completely, and new buildings can change the landscape dramatically.

Getting your bearings

To understand Buenos Aires, you have to venture beyond the downtown area. Walk the daytime streets of residential areas, ride buses, sit in cafes, and, above all, talk – and listen – to the people. Their conflicting and emotional feelings about the city and the whole country are contagious.

Buenos Aires is not only enormous in relation to the population of the rest of Argentina, but is also one of the largest cities in Latin America. The federal district occupies 200 sq. km (77 sq. miles) and the entire metropolitan area spans over 2,915 sq. km (1,121 sq. miles). Approximately 12 million people, or one third of the country's population, live in the city and surrounding areas. Three million reside within the federal district.

Buenos Aires is marked to the north and east by the Río de la Plata and, on a clear day, you can see all the way across the mud-colored river to the Uruguayan coast. To the south, the city limit is marked by the Riachuelo, a shallow channel constructed to permit entrance to seagoing ships.

The city's landscape is varied. There are wide boulevards and narrow cobblestone streets. The downtown area boasts chic boutique windows, outdoor cafes, simple but elegant restaurants, and grand old cinemas and theaters. In residential districts, ornamental old apartment buildings, with French doors that open onto plant-filled balconies, stand side by side with modern buildings up to 20 stories high. Sycamore, acacia, and *tipuana* trees line the streets, providing

Colonial detail on Calle Florida.

BELOW: the old reflected in the new in Plaza de Mayo.
RIGHT: a mural of the colonial past.

shade for little boys playing soccer. There are innumerable parks and plazas where you may opt to go jogging, or simply sit quietly and watch the old men playing *truco* (a card game) or chess in the summer.

Map on pages 142–3

A city of barrios

There are 47 barrios in Buenos Aires, each with its own special history and character. With few exceptions, the neighborhoods have a Roman grid structure around a central plaza with a church. Most barrios also have a main street for commerce, often with a two-story shopping mall, as well as a butcher, baker, and vegetable and fruit stand. A sports club, a movie theater, a pizzeria, and an ice-cream parlor also form part of the typical barrio.

The social atmosphere in these neighborhoods is much warmer than in the busy downtown area, where pedestrians, as in most big cities, are on the run and will barely stop to give the time of day. In a barrio, it is very likely that a lost tourist will be rescued by helpful and curious residents.

To grow up in a barrio is to acquire a special allegiance to it; soccer teams from each club compete in national competitions that create passionate rivalries among many of the districts.

In order to get a sense of Buenos Aires' layout, it is useful to simplify and talk about major blocks of the city. From Plaza de Mayo, two diagonal avenues extend to the northwest and southwest (Avenida Roque Sáenz Peña and Avenida Julio A. Roca). The central track between the two is the most populated area of the city. To the south is the oldest part of the city, including San Telmo and La Boca, where many working-class and some middle-class people live. To the north are the barrios of Retiro, Recoleta, and Palermo, where the wealthy moved

BELOW: the colorful barrio of La Boca.

when yellow fever hit the southern district in the 1870s. A fourth zone lies to the
west. With the opening of two railway lines – the Once line that runs along
Rivadavia, and the Retiro line that runs northwest along the river – new barrios
such as Palermo Viejo began to spring up.

The center of Buenos Aires

The center is truly the city's "downtown," and while most *porteños* live in outer
barrios, everyone comes here, either to work, to eat, or to find entertainment.
Residential barrios have their own mini commercial areas, so that except to
visit friends, many *porteños* never cross the city; they simply head downtown.

As in every big city, there are many hurried, well-dressed businesspeople in
the center of Buenos Aires, but there are also Argentines here enjoying the
bookstores, the movies, the theater, the cafe conversations on every imaginable topic, the plazas, the shopping, and the political and cultural street life.
Some streets, like Florida, Corrientes, and Lavalle, are for strolling, and are
filled with leisurely visitors come to walk, watch, and be watched. A two-hour
walk around the center starting at the Plaza de Mayo provides a quick introduction to the government buildings as well as the commercial, financial, and
entertainment districts.

Plaza politics

BELOW: Plaza de
Mayo, the scene of
many key historical
events and protests.

Buenos Aires began with the **Plaza de Mayo ❶**, today a strikingly beautiful
square with its tall palm trees, elaborate flower gardens, and a central monument,
set off by the surrounding colonial buildings. The plaza has been and still is the
pulsating center of the country. Since its founding in 1580, as the Plaza del

Fuerte (fortress), many important historical events have been celebrated or protested against here.

The most eye-catching structure in the plaza is unquestionably the **Casa Rosada**, the seat of the executive branch of the government, which has recently been renovated. Flanking it are the Banco de la Nación, the Catedral Metropolitana, the Palacio Municipal (city hall), and the Cabildo (town council).

The Casa Rosada was originally a fortress overlooking what is now the **Plaza Colón**, but was at that time the river's edge. When attacks by the indigenous inhabitants subsided, the plaza became Plaza del Mercado, a marketplace and social center. The name and role of the plaza changed again with the British invasions of 1806 and 1807, when it became the Plaza de la Victoria. Finally, following the declaration of independence, the plaza assumed its present name, in honor of the month of May in 1810 when the city broke away from Spain.

The date also marks the first mass rally in the plaza, on this occasion to celebrate independence. Subsequently, Argentines have poured into the plaza to protest and celebrate most of the nation's important events. Political parties, governments (de facto and constitutional), and even trade unions and the church call people into the plaza to demonstrate their symbolic power.

Historic demonstrations

Salient events in the history of the Plaza de Mayo include the October 17, 1945 workers' demonstration, organized by the General Confederation of Labor to protest the brief detention of then vice-president Juan Perón. Ten years later, the airforce bombed the plaza while hundreds of thousands of Perón's supporters were rallying to defend his administration from the impending military coup. In 1982, Argentines flooded the plaza to applaud General Galtieri's invasion of the Malvinas/Falkland Islands. A few months later, they were back again, determined to oust the military government for having lied about their chances of defeating the British. In 1987, the plaza was jammed with 800,000 *porteños* demonstrating against a military rebellion, and again at the end of 1989, protesting President Menem's pardon of convicted generals.

But the most famous rallies have been those of the *Madres de la Plaza de Mayo* – the mothers of the many people who disappeared during the "dirty war" *(see page 62)*. The Mothers now operate from a building close to the Congress, where they continue to put pressure on politicians to uncover the truth about these dark years.

During the last years of the military regime, young people accompanying the Mothers would taunt the menacing army and police units with chants of, "Cowards, this plaza belongs to the Mothers." The white headscarves the Mothers traditionally wear at all the demonstrations have been depicted around the base of the pyramid, marking their weekly route.

The Pink House

Leaders of the nation traditionally address the masses from the balconies of the **Casa Rosada ❷**,

Map on pages 142–3

The Plaza de Mayo has a central pyramid that was built on the first centennial of the city's independence.

BELOW: Santa enjoying Christmas in the sunshine.

Young porteño *facing up to a guard at the Casa Rosada.*

an architecturally imbalanced building constructed on the foundations of earlier structures in 1894. Sixteen years earlier, President Sarmiento had chosen the site for the new government house. There are several explanations for why he had it painted pink, the most credible of which is that it was the only alternative to white in those days. The special tone was actually achieved by mixing beef fat, blood, and lime. Some insist that Sarmiento chose pink to distinguish the building from the White House in Washington, D.C. Still others say that pink was selected as a compromise between two feuding parties, whose colors were white and red.

The **Museo de la Casa Rosada** (open weekdays, except Wed, 10am–6pm and Sun 2–6pm; guided tours 11am and 4pm weekdays and Sun 3.30pm and 4.30pm; free admission) is a small gallery that contains antiques and objects identified with the lives of different national heroes. The entrance is on Avenida Yrigoyen. The Grenadiers Regiment guards the Casa Rosada and the president. This elite army unit was created during the independence wars by General San Martín, and its soldiers wear the same blue and red uniforms that distinguished them in those times. Between 6 and 7pm each day, they lower the national flag in front of the Casa Rosada. On national holidays the Grenadiers often parade on horseback, and they accompany the president on his public appearances.

Church and state

The **Catedral Metropolitana** ❸ (open daily except Sat pm and Sun am. Guided tours in Spanish Mon–Fri 11.30am) is the next historic building on the plaza and the seat of Buenos Aires' archbishopric. The cathedral's presence in

this highly political plaza is appropriate. The Catholic church has always been a pillar of Argentine society, and since the city's founding, the church has shared the Plaza de Mayo. In a mural at the northern end of Avenida 9 de Julio, two symbols are used to illustrate the founding of the city: a priest and a spade, the latter representing the military.

The cathedral was erected over the course of several decades and was completed in 1862. It was built, like the Cabildo and the Casa Rosada, upon the foundations of earlier versions. There are 12 severe neoclassical pillars at its front that are said to represent the 12 apostles. The carved triangle above reputedly portrays the meeting of Joseph and his father Jacob. This section is generally considered to be the work of architects, although a theory persists among some that it was created by a prisoner, who was then set free as a reward for its beauty.

Inside are five naves housing important art relics. The oil paintings on the walls are attributed to the Flemish painter, Sir Peter Paul Rubens (1577–1640). There are also beautiful wood engravings by the Portuguese Manuel Coyto de Couto.

For Argentines, the most important aspect of the cathedral is the tomb of General José de San Martín, liberator of Argentina, Chile, and Peru. San Martín, who died during his self-imposed exile in France, is one of the few national heroes to be revered by Argentines of all political persuasions.

The first eye-catching building on Avenida de Mayo on the way from Plaza de Mayo is the **Palacio La Prensa** ❹, until recently housing Argentina's oldest and most conservative national newspaper. It is located opposite the Cabildo and adjacent to the Palacio Municipal, an ornamental old building

Map on pages 142–3

On the steps of the cathedral on Flag Day (Día de la Bandera).

BELOW: grandiose sculpture on the Avenida del Libertador.

with an enormous pentagonal clock in its tower. The La Prensa building, which now houses the Casa de la Cultura of the city of Buenos Aires, is French-style in architecture, unlike most of the Spanish-style Avenida de Mayo, and the ground floor is worth a look for its stained glass, decoration, and woodwork.

Across the Avenida de Mayo, and on the western end of the Plaza de Mayo, is the **Cabildo ❺** (town council), a key historic building and perhaps the greatest patriotic attraction in Argentina. School children are brought here and told how their forebears planned the nation's independence.

The town council has been on this site since around the time of the city's founding in 1580, although the present building was constructed in 1751. Originally, it spanned the length of the plaza with five great arches on each side. In 1880, when Avenida de Mayo was built, part of the building was demolished. And once again, in 1932, the Cabildo was further reduced, this time to its current size, with two arches on either side of the central balconies.

The Cabildo also houses an historic museum, the **Museo del Cabildo** (open Tues–Fri 12.30–7pm; Sun 3–7pm; free on Fri), exhibiting furniture and relics from the colonial period. Behind the museum is a pleasant patio, which features a simple outdoor snack bar and on Thursday and Friday afternoons you will find a small arts and crafts fair. Continuing around the plaza, on the southeastern corner is the **Antiguo Congreso Nacional ❻** (open for guided tours Thur 3–5pm; library open Mon–Fri 1–7pm), the former House of Congress, built in 1864. It served as the seat of government until 1906 and since 1971 it has been used by the National Academy of History as a conference center, with a history library.

BELOW: balancing the national diet of beef.

La City

The main banking area of Buenos Aires, known as "La City," extends four blocks north from the Plaza de Mayo to Corrientes along the parallel streets in between, and west for three blocks as far as pedestrianized Florida. Here you can find the major national as well as international banks.

Opposite the Antiguo Congreso Nacional, at the northeastern corner of Plaza de Mayo, is the **Banco de la Nación ❼**. The old Teatro Colón was on this site before it reopened on Plaza Lavalle in 1908. The imposing marble and stone bank was inaugurated in 1888. On the first floor is the **Museo Numismático** (open Feb–Dec Mon–Fri 10am–3pm; free admission), whose entrance is at Bartolomé Mitre 326. Apart from a large collection of coins, notes, and medals, the museum has a private research library and offers tours of the bank itself, available by prior appointment.

Nearby, at San Martín 216, the **Banco Central** (open Tues–Thur 10am–2pm) also has a currency museum. With some 14,000 exhibits, it claims to be the biggest of its kind in the Americas.

The **Bolsa de Comercio ❽** (stock exchange) (open Mon–Fri 10am–5pm) is located three blocks from the Plaza de Mayo, at 25 de Mayo between Sarmiento and Corrientes. The building was inaugurated in 1919, and its features such as woodwork and metalwork, the cupola, and the internal staircase are worth a look. Also within this area are the **Basílica de la Merced ❾**, at Reconquista and Perón, an 18th-century church and convent with lovely gardens and a restaurant in the patio offering one of the few peaceful oases in central Buenos Aires.

There has been a church on the site since 1712, and there was a convent here from 1600 to 1823. At San Martín 336, between Sarmiento and Corrientes, is the **Museo y Biblioteca Mitre ❿** (open Mon–Fri 1–6pm; free admission), which includes oil paintings, the personal effects of President Mitre, important historical and map libraries, as well as a currency museum. In front, at San Martín 322 is the **Museo de la Policía Federal ⓫** (open Tues–Fri 2–6pm) containing exhibits charting the history of a police force whose actions have not always gained widespread admiration.

The southern quarter

The expansion of Buenos Aires in the 17th century first occurred toward the south, making the southern quarter one of the city's oldest residential areas.

There are three areas of interest to most tourists: La Manzana de las Luces ("The Enlightenment Block"), one block south of the Plaza de Mayo; San Telmo, historically a fascinating barrio and today inhabited by artists and antiques dealers; and La Boca, at the southeastern tip of the city, which is famous for the pastel-colored tin houses where dock workers used to live, and for the raucous restaurants where tourists come for a lively evening's entertainment.

La Manzana de las Luces ⓬ refers to a block of buildings that were constructed by the Jesuits in the early 18th century. The church of San Ignacio,

Map on pages 142–3

TIP

The Feria de las Artes, on the Plazoleta de los Franciscanos, at the corner of Alsina and Defensa, is a weekly market offering a good selection of arts and crafts (Sundays noon–6pm).

BELOW: many rich *porteños* employ professional dog walkers.

The interior of the Farmacia la Estrella, whose shelving is crafted from Italian walnut.

the old Jesuit school, and underground tunnels are bordered by calles Bolí-var, Alsina, Perú, and Moreno.

The area was originally granted to the Jesuits at the end of the 17th century. In 1767, the Spanish Crown withdrew the gift, in light of what was perceived as the group's increasing power. In fact, of principal concern in this case, as with Jesuit missions throughout the world during this period, were the egalitarian principles practiced by the priests within their social organizations. Today, La Manzana de las Luces serves as a cultural center, but guided tours detailing its historical past are available for a small charge (Sat and Sun 3.30pm and 5pm).

Despite the repression against the Jesuit order, many of the churches still stand, the oldest of which is **San Ignacio de Loyola** ⓭ (open during Mass, Mon–Fri 7pm), at the corner of Alsina and Bolívar 225. This impressive baroque church, which is also the oldest of all the remaining six colonial churches in Buenos Aires, was founded in 1675 and completed in 1735.

Walking south on Defensa from the Plaza de Mayo, one finds the **Farmacia la Estrella**, a 19th-century drugstore with marvelous metaphorical murals on the ceiling and walls portraying disease and medicine.

On the second floor of the same building is the **Museo de la Ciudad** ⓮ (open daily 11am–7pm). The small museum features rotating exhibitions of aspects of the city's past and present, including architectural photo studies and curios, such as old postcards of the city.

On Defensa and Alsina is the **Basílica de San Francisco** ⓯ and the **Capilla de San Roque**. The main church, finished in 1754, is the headquarters of the Franciscan Order. Parts of the neoclassical building were rebuilt

BELOW:
tango and the
news in San Telmo.

at the end of the 19th century, in imitation of the German baroque styles in vogue at the time. The chapel was built in 1762.

San Francisco was severely damaged in 1955, as were a dozen other churches, when angry Peronist mobs attacked and set fire to them. The violence was a response to the Catholic church's opposition to the Peronist government, and its support for the impending military coup.

The **Basílica de Santo Domingo** ⑯, located at Belgrano and Defensa, is another important church that was partially burned in 1955, including the destruction of much of the principal altar. This former convent contains the mausoleum of independence hero General Manuel Belgrano. The basilica (correctly known as Nuestra Señora del Rosario) was inaugurated in 1783, although there has been a church on the site since 1600, and it is famous for its organ, which is often used for recitals.

One block north, at Moreno 350, the **Museo y Biblioteca Etnográfico J.B. Ambrosetti** ⑰ (open Feb–Dec Wed–Sun 2.30–6.30pm) has the largest archeological and ethnographic collection in Argentina, including a 1,200-year-old mummy and ceramics from the pre-Columbian era. The early 19th-century building was formerly the Law Faculty of the University of Buenos Aires.

The **Museo Nacional del Grabado** ⑱ (open Mon–Fri & Sun 2–6pm) at Defensa 372 offers exhibitions of works by contemporary and 19th-century engravers, and includes a library.

San Telmo – bohemian Buenos Aires

Like Greenwich Village in New York, **San Telmo** used to be one of the city's more run-down areas, until history, architecture, and low rents in the 1960s

The basilica of Santo Domingo contains four British flags captured during the British invasions of Buenos Aires in 1806 and 1807, as well as two Spanish flags taken by General Belgrano during the wars of independence.

BELOW: an antiques shop in San Telmo.

caught the attention of artists and intellectuals who began to revive the area. Attractive studios, restaurants, and antiques shops began to replace the decaying tenements. An open-air Sunday flea market in the central plaza has brought in enough tourists to nourish the new business ventures. While San Telmo is now one of the principal tourist stops, the neighborhood maintains its historic authenticity and its vitality. **Plaza Dorrego**, the site of the Sunday flea market, is proof of this. Weekdays, it remains a fascinating spot, where old people who have lived all their lives in the barrio, many of whom still speak with an Italian accent, meet to talk and to play chess and *truco*.

San Telmo grew during the 18th century as a rest stop for merchants en route from the Plaza de Mayo to the warehouses along the Riachuelo. Next to the Plaza Dorrego was a trading post for imported goods. On adjacent streets, *pulperías* (bar/grocery stores) quickly sprang up to accommodate passersby.

Except for the Bethlemite priests who had established themselves in the San Pedro Church, the area's first residents were Irish, blacks, and Genoese sailors, whose rowdy drinking habits made the *pulperías* notorious.

In the early 19th century, many important families built their homes along **Calle Defensa**, which connects Plaza de Mayo and Plaza Dorrego. During this period, a typical home had three successive interior patios, and only the facade would change, as new architectural styles arrived. The first patio was used as living quarters, the second for cooking and washing, and the third for the animals.

In the 1870s, a yellow fever epidemic swept through San Telmo, killing more than 13,000 people during a three-month period. At the time, it was widely believed that the fog off the Riachuelo carried the disease. Those who could fled San Telmo and built homes just west of the downtown area, approaching what is now called Congreso, and in the northern section, now called Barrio Norte.

In the 1880s and the subsequent three decades, San Telmo received poor European immigrants, particularly Italians, who were arriving in Argentina. Many of the old mansions and chorizo houses *(see margin note)* were converted into *conventillos* (one-room tenements that open onto a common patio), in order to accommodate the flood of new families.

Tango, jazz, and eating out

A walk through San Telmo begins at the corner of Balcarce and Chile, the northern edge of the barrio. There are several of the city's oldest and most prestigious tango bars nearby *(see Travel Tips, page 355)*.

Crossing Chile on Balcarce, you come to a two block-long cobblestone street called **San Lorenzo**. To the right are beautiful old houses, many now nightclubs. Others, some with interior patios, have been converted into apartments, studios and boutiques. At San Lorenzo 319 are **Los Patios de San Telmo**, a renovated house open to the public, which contains numerous artists' studios and a bar. The brick and wood ceilings date back at least 200 years.

Balcarce continues across Independencia and is one of the prettiest streets in San Telmo for strolling,

Nineteenth-century homes in San Telmo were called chorizo (sausage) houses because of their linear shape.

BELOW: lace stall, San Telmo market.

and for more live music venues. The next block is **Pasaje Giuffra**, another narrow, cobblestone street, where many of the old *pulperías* used to be.

Further down, **Carlos Calvo** is an attractive street with numerous restored colonial houses, several of which have been converted into elegant restaurants. Half a block past Carlos Calvo at Balcarce 1016 is the old home of the Argentine painter **Juan Carlos Castagnino**, whose murals from the 1950s adorn the ceiling of the Galerías Pacífico shopping mall on Florida. After he died, his son converted Castagnino's home into an art museum.

On this same block on the right is the **Galería del Viejo Hotel** (Balcarce 1053), another old *conventillo* that has been renovated and now serves as an arts center. Two stories of studios open onto a central plant-filled patio. Visitors may wander through the complex and watch the artists at work. Weekends are the best time to visit.

Calle Humberto 1 is the next block. Turning right, you come upon the old **Iglesia de Nuestra Señora de Belén** . The church was built by Bethlemite priests in 1770, and was temporarily occupied by the British invaders in 1807. Next door, at Humberto 1 378, is the ghoulish **Museo Penitenciario Nacional**  (Wed–Fri 3–6pm, Sun 11am–6pm), on the site of a former jail, which operated until the 1870s. This museum offers such delights as exhibitions of leg irons and other prison paraphernalia. Guided visits of the museum, which also offers occasional art exhibitions, can be arranged on request.

Across the street is the **Escuela G. Rawson**, a former convent that was the first school of medicine in Buenos Aires. Next door is a plaque commemorating the site of an old *pulpería*, operated by a woman named Martina Céspedes. During the British invasion, Señora Céspedes and her daughters enticed British

Sunny balcony of a cafe in San Telmo.

BELOW: the baroque church of Nuestra Señora de Belén.

If, after visiting the flea market, you still want more open-air browsing, one block north of Plaza Dorrego, on Carlos Calvo, is San Telmo's municipal market, which sells fresh meat, fruit, and vegetables.

BELOW: colorful clutter of a typical La Boca house.

soldiers into their bar, tied them up, and turned them over to the Argentine Army. Although one of her daughters reputedly married a captured British soldier, the mother was eventually rewarded for her brave deeds with the title of Captain of the Argentine Army.

Sunday flea market

Finally, we are upon **Plaza Dorrego ㉑**, the center of San Telmo's commercial and cultural life and the site of the Sunday flea market, with junk jewelry, second-hand books, antiques, and some handicrafts. Surrounding the plaza are several restaurants, bars, and antiques shops that are fun to wander through. Another charming shopping mall is **Galería El Solar de French**, on nearby Calle Defensa. It has been redone in a colonial style, with flagstone floors, narrow wooden doors, birdcages, and plants hanging from wrought-iron hooks along the patio.

Located two blocks south of the plaza, at Avenida San Juan 350, is the **Museo de Arte Moderno ㉒** (open Tues–Sun 11am–8pm; free on Wed; closed Feb). The museum is housed in the former Massalin y Celasco cigarette factory, an attractive building with a brick facade. It houses the Ignacio Pirovano collection of major 20th-century painters, as well as temporary exhibitions of international art.

Parque Lezama is just four blocks south of Plaza Dorrego on Defensa. Many believe that this little hill was the site of the first founding of the city. Later it was the home of Gregorio Lezama, who converted it into a public park. By the end of the 19th century, it was an important social center, with many amenities such as a restaurant, a circus, a boxing ring, and a theater. Today, the park is somewhat run-down, and the view is no longer attractive

Map
on pages
142–3

due to the surrounding construction and heavy traffic. There is a fountain built to commemorate one of the city's founders, Pedro de Mendoza, and the old mansion still holds nostalgic memories and has been converted into the **Museo Histórico Nacional** ㉓ (open Tues–Sat 1.30–5.30pm), the national history museum at Defensa 1600. One of the museum's highlights is a room decorated with the furniture from the house in France where General San Martín ended his days.

Next to Parque Lezama is one of the city's most extraordinary sights: the onion domes of the Russian Orthodox Church. The church was opened in 1940 for the many Russian immigrants who settled in the area. The facade has a Venetian-style gold mosaic made in St. Petersburg. Nearby at the intersection of Defensa and Brasil streets is the Café Británico, one of the most traditional in Buenos Aires, named in honor of the British builders of the railway system.

The sheet-iron homes that can still be seen throughout La Boca and across the canal in Avellaneda were originally built from materials taken from the interiors of abandoned ships by Genoese sailors.

La Boca

The working-class neighborhood of **La Boca** ㉔ is at the southern tip of the city, beyond Parque Lezama, along the Riachuelo Canal. The barrio is famous for its houses made from sheet iron and painted in bright colors, and for its history as a residential area for Genoese sailors and dock workers in the 19th century.

La Boca came to life with the mid-19th century surge in international trade and the accompanying increase in port activity. In the 1870s, meat-salting plants and warehouses were built, and a tramway facilitated access to the area. As the city's ports expanded, the Riachuelo was dug out to permit the entrance of deep-water ships. Sailors and longshoremen, most of whom were Italian immigrants, began to settle in the area.

BELOW: graffiti inspired by art.

One painter's influence

The famous painter Benito Quinquela Martín took up the theme of color, traditional to his neighborhood, and made it his own. Quinquela was an orphan, adopted by a longshoreman family of La Boca at the turn of the 20th century. As an artist, he dedicated his life to capturing the essence of La Boca. He painted dark, stooped figures, set in raging scenes of port action. In one of his works (which Mussolini reputedly tried unsuccessfully to buy from him with a blank check), an immense canvas splashed with bright oranges, blues, and black, men hurriedly unload a burning ship.

Neighborhood residents took pride in their local artist, and were influenced by Quinquela's vision of their lives. They chose even wilder colors for their own homes, and a unique dialogue grew between residents and artist.

Quinquela took over an alleyway, known as the **Caminito**, decorated it with murals and sculpture, and established an open-air market to promote local artists. The brightly painted homes and colorful laundry hanging out to dry provide the background to this charming one-block alley. There are small stands, manned by the artists themselves, where watercolor paintings and other works of art are displayed for sale.

A walking tour

BELOW: taking a break at the Galerías Pacífico shopping center.

A stroll through La Boca begins at the Caminito. Heading north from the river, it is worth walking around the block and back to the riverside to get a sense of the normal residential street. The tin houses were not created for tourists but are, in fact, comfortable homes. Most have long corridors leading to interior apartments, and are graced by wood paneling. The cobblestone streets are shaded by tall sycamore

trees, and elevated sidewalks provide some defense against frequent flooding.

The **Vuelta de Rocha**, where the Caminito begins, consists of a small triangular plaza with a ship's mast. It overlooks the port area, which may be more accurately described as a decaying shipyard, and you may be accosted by the foul odors of the canal.

Fundación Proa is a small, modern museum with changing contemporary art exhibits and a cafe with a terrace offering good views of the waterfront. A new Malecón promenade leads from the Vuelta de Rocha along the river and is a good place for a stroll.

East along Pedro de Mendoza, the avenue parallel to the canal, at No. 1835 is the **Museo de Bellas Artes de La Boca** (open Tues–Sun 10am–6pm), the neighborhood's very own fine arts museum. The top floor was used by Quinquela as an apartment studio. Many of his most important paintings are here, and one may also see the modest apartment he used in his last years. The museum is a fun stop, if only to get the view of the shipyard depicted in his paintings. Another relic of the past is visible from here: the huge, rusting transporter bridge which used to carry vehicles over the Riachuelo.

Bar mural in La Boca.

Rowdy *cantinas*, rowdy soccer

Just past the Avellaneda Bridge is **Calle Necochea**, where rowdy *cantinas* contrast with the sedate restaurants in other areas of Buenos Aires. These lively music and dance clubs were originally sailors' mess halls, and their high spirits recall the jazz clubs of New Orleans.

Brightly colored murals of couples dancing the tango, speakers set out on the sidewalk blaring loud music, and somewhat aggressive doormen who

BELOW: Buenos Aires soccer teams River Plate and San Lorenzo fight for the ball.

compete for the tourist dollar, may combine to frighten off those who are not prepared. But the scene is not as seedy as it might appear. Families from the interior of the country are there for a festive night out. Old people are singing their favorite tunes and dancing amid balloons and ribbons. And the idea that a night out on Calle Necochea is a celebration of sailors returning home is definitely preserved. Much of the action is concentrated between calles Brandsen and Olavarria. Two blocks west is **Avenida Almirante Brown**, the main commercial street in La Boca renowned for its excellent pizzerias. At the end of the street is the "Ghost Tower," said to be haunted by a local woman painter who threw herself from the top.

La Boca also boasts the country's most famous soccer team, **Boca Juniors**, and their stadium, La Bombonera ("the candybox"), located in the heart of the neighborhood, draws fans from all over the city. Diego Maradona, the internationally famous soccer star who carried Argentina to victory with his spectacular goals in the 1986 World Cup, played here.

Puerto Madero

Back at the Plaza de Mayo, and east toward the river, is the vibrant, renovated docklands area of **Puerto Madero** ㉕. Walking from Plaza de Mayo, cross Avenida Alem, where at Sarmiento and Alem, two blocks east of the plaza, you'll find the **Correo Central** (main post office), an ornate French-style building (open Mon–Fri 10am–8pm). Crossing Avenida Madero and Avenida Alicia Moreau de Justo, you will finally reach the string of renovated port buildings that runs from Avenida Córdoba at the northern end to the Buenos Aires–La Plata Highway at the southern end. The original waterfront port buildings,

BELOW: Café La Biela, in Recoleta.

CAFE LIFE

The social life, and to a great extent the business and cultural life of Buenos Aires revolves around cafes, or *confiterías*, as they are known in Argentina. "Meet me at the *confitería*" is the typical response to an invitation to go to the cinema or the theater, as well as to clinch a business deal or simply to get together for a chat. A coffee or a cognac in a favorite *confitería* is also the standard ritual for ending a night out on the town.

There are cafes on almost every street corner and they range from the most elegant to modest and cozy gathering places where neighbors exchange greetings or employees from nearby offices take a break to read the daily paper. Visitors to Buenos Aires often comment that only Paris rivals the city as a true "cafe society."

Historically, the rise of the cafe as an institution came from the high proportion of male immigrants, who were either single or whose wives stayed behind. These men came to the cafes for companionship, a smoke, or a game of dominos. Gradually, many cafes became associated with a particular clientele. Each political, artistic, and social group laid claim to its own cafe, so that even today many of the events that mark Argentine history were first discussed among friends or foes over a *confitería* table.

constructed by Eduardo Madero in 1887, have been turned into fancy office blocks and restaurants, where you can have a very elegant meal or a coffee. While this is the in place for lunch or dinner, the restaurants to be found here are among the most expensive in Buenos Aires – and not necessarily the best.

The Puerto Madero neighborhood has a pedestrian walkway extending the length of the port, and also includes yacht clubs and most of Buenos Aires' most modern tower blocks and hotels, in addition to the 19th-century port buildings. The most technologically advanced buildings in the area are the Telecom Tower and the Fortabat Tower, both near the Córdoba end of the district. At Dock 3, the **Fragata Sarmiento** (open daily 9am–9pm) is a 19th-century Argentine Navy frigate now serving as a museum. The ship, built in England in 1897, still has its original woodwork and furniture. A fresh round of building and renovation began in 2002, creating Puerto Madero Este. The symbol of this is the Faena Hotel and Universe complex built from a former grain silo by internationally renowned architect Philippe Starck for the local entrepreneur Alan Faena. Puerto Madero Este is, for the moment at least, the place to be seen in Buenos Aires.

A short distance away is the **Reserva Ecológica Costanera del Sur** ❷❻ (open daily 8am–7pm; free admission), a large open green space along the river which has been a nature reserve since 1986. There are four lakes and a revamped esplanade which make it an attractive area for walking. The reserve, which is very popular at weekends, is home to many species of water birds and mammals.

Returning to Plaza de Mayo and facing west, the view down Avenida de Mayo to the National Congress is spectacular, and the 15-block walk is a wonderful introduction to the city. The avenue was inaugurated in 1894 as the link

Map on pages 142–3

A menu from Café Tortoni, the most famous cafe in Buenos Aires.

BELOW: the graceful Puente de la Mujer of Puerto Madero.

between the executive branch and the Congress, most of which had been completed by 1906. It was originally designed to imitate a Spanish avenue, with wide sidewalks, gilded lampposts, chocolate shops, outfitters' emporiums, and old Zarzuela theaters. Today, however, there is a mixture of influences with local adaptations that defy classification. As in much of the city, "neoclassical," "French," "Italian," and "Art Nouveau" are terms that do not adequately describe the special combination of influences seen here. Nor is there a traditional coherence from one building to the next; ornamental buildings stand side by side with others that are simple and austere.

Plaza del Congreso is used as the zero kilometer mark for maps of Argentina.

Ornamental lunch

There are several well-known restaurants and cafes along the way, including **Café Tortoni** (Avenida de Mayo 825), a historic meeting place for writers and intellectuals. Apart from the famous customers said to have frequented the cafe, the ornamental interior makes the place worthy of at least a glimpse. Marble tables, red-leather seats, bronze statues, and elaborate mirrors create the most regal of atmospheres. In the evenings the cafe hosts various theater and music shows, the most common being tango or jazz. Across the avenue is the almost equally famous London City cafe, opened in 1954. It was here that novelist Julio Cortazar sat to write one of his first novels, *The Prizes*.

At Avenida de Mayo 500 is the Perú subway station. The line from here, Línea A, was the first in South America, opened in 1913. The station still has its original architecture.

The Spanish-style **Teatro Avenida** ㉗, inaugurated in 1908, is at Avenida de Mayo 1212. Closed down since 1979 as a result of a fire, the building has been renovated and was re-opened in 1994. The beautiful 1,200-seat theater offers regular theatrical and musical performances, usually by Spanish companies or with a Spanish theme, and it is also used for conferences.

Avenida de Mayo ends at the Plaza Lorea, just before the Plaza del Congreso.

BELOW: singing from the heart at Café Tortoni.

Pizzas, pigeons, and politics

The next block is the **Plaza del Congreso** ㉘. The plaza is a wonderful place for people-watching on warm summer evenings. Old and young eat pizza and ice cream on the benches among the pigeons, enjoying the civilized atmosphere. There is a dramatic fountain with a galloping horse and little cherubs, and at night, classical music booms out from below the falls. There is a monument above the fountain that honors "two congresses" – the 1813 assembly that abolished slavery, and the 1816 congress of Tucumán that declared the country's independence.

It is also here that groups come to protest about issues of the day in front of Congress and the congressional offices. You could well run into senior citizens complaining about the low level of state pensions, or the *piqueteros*, several well-organized groups of the unemployed who often block roads and hold demonstrations not just here but throughout the country.

The green-domed **Palacio del Congreso** ㉙ houses the Senate on the south side and the House of Representatives on the north (Rivadavia entrance). The green color was not in evidence when the building was inaugurated in 1906, but the dome was made of copper which over time developed its present green shade. Congressional sessions, which normally run from May 1 to September 30, are open to the press or those with a pass, available at the annex of the House of Representatives across Rivadavia. Guided tours are offered in Spanish, English, and French. The interior is decorated with appropriate pomp: large paintings, bronze and marble sculptures, luxurious red carpets, silk curtains, and wood paneling. The central hall (Salón Azul) is especially impressive, lying under the dome and including a huge two-ton crystal chandelier dating from 1910. Next to the Salón Azul is the Salón de los Pasos Perdidos, where delegations are received and where former Argentine presidents have lain in state. The building also boasts an extensive library, open Monday to Friday, 8am–8pm.

Across Rivadavia is a modern wing of the **House of Representatives**. Construction work began in 1973, but halted with the military coup of 1976. With the return to democracy in 1983, building resumed, and the wing was inaugurated in 1984.

The street that never sleeps

Congress is located at the corner of Rivadavia and Callao. Callao runs north from Rivadavia, and four blocks down is **Avenida Corrientes**, another principal street for *porteños*. Some of its bustle has recently been hijacked by Sante Fe, which has a very American feel, but Corrientes appeals to those who support local rather than imported culture. So, while there are neon lights, fast-food restaurants

Map on pages 142–3

TIP

Rivadavia (allegedly the longest street in the world) is a key street in Buenos Aires, dividing the city into two; street names change at its crossing and street numbering begins here as well.

BELOW: the National Congress building.

Argentine Writers and Buenos Aires

Argentina's capital has fascinated generations of authors. One of the earliest Argentine stories, *El Matadero (The Slaughterhouse)* by Esteban Echevarría (written in 1830 during the dictatorship of General Rosas) already pointed up the contrast between the sordid and often bloody reality of the capital and its symbolic dimensions. Perhaps the country's greatest writer, Jorge Luis Borges, once even suggested in a poem that Buenos Aires had such a mythical force it could never have been founded by man. In some of his other poems, however, he wrote of the grimness of its "butcher's shops."

In the 1920s and 1930s Borges looked back to those 19th-century days. In short stories such as *El Sur (The South)*, Buenos Aires is still a frontier town where violence is always close to the surface. In others, he emphasizes the mystery of a vast city in which individual identity can so easily be lost. Borges

was part of a thriving scene which made Buenos Aires one of the most important centers of literary production in the Hispanic world.

This anxiety of lost individuals comes to the fore in the work of another essential 1930s Buenos Aires writer, Roberto Arlt. His novel *Los Siete Locos (The Seven Madmen)* depicts the chaos of an immigrant society with all its crazy dreams of riches and utopias, which often end in suicide and murder. The harshness of life in Buenos Aires was also the theme of many of the best tango lyrics of this decade, written by world-weary men such as Enrique Discépolo, and sung by men whose appearance and voice spoke of danger and the cheapness of life in the turbulent city.

During the Peronist period, novels such as *Adán Buenosayres* by Leopoldo Marechal again showed Buenos Aires in a heroic, almost mythical light. But writers who were anti-Peronist, such as Julio Cortázar, also wrote memorably about their city: nowhere more so than in his greatest novel *Rayuela (Hopscotch)* which depicts characters divided between living in Paris and a nostalgic love for the street-corner towers of Buenos Aires. Manuel Puig also wrote books full of the voices and predicaments of lower middle-class people in the barrios of the capital, living their circumscribed, disappointing lives in the midst of this vast metropolis.

The dark days of the 1970s and 1980s have still to be adequately explored in Argentine literature, but Tomás Eloy Martínez has made fiction out of the myths of Peronism – and indeed Perón himself in *La Novela de Perón (The Perón Novel)* and in *Santa Evita*. More recently, Eloy Martínez has returned to the streets of Buenos Aires and the city's nostalgic atmosphere in *El Cantor de Tango (The Tango Singer)*.

The newer generations of Argentine writers have been exploring the myriad private worlds that co-exist in the city. In his collection of short stories, *La Novia de Odessa (The Bride of Odessa)*, Edgardo Cozarinsky describes the city's 20th-century Jewish heritage, while in *Pasado (The Past)*, Alan Pauls shows how the city is a complex, living world.   ❑

LEFT: Jorge Luis Borges in a bar in downtown Buenos Aires in 1973.

serving good local cuisine, movie theaters, and music stores on Corrientes, the atmosphere is intellectual rather than gaudy.

There are little bookstores everywhere, *kioscos* (newsstands) with a wide selection of newspapers, magazines, and paperbacks, and old cafes where friends gather for long talks. The international and national films on show also reflect the serious interests of the moviegoers; you'll find European art-house cinema here, whereas Santa Fe is more likely to feature the latest Hollywood hit. The bookstores are traditionally one of Corrientes' greatest attractions. They are single rooms, open to the street, selling both secondhand and new books. Some patrons come to hunt for old treasures, or the latest bestseller. Others use the bookstores as a meeting place. The stores stay open way past midnight, and, unlike other Buenos Aires shops, you may wander in and out without being accosted by aggressive salespeople.

Coffee and culture

Another endearing feature of Corrientes and adjoining streets is the cafe life. There are hundreds of old cafes, with tall, wood-framed windows that are left open when it's warm. A small table next to the window permits the lone thinker to gaze at the street life, and to write or read in a relaxed atmosphere. But going out for coffee in Buenos Aires is also a social encounter. Even if it is a *licuado* (fruit and milk shake) that you finally indulge in, "having a coffee" means an intimate moment with a friend. And without a doubt, the nicest aspect of these coffee breaks is that the waiter will never hurry you.

On the 1500 block of Corrientes, next door to each other are **Liberarte** and **Librería Gandhi-Galerna**. These are both combinations of bookstore, cafe, and performance space, where the artsy and the intellectual gather to browse for books, sip coffee, or take in poetry readings, plays, or music. Both are open in the evening.

Free culture

At Corrientes 1530 stands the **Teatro Municipal General San Martín** ③⓪. This chrome and glass building was inaugurated in 1960 and is the largest public theater in Argentina, with five stages and an estimated half a million spectators each year. There is a year-round program of free concerts, plays, film festivals, lectures, and musical performances, and the theater has a permanent company. There is also a contemporary ballet company and a group of puppeteers. This is also the headquarters for the important biennial International Theater Festival. Within the building, you'll also find the Leopoldo Lugones cinema, offering film retrospectives, international cinema, and avant-garde works.

In the block behind the theater, at Sarmiento 1551, is the **Centro Cultural San Martín** ③①, a sister building with an equally important flurry of cultural activity. The **City Tourism Bureau** is on the fifth floor, where you can pick up maps, hotel information, event listings, and a schedule of free, guided city tours.

Further down Corrientes, are the main commercial theaters in Buenos Aires: the Opéra, the Gran Rex,

Map on pages 142–3

A modern sculpture at the Centro Cultural General San Martín.

BELOW: Las Violetas tea rooms on Avenida Rivadavia.

For a taste of
Corrientes of years
past, go to **La Giralda**
on the 1400 block.
Here the white-coated
waiters serve the
house specialty of
chocolate y churros
(thick hot chocolate
and delicious hot, fried
sugary dough sticks).

BELOW: the opulent
Teatro Colón.

and El Nacional, which re-opened in 2000 after a disatrous fire in 1982. Also on Corrientes is a plaque that is a must for all lovers of traditional tango as it marks the spot where the Corrientes 348 apartment block once stood: the address is the title of one of the most famous tangos of the 1930s *(see page 89)*.

The tradition of free concerts, seminars, and other cultural activities is one of the most striking aspects of life in Buenos Aires. If anything, the activity has gained momentum in recent years, despite the economic crisis, and was undoubtedly boosted by the 1980s return to democracy *(see page 69)*. For visitors, both these centers are a fine introduction to the contemporary cultural scene in Buenos Aires and the rest of the country.

Plaza Lavalle is another center of activity in the area. It is two blocks north of Corrientes at the 1300 block. The **Federal Justice Tribunals** are at one end of this historic plaza, and the internationally renowned Teatro Colón is at the other. The plaza first served as a dumping ground for the unusable parts of cattle butchered for their hides. In the late 19th century, it became the site of the city's first train station, which later moved to Once. In the plaza today there is a beautiful statue and fountain commemorating Norma Fontenla and José Neglia, two dancers from the Colón ballet killed in a plane crash with nine other members of the ballet troupe in the 1970s.

Colón opera house

The **Teatro Colón** 32, Buenos Aires' opera house, occupies the entire block between Viamonte, Lavalle, Libertad, and Cerrito (part of 9 de Julio). It is the symbol of the city's high culture, and part of the reason Buenos Aires became known in the early 20th century as the "Paris of Latin America." The theater's

elaborate European architecture, its acoustics – which are said to be near perfect – and the quality of performers who appear here, have made the opera house internationally famous.

Three architects took part in the construction of the building before it was finally finished in 1908. The original blueprint, however, was respected. It is a combination of styles – Italian Renaissance, French, and Greek. The interior includes colored glass domes and elaborate chandeliers. The principal auditorium is seven stories high and holds up to 3,500 spectators. There is a 612-sq. meter (6,590-sq. ft) stage on a revolving disk that permits rapid scenery changes.

Well over 1,000 people are employed by the theater. As well as its role as an opera venue, it is also the home of the National Symphony Orchestra and the National Ballet. In a recent rehaul that cost millions of dollars, a huge basement was added, creating storage space for the sets, costumes, and props and working space for the various departments.

The Colón's season runs approximately from April to November. An interesting guided tour of the opera house is available in Spanish and English, Monday to Friday, on the hour from 11am–3pm, and Saturdays from 9am–noon. Also within the Colón, with the entry on Viamonte 1180, is the **Museo del Teatro Colón**, which includes original costumes and props as well as documents, and the **Museo de Instrumentos Antiguos**, with a collection of antique musical instruments (both museums open Mon–Fri 9am–4pm; Sat 9am–noon). In addition, there is also a library, with a wealth of material on opera and classical music (open Mon–Fri 9.30am–5pm).

One block from the front of the Colón, along the Plaza Lavalle, is the beautiful **Sinagoga Central**, the principal synagogue of Argentina's 1 million-strong

Map on pages 142–3

One of the treasures of the Teatro Colón is its central chandelier. Made in France, it measures 7 meters (23 ft) in diameter, holds 700 light bulbs and weighs 2½ tons.

BELOW: Plaza Lavalle's Fountain of the Dancers.

Jewish community (open Mon–Fri 8am–6pm). In front of the synagogue a series of concrete barriers has been erected, like most other synagogues and buildings linked to the Buenos Aires Jewish community: this came in the aftermath of the 1992 car bombing of the Israeli Embassy and the 1994 car bombing of the Jewish mutual society AMIA, in which 84 people were killed. Barricades to prevent cars from parking and the deployment of permanent guards are aimed at preventing further such attacks. Within the synagogue is the **Museo del Israelita** ③③ (open Tue–Thur 4–6pm). This small museum has a collection of religious artifacts and objects documenting the history of the Jewish community in Argentina.

Turning right off Libertad onto Córdoba brings you to the beautiful Spanish-style **Teatro Nacional Cervantes** ③④, inaugurated in 1921, designated the National Theater in 1933 and declared a national monument in 1995. The theater, which has three stages – the principal, large hall with red-velvet seats and curtains and abundant gilt decoration; the 150-seat Sala Argentina, used for chamber music; and the presently closed Salón Dorado – has been remodeled on several occasions. Within the theater is the small **Museo del Teatro Nacional Cervantes** (open Mon–Fri 1–6.30pm), which includes exhibits on Argentina's most important actors, costumes, programs, and manuscripts from important plays.

World's widest avenue

You could not have missed **Avenida 9 de Julio**. The world's widest avenue, according to the Argentines, is 140 meters (460 ft) from sidewalk to sidewalk. Everything about it is big – big billboards, big buildings, big *palos borrachos* (drunken trees) with pink blossoms in the summertime, and, of course, the big Obelisk.

BELOW: the Obelisk that *porteños* love to hate.

The military government of 1936 decided to demolish rows of beautiful old French-style mansions to build this avenue. Much of the central block is now occupied by parking lots. The only mansion to survive was the **French Embassy**; its occupants refused to move, claiming it was foreign territory. There is a sad view of its barren white wall facing the center of town, testimony to the tragic disappearance of its neighbors.

The **Obelisco** ③⑤, which rises sharply up towards the clouds at the intersection of Diagonal Norte, Corrientes, and 9 de Julio, was erected in 1936 in commemoration of the 400th anniversary of the first founding of Buenos Aires. Three years after the monument was erected the City Council voted 23 to 3 to tear it down. However, the order was not taken seriously and the Obelisk still stands today.

Pedestrian thoroughfares

Crossing 9 de Julio on Corrientes you enter the heart of the Buenos Aires business district. Here, it is worth going up to Lavalle, one block north, since the best stretch of Corrientes is back across 9 de Julio, as far as Callao. Lavalle, like Florida several blocks down, is a brash pedestrian street. At night, it is filled with young moviegoers, since, in a four-block stretch, there are many movie theaters. This is despite the fact that in recent years, a number have been closed down or turned into bazaars or evangelical temples. As more cinemas have been built in neighborhood shopping centers, the temptation to go downtown has been reduced. There are also pizza parlors, cafes, restaurants, and several shopping malls. Lavalle is also the main gay cruising street in the city.

Map on pages 142–3

Books, burgers, and art

Avenida Florida, also closed to motor vehicles, is the principal shopping district downtown. The promenade, punctuated occasionally with *kioscos* and potted shrubs, is packed with shoppers throughout the day, as well as folk musicians, pantomime artistes, and others passing the hat. There is a leisurely pace here, and, because of the crowds, it is not a good route for anyone needing to get somewhere in a hurry.

British-style post box on Florida.

The shopping on Florida is slightly more expensive than in other districts downtown, although the posh end of the street is between Corrientes and Plaza San Martín; between Corrientes and Rivadavia, Florida becomes decidedly more cut-price. As elsewhere, most shops are one-room boutiques, many in interior shopping malls that exit onto adjacent streets. They sell clothes, leather goods, jewelry, toys, and gifts. Leather continues to be the best buy for foreigners. **Centro Cultural Borges** on Viamonte and San Martín was constructed in 1995. It is a theater and arts venue which commemorates, rather than features, the great writer.

The most centrally located mall is the **Galerías Pacífico**, between Viamonte and Córdoba. It is part of an early 20th-century Italian building that was saved from demolition because of the frescoes on the ceiling of its great dome. These

BELOW: getting the party started at Club Niceto in Palermo.

are the work of five Argentine painters: Urruchua, Bern, Castagnino *(see page 159)*, Colmeiro, and Spilimbergo. Renovated in 1990, its spacious, air-conditioned interior provides a welcome relief from the bustle of Florida, with a good selection of shops, cafes, and crafts stalls.

There are also cafes along Florida, which offer a chance to relax from the busy street. The street ends at the Plaza San Martín and the entrance to **Ruth Benzacar Gallery** (Florida 1000), an underground art gallery dedicated to Argentine contemporary artists. At the southern end of Florida, toward Plaza de Mayo is the financial district. Tall banks and exchange houses line the narrow streets. It was here that the worst riots took place at the end of 2001, when demonstrators attacked many of the foreign banks. These were boarded up for many months afterwards, and Florida lost some of its appeal, as the better-off Argentines preferred to visit suburban malls with better security.

The northern quarter

The northern district, which includes the Retiro, Recoleta, and Palermo barrios, is the city's most expensive residential and commercial area. Elegant mansions built at the turn of the 20th century are immediately reminiscent of Paris, although the architectural styles are actually a mixture of different influences.

Until the end of the 19th century, this area was unpopulated, except for a slaughterhouse on the site of the Recoleta Plaza. Much of the area was under water. In the 1870s, following the yellow fever epidemic, many wealthy families from the south moved north.

Great changes came in the 1880s when President Roca began a campaign to turn Buenos Aires into the Paris of Latin America. Prominent Argentines had trav-

BELOW: lining up for the bus outside Retiro train station.

eled to the French capital and were deeply influenced. They brought back materials and ideas for the transformation of Buenos Aires into a cosmopolitan city.

Roca's policies were and still are controversial. Critics supported a more nationalistic policy, oriented toward the development of the interior of the country. And yet, unquestionably, what was called the "Generation of the 80s" was responsible for making Buenos Aires the great city that it became.

A walking tour of the northern area begins at the eastern edge of the city center, where Florida ends at the corner of Plaza San Martín. At the northern end of Florida is **Plaza San Martín** ❸, one of Buenos Aires' ritziest neighborhoods. Facing the tree-filled plaza, at the corner of Santa Fe and Maipú, is the **Palacio Paz y Museo de Armas** ❼, formerly the residence of the Paz family (founders of the newspaper *La Prensa*) and now housing the Círculo Militar. The French-style building, partially modeled on the Louvre museum in Paris, is of architectural interest for its ornateness, while the Arms Museum (open Tues–Fri 3–7pm) houses a series of uniforms used by the Argentine Army, as well as antique weapons. The only part of the Círculo Militar open to the public is the library (Mon–Fri 9am–7pm).

Across Plaza San Martín at the end of Florida is the **Edificio Kavanagh** ❽, built in 1935 and one of the most striking buildings in Buenos Aires, as well as the tallest in the city at the time of its inauguration. The building, with 105 apartments, is notable for its narrow front and terraced facade. Behind it, at San Martín 1039, is the **Basílica del Santísimo Sacramento** ❾. Opened in 1928, it is the church of the majority of Buenos Aires' most traditional families, and particularly popular for weddings.

Within the Plaza San Martín itself is the black-marble monument to Argentine soldiers killed in the Falklands/Malvinas war, modeled on the Vietnam war memorial in Washington. Across Libertador is **La Torre Monumental** ❿ (open Wed–Sat noon–7pm; free admission) or "La Torre de los Ingleses," on Plaza de la Fuerza Aérea, donated by British residents to celebrate the centenary of the 1806 May Revolution. It includes four clocks whose faces measure 4.5 meters (nearly 15 ft) in diameter. The tower is open to the public.

On one side of the plaza is the **Retiro** train station, which includes the Mitre, Belgrano, and Sarmiento suburban railroads, and, at the far end, the renovated Retiro bus terminal, where most long-distance buses arrive and depart. The Retiro train station was opened in 1915; its design was based on the style of British train stations of the period; it is now sadly deteriorated, as all the long-distance train lines have closed.

To one side of the Retiro station, along Libertador, is the **Museo Nacional Ferroviario** ⓫ (open Tues–Fri 10am–5.30pm). This museum is housed in a rather dilapidated converted warehouse and contains old locomotives, documents, and other memorabilia illustrating the former glories of the Argentine railroad network. Outside is an eccentric collection of modern-art sculptures created out of scraps of train and car parts. On the other side of the plaza is the modern, 24-story Sheraton Hotel, and still further to the south, a series of high-rise

Map on pages 142–3

Map on pages 142–3

TIP

The Subte (subway) in Buenos Aires is the oldest in South America and contains many of its original features. Look out for the ceramic murals that decorate many stations, including Retiro, Catedral, Jujuy, and Palermo.

BELOW: Edificio Kavanagh on Plaza San Martín.

mirrored glass and chrome office buildings known as the **Torres Catalinas**, completed in the late 1970s.

Just to the west of Plaza San Martín, at Suipacha 1422, is the **Museo de Arte Hispanoamericano Isaac Fernández Blanco** ㊷ (open Tues–Sun 2–7pm; tel: 4327 0272 to arrange a guided tour in English), set in a former stately home and including collections of colonial and post-independence artwork and silver objects from all over South America.

Chic shoppers

Before setting off to visit the Recoleta, those interested in shopping may want to take a detour to Avenida Santa Fe, one of the principal commercial districts. The busiest area is between Callao and 9 de Julio avenues. Here, there are innumerable shopping malls, replete with little boutiques selling clothing, shoes, chocolates, leather goods, linens, china, and jewels. But perhaps the greatest attraction is watching the young *porteños* from Barrio Norte, decked out in the latest Parisian styles, and simply out for a stroll. The Ateneo bookshop has relocated here, at No. 1860, from Florida, and is known as **El Ateneo Gran Splendid**. Located in an old theater, it is the largest bookstore in Latin America.

Evita's final resting place

The **Recoleta**, often referred to as Barrio Norte, is adjacent to Retiro on the northern side. A 20-minute walk from Plaza San Martín, along elegant Avenida Alvear to the Recoleta Cemetery provides a pleasant introduction to buildings that remind one of what some *porteños* call their golden years (1880–1920).

Among the many trees shading the street cafes opposite the Recoleta Cemetery is a giant rubber tree (Ficus macrophylla), brought here from Australia more than 100 years ago.

BELOW: a deli counter at the Patio Bullrich shopping center.

The **Cementerio de la Recoleta** ⓭ (open daily 7am–6pm) is the burial ground for the rich and famous, and the most expensive property in the country. Entering the gates, you have the sense of walking into a city in miniature, and, in fact, it provides an architectural and artistic history of Buenos Aires from its inauguration in 1882. The nation's great leaders, as well as their enemies, are buried here. The schisms of the rest of Argentine society are reflected here, not only in terms of the conflicting architectural styles, but, astonishingly, in disagreement about who is buried here and why. For example, one of the most visited tombs is that of Evita Perón. Nevertheless, despite the fact that she is listed in the cemetery's own map-guide, tourism officials have been known to deny that Evita is buried here, explaining that she is not of the "category" of people entombed in the Recoleta. In fact, she is buried here with other members of the Duarte family, 9 meters (30 ft) underground to keep her enemies from stealing her body, as happened in 1955.

Exclusive enclaves

Many of the city's most sumptuous palaces lie along Avenidas Tres Arroyos and Alvear. At Alvear 1300, is **Plaza Carlos Pellegrini,** where two great mansions, the **Brazilian Embassy** and the exclusive **Jockey Club**, are located.

Some of the best-quality and most expensive shops are situated along **Alvear**. At No. 1777 and No. 1885 there are elegant malls, ideal for window-shoppers. And at the 1900 block is the stately **Alvear Palace Hotel**, which also has its own arcade of chic boutiques.

Running parallel to Alvear one block down the hill toward Avenida Libertador is **Posadas**, where at the 1200 block you'll find **Patio Bullrich**, prob-

Map on pages 142–3

BELOW: the Basílica de Nuestra Señora del Pilar.

ably the most exclusive shopping mall in Buenos Aires. This former slaughterhouse *(see page 187)* stretches through to the next street, and houses not only stores and boutiques, but a cinema and various cafes. Directly across from it lies the modern **Caesar Park Hotel**.

Also parallel to Alvear, but on the other side to Posadas, runs **Avenida Quintana**, which ends at the **Plaza Ramón Cercano** and the Recoleta Cemetery. Here, you can browse in more boutiques, or stop for croissants and coffee at **La Biela** or **Café de la Paix**, two of the city's traditional social gathering sites, or one of the other numerous sidewalk cafes and modern American-style theme restaurants overlooking the plaza. This is one of the places to see and be seen among the Argentine wealthy and beautiful.

Just to the left, along the pedestrian street **Ortíz** (which merges with **Junín** after a couple of short blocks), are some of the renowned restaurants of the city, most with indoor and outdoor seating. Under the shade of a giant rubber tree, you have a view of the entrance to the Recoleta Cemetery; the handsome **Pilar Basílica**, an American baroque convent which is now used as a cultural center; and a series of attractive and well-kept parks and gardens.

Despite its modern-day refinement, the Plaza Ramón Cercano has a very gory past. It used to be the sight of a *hueco de cabecitos*, a dumping ground for heads of cattle slaughtered for their hides. As in the case of other *huecos*, a little stream flowed past the area, where other waste was thrown. The meat was not consumed, and black women were reputedly employed to drag away the carcasses.

The stream was piped underground in the 1770s and the Recoleta priests began to fix up the area, converting it into an orchard and vegetable garden.

Sign of the Automóvil Club Argentino (ACA), the motoring organization, whose headquarters are on Avenida del Libertador 1850.

BELOW: the Floralis Genérica in Plaza Naciones Unidas.

Until the 1850s, the Río de la Plata ran up to the edge of the plaza, covering what is now Avenida del Libertador. Under Rosas' administration this area began to be filled in. It was not until the 1870s that the population, mostly the wealthy, started to migrate to this northern barrio.

The **Basílica de Nuestra Señora del Pilar**  was built between 1716 and 1732. Subsequent restorations have been faithful to the original Jesuit simplicity of its architects, Andres Blanqui and Juan Primoli. Many of the building materials, such as wrought-iron gates and stone, were brought from Spain. It may be recalled that there is no rock in Buenos Aires, since the city lies on part of the pampas, and it was not until much later that stone was transported from an island in the delta. Among the historic relics contained in the church is a silver-plated altar, believed to have been brought from Peru. Like many other colonial churches, during the British invasions it was used as a hospital by foreign soldiers. Today, it is where some of the city's elite get married.

The **Centro Cultural Recoleta** ⑮ (open Tues–Fri 2–9pm; Sat and Sun 10am–9pm), just next door to the church, is housed in a former convent. There is always a flurry of activity inside this large arts center, which features a changing program of photography, painting, and sculpture exhibits, plus a theater, and dance and music performances. On Sundays, the grassy plaza which slopes down towards the river fills with people enjoying one of the largest arts and crafts fairs in the city.

Parks and patriachs

Down the hill from the Recoleta is Avenida del Libertador, and on the far side, before you reach Avenida Figueroa Alcorta, there is a series of parks

Maps on pages 142 and 179

BELOW: Paseo del Rosedal, one of several parks in Palermo.

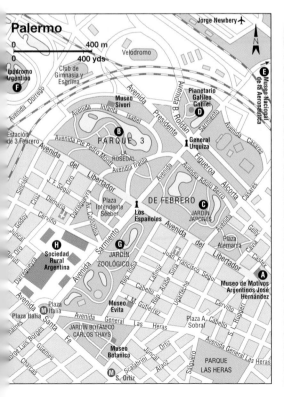

and gardens that are great for joggers interested in seeing more than the pretty woods and fields of Palermo. On the way down the hill is one of the most spectacular of Buenos Aires' monuments, a mounted statue of **General Alvear**.

Alongside the monument is the **Palais de Glace** ⓐ, a late 19th-century exhibition center, that has since been used as an ice-skating rink and cabaret and nightclub and is once again an exhibition center. The complex has housed the National Fine Arts Salon since 1932, and was re-modeled as the National Exposition Rooms in 1978. The Palais de Glace offers an ongoing series of temporary exhibitions (open daily 2–9pm).

Two blocks away at Libertador 1473 is the National Fine Arts Museum, the **Museo Nacional de Bellas Artes** ⓐ (open Tues–Fri 12.30–7.30pm; Sat and Sun 9.30am–7.30pm; free admission). It contains some 10,000 works, including the best collection of 19th- and 20th-century Argentine paintings in the country, as well some excellent paintings and sculpture by major foreign artists, including Rembrandt, El Greco, Goya, Degas, Gauguin, Rodin, Manet, and Monet. Opposite the museum, on the northern side of Avenida Figueroa Alcorta, is the Floralis Genérica, a giant steel rose that opens and closes with the sun.

Almost at the end of this row of plazas is the **Chilean Embassy**. Behind it lies one of the prettiest public gardens in the area. Nearby is the reconstructed house, **Grand Bourg** (open Mon–Fri 9.30am–5pm), from France, where the hero of the independence wars, General José de San Martín, spent the last 10 years of his life. In front of the building a series of statues represents some of the liberation fighter's closest fellow campaigners.

Statue of General Urquiza on Avenida Sarmiento and Figueroa Alcorta.

BELOW: a warm welcome at one of Buenos Aires' many cafes.

Erasing the past

On Avenida del Libertador, between Agüero and Austria, you will find the **Biblioteca Nacional** ⓐ, the national library which was under construction for 30 years and only inaugurated in 1992. The building is located on the site of the former Unzué Palace, which became the presidential palace and was torn down in 1955 because the military government considered it "contaminated" by the fact that the Peróns had lived there (and Evita died in the building). A statue of Evita was erected in the plaza in 1999.

The concrete library has several million books and a newspaper library, with extensive reading rooms and park space outside with benches for readers. It also contains exhibits including a first edition of Don Quixote and a desk used by the novelist Jorge Luis Borges, once director of the library (guided tours in Spanish Mon–Sat 3pm).

Palermo's palaces

The neighborhood of the rich and famous, **Palermo Chico**, is just around the bend. In fact, you'll have to weave around several bends in order to get a sense of this exclusive neighborhood. It is a cozy nest of palaces, set off from the rest of the city by its winding streets, that seems to exclude those from outside its boundaries. An assortment of movie stars, sports heroes, and diplomats make up this unusual community.

Maps on pages 142 and 179

The area was built up, together with the Recoleta area, in the 1880s. Many of the old French-style mansions are now used as embassies, since the original owners have been unable to maintain such an exorbitant standard of living. There are also many new wood- and brick-built homes with classic red-tile roofs, but apart from their well-kept gardens, they can hardly compete with the great stone palaces.

One of those classic palaces can be found at Libertador 1902. The **Museo Nacional de Arte Decorativo** and the **Museo Nacional de Arte Oriental** ⓭ (both museums open Tues–Sun 2–7pm; free on Tues) are located in a French-style mansion, primarily in Louis XVI style, which contains European and Oriental paintings, porcelain, and sculptures.

Also in Palermo Chico, at Libertador 2373, is the **Museo de Motivos Argentinos José Hernández** Ⓐ (open Wed–Fri 1–7pm; Sat–Sun 10am–8pm; free admission), which contains a spectacular collection of 19th-century silver pieces, including the traditional gaucho tack and tools of the trade, and an exposition of crafts from the interior of the country on sale to the public. There is also a library specializing in Argentine folklore.

An important recent addition to Buenos Aires' architectural and cultural landscape is the **Museo de Arte Latinoamericano de Buenos Aires** (MALBA) at Figueroa Alcorta 3415 (open Wed noon–9pm; Thurs–Mon noon–8pm) which was inaugurated in 2001. This impressive, purpose-built gallery houses the most comprehensive collection of 20th-century Latin American art in South America.

BELOW: the Museo Nacional de Arte Decorativo.

Parks and gardens

Few cities in the world have an infrastructure like Buenos Aires for recreation, and this is undoubtedly a key to understanding *porteños*. In the parks of Palermo, the frenzy of the city subsides and *porteños* refuel with the oxygen from the sumptuous vegetation. There are families picnicking, men working out with their buddies, young couples on the grass who have escaped the stern supervision of their parents, and, of course, lots of babies. The parks are a constantly changing scene of people, bicycles, and dogs. As Buenos Aires has relatively little open green space in comparison with other cities of similar size, the series of parks and woods in Palermo is a very welcome relief. At the same time, the neighborhood is less crowded with large apartment buildings and office blocks than much of the city, with some areas still dominated by one- or two-story houses in late 19th-century style.

A pleasant but lengthy jaunt through Palermo may begin in Palermo Chico. But the heart of the park area, **Parque 3 de Febrero** , is six blocks further down Figueroa Alcorta Avenue from the tip of Palermo Chico.

The park includes 400 hectares (1,000 acres) of fields, woods, and lakes. There are several points of interest near and within it. These include a zoo, botanical gardens, and the extroadinarily lush **Jardín Japonés** ❻ (Japanese Garden), which provides a pleasant spot for strolling. There are also tennis courts and a golf course, as well as polo and horseback riding facilities. Many people, however, simply come to sprawl out on the well-trimmed grass to begin work on their tans before hitting the beaches of Mar del Plata or Punta del Este.

Situated to the right on Avenida Sarmiento is the **Planetario Galileo Galilei** ❼, which sits next to a small artificial lake. The planetarium features a

Eco-friendly waste disposal unit.

BELOW: the *hipódromo* in suburban San Isidro.

changing astronomy show on Saturday and Sunday at 3pm, 4.30pm, and 6pm.

The intersection of Figueroa Alcorta and Avenida Sarmiento (not to be confused with Calle Sarmiento downtown), the wide avenue that crosses the park, is marked by an enormous statue of General Urquiza, who became president when he overthrew Rosas in 1852. Past Figueroa Alcorta is the Costanera Norte, where the metropolitan airport Aeroparque Jorge Newbery is located. Nearby at Rafael Obligado 4500 is the **Museo Nacional de la Aeronáutica E** (open Tues–Fri 8am–noon, Sun; 2–6pm in winter Tues–Fri 8am–noon, Sun, 3–7pm in summer), which has an exhibition of military aircraft in service from 1937 to 1973.

To the left on Sarmiento is **Avenida Iraola**, which leads to the heart of Palermo's parks and lakes. There are paddle boats for hire and a storybook pedestrian bridge that leads to rosebush-lined gravel paths with stone benches every few yards. Ice-cream vendors also sell warm peanuts, sweet popcorn, and candied apples, and still others specialize in *choripánes* (sausage sandwiches) and soda. A cafe overlooks the most crowded area of the lake.

The enclosed park beside the lake is called La Rosedal and is open 8am–7pm daily. Iraola weaves around the lake and back to Libertador and Sarmiento, where another large monument marks the intersection. This one was a gift from the Spanish community, and is surrounded by a pretty fountain pool. Heading back down Avenida Sarmiento and taking a left on Avenida Libertador are two of Palermo's other attractions. The **Hipódromo Argentino G**, or horserace track, is located at the corner of Libertador and Dorrego, and races are usually held on Monday and Friday, starting around 3 or 4pm. Across the street is the **Campo de Polo**, the attractive polo fields where in springtime the Argentine

BELOW: the canine star of *Bombón el Perro*, Carlos Sorin's award-winning film.

NEW ARGENTINE CINEMA

More than one hundred years ago, Argentina was one of the first countries in the world to experiment with, and show, film, and this cinematic tradition has continued to this day. In recent years, with the increased freedom which came after the end of the military dictatorships, there has been a resurgence of national cinema. In the 1980s and early 1990s, many directors tried to shed light on the dreadful things that had happened in their country, in films such as *La Historia Oficial (The Official Story)*, directed by Luis Puenzo.

Now in the 21st century a newer generation has appeared, telling stories that often combine accomplished technical and production skills with innovative direction and narrative. Films like *Nueve Reinas (Nine Queens)* directed by Fabián Bielinksy, *El Hijo de la Novia (Son of the Bride)* directed by Juan José Campanella, and *Bombón el Perro (Bombon the Dog)* directed by Carlos Sorin, have won international recognition and audiences both abroad, and perhaps more importantly, in Argentina itself. The devaluation of the peso has also meant that international film companies come to Argentina to make films, while the local cinema industry is producing as many as 60 home-grown films a year.

Maps on
pages 142
and 179

elite come to take in afternoon matches. Walking down Dorrego you can catch a glimpse through the bushes surrounding the fields.

Kiddies and creatures

Avenida Sarmiento continues up away from the parks and toward **Plaza Italia**. Here at the intersection is the entrance to the **Jardín Zoológico ❼** (open Tues–Sun 10am–6pm), a pleasant zoo with a variety of monkeys and birds native to South America. Although renovated in the 1990s, some find the conditions for the animals disturbing.

Across Sarmiento from the zoo's main entrance is the **Sociedad Rural Argentina ❽**, an exhibition complex run by the powerful association of Argentina's large-scale farmers. Their biggest event is the Exposición Rural, a cattle, horse, and agro-industries show, but many other events are held here for the general public as well, from auto shows to tributes to foreign countries.

Plaza Italia is at the intersection of Las Heras, Santa Fe, and Sarmiento avenues. The plaza holds no special charm except for its intense activity. Weekends in the area are especially fun. To the right, down Avenida Santa Fe, there is a street fair known as the "hippie market." Here, the individual stands are often run by young beard-and-sandal types, who make the ceramic mugs and ashtrays, leather shoes, belts, and handbags, the jewelry, and the embroidered and tie-dyed clothes you see on sale. On the last block, the stands sell secondhand books and magazines.

BELOW: rush hour on Avenida Santa Fe.
RIGHT: the Obelisk and Avenida 9 de Julio by night.

Soho and Hollywood

Just beyond Plaza Italia is Palermo Viejo. In recent years, this has become the trendiest area of all Buenos Aires. Not only is it full of restaurants and bars for the young crowd, but many young media types have moved into and renovated old houses in an area that was originally intended as a model workers' "village" (Pasajes de Palermo Soho, especially Russel, Santa Rosa, and Soria streets). The area starts with Calle Jorge Luis Borges, whose family lived here until 1914 (their home is now demolished). A little further on is a square which marks the center of Palermo Soho and which is dedicated to another famous 20th-century Argentine writer, Julio Cortázar.

On the far side of the railway lines there is an even trendier neighborhood, known simply as Hollywood, as this is the center of Buenos Aires' thriving television and film industry. Bars and restaurants here go in and out of fashion in a matter of weeks.

Belgrano

Beyond Palermo to the west (accessible on Line D of the subway) is the barrio of Belgrano, a well-to-do neighborhood that also has a thriving nightlife and social scene, and an important university campus. Belgrano is characterized largely by expensive high-rise apartment buildings, but it also includes the so-called Barrancas de Belgrano, a green hill which stands out in the general flatness of Buenos Aires, as well as the **Museo Histórico Sarmiento**, at the corner of Cuba and Juramento. ❑

THE ARCHITECTURE OF BUENOS AIRES

With its grand nationalistic monuments and colorful neighborhood backstreets, the capital reflects the country's turbulent history

The eclectic architecture of Buenos Aires was once described as being composed primarily of architectural styles which are painful to the eyes. Although its sometimes garish attempts to resemble Paris or New York do somewhat justify this description, Buenos Aires also boasts beautiful buildings ranging from more austere colonial styles to baroque, neo-classical, rather fantastic French designs, and inventions which blend these styles and could be described as purely *porteño*. The city center and hyper-fashionable Puerto Madero accommodate tall steel and glass office buildings with all the latest technology, jockeying for space with the old docks of the port area and with classic and increasingly unkempt public buildings.

A DIFFERENT PERSPECTIVE

Look down on the city from a tall building, or look at the side and back of the buildings whose impressive facades first meet the eye, and the difference is striking; the elaborate facades are virtually stuck on to square, unadorned buildings which often resemble rabbit hutches more than stately homes or *belle époque* buildings. The importance given to the facade in comparison with what lies behind it gives a clue to a wider *porteño* way of thinking.

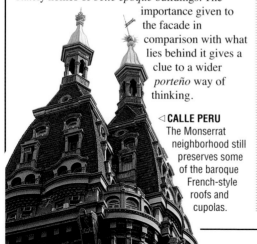

◁ **CALLE PERU**
The Monserrat neighborhood still preserves some of the baroque French-style roofs and cupolas.

▷ **CALLE CAMINITO**
Colorful buildings on Calle Caminito in the southern barrio of La Boca, whose brightly painted houses recall the first Italian immigrants.

△ **MODERN MONUMENT**
The slim, distinctive profile of the Kavanagh Building, which in the 1930s was Latin America's first skyscraper.

△ **DON'T CRY FOR ME...**
It was from Government House, known as the Casa Rosada, that Perón and Evita addressed their followers in the Plaza de Mayo.

▷ **STUNNING THEATER**
The spectacular Teatro Colón, an acoustically near-perfect temple to music and dance realized in gilt, crystal, marble, and velvet.

TEMPLES OF SHOPPING

As in other world cities, the shopping mall has become increasingly a social and cultural reference point in Buenos Aires, with a rising number growing up in and around the city in the past decade. Some malls have been installed in old and renovated buildings, such as Patio Bullrich in a beautiful building which was once a slaughter-house; Galería Pacífico in a one-time railway station; or the Abasto shopping center in the former central fruit and vegetable market. One of the most popular purpose-built malls is the Alto Palermo mall, located at the upmarket corner of Santa Fe and Coronel Diaz. Alto Palermo is a two block-long steel and glass-roofed structure spread over three stories. While Alto Palermo offers a number of clothing stores, its principal attractions, and those of other "shoppings," probably lie in the food hall and cinemas that represent the hub of social activity. Among the movie houses and chic boutiques are fast-food outlets, from McDonald's to a kosher deli, offering a place to meet, eat, see, and be seen – one of the most beloved pastimes of *porteños*.

◁ **HEART OF THE NATION**
The elegant Cabildo, where Argentine independence took its first steps in 1810, and the Plaza de Mayo, scene of many protests.

△ **HEROIC STATUE**
From his charging steed, The Liberator, José de San Martín, contemplates his elegant surroundings in the leafy Plaza San Martín.

◁ **WATER WORKS**
The outrageously elaborate Obras Sanitarias building was the headquarters for the state water and sewage company and is now a national monument.

AROUND BUENOS AIRES

Despite the enormous sprawl of the capital city, it's relatively easy to head out for a day or so – to a quiet ranch in the country or to an elegant riverside resort

Map on page 190

From Buenos Aires there are many possibilities for trips to nearby small towns in the pampas, north along the river to the delta and its islands, or east along the coast as far as the provincial capital, La Plata. Most of the attractions described below can be seen in a day, but if you are in need of a longer break from the city bustle, a good range of accommodations is available.

Suburban side trips

Among the attractive northern suburbs easily reached by train from Retiro or by bus are Olivos (where the presidential residence is located), and San Isidro. Both are also served by the Tren de la Costa railroad, an elaborate sightseeing line which leaves from Retiro and ends at the huge Parque de la Costa amusement park in Tigre, on the Río Luján. Passengers can use one ticket to get on and off at any of the stations en route, many of which are linked to shopping malls, riverside restaurants, and sports clubs. **Olivos ❶** has a couple of yacht clubs and a number of elegant European-style residences, as well as outdoor tea rooms and fresh air. Fishing can be done here, from a jetty managed by the local fishing club, the Club de Pescadores, which also operates catamaran cruises, sailing downriver as far as the delta on weekends and public holidays.

To the north, **San Isidro ❷** has an important horse-racing track, belonging to the Jockey Club and inaugurated in 1935. The Hipódromo de San Isidro is on Avenida Santa Fe, at the junction with Márquez, flanked by the golf course and polo club. Races are on Wednesday and Saturday 3–9pm; Sunday 2–9pm. The **Museo Municipal Histórico** (open Tues, Thur, Sat, and Sun 2–6pm) housed in the country house *(quinta)* of the Pueyrredón family, on Rivera Indarte 48, is also worth a visit. Both Olivos and San Isidro are located along the continuation of Avenida del Libertador and have traditionally been home to most of Buenos Aires' English-speaking community.

Up the delta

Tigre ❸ is an old town situated at the mouth of the delta. Tropical fruit brought by boat from the northern provinces is deposited here en route to Buenos Aires. But the principal economic activity revolves around the summer tourists and weekenders who come to fish, row, water ski, and cruise the winding channels that flow past hundreds of little islands, many of them dotted with weekend houses built on stilts. While it is only 28 km (17 miles) from downtown Buenos Aires, the air is clear, the vegetation subtropical, and the rhythm of activity less hurried.

LEFT: peaceful reflection at La Plata Cathedral.
BELOW: one of the many water birds seen in the delta.

TIP

Empresa Cacciola operates guided tours to Isla Martín García. The full-day cruises depart from Tigre daily at 7.30am, returning at 7pm, and include lunch on the island (tel: 4394 5520).

There is almost no crime, and it is said that the dogs never get sick because of special immunities gained from drinking the brown river water. There's a recommended fruit market, **Puerto de Frutos**, at Sarmiento 160 which takes place daily and is joined by a lively crafts market at weekends.

After touring the charming plant-filled residential area of the town, you should head for the main drag along the riverside, **Paseo Victorica**. Old English rowing clubs and *parrillas* (steak restaurants) line the street. There are several small docks where you can pick up rides on *lanchas* (taxi boats). Several larger ferries run two-hour cruises, which leave from the dock next to the train station. They also operate a regular daily service through the delta, allowing passengers to alight at various points and continue or return by the same or another company. Boats may also be rented for floating parties, and there is a ferry that crosses over to the Uruguayan beaches.

A train runs from the Retiro station to downtown Tigre, taking about 45 minutes, or you can join the Tren de la Costa at Maipú station. Alternatively, bus No. 60 starts in Constitución and winds through downtown to reach Tigre. Ask before getting on the bus because there are many different routes, and be prepared for a long journey. You can get more information on bus services from Tigre town hall, tel: 4512 4497/8; or the tourist office, tel: 4512 4498.

Unless you are planning a visit, don't get on board the **Tren de la Costa** which also goes to Tigre, but drops you off in the middle of the **Parque de la Costa** at the Delta station. This new amusement park is set in 16 hectares (40 acres) and includes mock Victorian buildings, rides, and concerts and other live performances. For more information on the park and the train, tel: 4732 6300.

BELOW: sunset at Chascomús.

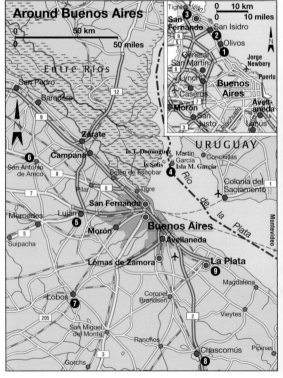

Island reserve

Three hours from Tigre by boat is the **Isla Martín García ❹**, the largest in the delta. The island, which was once a fortress and center of naval battles in the wars of independence, and where presidents Hipólito Yrigoyen, Juan Perón, and Arturo Frondizi were briefly detained, is now a nature reserve with a wide variety of flora and fauna, including water birds and deer. The island also has a small historical museum, a hotel with a good restaurant, and a modern lighthouse.

Luján

One of the oldest cities in the country, **Luján ❺**, is visited today by millions of Argentine tourists every year because of its religious importance. It lies 63 km (40 miles) west of Buenos Aires, along the Luján River. Trains leave from the Once station, and take two hours, stopping at every little town in the pampas along the way.

The **Basílica Nuestra Señora de Luján** (open Mon–Fri 10am–5pm; Sat–Sun 10am–6pm) is a magnificent Gothic structure, built over a period of 50 years and completed in 1935. The principal attraction of the basilica is a statue of the **Virgen de Luján**, which is housed in its own chapel behind the main altar. Legend has it that in 1630 the statue was sent by wagon from Brazil, and the wagon wouldn't continue until the Virgin was taken off. Here she has remained, and now she is the patron saint of Argentina. Every year in October, hundreds of thousands of young Catholics make a pilgrimage from Buenos Aires, arriving on foot in honor of the saint.

The Luján River runs through the city, and in colonial times boats heading to

Map on page 190

Field of sunflowers by the roadside on Ruta Nacional 8.

BELOW: racehorses at San Isidro.

Cannon outside the Ricardo Güiraldes Gaucho Museum in San Antonio de Areco.

BELOW: Estancia Los Patricios, San Antonio de Areco.

the Northwest were checked here for contraband. When there have been no recent rains, the river is a place of recreation for residents and tourists.

There are several museums in Luján. The **Complejo Museográfico Enrique Udaondo**, in a beautiful old colonial building, shows relics of Argentina's customs and history. In an annex is the **Museo del Transporte**, which has an interesting collection, mostly of horse-drawn carriages but also a flying boat, *Plus Ultra*, which was the first plane to cross the South Atlantic, in 1926. Both museums are open Wed–Fri noon–6pm; Sat and Sun 10am–6pm. There is also the **Museo de Bellas Artes** (open daily 1–6pm), in Parque Florentino Ameghino, dedicated principally to contemporary Argentine art.

On national and religious holidays there are gaucho competitions on horseback that are quite spectacular. Most of the competitors are in fact descendants of gauchos and now work as farm hands, although costumes and saddles are saved for these special occasions.

Gaucho country

Some 50 km (30 miles) further northwest of Buenos Aires, on RN8, is the town of **San Antonio de Areco** ❻, a typical town of the cattle-raising area of the pampas. There are a number of estancias (ranches) here which can be visited, including the **Estancia La Porteña** where famous author Ricardo Güiraldes (who wrote the gaucho classic *Don Segundo Sombra*) once lived. The **Ricardo Güiraldes Gaucho Museum** (open Wed–Mon 11am–5pm) includes extensive grounds on the river with numerous indigenous plants, while the **Gaucho Silver Museum and Workshop** at Alvear and Alsina is open daily 8.30am–12.30pm and 3–8pm.

In the second week of November, San Antonio de Areco celebrates Tradition Week, with gaucho shows, horse races and breaking, and gaucho parades. Several estancias in the area offer visits and accommodations, as well as gaucho shows and traditional *asados (see page 346).*

Heading south

There are also a number of possible outings to the south of Buenos Aires that offer fresh air, green space, and other attractions. Passing **Ezeiza**, the area which includes both the international airport and the wide-open spaces of the local forests, is the small pampas town of **Lobos** ❼, about 95 km (59 miles) from Buenos Aires on RN3. The town is known primarily for its *laguna*, a large lake used for fishing and windsurfing, and as the possible birthplace of Juan Perón.

The house in which Perón was said to have been born, located at Buenos Aires 1380, is the **Museo Juan Domingo Perón** (open Wed–Sun 10am–noon and 3–6pm) containing some of the ex-president's personal effects, including a letter written to Evita from his prison cell on Martín García.

Some 120 km (75 miles) south of Buenos Aires on RN2, going toward Mar del Plata, is the city of **Chascomús** ❽, located on the largest of the chain of lakes south of the capital. The attractive colonial city is the center of a prosperous agricultural region, and its buildings are well-preserved and stand on wide tree-lined streets with green plazas. The Laguna de Chascomús offers fishing, boating, water-skiing, and other water sports, while the Chascomús Riding Center offers horseback rides.

The town has a well-developed tourism infrastructure (the tourist office is located at Costanera España, on the *laguna*; open daily 9am–6pm) and has a variety of attractive restaurants along the lake front offering fresh fish (primarily *pejerrey*) and *parrillada mixta*. There are a number of estancias offering accommodations and shows for tourists, as well as the **Fortín Chascomús** fort (tel: 03241-424 993), scene of battles against the Araucanians in 1780.

La Plata

A 1½-hour train ride south from Buenos Aires' Constitución train station will take you toward La Plata. Just beyond the city, you pass through an industrial belt populated by poor, working-class people. Shanty towns line the tracks.

Traveling by road, some 38 km (24 miles) from Buenos Aires, where routes 1 and 14 split, is an estancia that used to be owned by the Pereyra family. It was expropriated by Perón and transformed into a recreational park, where people who live in the area can come to relax. Adjacent is a zoo, where the animals run wild and visitors can drive safari-style through the countryside.

La República de los Niños (open daily 10am–6pm; tel: 0221-484 1409), a recreational center for children, known as the Argentine "Disneyworld," lies 14 km (9 miles) further south. Built by Evita Perón, it celebrated its 50th anniversary in 2001.

A few more miles down Ruta 1, you'll reach the city of **La Plata ❾**. Despite being only 56 km (35 miles) south of Buenos Aires, it is representative of many provincial cities in Argentina. The capital of the province of Buenos Aires, life is less frantic here and the city's inhabitants enjoy an independent political and cultural life.

The city was founded in 1882 by Dr Dardo Rocha, and conceived by Pedro Benoit, who planned its tidy layout with its numbered horizontal/vertical streets, and diagonal avenues. Just off Plaza San Martín is the Legislatura, the Palacio del Gobernio, and the Pasaje Dardo Rocha, a large cultural center. The Gothic Catedral de La Plata is on the Plaza Moreno, and across the plaza you'll find the Palacio Municipal. One block away, between calles 9 and 10, is the Teatro Argentino.

The **Paseo del Bosque** is a series of pretty parks in the center of the city, with lakes, a zoo (actually much more complete than the Buenos Aires zoo), an observatory, and a theater, **Anfiteatro Martín Fierro**. The Paseo del Bosque is also home to the **Museo de Ciencias Naturales** (open Tues–Sun 10am–6pm), which was founded in 1884. This museum has many fascinating geological, zoological, and archeological exhibits, and is considered the best of its kind in all of South America. The **Museo Provincial de Bellas Artes** (open Mon–Sat), at 525 Calle 51, has an excellent collection of Argentine paintings and sculpture. ❑

Chascomús is the birthplace of Dr. Raúl Alfonsín, former president of Argentina (1983–89).

BELOW: main plaza of San Antonio de Areco.

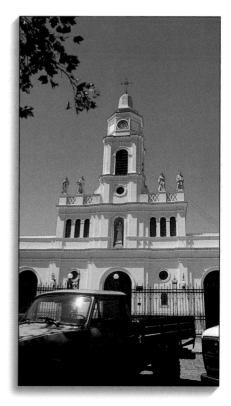

MAR Y SIERRAS

*The Atlantic coast is the playground for Buenos Aires'
rich and beautiful set, while inland in the sierras is some fine
countryside for walking, cycling, and horseback riding tours*

Map on page 198

I f your interests tend at all toward the sociological and anthropological, then
this is the place to come. Here along the extensive Atlantic coast, where the
hills roll down to the sea (giving rise to the popular name Mar y Sierras) is
an array of resorts for all tastes and bank accounts. Here one can see the
Argentines at play.

Although their country is enormous, and has an astonishing variety of
appealing destinations, few Argentines explore it. Instead they head for the
beach. Year after year, they return to the same spot, often renting the same
changing *cabaña* (beach hut) every time. This fostering of a second home leads
to a real sense of community in each resort. Families who may live far apart during much of the year see each other each summer, watch each other's kids grow
up, and keep up-to-date with the community gossip.

Along these beaches, the older folks pass the day playing the card games of
truco and canasta, while the young swim and play paddle ball and volleyball.
Young women pose in their *cola*-less bikinis (this translates as tail-less; the
backsides of these suits are strikingly short on fabric), and everyone seems
relaxed and happy to escape the mania of city life.

The Argentines are fiercely proud of their riviera. Keen competition exists
among all the resorts of the South Atlantic, and some
of Argentina's hot spots consider themselves rivals of
such places as Punta del Este, in Uruguay. Fashions
are kept up to the minute, and many fads actually start
here. The smart set insist on being seen here at least
once during the summer season.

So, if your exposure to Argentine society has been
mostly to people burdened with the pressures of
porteño life, it's not a bad idea to visit the coast, where
everybody is smiling. It's not a bad spot to take a
vacation either.

Coastal developments

The main strip of this popular vacation coast extends
from San Clemente del Tuyú to Mar del Plata, the hub
of the Atlántica area. Though founded late in the 19th
century, Mar del Plata was at first a resort for well-to-
do *porteños*, i.e. for those residents of Buenos Aires
who could afford the 400-km (250-mile) journey to
the then solitary cliffs near Punta Mogotes. Early on,
this journey was made by train, and later by car. Only
in the mid-1930s did Mar del Plata really start to
boom. This was due mainly to two developments: the
opening of the casino, with its 36 roulette tables (in
those days the largest gambling place in the world),
and the paving of the RN2, which brought Mar del
Plata to within four hours by car from Buenos Aires.
The road has been repaved and widened, cutting the

PRECEDING PAGES: an off day near Mar del Plata. **LEFT:** checking the nets. **BELOW:** Mar del Plata beach.

journey time further. With the construction of still another road along the coast (Ruta 11), smaller seaside resorts started to sprout up north and south from Mar del Plata. Before long, each of these places acquired a character of its own; some preferred by the elderly, others by youth, some by those who like rock music, and some by the lovers of tango dancing.

By road, train, or airplane

Until fairly recently, an excursion to the vacation coast was a small adventure. Muddy roads made access to many of the smaller villages very difficult, but today the entire coastline is easily reached. While the roads are now excellent, be warned that there are four toll stops between Buenos Aires and Mar del Plata and the roads can get very crowded during weekends and holidays. For one person traveling alone, it's cheaper to go by long-distance buses which serve most of Mar del Plata's sprawl, or even by air: in summer, services are inexpensive and frequent, and you can often pick up special promotional offers. Most flights con-

Waiting for the afternoon catch.

Mar y Sierras

0   100 km

0   100 miles

nect Buenos Aires and Mar del Plata, but some of the smaller resorts can be reached by air, including Santa Teresita, Pinamar, Villa Gesell, Miramar, and Necochea. Traveling by rail, Mar del Plata and Miramar can be reached by the Roca train which departs from Constitución station in Buenos Aires twice a week, taking less than six hours to make the journey south.

Fishermens' retreats

Heading south on Ruta 11 from Buenos Aires, the first resort town is **San Clemente del Tuyú** ❶, located at the northern point of **Cabo San Antonio**, the most easterly point of continental Argentina. It is adjacent to Bahía Samborombón, the muddy mouth of the Río Salado and other, smaller rivers of the pampas. The bay is rich with fish that come here to feed.

Mundo Marino is one of the few "marine worlds" in South America, and is particularly popular among fishermen who arrive hoping to catch the *corvina negra* or *corvina rubia*, fish used in soups and stews and regarded as a delicacy. There are numerous well-equipped campsites to stay in, as well as many other sports facilities.

A small stretch of land juts out between the bay and the ocean, an area called **Punta Rasa**. Here you can visit the **El Faro San Antonio** (open daily 9am–7.30pm), an iron lighthouse built in 1890 which, at 63 meters (207 ft) high, offers remarkable views. Also in Punta Rasa is an ecological reserve for migratory birds, which visit in spring and autumn on their journey between Alaska or Canada and Tierra del Fuego. The Estación Biológica Punta Rasa became the Alas de la Bahía (wings over the bay) visitor center in 1997 with an impressive audiovisual show on local migratory birds.

A further 22 km (14 miles) south on Ruta 11 is another well-developed resort town, **Santa Teresita**. In addition to the popular beach, long fishing pier, and many seafood restaurants, there is a golf course, horseback riding, and various campgrounds.

Heading south on Ruta 11, you'll find resort towns one after the other, in a rather developed 26-km (16-mile) stretch of coastline. **Mar del Tuyú** ❷ is the capital of the so-called Coast municipality, which includes all the following towns: Costa del Este, Aguas Verdes, La Lucila del Mar, Costa Azul, San Bernardo, and Mar de Ajó. Mar del Tuyú itself is a small, quiet resort, most popular for its swimming and fishing off the pier. The resorts attract many tourists, but the beaches are wide and services abundant. San Bernardo is the largest resort, with high-rise condominiums and hotels.

Most visitors to this area come to swim, sunbathe, and walk along the narrow beach beside the high sand dunes, but many others come to fish. This, however, is simply for sport; when it comes to mealtime, most of these visiting fishermen retire to one of the area's countless tiny seafood restaurants, many of which specialize in Italian fare.

South from Mar de Ajó, the beach becomes increasingly solitary. The spaces between settlements become wider, and you can find more stretches of isolated pristine shore.

Map on page 198

TIP

To the west of San Clemente del Tuyú is a wildlife sanctuary which is one of the last remaining habitats of the once numerous pampas deer, and an important resting area for migratory birds.

BELOW: watching the waves roll in at Mar del Plata.

Shipwrecks, sand dunes, and lighthouses

Along this part of the coast you can see many old lighthouses made of iron and brick. Previously mentioned is El Faro San Antonio, in San Clemente. Another is near Punta Médanos, a rather barren and rocky area without many facilities, which also reportedly boasts a number of past shipwrecks, at the southern tip of Cabo San Antonio. The lighthouse here, built in 1893, stands 59 meters (194 ft) tall amid sand dunes (*médanos*), after which the place is named. The dunes cover an enormous stretch of coastline between Mar de Ajó and Pinamar, some of them now covered in vegetation but others still forming, and reaching up to 30 meters (98 ft) high.

Still more lighthouses can be found halfway to Mar del Plata (Faro Querandí), on the southern outskirts of Mar del Plata (Faro Punta Mogotes), and at Monte Hermoso. Some of these towers are over a century old, and many of them have shared in the area's long and fascinating history of maritime adventures and misfortunes. They are well worth a visit, from both an architectural and a historical point of view, although some may be under repair and closed to visitors. In a walk along the beach you will frequently encounter the stranded and disintegrating hull of some old windjammer or steamer.

Probably one of the loveliest of all the urban areas along the Atlantic coast is the one that comprises Pinamar, Ostende, Valeria del Mar, and Cariló.

Pinamar ❸ is a very fashionable spot which receives large numbers of tourists in January and Feburary. It is bordered by a pine forest, and the scent of the pines mixed with the salty sea air gives the town a bracing atmosphere. There are no sand dunes at Pinamar, which makes access to the beach easy, even by car. Accommodations range from four-star establishments down to

One of this area's many shipwrecks was the Anna, *a steamship from Hamburg. In 1894 it hit a sandbank near Punta Médanos, where it remained until 1967, when it was scrapped. One of the ship's masts was salvaged, however, to be used as a flagpost for the lighthouse.*

BELOW: basking in the sunshine on Mar del Plata's promenade.

modest, if not budget *hosterías* and *hospedajes* (hostels). Although hotels of all categories are available all year round, most people come for two weeks or a full month and therefore choose to rent an apartment at a price which is much cheaper than that of the most humble hostel. These apartments may be rented on the spot, or in advance in Buenos Aires. Pinamar is the most urban development along this part of the coast, with a number of high-rise apartment blocks and discos, which makes it a good spot for young people. Its range of sporting activities include everything from horseback riding to windsurfing.

Upmarket elegance

The Greater Pinamar area includes **Ostende** and **Valeria del Mar**, where some very high dunes are to be found. A casino is located just outside Valeria, on Ruta 11, the main road running parallel to the coast. A short distance south of Valeria, **Cariló** is a country club-style community dotted with elegant villas and shaded by pines, which also has a wide beach and some of the most beautiful and unspoiled wooded areas left on the coast. Cariló also has a tiny, attractive, and up-market town center, with shops and restaurants constructed in alpine style.

About 20 km (12 miles) south of Cariló lies **Villa Gesell** ❹. Founded by Carlos Idaho Gesell in 1940, the town was forested with pines with the intention of maintaining a small and tranquil tourist spot. Except for Avenida 3, its streets are still made of sand, which absorbs water better; trucks pass on a daily basis to water it all down. The town, with a long and very wide beach, also has a forestry reserve including a museum and archive with photos and documents relating to the foundation of the city. Outside the center is a horseback riding

TIP

The Pinamar region is a sports-lover's paradise, with golf courses, horseback riding centers, and even a "Tennis Ranch" run by former Argentine champion, José Luis Clerc.

BELOW: the Museo de Automovilismo Juan Manuel Fangio, Balcarce.

Catedral de San Pedro, Mar del Plata.

school, which offers classes and guided outings, and there is year-round fishing for shark, mackerel, and other fish from the pier. Villa Gesell is especially popular with young people, due to its many bars, discotheques, and skating rinks; and it also has several excellent campsites.

The main attraction between Gesell and Mar del Plata are the shady campsites at **Mar Chiquita ❺**, which is a small cluster of hotels and restaurants on the edge of a saltwater lagoon, and **Santa Clara del Mar**. Both, however, are some distance from the beach.

Pearl of the Atlantic

Shortly before you reach **Mar del Plata ❻**, the landscape changes dramatically. Approaching the city on the coastal Ruta 11, the high cliffs of Cabo Corrientes and the downtown skyscrapers built upon this rocky peninsula seem to grow from the sea like a mirage. It is a truly striking first impression which, as one gets closer, becomes no less impressive.

Mar del Plata is proudly called *La Perla del Atlántico* (the Pearl of the Atlantic) by its 700,000 residents. Accommodations range from first-class hotels to apartments available for short-term lease all year round. The city has well-groomed plazas, parks, boulevards, and several golf courses. Beyond the beaches and the sun lie perhaps the biggest attraction for the 3 million summer visitors, the colossal **casino** where you can try your hand at roulette, poker, *punta banca*, and other games. There are also several theaters, which feature mostly comedies,

Another major pastime in Mar del Plata is to see and be seen. In the past all of fashionable Buenos Aires felt obliged to be seen here at least once a year, either in the summer months from January to March, or even in winter. The

BELOW: the bright lights of the Mar del Plata fishing club.

devalued peso has led to a boom in Argentines vacationing in their own country, making Mar del Plata as crowded as ever. During the peak of the season the boutiques and galleries of **Calle San Martín** and the adjacent streets still bustle late into the night with the tanned and the beautiful.

International events

Mar del Plata has a number of important events throughout the year, such as the National Ocean Festival (first week of January), with a number of sporting events, the National Fishing Festival and Regatta in February, the International Film Festival in March, the International Jazz Festival in April, and the National Film Festival in November. In summer, its beaches are so crowded that the sand virtually disappears, although further from the center the beaches are somewhat less populated. A good place to observe the beautiful people and the locals is the Rambla, a wide pedestrian walkway which runs along the Bristol beach in the center of the city, past the Gran Hotel Provincial and the casino.

A visit to Mar del Plata would not be complete without sampling the area's specialties. At the fishing port, with its red and yellow boats along the quays, a raft of restaurants in the area serve good, fresh fish and seafood. You might also like to take the opportunity to buy well-made inexpensive woolens here, made by the locals during the winter months.

Some 60 km (37 miles) inland from Mar del Plata on RN226 is the city of **Balcarce ❼**, with 35,000 residents. The area is more hilly than most of the province of Buenos Aires, and Balcarce lies in a valley near La Brava. The city houses a satellite land station, of which a guided tour can be organized with the EMTUR tourist office in Mar del Plata. The **Museo de Automovilismo Juan Manuel Fangio** (open daily 10am–8pm; Mar–Dec until 6pm) in Balcarce is named for the town's most famous citizen, the five-time world champion racing driver who died in 1995. The museum contains many of Fangio's prizes as well as one of his racing cars, the Mercedes Benz Flecha de Plata. Near Balcarce are the Ojos de Agua caves as well as Laguna La Brava, a well-known fishing spot.

Solitary beaches

From Mar del Plata, the coastal road runs past the Punta Mogotes lighthouse (where there is a popular beach lined with seafood restaurants) toward Miramar. The scenery along this 40-km (25-mile) stretch is very different from that at the northern end of the Atlantic coast. Instead of dunes and sandy beaches, the sea is met by cliffs. The road runs along the very edge, offering travelers a splendid view of the ocean, and the spectacle of Mar del Plata disappearing into the distance.

About halfway between Mar del Plata and Miramar is Chapadmalal, where the presidential vacation residence is located. The area has a tourism complex opened in the 1950s by the Eva Perón Foundation for students, pensioners, and low-income families, which has a privileged position on a quiet beach and is still much in demand.

Map on page 198

TIP

While in Mar del Plata, be sure to try one of the famed *alfajores marplatenses*. These are biscuits filled with chocolate or caramel, and are a favorite for afternoon tea.

BELOW: on the crest of a wave.

Miramar ❽ is infinitely less developed and much quieter than Mar del Plata, yet the main beachfront is overshadowed by towering apartment buildings. But the beach is very wide here and it's not difficult to escape the crowds. There is plenty of open space for many outdoor sports, including bicycling, horseback riding, tennis, jogging, or just walking. For a break from the sand and surf, Miramar boasts a lovely, large, wooded park, Vivero Florentino Ameghino, complete with picnic spots and walking trails.

Between Miramar and Necochea, the seaside resorts become sparser. Along this 80-km (50-mile) section of shoreline, there are only three places with facilities for vacationers: Mar del Sur (which has beautiful, deserted and windswept beaches), Centinela del Mar, and Costa Bonita.

At **Necochea** ❾, a pleasant city 125 km (78 miles) from Mar del Plata, the Río Quequén empties into the sea. There is a large port, from where fishing excursions depart daily, a developed beachfront, and a proper city center. Beyond the beach, an interesting trip is 15 km (9 miles) up the river to the Parque Cura Meucó, where you can relax and enjoy the small waterfalls.

There are even fewer developed beaches south of Necochea. **Claromecó**, about 150 km (93 miles) to the south, is one of the most attractive.

Peace and quiet

One place that is highly recommended is **Monte Hermoso** ❿, some 110 km (68 miles) further down the coast. Visited by Darwin during his voyage on the *Beagle*, and since then well known for its wealth of fossils along the shore, Monte Hermoso has a broad beach of fine white sand, shady campsites, and a venerable lighthouse. The lack of crowds make this peaceful place well worth

Bahía Blanca has been dubbed the "capital of basketball" in Argentina. Top players Emanuel Ginóbili and Juan Ignacio "Pepe" Sanchez were born here and played for local club Estudiantes de Bahía Blanca. They went on to win gold for Argentina in the 2004 Olympics.

BELOW: the docks at Bahía Blanca.

exploring. There is a large YMCA campsite just outside Monte Hermoso, which also offers hotel accommodations, and the town has an artisans' market. Sunbathing opportunities may, however, be limited by the fierce wind which sweeps the area most of the time, as the southern coast of Buenos Aires is much less protected from South Atlantic winds than the eastern coast. It is here, at Monte Hermoso, that the Argentine vacation coast ends.

Map on page 198

About 90 km (56 miles) further along the southern coast from Monte Hermoso, and some 660 km (410 miles) southwest of Buenos Aires on RN3, is the city of **Bahía Blanca ⓫**. Located on the largest bay in southern Argentina, it is a major industrial center and port with more than 300,000 inhabitants. The most important civic buildings are located on the **Plaza Rivadavia**, including the town hall, cathedral, court buildings, library, and the newspaper offices of *La Nueva Provincia*.

The city has several interesting museums. The **Museo Municipal de Ciencias** (open Tues–Fri 9am–noon and 4–8pm; Sat–Sun 3–6pm), on Alsina 425 is a natural history museum with some interesting exhibits. The **Museo del Puerto**, on Guillermo Torres 4131 (open Mon–Fri 9am–noon; Sat–Sun 3.30–7.30pm; closed Jan) contains old photographs and other memorabilia of the town's industrial past. In the **Mercado Victoria** area, formerly the central export market for hides and wool, there remains an British neighborhood of houses constructed in the 19th century by the railway companies for their British employees.

Into the sierras

Some 80 km (49 miles) north of Bahía Blanca, and entering the sierras area of the province, is the small town of **Tornquist ⓬**, founded in 1883 and filled

BELOW: grazing livestock in the sierras.

Map on page 198

with pines and attractive gardens. The Santa Rosa de Lima church is made of stone and especially pretty. Nearby is the former residence of Ernesto Tornquist (an important 19th-century businessman responsible for much of the early development of the Atlantic coastal resorts), for whom it is named. The estate includes a castle of medieval design, a copy of Château d'Amboise in the French Loire Valley. Close to Tornquist is the **Parque Provincial Ernesto Tornquist**, which has an ecology center containing information on its flora and fauna, from where guided tours of the park can be made. The Cerro Bahía Blanca mountain and the Toro cave grotto are found in the park.

Beyond the park to the south on Ruta 72 is the attractive town of **Sierra de la Ventana** ⓭, the principal tourist center in the area. Surrounded by three rivers, the town has beaches, walking sites, and campgrounds, as well as a golf course. It is also a center for the production of herbs, and visits to herbal plantations can be arranged at the tourist office, as well as guided walking, bicycle, or horseback riding excursions in the mountains. The town is located in the sierra, and the Confitería El Mirador offers panoramic views of the area. Nearby is **Cerro Tres Picos**, the highest mountain in the pampas area at 1,239 meters (4,065 ft).

Lagoons and lakes

North of Tornquist, on RN33, is **Guaminí** ⓮, in the southwest of Buenos Aires province close to the border with La Pampa. The town, a central fortress in the Conquest of the Desert in the 1870s, is located on the Laguna del Monte. One of the largest lagoons in the province, it has a beach and fishing clubs, as well as an island with an antelope reserve. In the town itself, the former fort (now the police station) and the **Museo Histórico** (open daily, 3–8pm) are worth a visit. Some 40 km (25 miles) further west lies **Carhué** ⓯, also originally a fort and now a spa town. Carhué is located near **Lago Epecuén**, a large saltwater lake known for its curative properties, which swallowed up the nearby town of Villa de Epecuén during the 1985 floods.

The principal city in the sierras is **Tandil** ⓰, located some 360 km (240 miles) from Buenos Aires. The city was founded in the early 19th century and is an important tourist center, especially in Holy Week, when celebrations are held at Mount Calvary and the Passion play is enacted.

Tandil found fame as the site of the "moving rock," a 300-ton stone which perched precariously on the edge of a cliff, and trembled for some 30 years before finally falling in 1912. Efforts to return the stone to its original site failed, but its memory is still widely celebrated. Tandil has a large park and lake (Lago del Fuerte) nestling at the foot of the hills in the south of the city. The city houses the **Museo Tradicionalista Fuerte Independencia** (open Tues–Sun 4–8pm), which includes exhibits from the history of life in Tandil, such as a hansom cab and carriages, and rooms to rent in the old estancia school.

In the sierras surrounding the city are several estancias, which offer accommodations as well as a range of day visits with outdoor activities. The luxurious **Estancia Acelain**, 50 km (31 miles) from Tandil, has an Andalusian-style mansion, pool, and gardens (*see page 346*). ❑

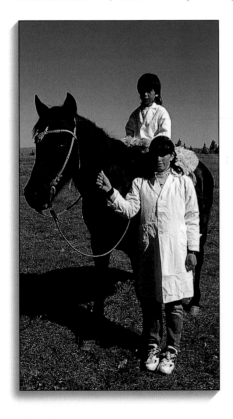

BELOW: school transport.
RIGHT: fishing boats in Mar del Plata.

THE CENTRAL SIERRAS

This landlocked region offers some exquisite Jesuit architecture in and around the historic city of Córdoba, as well as excellent outdoor activities in the surrounding countryside

Map on page 220

The province of Córdoba could in many respects be considered the heartland of Argentina. It lies about midway between the Andes and Buenos Aires and the Atlantic coast. Beyond geography, Córdoba represents much that Argentina is known for. Its economy is based not only on farming and ranching, but also on commerce and agro-related and automotive industries.

Approaching Córdoba from Buenos Aires, one drives across miles and miles of stunningly flat pampas before reaching the gentle waves of the central sierras. Along the open plains or in the hidden valleys you can stumble upon a variety of characteristically Argentine scenes: a vast herd of the country's famous grass-fed cattle, or an animated scene of gauchos branding cattle in a rough-hewn country paddock, or a farm specializing in the breeding and training of world-class racing horses and polo ponies.

Aside from the chance encounters, there is much that the traveler can set out to see and do here. The city of Córdoba, Argentina's second largest, holds some of the country's finest examples of colonial architecture, both secular and religious. The province's mountain landscapes, embellished by numerous lakes, rivers, and streams, are an ideal environment for trekking, horseback riding, water sports, and fishing, among other options.

During the summer, the village of Villa Carlos Paz, near the provincial capital, becomes the country's second-biggest tourist destination after Mar del Plata. Here, as in other quaint mountain villages, summer visitors have their choice of many cultural and musical events. The most famous are the folk festival in Cosquín and the Oktoberfest beer festival organized by the German community in Villa General Belgrano.

PRECEDING PAGES: symmetrical church facade in Córdoba **LEFT:** gilt ceiling of Córdoba Cathedral. **BELOW:** modern sculpture in Villa Dolores.

Historic Córdoba

The city of Córdoba dates back to colonial times. One of the oldest cities in the country, it was founded by Jerónimo Luis de Cabrera in 1573. Cabrera came from Santiago del Estero in the north, following the Río Dulce, and settled his people by the Río Suquía. It is interesting to note that when information about these new, not yet settled areas was recounted in Peru by the early adventurous surveyors, some of the characteristics that have made Córdoba attractive were already mentioned. It was said that these lands had low mountains, plenty of fish in the many streams and rivers, an abundance of wild birds and animals (rheas, deer, pumas, armadillos, otters, hares, partridges, and much more), beautiful views, and weather like Spain.

In these few words lay the allure, the charm of the Córdoba region, the same charm which draws Argentines to visit the hundreds of little towns, inns, and campgrounds every year.

Grinding stone and mortar of the Comechingones.

When Cabrera arrived in the Córdoba region in 1573, it was populated by three principal indigenous groups: the Sanavirones in the northeast, the Comechingones in the west, and the Pampas in the plains.

Though a few confrontations did take place between the Spanish and the indigenous peoples, the latter were labeled "peaceful and cooperative" by the Spaniards, a commentary dictated by the contrast between these groups and other very bellicose tribes of the northwest, south, and east of the country.

The Pampas were nomadic groups who roamed the plains. The Sanavirones and Comechingones lived in caves or crude adobe houses surrounded by thorny bushes and cactus fences. They were organized in tribes led by *caciques* (chiefs) and they lived by hunting, gathering, and agriculture. Their religion centered around the sun and the moon, and there were three or four main languages and many dialects in the area. It is estimated that there were between 12,000 and 30,000 people in the area at the time of the Spanish conquest.

The discovery by the Spaniards of metal sources and stone for quarrying in the mountains more than justified in their eyes the foundation of a new city.

One hundred years after its foundation, Córdoba manifested the characteristics which are still seen as its trademark. The little village had flourished religiously and culturally. By that time it boasted an astonishing number of churches, chapels, and convents erected by the Jesuits, the Franciscans, the Carmelites, and others; it had a Jesuit-run university, the oldest in the country, erected in 1621 (now called the Universidad Nacional de Córdoba); the local economy was supported by a variety of agricultural products (corn, wheat, beans, potatoes, peaches, apricots, grapes, and pears), and by extensive and ever-growing herds of wild cattle.

BELOW: the church of Candonga, in the sierras of Córdoba.

The mountains and "the tree"

In Córdoba one finds the stark juxtaposition of the impossibly flat pampas with the rolling sierras, the first mountain chain one encounters when moving west toward the Andes. As one approaches across the plain, the hills appear like great waves breaking on a beach.

There are three chains of mountains in the western part of the province of Córdoba, all of which run parallel to each other, from north to south. They are the Sierra Chica in the east, the Sierra Grande in the center, and the Sierra del Pocho (which turn into the Sierra de Guasapampa) in the west. The highest peak in the province is Champaquí, which reaches a height of 2,884 meters (9,462 ft). The Sierras de Córdoba are neither as high nor as extensive as many of the other mountain formations east of the Andes. Their easy accessibility, their beauty, their dry weather, magnificent views, and good roads, as well as the myriad of small rivers and watercourses have established for Córdoba a strong reputation as an ideal spot for rest and recuperation.

Most of the rain falls in the summer and is heavier in the eastern section, where the hills look very green and lush, although it is mostly bushes and low thorny thickets. Toward the piedmont of the eastern hills, larger trees grow in greater abundance. Among these trees, the friendly *algarrobo* deserves special mention. From prehistoric times right up to the present it has been used by the local populations as a shade-giving tree, and as a source both of fruit and wood for fence posts and for fires. The fruit is used to make various foodstuffs, including *patay*, a hard, sweet bread. The *algarrobo* is also one of the trees most resistant to drought, and because of all these virtues, it is sometimes simply called "the tree" by the locals.

Map on page 220

The city of Córdoba was founded on 24 June 1573 as Córdoba La Llana de la Nueva Andalucía, a likely reference to its sunny Mediterranean climate.

BELOW: the rocky landscape around La Cumbrecita.

Bird songs

The fauna of the region is not as rich as when the Spaniards first arrived, but is still plentiful enough in some hidden areas to support seasonal hunting. Pumas, or American lions, still roam the hills but are few and isolated. Guanacos are not a common sight around most of the vacation resorts but can be seen toward the higher western areas. Hares abound and are hunted and eaten, as are partridges and vizcachas. Several types of snake can be found, including rattlesnakes and coral snakes, but the steady invasion of most places in the mountains by residents and visitors has decreased their numbers. Foxes are also occasionally seen, and there are countless species of birds, including condors, in the area.

Córdoba has a dry continental climate, with cooler, wetter weather in the sierras and warmer and drier weather in the plains to the south and east of the province. Though the summer, with its hot days and cool nights, is the favorite season for most visitors, the winter is not without its charm. Because the rains are seasonal, occurring in spring and summer, the views change dramatically.

Across the pampas

The easiest access to the city and province of Córdoba is from the south and east. Leaving from Buenos Aires, the visitor has the choice of traveling by plane, bus or car. Buses are fast, offer a wider variety of schedules and are modern, spacious, and comfortable. There are several companies that make the Buenos Aires–Córdoba run with options to stop in Rosario and a few other large towns (which takes under 9 hours).

If the trip from Buenos Aires is made by land, there are two main ways to go to Córdoba. The shortest is via Rosario, a city of over 1 million inhabitants

The rich wildlife in this region attracts many visitors – these days most are armed only with cameras and binoculars.

BELOW:
bright young
sparks in Córdoba.

located 300 km (185 miles) northwest of Buenos Aires, using Ruta 9. The other choice is using Ruta 8, a slightly longer but quieter and quainter road, which runs parallel to the south, passing through some traditional agricultural towns such as San Antonio de Areco *(see page 192)*, Pergamino, Venado Tuerto, and Río Cuarto. In both cases, the visitor will pass through miles and miles of pampas (plain, flat, and very rich terrain) dotted with small towns and huge plots planted with corn, wheat, soya, and sunflower. Everywhere there are enormous herds of cattle (Aberdeen Angus, Hereford, Holando-Argentina) and horses. The roads are quite good and offer the basic commodities (hotels, small restaurants, cafes, gas stations) in almost every town along the way.

Córdoba can also be reached easily from the west (either Santiago, the Chilean capital, or Mendoza) by plane and bus and from the north (Santiago del Estero, Salta, Tucumán, Jujuy) by plane, bus, and train. All buses arrive at the **Terminal de Omnibus**, located at Boulevard Reconquista 380.

Spanish grid

The city of **Córdoba ❶** has a population of approximately 1.3 million. The basis of its economy is agriculture, cattle, and the car industry. Its key location, at the crossroads of many of the main routes, established its early importance and fostered its rapid growth. Although Buenos Aires, with its excessive absorption of power and people, has always tended to overshadow the rest of the country, Córdoba and its zone of influence is the strongest nucleus found in the vast interior of Argentina.

Córdoba, like most Spanish-settled cities, was designed with a rectangular grid of streets, with the main plaza (Plaza San Martín), the cathedral, and the main

TIP

The airlines Aerolíneas Argentinas, Austral, and Southern Winds have several daily flights from Buenos Aires to Córdoba which take about an hour.

LEFT: Córdoba cathedral.
BELOW: El Arco, Córdoba.

Maps:
Area 220
City 216

TIP

If you are planning a trip to the country, make sure to visit Córdoba's provincial tourist office, the Dirección Provincial de Turismo, at Tucumán 360, which offers a wide range of information about the nearby sierras.

buildings in the city center. It is therefore easy for tourists to find on a map the different sites of historical, architectural, or artistic interest within the city.

Because many of the early buildings of Córdoba were either religious or educational, time and progress have spared a great number of them, leaving visitors and residents with a rich treasure-trove of colonial chapels, churches, convents, and public buildings amid the modern surroundings.

There are several tourist offices, including in the downtown area, at the airport and inside the bus terminal. The main office for city tourism is located in the **Recova del Cabildo** Ⓐ (Independencia 30; open Mon–Fri 8am–9pm, Sat–Sun 9am–1pm and 3–7pm), with information about walking tours, special events, museum exhibits, maps, and historical background.

Church circuit

The religious *circuito* (circuits being the various tours that are recommended by the city tourist office) covers most of the oldest colonial religious buildings. An

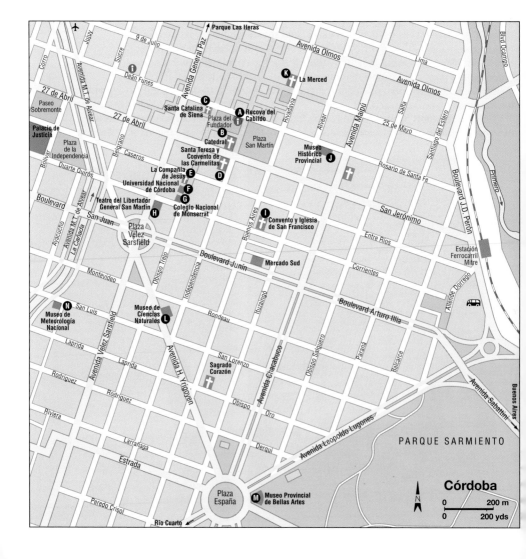

Map
on page
216

ideal walking tour around the city center, which you can make unaccompanied or with a guide, begins at Plaza San Martín. Though its site was originally decided on in 1577, the final consecration of the **Catedral** Ⓑ took place in 1784, after collapses, interruptions, and changes. These delays account for the many artistic styles visible in the architecture. It has been described by the architect J. Roca as having a classic Renaissance portico and a baroque dome and steeple, with influences of indigenous origin in its towers. A large wrought-iron gate completes the picture. The cool, shady interior of the church, located on the western side of **Plaza San Martín**, is divided into three large naves, separated from each other by wide, thick columns (which replaced the smaller original columns that were not strong enough to support the building). The main altar, made of silver, is from the 19th century; it replaced the original baroque altar which is now in the church of Tulumba.

El Cabildo, Córdoba.

The church and convent of **Santa Catalina de Siena** Ⓒ (open at Mass hours: Mon–Sat 7am, Sun 8am, 9am, and 7.30pm), located behind the cathedral, off the pedestrian street Obispo Trejo and at the end of the Pasaje Cuzco, was founded in 1613 by a wealthy widow, Leonor de Tejeda y Mirabal, who converted her home into the province's first convent. The current building dates from the end of the 19th century, and is noted in particular for its dome.

The **Iglesia de Santa Teresa y Convento de las Carmelitas** Ⓓ (Church and Monastery of the Carmelite Nuns, also called Las Teresas; open at Mass hours: 8am daily) was founded in the early 17th century. It was completed in 1717 but was heavily renovated during the latter half of the 18th century and many of the buildings date to this later period. The main altar has a large baroque sculpture of Santa Teresa de Jesús and the wooden choir is an example of fine woodwork. In the monastery there is a religious art museum, the Museo de Arte Religioso, in which many of the objects once belonging to the cathedral are now exhibited. The entrance is on Calle Independencia and the complex is located opposite the cathedral.

BELOW:
the narrowest
building in the
world, Córdoba.

The Jesuit complex

Built on the original site of a small shrine, dating from 1589, the Jesuit complex is located on Calle Caseros, two blocks from the cathedral. It was declared a World Heritage Site in 2000.

The group of buildings is made up of the church, the Capilla Doméstica and the living quarters. Originally it also encompassed the Colegio Máximo and the university, both of which are now national institutions.

The church, **La Compañía de Jesús** Ⓔ (open Mon–Sat 8am–7pm, Sun at Mass hours) dates to the 17th century. One of its notable details is an arch made of Paraguayan cedar, in the shape of an inverted boat's hull. The church interior is lined with cedar beams and the roof is made up of beams and tiles. The tiles were joined with a special glue, which after 300 years is still tightly weatherproof. Many of the baroque altars, including the one made of cedar, date to the 18th century and the Carrara marble work on the walls is 19th century.

The Capilla Doméstica is also from the 17th century. Here, the ceiling was constructed of

A traditional evening out in Córdoba would include attending a *peña*, where locals and visitors gather to drink wine, eat empanadas, and listen to folk music.

wooden beams and canes tied with rawhide, which were placed between the beams and then plastered and covered with painted cloth.

Within the Jesuit complex is located the **Universidad Nacional de Córdoba** (Rectory of the University of Córdoba; open Mon–Fri 8am–9pm, Sat 8am–noon). Opened in 1613, it is the oldest university in South America. Now a museum, the rectory includes the university library, as well as cloisters, gardens, and a monument to university founder Bishop Trejo y Sanabria.

Another academic institution located within the Jesuit complex is the traditional **Colegio Nacional de Montserrat** (Montserrat National College; open Mon–Fri 8am–9pm during term), a secondary school which until 1998 was open only to boys. The college was founded by Ignacio Duarte Quirós in 1687, and since 1907 has been a dependency of the university. The building was reconstructed in 1927 and is primarily notable for the clock tower at one end, as well as a mural by Claudio Boggino in its central salon (open Mon–Fri, mornings only).

Across from the Montserrat on Duarte Quirós, between Velez Sarsfield and Obispo Trejo, is the **Teatro del Libertador General San Martín** , formerly known as the Teatro Rivera Indarte and constructed in 1887. The theater, which is considered to have outstanding acoustics, still offers performances and includes the **Museo del Teatro y de la Música** (open Mon–Fri 9am–noon), with photographs, scores, and programs from the history of the theater.

The **Convento y Iglesia de San Francisco** (Church and Convent of Saint Francis) is located at the corner of calles Buenos Aires and Entre Rios, two blocks from the cathedral. The land for the church was given to the Franciscan Order by the founder of the city, Jerónimo Luis de Cabrera. The first chapel was

BELOW: Paseo de las Flores, one of Córdoba's pedestrianized shopping streets.

built in 1575; this original chapel and a second one which replaced it no longer exist. The current structure was initiated in 1796 and finished in 1813. Within the complex, the room named Salón de Profundis is original.

Map on page 216

Ethnic artifacts

Also worth mentioning is the **Museo Histórico Provincial ❿** (Provincial History Museum, open Tues–Fri 9am–1pm and 3–7pm, Sat–Sun 10am–1pm), an outstanding example of colonial residential architecture, located in the mansion of the Marquis de Sobremonte, the last colonial mansion left in the city, on calles Rosario de Santa Fe and Ituzaingó, three blocks from the cathedral. The building was constructed in the 18th century and occupied by the governor of Córdoba. It hosts a large collection of indigenous and gaucho artifacts, old musical instruments, ceramics, and furniture.

Located in the corner of 25 de Mayo and Rivadavia, only three blocks from the cathedral, is the **Basílica de La Merced ❾**. The present building was finished in 1826 over foundations dating from the1600s. The main altar, executed in 1890, and the polychrome wooden pulpit from the 18th century, are two of the outstanding attractions of the interior.

In the southern part of the city is the huge **Parque Sarmiento**, near the Barrio Nueva Córdoba and the **Ciudad Universitaria**, which houses all of the university's faculties in buildings of different eras and designs. The park has a lake with two islands, a Greek theater, a zoo, and the Córdoba Lawn Tennis Club. It was designed in the late 19th century by French landscape architect Carlos Thays.

Renowned 19th-century French landscape architect Carlos Thays was responsible for the layout of Parque Sarmiento in Córdoba, as well as designing other city parks in Mendoza, Tucumán, and Buenos Aires.

Beyond the city center

The **Museo de Ciencias Naturales ❶** (open Mon–Fri 9am–noon; with daily guided tours), located at Yrigoyen 115, includes exhibits on geology, botany, paleontology, and zoology relating to the history and flora and fauna of the province.

At Parque Sarmiento's main entrance, located on Plaza España, is the **Museo Provincial de Bellas Artes ❿** (open Tues–Sun 11am–7pm), opened in 1916 and offering special art exhibitions, a library, and cultural activities. Another fine arts museum, the **Museo de Bellas Artes Dr. Génaro Perez** (open Tues–Fri 9.30am–1.30pm and 4.30–8.30pm, Sat–Sun 10am–8pm), is located in the Palacio Garzón, on the Paseo de la Ciudad two blocks north of the cathedral and has permanent exhibitions of Argentine three-dimensional art.

To the west of the center, near the canal at San Luís and Belgrano, is the **Museo de Meteorología Nacional ❾** (National Meteorology Museum and Observatory; open Tues–Fri 9am–1pm and 3–7pm, Sat 8.30am–12.30pm), founded in 1871 by President Sarmiento and Argentina's principal observatory.

Another huge park, located on the western edge of the city, is the **Parque San Martín**, located by the Río Suquía and close to the Córdoba stadium and the University of the Environment. This beautiful park, also designed by Carlos Thays, includes the **Centro de Arte Contemporáneo** (open Tues–Sun 4–8pm),

BELOW: mosaics in Basílica de la Merced, Córdoba.

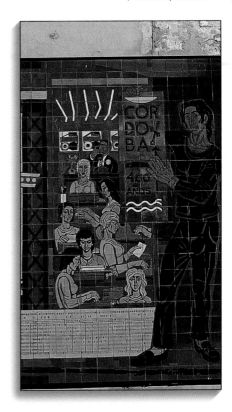

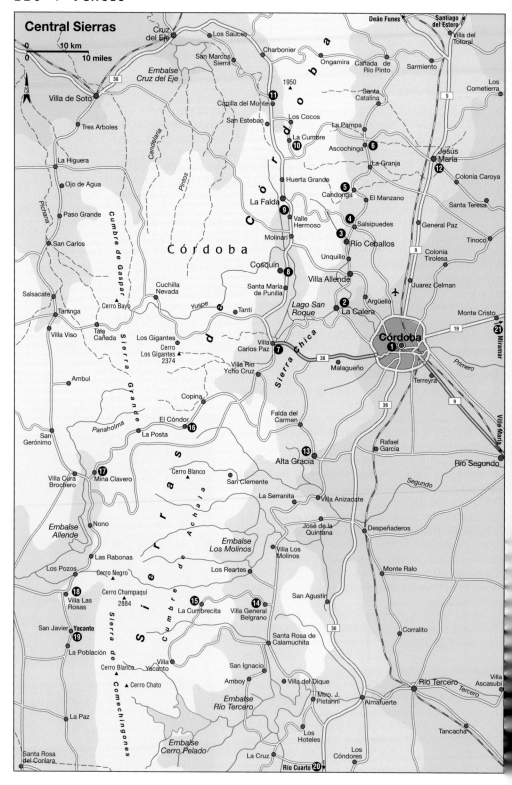

Central Sierras

0   10 km
0   10 miles

38

N

Deán Funes

Santiago del Estero

Villa del Totoral

Cruz del Eje

Los Sauces

Charbonier

Ongamira   Cañada de Río Pinto   Sarmiento

Los Cometierra

San Marcos Sierra

Santa Catalina

9

Villa de Soto

Capilla del Monte   11   1950

Tres Arboles

San Esteban

Los Cocos

La Cumbre   10   6   La Pampa

Ascochinga

Jesús María   12

La Higuera

La Granja

Colonia Caroya

Ojo de Agua

Huerta Grande   5   Candonga   El Manzano

Santa Teresa

Paso Grande

La Falda   9   Valle Hermoso   4   Salsipuedes   General Paz

San Carlos

Molinari   3   Río Ceballos   9   Colonia Tirolesa   Tinoco

Córdoba

Unquillo

Salsacate

Cosquín   8   Villa Allende   Juarez Celman

Cuchilla Nevada

Santa María de Punilla

Taninga

Cerro Bayo   Yuspe   Tanti   Lago San Roque   2   Argüello   Monte Cristo   21

Villa Viso   Tala Cañada   La Calera   19   Miramar

Los Gigantes   Cerro Los Gigantes 2374   Villa Carlos Paz   7   Córdoba   1

Ambul   Villa Río Ycho Cruz   38   Malagueño   Terreyra

San Gerónimo   Copina   Falda del Carmen   36

El Cóndor   16   La Posta   Panaholma

Rafael García

Villa Cura Brochero   17   Mina Clavero   Alta Gracia   13   Río Segundo

Cerro Blanco   San Clemente   Segundo

Embalse Allende   Nono   La Serranita   Villa Anizacate

José de la Quintana   Despeñaderos

Las Rabonas   Embalse Los Molinos   Villa Los Molinos   Monte Ralo

Los Pozos   Cerro Negro   Los Reartes

Villa Las Rosas   18   Cerro Champaquí 2884   La Cumbrecita   15   Villa General Belgrano   14   San Agustín   Corralito

San Javier   Yacanto   19

La Población

Villa Yacanto   San Ignacio   Santa Rosa de Calamuchita   36

Cerro Blanco   Amboy   Villa del Dique   Río Tercero   Villa Ascasubi

Cerro Chato   Mtro. J. Pistarini   Almafuerte   Tercero

Embalse Río Tercero

La Paz   Embalse Cerro Pelado   Los Hoteles   Los Cóndores   Tancacha

Santa Rosa del Conlara   La Cruz   Río Cuarto   20

which exhibits permanent as well as temporary works of modern art; an exhibition center, and a campground. Also by the river is the **Parque Las Heras**, extending from the Centenario Bridge to the Antártida Bridge, which includes a monument to famous tango singer Carlos Gardel.

Maps:
Area 220
City 216

The contemporary city

Córdoba might be better known for its colonial charm, but the modern city also has much to offer visitors. A few blocks from the city center is **La Cañada**, the tree-lined canal that runs through town, a lovely place to walk in the evening or at quiet times of day. On Saturday and Sunday there is an art and crafts fair on the corner of La Cañada and A. Rodríguez. The Rincón de los Pintores (the Painters' Corner) is a gallery devoted to the work of local artists, and is located inside the Centro Muncipal de Exposiciones Obispo Mercadillo at Rosario de Santa Fe 39. *Peatonales* (pedestrian streets) in the city center are lined with cafes, bookstores, and boutiques – popular sites for university students. This is a good place to sit and relax, do some window shopping, or watch people strolling by. Also close by are numerous movie theaters showing current releases.

Córdoba has many popular street cafes.

Village fiestas

Once you have had your fill of the city of Córdoba, a trip to the surrounding country is highly recommended if you have the time. The local tourism authorities have laid out a number of routes which will lead the dedicated traveler up into the mountains, along paved and unpaved roads to tiny villages, lakes, streams, campsites, and spectacular views. While these routes can be undertaken by public bus, private transport is necessary to really explore the area.

BELOW: a Germanic-style cafe in Villa General Belgrano.

THE JESUITS IN CORDOBA

During the 17th and 18th centuries, the city of Córdoba was the spiritual and administrative center of the Jesuit movement in the Americas, whose activities covered all of north and west Argentina and much of central South America.

The chief goal of the Jesuits was a spiritual one – to convert the heathen souls of the indigenous population and to further the religious education of their brotherhood. However, as they attracted an increasing number of native converts into their missions, the Jesuits developed their own economic system, abolishing forced labor and replacing it with a productive, communal economy.

With a steady flow of new missionaries from Europe, together with large donations of money and property, the Jesuit "empire" grew spectacularly. The highly skilled communities built fabulous missions, comprising churches, residences, and estancias, filled with finely crafted furniture, ironwork, and silverware. By the time of their expulsion in 1767 by Spain's King Carlos III, the Jesuits had established a network of centers in and around Córdoba, including La Calera, Estancia Santa Catalina, Jesús María, and Alta Gracia *(see map on opposite page)*, the remains of which can be visited today.

TIP

Laguna Azul is a popular bathing pool converted from a disused quarry, near the Mal Paso Dam on the Río Suquía, outside La Calera.

Side trips from Córdoba

Among the shorter day excursions from Córdoba is **La Calera** ❷, some 15 km (9 miles) to the west of the city and now one of the dormitory communities for those working in the city. Located at the foot of the sierras, La Calera stands near the Mal Paso Dam on Río Suquía, which offers attractive views over the reservoir. Within La Calera, surrounded by former limestone quarries started in the 17th century, are the ruins of a Jesuit chapel and of the former lime mills and furnaces. The town also has a municipal beach on the river, which gets extremely busy in the summer.

About 40 km (25 miles) to the north of Córdoba is **Río Ceballos** ❸, a delightful town in the sierras and also home to many of those working in the city. The Ceballos River runs through the center of town, set among green hills, and at the far end of the town is La Quebrada reservoir and park. Slightly farther up (or about two hours' walk on foot) are two waterfalls, the Cascada del Aguila and the Cascada de los Hornillos. Río Ceballos also has a casino and is a popular summer watering hole for those seeking a quieter getaway than the nightlife of Villa Carlos Paz. Between La Calera and Río Ceballos are a number of other purely residential towns such as Villa Allende and Unquillo, which are well worth passing through because of their attractiveness.

One of the most popular visits is to **El Valle de la Punilla**, which extends north from the city of Córdoba on Ruta 38 toward **Cruz del Eje**. This route passes through, or close to, most of the small resort towns of the region. Among these towns is **Salsipuedes** ❹, about 30 km (19 miles) north of Río Ceballos. The town is located in an area of great natural beauty and has a riverside beach area for tourists. Passing Salsipuedes, after about another 20 km (12 miles)

BELOW: a river running slowly through the sierras.

brings you to the tiny village of **Candonga** ❺, located on the dirt road on the way to Cerro Azul. There is an 18th-century chapel here, the **Capilla de Candonga**, which was formerly part of the Santa Gertrudis Jesuit estancia. A larger Jesuit site is located in **Ascochinga** ❻, north of Salsipuedes on a road that offers great natural beauty and a great selection of German pastry shops. Ascochinga has the former Jesuit **Estancia Santa Catalina**, including a church and cemetery and the ruins of a seminary. The complex can be seen from outside (the key to the church can be requested from the caretaker) and is an exceptional example of colonial architecture from the early 18th century.

Some 39 km (24 miles) to the west of Córdoba is **Villa Carlos Paz** ❼, famous for its busy nightlife, its casinos, restaurants, and clubs, and the sports activities centered around San Roque reservoir. It is immensely popular with Argentines, with handsome chalets, comfortable hotels, and streets packed day and night with tourists (during the high season).

Music festivals

About 18 km (11 miles) directly north of Carlos Paz is **Cosquín** ❽, a quaint village famous for its Argentine and Latin American folk music and dance festival in the second half of January *(see page 353)*. Another 15 km (9 miles) north along the narrow, well-paved road brings you to the village of **La Falda** ❾, which holds a festival celebrating the folk music of Argentina's immigrants, along with tango, in the first week of February. At other times of the year, golfing, swimming, horseback riding, and sailing can be enjoyed. La Falda has an archeological museum and a museum of miniature locomotives.

About 11 km (7 miles) further north lies **La Cumbre** ❿. This town, on Río

The town of La Cumbre is noted for its well-tended gardens and large brick buildings, built by British immigrants.

BELOW: the Jesuit complex at Alta Gracia.

Map on page 220

German immigrants in Villa General Belgrano celebrate a hearty Oktoberfest every year.

San Gerónimo, offers excellent trout fishing from November to April, as well as golf, tennis, and swimming facilities. Its altitude of 1,142 meters (3,768 ft) creates a very pleasant climate and it has become known as a writers' haven. In 1999 it hosted the Paragliding World Cup and achieved international fame.

Another 15 km (9 miles) along the same road (106 km/66 miles from Córdoba) will take the visitor to **Capilla del Monte** ⓫, a town which celebrates its Spanish Festival in February. You can enjoy hiking, rock climbing, swimming, and serenity in this town in the heart of the sierras.

Cutting across country to the east for some 65 km (40 miles) on to Ruta 9 brings you to the large town of **Jesús María** ⓬, also associated with the Jesuits. The Jesuit **Estancia Jesuítica San Isidro Labrador**, one of the earliest vineyards in Argentina, on the outskirts of the town, comprises a church, residence, and museum (open daily). There is another former Jesuit school in town: the **Casa de Caroya**. The city also has a national festival of folklore and rodeo, held in the first half of January at an amphitheater next to San Isidro Labrador.

Gaucho games, maté, and cakes

Another former Jesuit settlement is **Alta Gracia** ⓭, some 36 km (24 miles) southwest of Córdoba city. This is a charming, prosperous town which welcomes tourists but is not overwhelmed by the kinds of crowds found in Carlos Paz. One of the main attractions is the Jesuit complex, a veritable jewel of colonial architecture, containing the Iglesia de la Merced (open during Mass hours) and the Residencia Jesuítica (open daily). Alta Gracia is most famous for a more recent inhabitant, however. In 2001, the **Museo Casa de Ernesto Che Guevara** (open daily) was opened – the legendary revolutionary hero spent his teenage years here when a doctor recommended the town's dry air for his asthma.

BELOW: handicrafts for sale in the sierras.

A short excursion into the hills behind Alta Gracia toward La Isla, on the Río Anizacate, leads over a passable dirt road, past small farms with spectacular views of the beautiful river. With luck, somewhere along this route, or another in the sierra region, you just might come upon a group of locals branding their cattle and be invited to eat a barbecue *(asado)*, drink strong red wine, and throw the *taba* (a gaucho game of chance played with the left knee bone of a horse).

Leaving Alta Gracia behind and returning to the main route, continue on south and enter the sierras on a well-paved but winding road. Twenty picturesque kilometers (12 miles) later the Embalse Los Molinos appears. This is a favorite spot for the people of the region to practice various aquatic sports, or have a meal by the dam, high above the lake.

Another 20 km (12 miles) brings you to **Villa General Belgrano** ⓮, a town purportedly founded by sailors from the ill-fated *Graf Spee*, who chose not to return to Germany. Villa General Belgrano has a decidedly German character, with its charming chalets and well-kept gardens. As might be expected, the town celebrates an Oktoberfest during the first week of that month and don't leave town without sampling some of the famous homemade cakes. A bit further to the south is the Embalse Río Tercero,

Map
on page
220

part of a series of seven lakes beginning with Los Molinos, all of which offer beautiful mountain scenery. Embalse Río Tercero is the largest lake in the area. The town of Embalse at the tip of the lake offers reasonable tourist facilities.

The tiny town of **La Cumbrecita** ⓯ nestles at the foot of Las Sierras Grandes, 40 km (25 miles) down an unpaved road west of Villa General Belgrano. Visitors will find many nature paths just outside town, crossing small rivers and waterfalls, and meandering among varied plant life, including a small forest of cedar, pine, and cypress trees. La Cumbrecita is relaxing and quiet, with attractive houses and gardens along the side streets. On the road between Villa General Belgrano and La Cumbrecita there's a view of **Cerro Champaquí**, at 2,884 meters (9,461 ft), the highest peak in the sierras of Córdoba, and which can be climbed on foot or on horseback (around two hours in the latter case).

A more tranquil part of the sierras is the valley of Traslasierra (which means behind the mountains), reached by taking **El Camino de las Altas Cumbres** to the west, on the other side of the mountains from the La Punilla and Calamuchita valleys. On this road there is a panoramic view from **El Cóndor** ⓰, a lookout point at the site of the former Hotel El Cóndor. Some of the towns worth visiting in Traslasierra are Mina Clavero, San Javier, and Cura Brochero.

Mina Clavero ⓱ is located at the meeting of the Panaholma and Mina Clavero rivers, and houses the **Museo Piedra Cruz del Sur** (open daily in summer only), a museum of minerals, which has stone carvings and other crafts for sale. Further south is the former tobacco town of **Villa Las Rosas** ⓲, on the Río Gusmara, with a beach area. South of Villa Las Rosas is **Yacanto** ⓳, an upmarket resort built by British railways engineers, with grand summer houses and an exclusive hotel complex, the Hotel Yacanto, with its own golf course. Yacanto is also known for a well-documented UFO sighting.

Further exploration

The sierras of Córdoba offer countless possibilities to explore off the main tourist routes, following dirt roads to quiet villages in the mountains.

In the south of the province is the large city of **Río Cuarto** ⓴, located on the river of the same name, close to the southern lake district around Río Tercero and some 220 km (137 miles) from the city of Córdoba. Río Cuarto has a 19th-century cathedral located on Central Julio Roca, as well as the **Museo de Bellas Artes** (open daily), with an important collection by local and national artists and the **Museo Histórico Regional** (open daily except Mon), housed in a building dating from 1860, covering local history from the pre-Columbian era to the present day.

In the north of Córdoba province, on the shore of **Laguna Mar Chiquita**, the largest saltwater lake in Argentina, is the resort town of **Miramar** ㉑ which offers water sports, a center for balneotherapy, and the Reserva Provincial at Laguna Mar Chiquita, an important wetlands area for overwintering shore birds; the area has been made a Provincial Natural Reserve and Hemispheric Site of the Organization of Reserves for Beach Birds. ❑

BELOW: a rocky riverbed near La Cumbrecita.

THE NORTHEAST

This long sliver of land, squeezed in between Uruguay, Brazil, and Paraguay, is home to the famous Iguazú Falls, as well as ruins of Jesuit missions and a clutch of lesser-known natural attractions

Map on page 230

As with everywhere else in Argentina, the distances in the Northeast are considerable. Here, the major tourist attractions are few and far between and hurried visitors tend to fly to Iguazú and skip the rest. In so doing, they miss an overland journey that can be really worthwhile. The best way to do this journey is in a car, so that you can spend time in selected spots, although public transportation is quite extensive and reliable.

The two principal sites in Misiones – the 275 impressive and thundering cascades of Iguazú Falls and the Jesuit ruins at San Ignacio – should not be missed. Neither should the 2-km (1¼-mile) wide Moconá Falls on the Uruguay River on the border with Brazil. On the way to Moconá are 40 smaller cascades accessible by jungle paths in the Central Highlands, and the charming town of Oberá, a jumping-off point for expeditions to the falls.

Along the road to Misiones, in the slow-paced and friendly towns in Entre Ríos and Corrientes, there are churches, modest museums, and even small private zoos to see. In-between the towns, across a variety of terrains, there are provincial and national parks, such as the Parque Nacional El Palmar near Colón in Entre Ríos, with rare palm trees and abundant wildlife.

The most interesting park and nature reserve of all is the Esteros del Iberá lagoon and wetlands in Corrientes province, where intrepid travelers can see hundreds of bird and animal species, and look alligators and boa constrictors in the eye from small boats paddled by former poachers turned park rangers. (The ex-poachers' change of heart has a purely capitalistic motive: their salaries make it more profitable for them to protect the animals than to hunt them.)

Along the way, you can always break up the trip with a visit to a citrus farm, or a yerba maté plantation, to sample a gourd filled with the green tea that is Argentina's national drink.

Fantasy ferry journey

From 1550 to about 1920, the rivers of northeast Argentina were the safest, cheapest, and best way to see the country. For more than 350 years, vessels navigated the rivers, carrying goods, settlers, explorers, officials, and, in later years, tourists.

Today, however, the vast majority of visitors to this region, known as Mesopotamia, travel by road or air. Nevertheless, everything of any interest in northeast Argentina is on or close to a river, so one approach to getting to know this area, on paper at least, would be to use the river system to explore this corner of the country. On this hypothetical journey one will embark in Buenos Aires.

Soon after setting sail, the vessel will have to find the navigable mouth of the Paraná, as the river splits up

PRECEDING PAGES: waiting for the last boat home. **LEFT:** the steaming Iguazú Falls. **BELOW:** a barefoot Corrientes gaucho.

into many channels when it joins the Río de la Plata, forming a huge delta. Suburban **Tigre** is the gateway to this maze of waterways lined with weekend houses, each with its own small jetty. Here people have a restful time fishing, boating, or just getting away from the nearby metropolis. The delta has a life of its own from Monday to Friday: there are permanent residents, fishermen, citrus growers, and pulp-wood producers, all of whom lead the gentler and slower-paced life of river dwellers. Hotels and guesthouses are plentiful.

Upriver, **Zárate** is the site of a huge road and rail bridge complex which, when completed in 1979, at last joined Mesopotamia to Buenos Aires and made obsolete the double ferry connection which was susceptible to interruption by flood and drought water levels and was a fearful hassle.

On then to **Rosario ❶**, a large grain port which was once the second city in the country, though *rosarinos* may still debate the "once" bit. It is a large city, with a population of more than 1 million, although it suffered a major loss of population following the decline of its port, once the nation's second after Buenos Aires. The port was privatized in the mid 1990s and is again becoming a major hub of activity.

Rosario is not particularly geared toward visitors, but the early 20th-century and Art Deco architecture in the center of town gives some idea of its history. A pedestrian precinct in the city center passes through some of the oldest and most architecturally mixed parts of town. It is also worth visiting the monument to the national flag, the **Monumento a la Bandera**, which consists of a sweep of steps, an obelisk backed by a series of arches, and an eternal flame.

North to Santa Fe

Some 32 km (20 miles) upstream, on the western shore, is **San Lorenzo ❷**, and the **Convento de San Carlos**, built at the end of the 18th century and famous for being the site of a battle in the war of independence. Here, on

Map on page 230

February 3, 1813, the Argentine hero José de San Martín was pinned under his fallen horse. A Sergeant Cabral saved him, but in so doing was himself fatally wounded. The tree under which he died still stands in the grounds of the convent as a symbol of self-sacrifice.

Rosario is in the province of **Santa Fe**. It is by far the most important city in that province, but it is not the capital, a fact that *rosarinos* dislike intensely. This honor goes to **Santa Fe ❸**, a city some way upstream and the next port of call. First founded in the 1500s, somewhat north of its present location, it was lost early on to disease and indigenous harrassment. The new city was founded in 1573. Today, Santa Fe is a pleasant provincial town, steeped in tradition, but with modern amenities and little pretense. On the corner of Amenábar and San Martín is the ancient but beautiful church of **San Francisco**, surrounded by monastic buildings that house the province's **Museo Histórico** (open Mon–Fri 8.30am–noon, Sun 9am–noon and 4–7pm).

The town center also includes the **Catedral Metropolitana**, constructed in the 1750s, and at San Martín 1490 is the **Museo Provincial de Bellas Artes** (open Tues–Sun 10am–noon and 4–8pm). Here you will find a large collection of some 2,000 works of art by native and foreign artists. The city hosts a folklore festival of music and dance in the first week of February.

From Santa Fe there is a tunnel under the Río Paraná to the city of **Paraná ❹**, capital of the province of Entre Ríos. Paraná has fine parks, lovely buildings and churches, and views across the river. Inland, the undulating landscape is dotted with woods of native acacias and cut into chunks by smaller rivers and streams. Santa Fe, on the other shore, sits in lowlands as flat as a pancake, surrounded by lakes, marshes, and rivers. Its hinterland is all fenced off into square fields, with regularly spaced towns and villages.

San Martín's cell and final resting place, San Lorenzo.

BELOW: Monumento a la Bandera, Rosario.

Jungle ruins

About 80 km (50 miles) upstream near **Cayastá ❺**, old Santa Fe slept in oblivion until it was rediscovered in the 20th century. Previously hidden by vegetation of centuries' growth on the low bank of a small branch of the river, it is now being recovered as a historical site. Though it was a small town and entirely built of adobe (stone of any kind is hard to find in the pampas), there were seven different churches or religious orders represented here and it is an important historical site, although tourist facilities are minimal. Cayastá also offers panoramic views of the San Javier River and islands.

In the north of Santa Fe province is **Reconquista ❻**, a town of some 55,000 people where the late 19th-century port is currently undergoing renovation and a rise in shipping due to the dredging of the Paraguay and Paraná rivers. The large **Plaza 25 de Mayo** in the town center has a monument to the city's founder, General Manuel Obligado.

Passing into the province of Corrientes, the second-largest city is **Goya ❼**, located on the Río Paraná and a well-known draw for *surubí* (a large tropical catfish) angling enthusiasts, as well as the headquarters of the local Philip Morris cigarette manufacturing subsidiary, Massalin Particulares. Goya has a 19th-century cathedral on the Plaza Mitre, river walks, and

the **Capilla del Diablo** (on RN12, in Colonia Carolina, ask owners for permission to enter), constructed by immigrants in the early 20th century and featuring a carving of the Virgin Mary in a block of carob wood, as well as additional carvings including serpents and other apparently diabolical designs.

There is still a ferry in operation between Reconquista and Goya, and for those interested, the trip across gives you a good feel for the entire stretch of the Paraná River. It takes from four to six hours and goes along a network of waterways, wending between islands with wooded shores.

Resistencia ❽, with over 400,000 inhabitants, is the capital of Chaco province on the edge of the Gran Chaco, the heart of South America. These flat swampy lowlands stretch from Argentina into Paraguay and Bolivia, and as far as southwestern Brazil. Resistencia, founded in 1750, grew rich on agricultural produce and through exporting the local quebracho plants for tannin extraction. It is now famous as the "capital of sculpture," with more than 300 pieces scattered through the city. It is linked by bridge to **Corrientes**, capital of the province of the same name. The latter, on the east bank, sits high, while Resistencia lies among the swamps. In the subtropical heat, Corrientes is one of the most laid-back cities in Argentina, closer in spirit to Asunción in Paraguay. Its central streets, with many murals and stores selling local indigenous handicrafts, make it an interesting place to visit. There has also been a revival in the regional guitar music of *chamame*, which is featured in several places in the city, and an increasingly popular carnival during the last days before Lent, with floats, music, dancing, and fancy dress. About 25 km (15 miles) inland from Corrientes, the small town of **San Luis del Palmar** ❾ has retained the flavor of colonial times. East of the town is the **Parque Nacional Mburucuyá** which is worth a visit for its quebracho forests.

Gauchos on an empty back road in Corrientes.

BELOW: Convento de San Carlos, San Lorenzo.

THE RUINS OF SAN IGNACIO MINI

Among the 30 or so Jesuit missions whose remains have survived in northeast Argentina, San Ignacio Miní is the largest and best preserved. For its historic and architectural importance, the site has been declared Patrimonio Histórico Cultural de la Humanidad by UNESCO.

Founded in 1610 on what is now Brazilian territory in the north of Misiones province, San Ignacio suffered continual slave raids from the Portuguese colony and was forced to move twice, finally settling in its current location near Posadas, by the Río Paraná, in 1696.

Throughout the 18th century the mission grew to become one of the most important in the region, inhabited by more than 3,000 Guaraní converts. Following the expulsion of the Jesuits in 1767, however, San Ignacio, along with all the missions, fell into decline until, in the 19th century, it was destroyed and its occupants ejected.

Miraculously, much of the original complex has survived today, aided by some careful restoration work. Entering San Ignacio via a wide, tree-lined avenue, visitors are confronted by the towering red sandstone walls of the church and adjoining buildings. Encroaching vegetation drapes some outlying ruins and a nightly son et lumière show recreates the atmosphere of the Jesuits' glory days.

A short distance beyond Corrientes, you reach the confluence with the Río Paraguay. It is about here, at **Paso de la Patria** , that fishermen from all over the world congregate to try for dorado, the "fightingest fish in the world." Lodging, boats, guides, and equipment are available from July to November.

Map on page 230

Pilgrims' progress

Incongruous and out of the blue, the huge church dome at **Itatí** ⑪ can be seen from up to 24 km (15 miles) away across the plains. This dome is said to be the "most impressive" after St Peter's in Rome. It tops the basilica where many pilgrims converge to venerate the miraculous Virgin of Itatí, housed in the adjoining shrine. For sheer bad taste it is hard to beat the local *santerías*, which sell plaster statues of the virgin and saints, and other religious articles.

The gigantic hydroelectric dam, **Represa Yacyretá**, has become the chief tourist attraction of the once-sleepy Corrientes town of **Ituzaingó** ⑫, some 330 km (205 miles) east of Resistencia, which is recommended for its beaches, zoo, and fishing. The multimillion dollar dam meant nearly 50,000 people were forced to relocate. Free tours are available several times daily.

Just southwest of Posadas, the character of the river changes; the wide, shallow sweeps change to a boxed-in area between steep, high banks in rolling country. Upstream from here, the river cuts through a basalt flow originating some 1,290 km (800 miles) away in Brazil.

Prize dorados drying in the sun.

Jesuit missions

Another 140 km (87 miles) upstream is **Posadas** ⑬, the provincial capital of Misiones, with some 300,000 inhabitants. Posadas' Paraguayan market is open

BELOW: the Jesuit ruins of San Ignacio Miní.

everyday at calles San Martín and Roque Pérez, while a bridge crosses the river to Encarnación in Paraguay itself. The tropical spirit of the region is best appreciated at Carnival time when it seems the whole city joins in the celebrations. The city has the nearest main airport to the increasingly popular Iberá wetlands *(see page 238)*.

The Jesuits were the real pioneers in Misiones; indeed, it is from their work that the province gets its name. They arrived early in the 17th century, and proceeded to settle and convert the Guaraní natives in some 30 missions. Their success led to clashes, first with slave traders in the area and then the Iberian governments, first Portugal, then Spain. They were finally expelled in 1777, and left behind them the mission buildings and lots of unprotected and slightly Christian souls.

Some 20 km (12 miles) southeast of Posadas is the small town of **Candelaria**, which has a beach area on the Río Paraná, as well as the Jesuit ruins of Nuestra Señora de Candelaria, which was founded in 1689 and was the Jesuit seat in the area until the order's expulsion. A few kilometers further north on RN12 are the towns of **Santa Ana**, 30 km (19 miles) away, and **Loreto**, both of which also have Jesuit ruins dating from the same period. In addition to the ruined missions, Candelaria has both natural forests and planted eucalyptus and pine plantations, as well as the **Parque Provincial El Cañadón de Profundidad**, with a river, waterfall, canyon, and small campsite.

Of the 12 mission ruins that have been restored to date in Misiones, the best-known is **San Ignacio Miní ⑭** (open daily 7am–7pm, with a son et lumière show at 7pm in winter and 8.30pm in summer), 55 km (34 miles) east of Posadas on RN12. It is best to amble around the ruins at dawn or dusk, when you can be alone and when the light plays wonders on the red stone. It is then that you can commune with the spirit of what was begun in the name of humanity.

BELOW: bird's-eye view of the *Garganta del Diablo* (Devil's Throat) of the Iguazú Falls.

Northern settlers

Some of the villages of Misiones have a flavor peculiar to themselves. Wooden houses and churches are made from local materials, but the ideas which inspired them came from northern Europe – the origin of most of the settlers. Immigrants from Germany, Poland, Switzerland, Sweden, and France settled in this area, which accounts for the fair-haired people seen everywhere.

Shortly before reaching Puerto Iguazú on the trip north from Posadas, and located on a bend in the Paraná River, is the small town of **Wanda** ⓯, where semi-precious stones are mined. The town is famous for its stone crafts, and has a commercial center where artisans sell regional crafts.

The end of this fantasy river trip is **Puerto Iguazú** ⓰, the head point of navigation, now that the Itaipú Dam has closed off the Paraná and since the Río Iguazú has its own natural barrier. This small town is fully geared for tourism, with a number of hotels, restaurants, taxis, exchange houses, and so on. As a town, it has little to save it from mediocrity, but it just happens to be the nearest settlement to the **Parque Nacional Iguazú** and the world-famous **waterfalls**.

An alternative to staying in Puerto Iguazú is to cross the border into Brazil, where its twin town **Foz do Iguaçu** offers better accommodations and restaurants, although these are no better value than those on the Argentine side. The more spectacular close-up views of the falls are on the Argentine side, where the entrance fee includes a lot more for your money.

Iguazú Falls

Amidst a spectacular jungle setting, the **Cataratas del Iguazú** Ⓐ lie on the Río Iguazú, which runs along the border of Brazil and Argentina. It is often

Maps:
Area 230
Falls 235

Lookout tower over the Iguazú Falls in the national park.

BELOW: walkway perilously close to the rim of the falls.

Iguazú Falls

0   5 km

0   5 miles
          Posadas

The lush forest around the falls is brimming with fauna and flora, such as this bromeliad.

said about this magnificent site that Argentina provides the falls and Brazil enjoys the view. Certainly the 550 meters (600 yards) of walks on the Brazilian side give the visitor a marvelous panoramic view of most of the falls but this is at something of a distance. The simple solution, if you are torn for choice but have enough time, is to visit both sides, which can be done in a day.

On the Argentine side, the falls can be experienced from a number of angles. The lower falls circuit is perhaps the most beautiful 1,000-meter (3,200 ft) walk in the world and should be done clockwise. It leads to the start of the **Isla San Martín** boat trip, which is free and recommended as it allows one to get right into the heart of the spectacle.

By far the most magnificent walk is the one right across the upper river, from Puerto Canoas to the **Garganta del Diablo** (the "Devil's Throat"), where the water plunges the entire 70 meters (240 ft) off the basalt flow into the cauldron below. Late afternoon till dusk is the best time to see the Garganta, both for the lighting at that hour and to watch the flocks of birds that swoop through the billowing mists on their way back to their nests for the night.

The park has many trails into the subtropical rainforest surrounding the falls. If you are attentive and lucky, there's a good chance of seeing some of the exotic wildlife that inhabits the area. At the **visitors' center B** you can get lists of the local mammals, birds, and plants. In 2001, a gas-powered, silent train service was completed. Leaving every 20 minutes from the visitors' center, it takes passengers to the start of the two walking trails. A US$18-million-dollar project also included improvement to facilities and the construction of a large car park.

BELOW: roseate spoonbill.

If you are looking for accommodations, the **Hotel Internacional C** is located on the premises of the park, and offers easy access to all the sites.

Iguazú and Itaipú dams

The Río Iguazú is some 900 km (540 miles) long above the falls and has been dammed. The forest clearing in the watershed permits the immediate run-off of rain, so the river floods, runs dry, runs dirty, "pulses" (due to week-day industrial energy demands), and, in general, behaves in a way unnatural to the trained eye. The stunning natural setting, however, offsets any disappointments.

The **Represa Hidroeléctrica Itaipú**, on the Río Paraná, 20 km (12 miles) north of Puerto Iguazú, is a joint enterprise between Brazil and Paraguay. Free guided tours (Mon–Sat 8am, 9am, 10am, 2pm, and 3.30pm) are well worth it, especially if one of the sluice gates is opened, creating a cascade of water to rival that of Iguazú.

Bitter tea

To return to Buenos Aires on the Río Uruguay would be impossible, due to the river's rapids. The first obstacle encountered is the **Moconá Falls**, some 230 km (143 miles) south by road, which are best viewed from the Brazilian side of the river. To see the falls, the nearest town is **El Soberbio ⑰**, which is also known as the national capital of essential oils, its principal export. The tiny town, founded only about 60 years ago by German and Italian immigrants, is

located on the Río Uruguay on the site of three river basins and three hill ranges. El Soberbio has both hotels and campsites, and you can arrange trips in small boats to the Moconá Falls; by crossing to Porto Soberbio in Brazil, the trip can also be made by land in good weather. The falls themselves are within the Parque Provincial Moconá, an ecological reserve, and consist of a 3-km (2-mile) long series of waterfalls of up to 12 meters (40 ft) high.

Maps:
Area 230
Falls 235

Yerba maté plantations

There are two towns of interest in the southwest of Misiones. **Obera** ⑱, about 90 km (56 miles) east of Posadas on Ruta 5, has settlers from many European countries. The second-largest city in Misiones, with a population of around 42,000, Oberá has a number of European-style buildings, especially of German influence, and the town hosts the National Festival of the Immigrant in its Parque de las Naciones. The city also houses the Museo de Ciencias Naturales Florentino Ameghino (natural science museum), on Barreyro and José Ingenieros (open Tues–Fri and Sat am only), as well as the Wendlinger bird sanctuary, on Haití and Díaz de Solís, containing native and foreign species.

About 100 km (60 miles) to the southwest of Oberá – and founded some 300 years before, in 1638 – lies **Apóstoles** ⑲, the capital of the yerba maté industry. The yerba maté tree is of the holly genus *(Ilex)*, though there the similarity ends. Its leaves are used in many South American countries to make a strong tea, sometimes called Argentina's national drink. Apóstoles has the **Museo y Archivo Histórico Diego de Alfaro** (open daily), on Belgrano 845, which includes exhibits on prehistoric culture, the Jesuits, the colonial period, and fine arts of the region.

Near Apóstoles are the Jesuit missions *(reducciones)* of **Santa María la Mayor**

The majority of the nation's favorite drink, yerba maté, is produced in large plantations in Misiones and Corrientes.

BELOW: spectacled caiman in the Iberá wetlands.

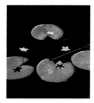

Insectivorous plants in the Iberá Lagoon, which allegedly keep the mosquito population down.

and **San Javier**. Santa María was one of the most important Jesuit missions in Argentina, after San Ignacio Miní *(see box on page 232)*, and was also one of the wealthiest, with extensive livestock and crop production. At present, the mission is permanently open to visitors as an archeological site, although it lacks tourist infrastructure and restoration plans have made little progress. San Javier, which was founded first in 1629, was an important cultural center with the first printing press in South America, and later became a fortress against attacks by slave traders from Brazil. The mission, on the outskirts of the small town of the same name, is located on the Río Uruguay, and the town also has a sugar mill and distillery.

Wetlands wildlife

On the eastern edge of the **Esteros del Iberá** (Iberá marshlands) is the tiny town of **Colonia Carlos Pellegrini** ㉒, which has a couple of lodges and a campground on the Iberá Lagoon and has been named an "ecological village" due to the nature of its buildings, constructed primarily of wood and adobe. The town also has bungalows and cottages to rent, making it a good base to visit the **Reserva Provincial del Iberá**. This huge area runs from Ituzaingó on the Río Paraná to Chavarría in the south, and accounts for nearly 15 percent of Corrientes province. It offers varied scenery, including a series of lagoons, forests, and many native species of plants and animals, including water fowl, alligators, and capybaras (huge rodents). Iberá is considered one of the most important, unspoiled ecosystems in Argentina, with reserves for endangered species such as foxes and swamp deer. The animals are being bred to preserve the species and may be quite tame within the reserves. The best way to view the wildlife is to stay at one of the lodges near the lagoon, where you can organize boat excursions *(see page 342)*, or enquire at the visitors' center just outside Carlos Pellegrini.

BELOW: Palacio de San José, near Colón, former residence of President Urquiza.

About 50 km (30 miles) south of Iberá is the city of **Mercedes** ㉑, a livestock breeding center, which hosts an annual livestock exposition as well as regional craft exhibitions. Within the city is the artisans' cooperative **Fundación Manos Correntinas** (corner of San Martín and Salta), which sells leather, stone, wood, and woolen crafts, as well as fine work in silver or bone. The city has museums of natural science (the largest in the area) and history, while the Nuestra Señora de las Mercedes church, on the main Plaza 25 de Mayo, includes a collection of fine robes, jewels, and a silver crown.

Some 76 km (47 miles) southeast of Mercedes, on the Río Uruguay and on the border with Brazil, is **Paso de los Libres** ㉒, a main transport route for the Brazilian port of Porto Alegre. The city has a casino, close to the Plaza Independencia, and the Laguna Mansa has camping and swimming facilities. It is located in one of the principal rice-growing areas in Argentina.

Yapeyú ㉓, some 60 km (37 miles) northeast of Paso de los Libres, was originally a Jesuit mission and later a Spanish garrison which was burned to the ground by the Portuguese in 1817. Its claim to fame is that the Argentine hero and liberator, José de San Martín, was born here. His father was a Spanish officer stationed at the garrison. The **Templete Histórico Sanmartiniano** (open daily), on Alejandro Aguado, displays some of San Martín's personal effects.

Concordia and Colón

Concordia is a large rural city about 450 km (280 miles) south of Yapeyú on RN14, and is the center of the citrus industry. When the **Embalse Salto Grande** dam just north of the city was planned, the Río Uruguay flowed clear. By the time the dam was finished, however, the river had become muddy due to deforestation. There is a question as to how long the dam will remain operative; it now effectively serves as a sedimentation tank although tours are available.

Heading south, you'll find the **Parque Nacional El Palmar** ㉕, which protects the 800-year-old yatay palms for which the park is named. Facilities for staying overnight are limited to campsites in the park and a motel in **Ubajay**, the nearby village. There are a number of interesting walking trails in the park, and some rare species of animals.

Colón is an old meat-packing town. A few kilometers to the west you will find the **Palacio de San José** (open daily), the former residence of General Justo José de Urquiza, who is famous for having ousted Juan Manuel de Rosas, the 19th-century dictator. The house is maintained as a National Historic Monument; its opulence has faded but it is still impressive.

About 30 km (18 miles) south of Colón is **Concepción del Uruguay** ㉖, situated on the Río Uruguay. Founded in 1783, it was one of the first provincial cities to join the rebels after the 1810 revolution against Spain, and also saw the beginning of the uprising led by General Urquiza against Rosas in 1851. The pronouncement by Urquiza was made at the pyramid located in the center of the **Plaza Francisco Ramírez**, where the casino and the **Basílica de la Inmaculada Concepción** are also located. The basilica was constructed in 1857 on the orders of Urquiza, who is buried here, and is noted in particular for its organ.

The city also has the **Museo Histórico Delio Panizza** (open daily), on Galarza and Supremo Entrerriano. Housed in a colonial residence, it contains a collection of colonial exhibits. Close to Concepción is the Banco Pelay beach and campground, with water sports and horseback riding.

Gualeguaychú ㉗, south of Concepción, is one of the largest cities in Entre Ríos province and is famous for its carnival, the largest in Argentina, which takes place during Lent. The city has an annual week-long carriage parade starting on October 12, considered a provincial festival. It also has folklore and horse-breaking shows throughout the year. The colonial city was sacked by the Italian nationalist Giuseppe Garibaldi in 1845, then residing in Uruguay and a supporter of anti-Rosas forces, and includes a number of interesting buildings such as the cathedral, located on Plaza San Martín, the **Museo de la Ciudad** (open Tues–Sun), on San Luis and Jujuy, and the **Museo Arqueológico** (open Mon–Sat), housed in the city's cultural center, on 25 de Mayo 734.

Just before the rail and road bridge at **Brazo Largo**, which crosses over to **Zárate** 140 km (87 miles) to the south, there is a side road east to **Paranacito**, a good place to get a feel for the marshy delta terrain. ❑

Map on page 230

The amount of concrete used in the construction of the Itaipú Dam (see page 236) is equivalent to building a two-lane highway from Lisbon to Moscow, according to company literature.

BELOW: yatay palms in Parque Nacional El Palmar.

THE NORTHWEST

Map on page 244

This extensive territory was home to Argentina's earliest settlers, and it contains some of the country's most rugged mountain landscapes

The northwest of Argentina is in large part a colorful, wind-sculpted high-altitude desert traversed by green river valleys. Blessed with as many minerals as rock colors, it is the epicenter of Argentina's colonial and pre-Columbian cultures; its elevation and dry, sunny climate have made it an ideal agricultural region for settlers over the past 10,000 years. The Calchaquí Valleys, named after one of the pre-Inca tribes that inhabited the region, occupy a 17,500-sq. km (6,800-sq. mile) area in the provinces of Salta, Catamarca, and Tucumán, that is home to small farmers and artisans. There are interesting yet modest ruins scattered throughout the Northwest, historical museums and monuments, traditional foods and music, and arts and crafts still made using ancient techniques. This is the most traditional region of Argentina, and the area where the size and influence of the indigenous population are still significant.

The Northwest comprises the provinces of Jujuy, Salta, Tucumán, Santiago del Estero, and Catamarca, which can be grouped into three distinct regions. The best-known are the *quebradas*, the arid, high *precordillera* (foothills of the Andes), characterized by multicolored desert hillsides, cacti and dry shrubs, deep canyons, and wide valleys. In stark contrast, the *yungas*, or subtropical mountainous jungle, are identified by dense vegetation, misty hillsides, and trees draped in vines and moss. Finally, there is the *puna*: cold, high-altitude and practically barren plateaux close to the Chilean and Bolivian borders.

PRECEDING PAGES: the church of El Carmen, Salta. **LEFT:** multicolored corn on the cob. **BELOW:** a typical church of the Northwest.

Salt flats and volcanoes

The southernmost region covered in this section, **Catamarca** offers stark geographical highlights. This province has the greatest altitude differences imaginable; toward Córdoba and Santiago del Estero in the east, the vast **Salinas Grandes** salt flats are barely 400 meters (1,300 ft) above sea level, while in the west, near the Chilean border, the **Ojos del Salado** volcano reaches the vertiginous height of 6,864 meters (22,520 ft), making it the highest active volcano in the world.

In the capital, **San Fernando del Valle de Catamarca ❶**, points of interest include the Catedral Basílica, containing the famous wooden Virgin of the Valley, discovered being worshiped by Amerindians in the 17th century; the convent of San Francisco; archeological and historical museums; and a permanent arts and crafts fair, best known for rugs and tapestries, located a few blocks from the center. The area around the central Plaza 25 de Mayo, including the Casa de Gobierno and the cathedral, is exceptionally pretty, with an attractive plaza full of citrus trees and views of the surrounding mountains.

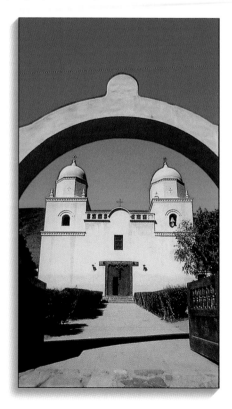

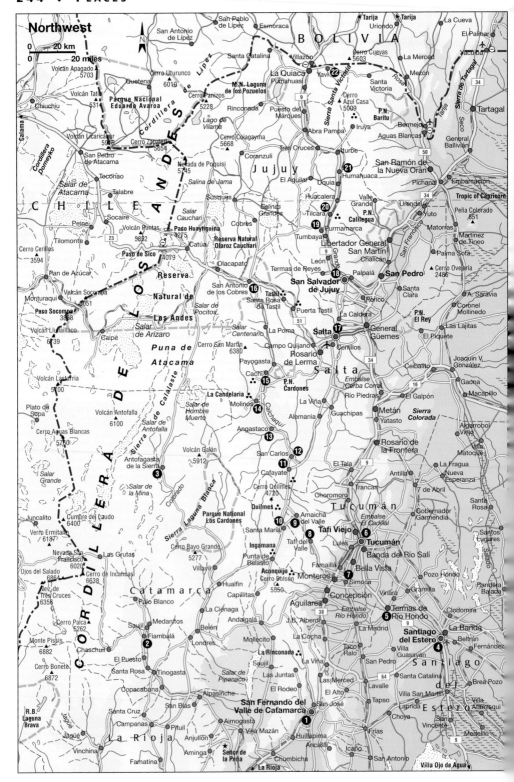

Around San Fernando del Valle de Catamarca

Map on page 244

The country around the capital is lovely, and several side trips are worth mentioning. Ruta 4 winds up north through hills and canyons, passing the two small towns of **El Rodeo** (37 km/23 miles) and **Las Juntas** (another 15 km/9 miles), both with services for visitors and recreational activities, including beach and water sports in a green valley setting. Heading east out of town on RN38 is the well-known **Cuesta El Portezuelo**, a winding road climbing out of the valley and up the lush mountainside, offering stunning views of the valley below.

Frozen stream beds on the puna.

Some 7 km (4 miles) to the north of the capital is **La Gruta de la Virgen del Valle**, where the Virgin of the Valley was discovered, and further along Ruta 32 is the **El Jumeal** dam *(dique)*, with fishing and a scenic view of the city. On Ruta 41, also north of the city, is a series of 19th-century chapels along the Río Valle, leading to the **Las Pirquitas** dam, forming a huge and beautiful lake used for fishing and water sports and offering spectacular views.

Time permitting, a trip to the old indigenous settlements scattered on RN40 is highly recommended. The road crosses the province through a series of valleys and riverbeds, surrounded by dusty mountains. These towns still give a strong impression of how they were hundreds of years ago, and their small museums, traditional chapels, and the spectacular landscape make for a worthwhile trip. The most visited of these towns are **Tinogasta**, **Belén**, and **Santa María**. Look for the thermal spas along the route, one of the most developed being at **Fiambalá** ❷, 48 km (30 miles) north of Tinogasta. Fiambalá, which is also famous for its woven ponchos, is an oasis surrounded by vineyards. Its thermal spa is located 15 km (9 miles) to the east of the town, in a ravine with waterfalls, and has been used for its curative waters since pre-Columbian times.

BELOW: vicuñas crossing a salt flat on the Altiplano.

For the adventurous, there is **Antofagasta de la Sierra** ❸, about 250 km (155 miles) north of RN40, located in the *puna* region of northern Catamarca. The remote Antofagasta is 3,500 meters (11,482 ft) above sea level and nearby are lagoons, volcanoes, and salt flats. High-quality textiles can be bought here, especially during March, when a craft and agricultural fair is held in the town.

Dusty flats

To the east of Catamarca lie the dusty flats of Santiago del Estero province. The capital of the province, bearing the same name, was founded by the Spanish in 1553, making it the oldest continuously inhabited city of the region. The city of **Santiago del Estero** ❹ is also home to the first university established in Argentine territory, and some very attractive colonial buildings remain near the central plaza.

There is not much to see in this region beyond *algarrobo* (carob) forests and cotton fields. However, there is one major attraction: **Termas de Río Hondo** ❺. Near an artificial lake, which offers a variety of sporting activities, the city and thermal spa of Río Hondo has developed into one of the most fashionable spas in Argentina, with upmarket (though not particularly good) restaurants, luxury hotels, and even convention facilities. Life here is as bustling in winter as it is on Mar del Plata's beaches in the summer months.

TIP

Running northwest of San Fernando, Ruta Nacional 40 and Ruta Provincial 43 leading to Antofagasta de la Sierra cross some of the remotest parts of the Northwest. Facilities are very limited and road conditions variable, so seek local advice before you set out.

A tropical garden

Not far north from Río Hondo the dusty desert gives way to a subtropical spectacle which surprises everybody who visits Tucumán for the first time. Here the almost endless aridity and scenic boredom of Santiago del Estero, Formosa, and the Chaco provinces is replaced abruptly by a cornucopia of tropical vegetation. It is for this reason that the province of Tucumán – the smallest of the 24 Argentine federal provinces – is popularly known as the Garden of the Republic. This climatic and visual contrast is most vividly marked along the Aconquija range, which has several peaks of more than 5,500 meters (18,000 ft). The intense greenery is juxtaposed with snowcapped peaks. The best time of year to visit is in winter (June–Aug), when the weather is usually warm and dry; in the summer months it is often stiflingly hot and heavy rains are common. Favored with copious rainfall, the province of Tucumán is one of the loveliest in Argentina. On the plains, farming and tobacco and sugar cane cultivation are the major economic activities. Around Tucumán, the provincial capital, one finds the smoky *ingenios* (sugar mills) which became in the 1830s the province's first industry and remain the principal economic source.

In addition to its very visible colonial past, **Tucumán ❻**, previously known as San Miguel de Tucumán, is the only city in the Northwest with a very large immigrant population, especially of Italian, Arab, and Jewish settlers. As a result, it has traditionally been a thriving commercial center with a pace of life more similar to Buenos Aires than to the slower-paced cities of the north. It was also the first industrial center in the Northwest which, together with its historical past as the main commercial center between Buenos Aires and Bolivia and Peru, make it a fairly cosmopolitan and very lively place.

BELOW: the sun-baked scenery around Salta.

The spacious **Parque 9 de Julio**, the baroque **Casa de Gobierno**, and several patrician edifices, together with a number of venerable churches, are reminders of the town's colonial past. This may best be appreciated by visiting the **Casa de la Independencia** (open Mon–Fri 9am–1pm and 4–6pm, Sat and Sun 9am–1pm). In a large room of this stately house, part of which has been rebuilt, the Argentine national independence ceremony took place on July 9, 1816.

Among the other museums worth a visit in Tucumán are those situated near the central **Plaza Independencia**: the **Museo Histórico de la Provincia** (open daily), located in the house of 19th-century president Nicolás Avellaneda; the **Museo Folklórico** (open daily), also including a craft shop and a restaurant; the **Museo Provincial de Bellas Artes** (open daily except Mon); and the **Casa Padilla** (open Mon–Fri), located next to the Casa de Gobierno, also offering crafts for sale.

The principal colonial churches in Tucumán are the **cathedral**, **San Francisco Church** (open daily), both located on the plaza; **Santo Domingo Church** (open Mon–Fri), on 9 de Julio and also operating as a school; and **La Merced**, on the corner of 24 de Septiembre and Las Heras, which houses a famous image of Tucumán's patroness, the Virgin of Mercy.

Local crafts and cooking

In the area near the main plaza and La Merced, on and around 24 de Septiembre, are various craft shops and a number of restaurants offering exquisite examples of regional cooking. The regional specialties include empanadas (meat pies) filled with diced beef, chicken, or occasionally tripe, as well as a number of

Tucumán's Casa de la Independencia puts on a nightly son et lumière show, re-enacting the city's key role in Argentina's independence (Wed–Mon 8.30pm).

BELOW: baking bread in a traditional adobe oven.

corn-based dishes such as *humita* (a stew made of corn, squash, onion, tomato, and spices), *locro* (a heavier corn-based stew which contains pig's feet and other cuts of pork and beef), and tamales (corn meal and shredded pork, wrapped in corn husks and boiled). In the artisans' shops, watch out for the black ceramics which are a regional tradition, often using pre-Inca designs, usually depicting the tatú, an animal similar to the armadillo.

Parque 9 de Julio

Some high-quality local handicrafts can be bought in Tucumán's craft fair.

Tucumán has a lively cultural output, with a fine university (most of whose buildings are located in the Parque 9 de Julio); a cultural center located on 25 de Mayo which offers daily lectures, debates, films and theatrical activities; a theater; and a casino. East of the city center is the elegant **Parque 9 de Julio**, designed by French landscape architect Carlos Thays in 1916, and including a lake, rose garden, polo ground, and show-jumping arena, theater, tennis club, an Italian garden, various cafes, and the house of Bishop Colombres, the early 19th-century bishop of Tucumán who founded the sugar industry. The house contains the **Museo de la Industria Azucarera** (open daily), which contains exhibits illustrating the process of sugar production. The beautiful park makes a relaxing break from the rather rushed pace of the city. However, care should be taken, especially after dark.

A few blocks to the south of the park is one of the most modern bus terminals in Argentina, which offers services to cities throughout the north and center of the country and as far afield as Buenos Aires. It also includes a shopping mall with restaurants and cinemas. An international airport is located 8 km (5 miles) east of town.

BELOW:
Tucumán Cathedral.

Side trips

However, it is not so much the town but its surroundings which make Tucumán worth an extended visit. Short excursions are highly recommended to **Villa Nougués** and to **San Javier**, high up in the Aconquija range. Both are summer resorts with hotel and restaurant facilities and splendid walks, and San Javier, at the top of the mountain, has a huge statue of Christ the Redeemer and a panoramic view. Both sites offer a splendid view of Tucumán, its outskirts, and the extensive sugar cane and tobacco fields. En route to Villa Nougués and San Javier, one passes through the pretty suburb of Yerba Buena, a rural setting where many of Tucumán's elite have their estates.

A visit to nearby **El Cadillal**, with its dam, artificial lake, archeological museum, and restaurants (where fresh *pejerrey* fish is served) is quite pleasant. Guided tours are available to some of the local sugar mills *(ingenios)*.

Once finished with the sightseeing tours in and around Tucumán, you may choose between two different roads to carry on toward the north. One choice is the main RN9, which passes by Metán and the Rosario de la Frontera spa and then winds through dense scrub forest and bushland to Salta and from there to Jujuy. But perhaps the better choice is to leave Tucumán, heading south. Passing through sugar cane fields, past several sugar mills, and the large town of Monteros, you come to **Simoca ❼**, "the sulky capital of Argentina," where on Saturdays the locals travel to town in their horse-drawn sulkies and offer produce, crafts, freshly prepared spices, and home cooking at a weekly fair which should not be missed.

From there, the road west travels toward **Acheral**. From Acheral, a narrow paved road starts climbing up through dense tropical vegetation, until it reaches a pleasant green valley, which is frequently covered by clouds. The winding road (not recommended for novice drivers) is spectacular, with lush vegetation, steep cliffs, waterfalls, and a river at the bottom of a ravine. Nearly half way to Tafí del Valle is a stopping place called **El Indio**, with a giant statue of an Amerindian, spectacular panoramic views, and a number of artisans, many offering high-quality craft items. The valley is dotted with tiny hamlets, the principal one being the old aboriginal and Jesuit settlement of Tafí del Valle.

Stone circles

Tafí del Valle ❽, situated in the heart of the Aconquija range at an altitude of 2,000 meters (6,600 ft), is considered the sacred valley of the Diaguitas, who, with different tribal names, inhabited the area. The valley is littered with clusters of aboriginal dwellings and dozens of sacred stone circles.

By far the most outstanding attractions at Tafí are the menhirs or standing stones. These stones, which sometimes stand more than 2 meters (6 ft) high, were assembled at the **Parque de los Menhires**, close to the entrance of the valley, by the government of General Antonio Bussi, moving them from their original positions when the La Angostura dam was built. The dam and lake are in an idyllic mountain setting. The town of Tafí itself, with a dry and cool mountain cli-

TIP

In spite of its relatively cool mountain climate, most businesses in the Northwest retain the siesta custom inherited from Spain, and close from noon until about 5pm.

BELOW: El Anfiteatro, an eroded river gorge near Cafayate.

Tucumán's patroness, the Virgin of Mercy, was made a General of the Argentine Army by General Manuel Belgrano because the Battle of Tucumán was won on the saint's day – September 24, 1812 – as a result of which La Merced Church where her image is kept still receives a general's salary from the army.

mate, is a favorite retreat for local residents, with beautiful views, coffee houses, and artisan crafts, foods (especially cheeses), and sweets.

From Tafí, a dusty gravel road winds up to **El Infiernillo** (Little Hell), at 3,000 meters (10,000 ft) above sea level. Just past this point the landscape changes dramatically once again, from rolling grass-covered mountains to the desert highlands.

Local tradition has it that at **Amaicha del Valle** ⑨, 56 km (35 miles) north of Tafí del Valle, the sun shines 360 days of the year. Some hotel owners are so fond of this bit of lore that they reimburse their guests if an entire visit should pass without any sun at all. The local hand-woven tapestries and the workshops certainly merit the visit. The town is a favorite vacation spot for residents of Tucumán, many of whom have weekend homes here. It has a permanent population almost exclusively of indigenous origin, which is the only indigenous community in Argentina to have been given the titles to its traditional lands (by the Perón government in the early 1970s).

Although Amaicha tends to be hot during the day throughout the year, the high altitude and sparklingly clear air make it cold at night even in summer: a sharp change in temperature which is refreshing and requires warm clothes, even at the height of summer.

In February every year, the traditional indigenous **Fiesta de la Pachamama** (Mother Earth Festival) is celebrated here, to give thanks for the fertility of the earth and livestock. An elderly local woman is chosen to play the part of the Pachamama, dressing up and offering wine to all participants. A recent rise in tourist interest has made the week-long festival somewhat more commercial, but it sticks to tradition and offers ritual ceremony, music, and dance.

BELOW: improvised seesaw.

Sun-blessed valleys

Leaving Amaicha to the south, you enter the colorful, sun-blessed **Santa María** and **Calchaquí** valleys, fertile landscapes fed by rivers of the same names. Together these valleys constituted one of the most densely populated regions of pre-Hispanic Argentina. Shortly after Amaicha, the road splits into two. To the left (the south) one soon reaches **Santa María ⑩** (in Catamarca province), with its variety of fine artisan products and wines, and its important red-pepper industry. In recent years the town has experienced a boom as a result of the huge Bajo La Alumbrera gold and copper mine nearby.

However, still better is to go straight ahead toward the north. Soon after you reach RN40 (the same RN40 recommended for exploring Catamarca, and Argentina's longest road), a short approach road leads to the archeological ruins of **Quilmes**, one of the country's most important indigenous sites *(see box on page 252)*.

The road goes on through forlorn villages like **Colalao del Valle** and **Tolombón** to **Cafayate**, leaving Tucumán province and crossing into Salta.

Shady patios

Though situated only 260 km/160 miles (about 3½ driving hours) from Tucumán, **Cafayate ⑪** should be earmarked in advance as a place to spend at least one night. There is more to Cafayate than the cathedral, with its rare five naves; its small museums of archeology and wine cultivation; its several bodegas (wine cellars), tapestry artisans, and silversmiths. It is the freshness of the altitude of 1,600 meters (5,300 ft) and the shade of its patios, overgrown with vines, that really enchant the visitor. The surroundings of this tiny colonial town

Map on page 244

The cardón *or* candelabra cactus, *a familiar site in the Northwest.*

BELOW: Parque de los Menhires, Tafí del Valle.

TIP

Some of the bodegas worth visiting around Cafayate are Etchart and Michel Torino, where guided tours and wine tastings are available.

BELOW:
Humahuaca,
Jujuy province.

are dotted with vineyards and countless archeological remains. In Cafayate, the exquisite white wines made from the Torrontés grape are produced, with guided tours of its vineyards a popular tourist attraction.

Two ways to Salta

There are two routes which lead from Cafayate to Salta. To the right, along RN68, the road winds through the colorful Guachipas Valley, also called **La Quebrada de Cafayate**. Along this valley, water and wind have carved from the red sandstone a vast number of curious formations which delight the traveler at every bend. It is a pleasant drive of less than four hours (about 180 km/ 112 miles), and is especially ideal for those who are in a hurry.

Others, who have more time and who are equally interested in natural beauty and history, could choose the longer route, following RN40. It snakes along the scenic **Calchaquí Valley**, which is irrigated by the Calchaquí, one of Argentina's longest rivers.

Every one of the many romantic villages along the Calchaquí Valley deserves at least a short sightseeing walk, in order to gain an appreciation of the fine colonial architecture and Hispanic art still largely preserved in this region. A stop at **San Carlos** ⑫, not far away from Cafayate, is especially worthwhile. This sleepy spot is said to have been founded no fewer than five times, first by the Spanish conquistadors as early as 1551, and later by waves of missionaries.

Soon after San Carlos the road becomes even more winding. From the chimneys of humble houses lining the way, the tempting aromas of traditional dishes is frequently perceivable. The traveler may smell *locro* and *puchero* (meat and vegetable stews), tamales *(see page 248)*, or *mazamorra* (a hot drink

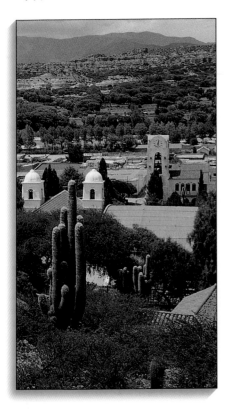

QUILMES

This vast stronghold of the Calchaquís, located in the Calchaquí Valley, near Santa María, once had as many as 200,000 inhabitants, and was the last indigenous site in Argentina to surrender to the Spanish, in 1667.

The Calchaquís were farmers cultivating a large area of land around the urban settlement, and they developed an impressively integrated social and economic structure. This undoubtedly helped their long resistance of the Spanish – both the invasion and conversion to Christianity.

Quilmes is a paradigm of fine pre-Hispanic urban architecture. Its walls of neatly set flat stones are still perfectly preserved, though the roofs of giant cacti girders vanished long ago. Local guides take the visitor to some of the most interesting parts of this vast complex, its fortifications (requiring quite a steep climb), its residential area, its huge dam, and its reservoir.

At the foot of the ruins is a small museum and a craft shop with very beautiful ceramics and tapestries for sale. The ruins are open daily from 9am–5pm, and within the complex there is a hotel and simple restaurant which is interesting for having maintained the architectural style and low profile of the ruins very successfully (although controversial for being built on part of the ruins themselves).

made from corn meal and sugar), as well as fragrant bread being baked in the adobe ovens that are hidden behind the dwellings.

The route briefly leaves the river bed and crosses the impressive **Quebrada de la Flecha**. Here, a forest of eroded sandstone spikes provides a spectacle, as the play of sun and shadow makes the figures appear to change their shapes. **Angastaco ⑬**, the next hamlet, was once an aboriginal settlement, with its primitive adobe huts standing on the slopes of immobile sand dunes. In the center there is a comfortable *hostería*. Angastaco lies amid extensive vineyards, though between this point and the north, more red peppers than grapes are grown.

Molinos ⑭, with its massive adobe church and colonial streets, is another quiet place worth a stop. *Molino* means mill, and one can still see the town's old water-driven mill grinding corn and other grains by the bank of the Calchaquí River. Across the river is an artists' cooperative, housed in a beautifully renovated colonial home, complete with a large patio, arches, and an inner courtyard. The local craftspeople sell only handmade goods, including sweaters, rugs, and tapestries. At **Seclantás** and the nearby hamlet of **Solco**, artisans continue to produce the traditional handwoven ponchos *de Güemes*, red and black blankets made of fine wool that are carried over the shoulders of the proud gauchos of Salta.

Cactus church

By far the loveliest place along the picturesque, twisting Calchaquí road is **Cachi ⑮**, 175 km (108 miles) north of Cafayate. Cachi has a very old church with many of its furnishings (altar, confessionals, pews, even the roof and the floor) made of cactus wood, one of the few building materials available in the area. Across the square lies the archeological museum (open Mon–Sat), prob-

Map on page 244

BELOW: eating out in Bermejo, near Salta.

The llama, sturdy beast of burden throughout the Andes.

a trail through Calilegua National Park.

ably the best of its kind in Argentina. With the permission of the museum's director, visitors are allowed into the vast aboriginal complex at **Las Pailas**, some 18 km (11 miles) away and partially excavated.

Here, as in Cafayate, you may decide to stay for more than just one night. An ACA *hostería* is situated magnificently atop a hill above old Cachi.

So clear is the air here that the mighty **Cerro Cachi** (6,300 meters/20,800 ft) seems to be within arms' reach. Inhabitants of this region are said to benefit from the crisp mountain air, and many live to a very old age.

For closer views of Mount Cachi and a glimpse of the beautiful farms and country houses, be sure to visit **Cachi Adentro**, a tiny village 6 km (4 miles) from Cachi proper. RN40 at this point becomes almost impassable, although you can visit the sleepy village of **La Poma**, 50 km (30 miles) to the north and partly destroyed by an earthquake in 1930. But the main tourist route runs to the east over a high plateau called **Tin-Tin**, the native terrain of the sleek, giant *cardón*, or candelabra cactus. The **Parque Nacional Los Cardones** was designated a national park in 1997 to protect the endangered and distinctive cactus.

Some 90 km (56 miles) to the north of La Poma is the town of **San Antonio de los Cobres** ⑯, although the road is in poor condition and frequently impassible in bad weather. The town is situated at an altitude of 3,775 meters (12,385 ft) and is on the route of the spectacular tourist train, El Tren a las Nubes *(see page 257–8).* Also nearby, on RN51, is the pre-Inca city of Santa Rosa de Tastil, discovered in 1903 and dating back to the 14th century. There is a small museum at the site, whose caretaker also offers guided tours around the ruins (open Tues–Sat 9am–5.30pm).

Down the spectacular **Cuesta del Obispo Pass**, through the multicolored

Quebrada de Escoipe and over the lush plains of the Lerma Valley the road stretches to Salta. From Cafayate to Salta, via Cachi, without stopovers, it is a demanding eight-hour drive.

Colonial gems

Salta ⑰, known as "Salta the beautiful," is probably the most seductive town of the Northwest, due both to its setting in the lovely Lerma Valley and to the eye-catching contrast of its old colonial buildings with its modern urban architecture. Salta is very proud – not to say snobbish – with respect to its colonial heritage, and many *salteños* consider themselves to be the only true criollos (native Argentines of Spanish parentage) "untainted" by generations of immigrants. The city is the most formal in dress and behavior in the region, and is the largest in northern Argentina, making it a good base to explore the area, which offers many opportunities for adventure tourism.

Salta has some valuable colonial gems, such as the Convento de San Bernardo (not open to the public), the Iglesia de San Francisco, and the Cabildo (city hall). The **catedral Ⓐ**, completed in 1882 and located on the Plaza 9 de Julio, houses the remains of heroes of the independence such as General Martín Miguel de Güemes. Opposite the cathedral on the plaza is the **Cabildo y Museo Histórico del Norte Ⓑ** (open Tues–Fri 9.30am–1.30pm and 3.30–8.30 pm), dating from 1626, which used to house the government of the viceroyalty until 1825. It was the seat of provincial government until the end of the 19th century. With its graceful row of arches, the Cabildo is particularly famous for the 16th-century statues of the Virgin Mary and *Cristo del Milagro* (Christ of the Miracle), washed up from a Spanish shipwreck on the Peruvian coast and credited

Maps:
Area 244
City 256

TIP

In the whole Northwest region many roads are impassable during the rainy summer season (approximately Christmas to Easter). Fall and spring (Apr–May and Sept–Nov) are the best times for a visit.

BELOW: traditional dance in the Calchaquí Valley.

with having performed miracles such as stopping a 1692 earthquake. The statues are paraded in a colorful procession every September 15th. The Cabildo also houses a very fine historical museum, which has ten rooms of archeological and colonial artefacts.

Art and history museums

Two blocks from the Cabildo, on the corner of Florida and Alvarado, is the **Museo de la Ciudad** **C** (open Mon–Fri 9am–1pm and 4–8pm, Sat 9am–1pm), once the residence of the Hernández family. Dating from 1870, it now houses the museum of the city of Salta. Also on Florida, at No. 20, is the **Museo de Bellas Artes** **D** (open daily 8.30am–1pm and 4.30pm–8pm, except Mon), located in the 18th-century Arias Rengel residence, the most important building left from the viceregal period. The house has been restored, and the museum has a fine collection of American art, in particular from local and Argentine artists, as well as paintings from the Jesuit Missions.

Another residence from the colonial period, the **Museo Uriburu** **E** (open daily except Mon), located on Caseros one block from San Francisco, has been renovated and houses a museum of the colonial era. Also in this area are a number of artisans' shops, primarily selling silver and alpaca products of high quality (the locally crafted silver, alpaca, and wooden maté holders are especially beautiful).

A few blocks further east of Museo Uriburu, on the corner of Caseros and Santa Fe, is the beautiful **Convento de San Bernardo** **F**. The convent, which is closed to visitors, has been occupied by the Carmelite Order since 1846, and is built around four cloisters with roofed galleries. The adjoining church is a

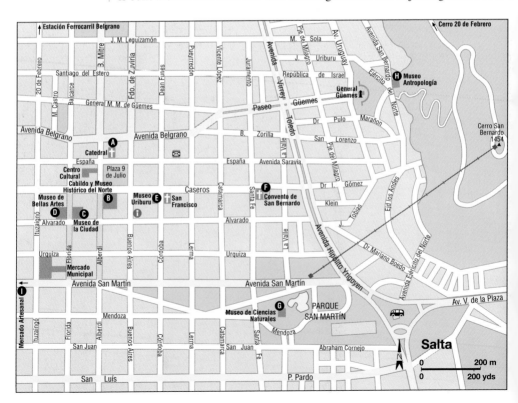

less elegant and more solid building, part of which remains from the original construction, which was destroyed by an earthquake in 1692, although the unadorned tower is thought to date from the 18th century.

Located a few blocks southeast of the Plaza 9 de Julio is the large **Parque San Martín**, which includes a statue by famous Tucumán sculptress Lola Mora; and at Mendoza 2, the **Museo de Ciencias Naturales** ⓖ (open daily) has exhibits of native plant and animal life from Salta and Jujuy, including examples of the tatú, a local type of armadillo, and of fossils of earlier fish and plant species.

The **Museo de Antropología** ⓗ (open daily except Sat), on Ejército del Norte and Polo Sur, contains a chronology of the cultural history of the Northwest and, in particular, an exhibition of pieces from Santa Rosa de Tastil, including weavings and a stone on which the "Tastil dancer" was carved. In 2004, a new museum, the **Museo de Arqueología de Alta Montaña** (MAAM; open 9am–1pm and 4–9pm) was opened on the main square. It contains the preserved bodies of three children sacrificed to the Inca gods, and all the objects they were buried with. Also well worth a visit is the **Mercado Artesanal** ⓘ (open daily 8am–8pm), located three blocks southwest of the Plaza 9 de Julio, with handicrafts by some of the indigenous tribes living in the vast province of Salta.

A superb view of the city can be enjoyed from atop **Cerro San Bernardo**, which can be reached by cable car from Parque San Martín; the cable car runs Mon–Fri 2–8pm, Sat–Sun 11am–1pm and 3–7pm.

A great railway journey

The **Tren a las Nubes** (train to the clouds) is now run purely for tourists, although it was closed for repairs during 2006 *(see page 258)*. As well as being

Maps:
Area 244
City 256

Convento de San Bernardo, Salta.

BELOW: the church of San Francisco, in Salta.

one of the highlights of Argentina, it is also one of the last remaining "great railway journeys" of South America. The train, fully equipped with dining car, bar, guide, and stewardess, leaves Salta's main station at 7 o'clock in the morning and enters the deep **Quebrada del Toro** gorge about an hour later. Slowly, the train starts to make its way up. The line is a true work of engineering art, and doesn't make use of cogs, even for the steepest parts of the climb. Instead, the rails have been laid so as to allow circulation by means of switchbacks and spirals. This, together with some truly spectacular scenery, is what makes the trip so fascinating.

After passing through **San Antonio de los Cobres**, the old capital of the former national territory, Los Andes, the train finally comes to a halt at **La Polvorilla Viaduct** (63 meters/207 ft high and 224 meters/739 ft long), an impressive steel span amid the breathtaking Andean landscape. At this point the train has reached an altitude of 4,197 meters (13,850 ft) above sea level. From here the train returns to Salta, where it arrives in the late evening, after a roundtrip of 272 km (169 miles), taking about 14 hours.

El Tren a las Nubes (train to the clouds) usually runs from March through October, but was recently closed for repairs and is due to re-open in 2007. Contact the Salta tourist office (see page 365) for further information.

Jungle retreat

Parque Nacional El Rey is located in the heart of the *yungas* or subtropical jungle region, 80 km (50 miles) east of Salta. It's a natural hothouse with tropical vegetation as dense and green as one can find almost anywhere in South America. Visitors who come to fish, study the flora and fauna, or just to relax, will find ample accommodations; there is a clean *hostería,* some bungalows, and a campground. The park is only accessible by car or prearranged transportation from Salta, and the best time to visit is between the months of May and October.

BELOW: Carnival in Purmamarca.

Jujuy

From Salta, a winding but wonderful mountain road, **La Cornisa**, takes you, in about an hour and a half, to **San Salvador de Jujuy** ⓲. Don't miss the extraordinary gilded pulpit in the **catedral** Ⓐ (open daily), carved by the local inhabitants. The cathedral dates from 1611, although most of the current building was completed in 1765 after being destroyed by an earthquake late in the 17th century. In addition to its famous pulpit, the cathedral has a beautiful chapel dedicated to the Virgin of the Rosary, as well as an outstanding 18th-century painting of the Virgin Mary. The tourist office is located nearby in the old railway station.

Among the other attractions of this colonial city are the **Casa de Gobierno** Ⓑ, across the **Plaza General Belgrano** from the cathedral. The classical building, completed in 1920, houses the first Argentine flag and coat of arms, created by independence hero General Belgrano and donated to the city in 1813. The Salón de la Bandera where the flag is on display is open Mon–Fri 8am–noon and 4–8pm. The front of the Casa de Gobierno has four statues, representing Peace, Liberty, Justice, and Progress, by Lola Mora, the Tucumán artist who was once director of plazas and parks in Jujuy. Facing the Casa de Gobierno is the **Cabildo y Museo Histórico Policial** Ⓒ, a 19th-century building re-constructed after it was destroyed by an earthquake in 1863. The Cabildo houses the city's police department and a small museum (open daily 8am–1pm and 3–9pm; free admission), which includes exhibits on the police's anti-drugs campaign.

Two blocks from the Cabildo, on Belgrano and Lavalle, is the beautiful church of **San Francisco** **D** (open daily 6.30am–noon and 5.30–9pm), situated on the site since the beginning of the 17th century, although the current building, maintaining the traditional style of Franciscan churches, dates from the 1920s. The church has a famous pulpit carved on the basis of traditional designs from Cusco in Peru and a notable wooden statue of St Francis – known locally as San Roque. Within the church is the **Museo de San Francisco** (open daily 8am–noon and 5–8.30pm), including the Stations of the Cross painted in Bolivia in 1780.

The local religious imagery is particularly notable for its rather gory nature, primarily because life for the indigenous communities who originally inhabited the area was so hard that early missionaries had to depict the sufferings of Christ and other religious figures in exceptionally horrific terms in order to make an impression on the locals. Statues in particular are prone to depict gaping and bloody wounds with more enthusiasm than is usually the case.

Among the other interesting museums in Jujuy are the **Museo Histórico Provincial** **E** (open Mon–Fri 8am–noon and 4–8pm, weekends 9am–1pm and 4–8pm), located in a 19th-century residence in which the hero of the Argentine union, General Lavalle, died in 1841 after his defeat by the federalists at the battle of Famaillá. The museum contains exhibits of 19th-century dress, as well as religious works of art, and a room is dedicated to the independence movement, including weapons captured in the battle of Suipacha.

Two blocks away, also on Lavalle, is the **Museo Arqueológico Provincial** **G**

Maps:
Area 244
City 260

Church bell tower, Casabindo.

BELOW: Easter procession in Tilcara for the Virgin of Copacabana.

TIP

A pleasant walk in the northern outskirts of Jujuy is to the road (Fascio) by the Río Grande, where some of the oldest and grandest homes in the city are located.

(open daily 9am–noon and 3–9pm), where exhibits including stone, ceramic, and metal objects from the region are on display. The oldest church in Jujuy is **Capilla de Santa Bárbara** Ⓖ dating from 1777 and including a collection of 18th-century religious paintings. Two blocks away, on Calle Lamadrid, is the **Teatro Mitre** Ⓗ, constructed in 1901. The Italian-style theater was restored in 1979. Two blocks to the east is the Mercado Municipal. The French-style railway station is located two blocks from the Plaza Belgrano, on Gorriti and Urquiza, while the bus terminal is a few blocks south of the Río Chico Xibi Xibi at the corner of Iguazú and Dorrego.

City park

Several blocks to the west of the plaza is the **Parque San Martín** Ⓘ, the city's only park which, although smaller than those of other Argentine cities, contains a swimming pool as well as a housing complex and a restaurant, La Mirage. Near to the park, on Bolivia 2365, is the **Museo de Mineralogía** (open Mon–Fri 9am–1pm), which belongs to the provincial university's geology and mining faculty. The museum includes exhibits of the mineral wealth of the province, detailing the history of its tin- and iron-mining tradition as well as its gold deposits.

A few miles from town, one can visit the **Termas de Reyes** spa, located in a narrow valley. The visit offers beautiful views of the city and of mountains and lakes in the area, as well as the opportunity to indulge in thermal bathing. Nearby is the Parque Provincial Potrero de Yala, a quiet spot amidst the lakes much favored by residents of the city.

Parque Nacional Calilegua occupies 76,000 hectares (188,000 acres) in the east of Jujuy province. Calilegua is primarily tropical *yunga* forest, like El Rey, although as the altitude climbs the topography changes to mountain jungle,

BELOW: fresh produce at Jujuy's Mercado Municipal.

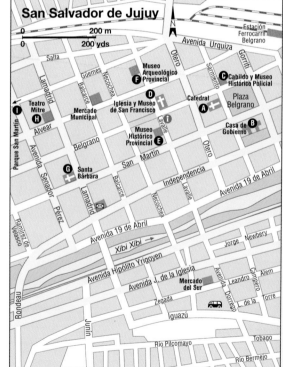

mountain forest, and eventually mountain plains. The park has a campsite, several rivers, and a wide range of wildlife, including wild boar and jaguars, in an exceptionally diverse ecosystem. In 2000, environmental groups lost their fight to stop a gas pipeline being constructed through the park.

Maps:
Area 244
City 260

The colorful Quebrada

RN9 climbs steadily up, and before long, the sun breaks through. Here, a wide and highly distinctive *quebrada* (gorge) is dominated by the Río Grande. This river receives torrential and often destructive rains in the summer, when the colors of the valley wall become more intense and delineated. The **Quebrada de Humahuaca** valley has been used for 10,000 years as an important passage for transporting both people and ideas between the Andean highlands and the plains of Jujuy below. In 2003 it was made a World Heritage Site.

Purmamarca ⓲ is a tiny village with the striking **Cerro de los Siete Colores** (Hill of the Seven Colors) towering behind the old adobe church. Around the shady square, local vendors sell wood carvings, handwoven carpets, and herbs to cure every possible ailment. After a short ride you come to **Tilcara ⓴**, famous for its huge pre-Columbian *pucará* (stronghold), built on a hill in the middle of the valley. The **Museo Arqueológico** (open daily) on the main plaza has a pre-Inca mummy and various other artifacts from Bolivia, Chile, and Peru. There is also a botanical garden, with specimens from the *puna* (high plateau).

At **El Angosto de Perchel** the Quebrada narrows to less than 200 meters (650 ft) and then opens into a large valley. Wherever the available water is used for irrigation, tiny fields and orchards give a touch of fresh green to the red and yellow shades of the river banks.

Floral painting from Tilcara's Easter festivities.

BELOW: a cemetery in the Quebrada de Humahuaca.

Map on page 244

TIP

South of Humahuaca, at Huacalera, a monument marks the exact point of the Tropic of Capricorn (23 degrees and 27 minutes south of the Equator).

BELOW: Iglesia de Candelaria, Humahuaca.
RIGHT: El Tren a las Nubes, Salta.

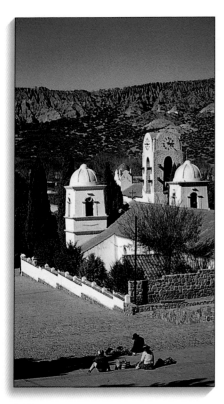

Desert chapels

Further up the valley lies the town of **Humahuaca ㉑**, which gives its name to the whole gorge. Previously an important railway stopover on the way up to Bolivia, it has suffered badly from the closure of the railway. Humahuaca lies at almost 3,000 meters (9,000 ft), so move very slowly to avoid running out of breath. Also avoid eating heavily or drinking alcohol prior to ascending: a cup of sweet tea is more beneficial at this altitude. Here one finds stone-paved and extremely narrow streets, vendors of herbs and produce near the former railway station, and an imposing monument commemorating the Argentine War of Independence. The museum of local customs and traditions is worth a visit. Most travelers pay only a short visit to this fascinating place, but a stay of several days is truly worthwhile, as many side trips can be made from here.

Some 9 km (6 miles) outside the town are the extensive archeological ruins of **Coctaca**. The true significance of this site is still largely unknown although scientists are studying it, and its secrets may soon be revealed. Other options include a journey to **Iruya**, a hamlet cradled amid towering mountains, 75 km (47 miles) from Humahuaca. An even more adventurous trip would be to **Abra Pampa** and from there to the **Monumento Natural Laguna de los Pozuelos**, where you can see huge flocks of the spectacular Andean flamingo, and vicuña herds grazing near the road. Near Abra Pampa there is a huge vicuña farm.

Here in the heart of the Altiplano or *puna* (with an average altitude of 3,500 meters/11,500 ft), are some of the most interesting villages in the Northwest, in a region inhabited for thousands of years before the arrival of the Spanish, and occupied by the Incas during the expansion of their empire southward from Bolivia. Many of the isolated villages have surprisingly large and richly decorated colonial churches, including those at Casabindo, Cochinoca, Pozuelos, Tafna, and Rinconada, which can all be reached by small access roads that wind through the peaceful countryside. RN9 continues all the way to **La Quiaca**, at the Argentine border, opposite the Bolivian town of Villazón. This has also suffered with the closure of the railway, but still has a colorful market.

Glowing gilding

Finally, as if saved for a happy ending to this excursion, there remains one of the most sparkling jewels of Argentina: the ancient **Iglesia de Nuestra Señora del Rosario y San Francisco**, in Yavi.

The tiny village of **Yavi ㉒**, on the windy and barren high plateau near the Bolivian border, lies protected in a small depression, about 15 km (9 miles) by paved road to the east of La Quiaca. Between the 17th and 19th centuries, Yavi was the seat of the Marqués de Campero, one of the wealthiest Spanish feudal possessions in this part of the continent. Though the chapel here was originally built in 1690, one of the later marquesses ordered the altar and pulpit to be gilded. The thin alabaster plaques covering the windows create a soft lighting which makes the gilding glow (open Tues–Sun 9am–noon and 3.30–6pm). This precious historical monument makes a fine conclusion to a rewarding journey through the plains and valleys and over the mountains of the Northwest. ❑

THE CUYO

The west-central area of Argentina is its main wine-growing region. It is also the location of whitewater rafting activities, fashionable ski resorts, and South America's highest peak, Aconcagua

Map on page 268

A rgentina is the fifth-largest wine producer in the world, and the Cuyo is the heart of that industry. The vines are nurtured by the melting snows of the Andes, and the mountains themselves add colorful drama to the scene. While the grape harvest takes place in March, a visitor at any time of the year can tour the bodegas (wine cellars) and sample the excellent wines. The cities of the area are some of Argentina's oldest, and although most have been rebuilt in modern times to repair damage caused by earthquakes, you can still learn a lot about Argentine history in the many regional museums. Opinions differ as to exactly what area is covered by the Cuyo, but in this section we include all the provinces from Mendoza in the south, through San Luis, to San Juan and La Rioja in the north.

Nestling high in the Andes is Aconcagua, the highest mountain in the world outside Asia. There are also numerous ski resorts in the area, most notably Las Leñas, which is becoming increasingly popular as an off-season vacation and competition site for skiers from the Northern Hemisphere. Mendoza's mountains and rushing white-water rivers have made it an adventure center attracting mountain climbers, rafters, hikers, and trail riders from around the world.

San Juan's wines are generally of lower price and quality than those of its neighbor Mendoza. Other points of interest in this province are the shrine to La Difunta Correa and the Reserva Provincial San Guillermo, home to guanacos, vicuñas, rheas, and condors. The largest nature reserve in the region is the Reserva Provincial Ischigualasto, which incorporates the Valle de la Luna and the Parque Provincial Talampaya in neighboring La Rioja province. You will find these and many more scenic attractions along the winding mountain passes and tree-lined country roads of the Cuyo.

PRECEDING PAGES: a shady road outside Mendoza. **LEFT:** the Cuyo's Andean backdrop. **BELOW:** a vineyard owner shows off his raw materials.

Colonial history

In the mid-16th century the Spanish colonies along the western coast of South America sought to expand their territories beyond the Andes, to the east, in what is today Argentina. They were driven by reports that these lands held a vast wealth of gold, similar to what had been found further to the north. Several of the early Chilean efforts at settlement were wiped out by repeated Amerindian attacks. Conquistadors from Peru had better luck, staking their claims to the north. In 1553, Francisco de Aguirre founded Santiago del Estero for the Spanish viceroyalty of Peru. It is the oldest surviving settlement in all of Argentina *(see page 37)*.

The explorers from Peru went on to found the towns of San Miguel de Tucumán (on a site earlier established by the explorers from Chile), Salta, and Xiu

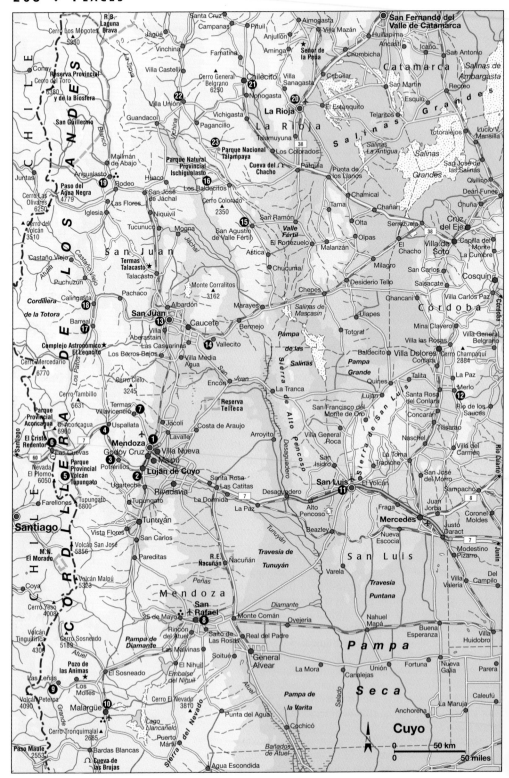

Xiu (Jujuy). The Chileans were finally successful in establishing their domain further to the south, in the Cuyo region, parallel to Chile's central valley. Although this eastern side of the Andes was barren and arid (Cuyo means "desert land" in the dialect of the local Huarpe indigenous culture), it was cut through by rivers flowing down from the high Andean peaks.

Map on page 268

First cities

The first permanent settlement in the Cuyo was established at Mendoza, a site chosen for its location across from Santiago at the eastern end of the Uspallata Pass, the major access through the Andes in the region. Pedro de Castillo founded the town in 1561, and named it for Hurtado de Mendoza, the governor of Chile. Not long after, the town was relocated several miles to the north.

In 1562, Juan Jufre founded San Juan, to the north of Mendoza, and a third town, San Luis, was started to the east, in 1598.

The Spanish Crown established the eastern viceroyalty of Río de la Plata in 1776 to accommodate the growing importance of the port of Buenos Aires. At this time, the Cuyo and the Peruvian holdings to the north passed to the jurisdiction of the new territory. However, the Cuyo remained isolated from the east for many years, and its strongest economic and cultural ties were with central Chile.

The isolation was broken in 1884, with the completion of the transcontinental railroad, and today the region is well integrated into the Argentine economy. It is the center of the country's wine industry, and a whole array of fruits and vegetables are grown for national markets. The area has also proved to be rich in mineral wealth, although not in the gold that the early explorers had hoped to find.

The region is the major supplier for the nation's vital petroleum industry, and uranium, copper, and lead mines are scattered throughout the mountains. One of the principal sources of provincial income in Mendoza is hydroelectricity; there are several hydroelectric projects, and the reservoirs created by the dams have made this a popular recreational area.

An Inca mummy, found in Panquegua, near Mendoza, is kept at the city's Museum of Natural History and Anthropology.

BELOW:
Mendoza in the mid-19th century.

Mendoza

Today, the Cuyo comprises the provinces of Mendoza, San Juan, San Luis, and La Rioja. The largest city is **Mendoza ❶**, with a total population of around 1 million inhabitants, located 1,060 km (659 miles) due west of Buenos Aires. Little remains today of the town's original colonial architecture.

The whole region is periodically racked by earthquakes, some of them quite severe. One such quake, in 1861, killed 10,000 and completely leveled Mendoza, and rebuilding was done with an eye to averting further disaster. Another in January 1985 left 40,000 homeless. The last major quake happened in 1997.

In spite of Mendoza's relatively modern appearance, it has a long history, of which its residents are very proud. It was from here, in 1817, that General San Martín launched his march with 40,000 men across the Andes to liberate Chile and Peru. The wine industry began in earnest in the mid-19th century, with the arrival of many Italian and French immigrants. This was due in large part to the progressive thinking

Snacks on wheels in Mendoza.

of a series of Mendozan governors who took positive steps to attract immigrants. Among other things, they paid agents at the port of Buenos Aires for each immigrant transported to the province; in particular, qualified engineers and vintners who were responsible both for designing the irrigation system that made cultivation possible in the desert province, and for the planting of vineyards and the construction of wineries. The strength of the wine industry, which has reached world-class standard for fine wines, is reflected in the annual grape harvest festival (Festival de la Vendimia), held in early March and featuring a beauty contest, fireworks, dances, and son et lumière shows in an Andean setting. Although wine remains a substantial part of the economy, it was the growth of the petroleum industry in the 1950s that brought real prosperity to the city.

Mendoza is much closer to the Chilean capital, Santiago, than to Buenos Aires, and with the cheap Argentine peso, many thousands of Chileans come to Mendoza on weekend shopping trips.

A clean and cultured city

While Mendoza is nothing like the metropolis that is Buenos Aires, it has its own charms, and a wealth of cultural activity. Transplanted residents from the capital boast a happy conversion to the more relaxed pace of Mendoza. *Mendocinos* often claim that the province is the most civilized in the country, with an unusually modernist and democratic tradition based on the concept that the successful development of the province is the result of the efforts of the inhabitants, rather than of the generosity of nature. The city is arguably the cleanest and certainly one of the most modern in the country, nestled at the foot of the mountains and offering a wide range of cinemas, theaters, concert halls, and other cultural activities.

BELOW: a blaze of lupins brightens up a city park.

The waters of the region have been put to good use, and the arid landscape has been transformed into a lush oasis. Some of the irrigation channels dug by the original Amerindian inhabitants are still in use, and many more have been added since. The city's low buildings lie along wide, tree-lined streets where channels of running water keep the temperature an agreeable measure below that of the surrounding dry lands, although in summer Mendoza has an extremely hot, desert climate. Even in winter, when the *zonda* windstorms sweep the city, the temperature can rise to Saharan levels.

Many homes have well-tended gardens, and there are parks throughout the city that serve the dual interests of recreation and safety in case of an earthquake. In the midst of the plentiful shade, it is astonishing to realize that all the millions of trees have been planted by the city's residents and developers. Not one of the poplars, elms, or sycamores is native to the region. Beyond and above all this greenery, to the west lie the Andes, which provide Mendoza with a spectacular backdrop of changing hues throughout the day and night.

Theaters and museums

At the center of the city of Mendoza is the **Plaza Independencia**. Several important buildings flank the

Map below

plaza; the oldest is the **Legislatura Provincial** (provincial legislature), which dates from 1889. Opposite this, on the northwestern corner is the 1925 **Teatro Independencia**, where theatrical and musical performances are held. In the center of the plaza, located underground, are the **Museo Municipal de Arte Moderno Ⓐ** (open Mon–Sat 9am–1pm and 4–9pm), a small gallery exhibiting modern works by local artists, with occasional temporary exhibitions; and the Teatro Municipal Julio Quintanilla, which puts on theatrical performances at weekends. Around the corner, at Sarmiento and 25 de Mayo, is the provincial **casino**, part of the same complex as the Teatro Independencia and Plaza Hotel. There is also an artisans' market on the eastern side of the plaza, facing Calle Patricias Mendocinas, where crafts are on sale Friday to Sunday.

Running east from the plaza, past the provincial legislature and the stock exchange, is the pedestrian Paseo Sarmiento, a lively place in the evening, with a number of attractive shops and outdoor cafes, populated by occasional street musicians. This leads to Avenida San Martín, Mendoza's main street.

Mendoza has a good selection of museums and other sites of interest. The **Museo del Pasado Cuyano Ⓑ** (open Tues–Sat 9am–1pm), located at Montevideo 544, two blocks south of Plaza Independencia and housed in a residence dating from 1873, includes the Historical Studies Board, as well as an exhibition on General San Martín, a collection of artifacts from Mendoza's history, a series of religious art and an arms collection. Archeology, anthropology, and paleontology buffs should enjoy the **Museo de Ciencias Naturales y Museo Arqueológico Ⓒ** (open daily except Mon), located outside the city center in Parque San Martín, at Las Tipas and Prado Español. The museum contains some pre-Columbian ceramics, along with a small folkloric collection, and includes

Monument to General San Martin in El Manzano Histórico in Tunuyán, south of Mendoza.

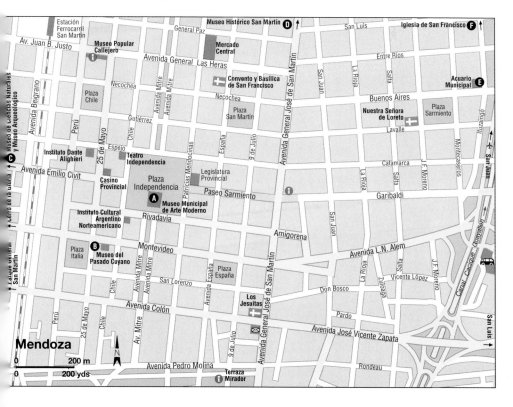

If you want a break from sightseeing, Las Heras is the place for shopping. Or pull up a chair at one of the shady sidewalk cafes clustered in the city center; most of these have good fast food, and some offer pitchers of *clérico*, the Argentine version of sangría, made with white wine.

BELOW: taking it easy in Mendoza's Parque San Martín.

archeological and zoological collections. The **Museo Histórico San Martín** **D** (open Mon–Fri 9am–12:30pm), at Avenida San Martín 1843, houses a collection dedicated to the General and his accomplishments.

Located underground at the junction of Ituzaingó and Buenos Aires, south of Parque O'Higgins, is the **Acuario Municipal E** (open daily 9am–9pm). The aquarium has one of the most important collections of fresh- and salt-water fish in Latin America, including species from both the Atlantic and Pacific, and aquatic animals such as giant sea turtles. The aquarium breeds some rare species not usually bred in captivity, and it makes a very interesting visit, especially for children.

Shady plazas

Mendoza has a number of plazas, of which the **Plaza España** is probably the most attractive. Donated by the Spanish Government in the 1940s, the Plaza España recreates an Andalusian square, complete with fountains and painted tiles imported from Spain; tile scenes include depictions of the founding of Mendoza in 1561. The plaza is one of four which form an extended square some three blocks distant from the Plaza Independencia, the others being Plaza Italia, Plaza Chile, and Plaza San Martín. The latter is located in the heart of the banking district, and has tall, shady trees and a statue of the Liberator. To the east of the city center, located near the aquarium and snake house, and two blocks south of the Parque Bernardo O'Higgins and the Teatro Municipal Gabriela Mistral, is another square, **Plaza Sarmiento**, flanked on its southwestern side by the Nuestra Señora de Loreto Church, which was rebuilt after being destroyed by an earthquake in 1861, and renovated in 1957.

North of Plaza Sarmiento, the **Plaza Pedro de Castillo**, formerly the Plaza Mayor, marks the site of the original, 16th-century city center, now preserved as the Area Fundacional. On the northwestern side of the plaza are the ruins of the **Iglesia de San Francisco** . Founded by the Jesuits in the 18th century as the Iglesia de Loreto, the church was destroyed by a massive earthquake in 1861, which flattened the whole city. Also on this plaza is the **Museo Histórico del Area Fundacional** (open Mon–Sat 8am–8pm, Sun 3–10pm), a comprehensive, modern museum containing exhibits and models of the original city and other archeological objects.

In this desert climate, hot summer days are followed by pleasantly cool nights, and there are restaurants which offer dining alfresco. **La Bodega del 900**, on the outskirts of town, has a dinner show on its patio, and a small wine museum in its cellar. There are several cafes and nightclubs perched along the foothills to the west. One of the most pleasant of these is **Le Per**, open until quite late, with its patio overlooking Mendoza.

Parque San Martín

On the western edge of the city lies **Parque San Martín**, crowned by the Cerro de la Gloria. Located at the foot of the Andes, the 420-hectare (1,038-acre) park has facilities for a wide variety of sports, including a soccer stadium built for the 1978 World Cup and a yacht club with an artificial lake. It was designed by French landscape architect Carlos Thays at the end of the 19th century, and has fine statues (most of them copies of well-known French sculptures); it also houses the Universidad Nacional del Cuyo. Further up the hill is the **Jardín Zoológico** (city zoo; open Tues–Sun 9am–6pm), with shaded walkways between open-air cages, which are pleasantly set among ponds, caves, and rockeries. The zoo contains some 700 animals, both indigenous and foreign species, including orangutans and lions.

At the top of the **Cerro de la Gloria** sits an ornate statue, the **Monumento al Ejército Libertador**, complete with bolting horses and Liberty breaking her chains. A bas-relief around the statue's base depicts various scenes of the liberation campaigns. The site also provides an excellent overview of Mendoza.

Behind the hill, in the southwestern corner of the park, is the **Teatro Griego Frank Romero Day**, an amphitheater built in 1940, and site of many of the city's celebrations, including the grand spectacle of the Festival de la Vendimia (Grape Harvest Festival). First held in 1963, this important festival takes place every year in March, and lasts over three or four days. During the first few days there are street performances and parades, and a queen of the harvest is chosen. The finale is a somewhat overproduced extravaganza, with dancing, fireworks, and moving light shows. This is Mendoza's annual opportunity to show off its hard-earned wealth.

Just to the south of Mendoza, in the town of **Luján de Cuyo** ❷, is the Museo Provincial de Bellas Artes Emiliano Guiñazú, on Avenida San Martín 3651 (Mar–Oct, Tues–Fri 9am–6:30pm; Sat and Sun 3–7:30 pm). The museum is known as the Casa de Fader as it was inau-

Maps:
Area 268
City 271

TIP

There are several tourist information offices around Mendoza; the main Centro Municipal de Información Turística, a kiosk at the corner of San Martín and Garibaldi, is quite helpful (open Mon–Fri 9am–12.30pm and 4–8pm).

BELOW: Maipú, outside Mendoza.

Frieze of the grape harvest, Luján de Cuyo.

gurated on the birth date of Spanish painter Fernando Fader, who lived in Mendoza for some years in the early part of the 20th century. Fader's murals decorate some of the walls of the museum, formerly the summer residence of Emiliano Guiñazú. The museum includes formal gardens, as well as collections of foreign and Argentine artists, local landscape painters, and an exhibit of Fader's work.

Mendoza's bodegas

Scattered across the fertile plain around Mendoza are nearly 2,000 different vineyards, some of which are small family operations, others huge and foreign-owned. All of this cultivation is made possible through an extensive network of irrigation channels, originally laid in pre-Columbian times and extended during the colonial era. The area is blessed with a heady combination of plentiful water, sandy soil, a dry climate, and year-round sunshine, which makes for enormous grape yields.

The first vines were planted in the Cuyo by Jesuit missionaries in the 16th century, but production really took off in the mid-1800s with the arrival of Italian and French immigrants. Many of them simply worked as laborers in the fields, but a knowledgeable few contributed European expertise that greatly refined the industry. Toward the end of the 19th century, Mendoza was finally linked by rail with Buenos Aires and, by the 1920s, with the opening up of many more vineyards, the region had become one of the world's leading wine producers.

A number of vineyards are right on the outskirts of Mendoza. Tours can be arranged through a travel agent, but a more pleasant way to make the rounds is by getting a map, renting a car, and finding them yourself *(see page 284)*. This provides the opportunity to meander down the lovely country lanes lined with

BELOW: the pass at Villavicencio.

poplars and wildflowers, and to get a sense of the Cuyo's lifestyle. Local cycling fanatics come out in packs and, with luck, you might even catch sight of old men playing a lazy afternoon game of *bocci* (bowls). In Maipú, some 15 km (8 miles) southeast of Mendoza, there is the **Museo Nacional del Vino** (National Wine Museum) in a building that originally belonged to the Giol winery.

Map on page 268

Daytrip to Chile

One of the most spectacular trips to be made from Mendoza is up the **Uspallata Pass** to the border with **Chile**. It is an all-day excursion of some 210 km (131 miles), passing through the flat, irrigated oases and climbing to over 3,000 meters (9,840 ft) beyond Puente del Inca, in the shadow of Cerro Aconcagua. Organized tours are available from Mendoza, but hiring a car will allow you to avoid being herded around. Either way, you should start early in the morning to allow enough time to see all the sights en route.

However, unless you're carrying on through Chile, driving independently is only recommended outside the winter months (July–Sept). Although the roads are paved throughout, conditions in the upper reaches are often icily treacherous during these months, and snow and rock slides are common.

At any time of year it is worth taking some warmer clothes for these cooler altitudes. Also be aware that altitude sickness can be a problem, as you climb from 750 meters to 2,500 meters (2,500 ft to 8,200 ft). Those requiring visas for Chile should get them in Mendoza, as they will not be issued at the border.

You begin the trip by heading south from Mendoza on Route 7 to **Luján**. Turning right at the town square, you get onto Highway 7, which carries you up into the pass. This stretch of road, the Camino de los Andes, is part of the vast

La Virgen de la Carrodilla, patron of the grape harvest.

BELOW: the Puente del Inca, a natural rock bridge.

Pan-American Highway. Throughout the centuries, even before the time of the Incas, the pass was used to cross the mountains.

Immediately the landscape becomes more barren as you leave behind the irrigated greenery of the lowlands to follow the Mendoza River up the valley. Trees give way to scrub and the occasional bright flower.

The first spot you will pass in the valley is the **Cacheuta Hot Springs**, located at a lovely bend in the river in the grounds of the Centro Climático Termal Cacheuta (Cacheuta Thermal Springs Center).

Thirteen km (8 miles) beyond is **Potrerillos ❸**, a scenic oasis where many *mendocinos* have summer homes to escape the heat. The **Potrerillos Hotel** has terraced gardens overlooking the valley, along with a swimming pool and facilities for tennis and horseback riding. There is also a campsite nearby. Up from Potrerillos, at the end of a side road, is the ski resort of **Vallecitos**, reputedly the oldest in Argentina. The resort is open from July through September. Continuing up the valley for another 105 km (65 miles), you reach the town of **Uspallata ❹**, set in a wide meadow. Further up again, the valley widens at Punta de Vacas (Cattle Point), where long ago the herds were rounded up to be driven across to Chile. It is at Punta de Vacas that you submit documentation if wishing to continue across the border. About 10 km (6 miles) beyond Punta de Vacas lies the ski resort of **Villa Los Penitentes**, which has a ski school, and several hotels and restaurants. Buses bring skiers up for day trips from July through September. Across the valley is the strange formation for which the resort is named; tall rock outcroppings look like hooded monks ("the penitents") ascending toward the cathedral-like peak of the mountain. In winter, windswept ice on the rocks heightens the illusion.

The Potrerillos Hotel was the base for the Dutch soccer team during the 1978 World Cup, hosted (and won) by Argentina.

BELOW: the Río Mendoza, near Potrerillos.

Aconcagua

Off to the left of the road, a few kilometers further on, is a desolate, melancholy sight: the Cementerio de los Andinistas is a small graveyard for those who have died in the attempt to scale nearby Cerro Aconcagua. A couple of kilometers beyond this is the **Puente del Inca**, a natural stone bridge made colorful by the sulfurous deposits of the bubbling hot springs beneath it. There is a hostel used particularly by Aconcagua expeditions, as well as gift stalls selling an unusual line in souvenirs – objects solidified in the mineral waters.

Just a few kilometers up the road lies the most impressive sight of the whole excursion. There is a break in the wall of rock and, looking up the valley to the right, you can see the towering mass of **Aconcagua**, at 6,962 meters (22,840 ft) the highest peak in the Western Hemisphere. The mountain is at the center of the Parque Provincial Aconcagua, an important nature reserve. Another important trekking site is **Parque Provincial Volcán Tupungato 5**, located just south of Puente del Inca and dominated by the 6,800-meter (22,310-ft) Tupungato Volcano, surrounded by glaciers and also served by organized treks.

Aconcagua means "stone watchtower" in the Huarpe dialect. It is perpetually blanketed in snow, and its visible southern face presents a tremendous 3,000-meter (10,000-ft) wall of sheer ice and stone. The clear mountain air creates the illusion that Aconcagua lies quite close to the road, but the peak is actually 45 km (28 miles) away. You can walk as far as **Laguna de los Horcones**, a green-colored lake at the mountain's base. Most expeditions tackle the northern face. The best time to attempt the climb is mid-January to mid-February. Further information can be obtained in Mendoza at the Club Andinista on F.L. Beltrán 357 (tel: 0261-4319 870), or on the Aconcagua website (www.aconcagua.com).

The statue of El Cristo Redentor, *on the Argentine-Chilean border, was transported in pieces by rail from Buenos Aires, and made the last leg of its journey by mule.*

Christ the Redeemer

The last sight to see before heading back is the statue of Christ, which marks the border with Chile. On the way there, the road passes the town of **Las Cuevas**, where the road branches. To the right is the tunnel for road and rail traffic to Chile (passenger rail service has been suspended due to lack of customers). To the left is the old road to Chile, which climbs steeply over rock and gravel to **La Cumbre Pass**, at an altitude of 4,200 meters (13,800 ft). At the top is the 8-meter (26-ft) high statue of **El Cristo Redentor 6**, erected in 1904, in commemoration of an international border pact signed with Chile. It is most interesting for the bits of colored rag tied onto it by visitors, in hopes of having prayers answered. The best reward for having made it up this far is the view over the mountains. In every direction, the raw steep peaks of the Andes reach up, the tips still catching the late-afternoon sun. The perfect cap for the journey is to catch sight of a condor soaring at this lonely altitude, so keep your eyes open.

BELOW: the south summit of Cerro Aconcagua.

Jet-set skiers

Another day trip from Mendoza is to **Villavicencio 7**, the hot-spring spa 45 km (28 miles) to the northwest

River rafting on the Río Mendoza is suitable for all ages, with no experience necessary. Day trips are organized by several agencies in Mendoza.

BELOW: off-piste skiing at Las Leñas.

along Ruta 5, with many hotels and baths. Villavicencio also produces some of Argentina's best-known mineral water.

If you're heading south toward Patagonia, it is worth stopping at the agricultural oasis of **San Rafael** ⑧, some 240 km (150 miles) south of Mendoza. Nearby hydroelectric projects have created reservoirs, which have become centers for vacationers. San Rafael is Mendoza's second-largest city, as well as one of its most modern. Like in the city of Mendoza, local residents have kept the desert at bay through planting hundreds of trees and creating parks. The city is on the Río Diamante; there is a park and campsite with a small zoo on an island in the middle of the river, as well as the **Museo Histórico Natural**, a small but eclectic museum with five rooms on botany and zoology, geology, anthropology, history, and local folklore (open Mon–Fri 8am–1pm and 3–8pm; Sat and Sun 8am–8pm).

In the city center, on Bernardo de Irigoyen 148, is the **Museo de Bellas Artes**, with a small exhibition of art (open Mon–Fri 9am–1pm). Some 92 km (57 miles) to the south of San Rafael is Mendoza's largest hydroelectric plant, El Nihuil, which has a dam and reservoir where water sports such as windsurfing and fishing are practiced.

Skiing at Las Leñas

To the southwest of San Rafael, in the **Valle Hermoso** (Beautiful Valley), is the ski resort of **Las Leñas** ⑨ at 2,250 meters (7,400 ft) up in the Andes. This is becoming quite the place for the chic set of both hemispheres to meet between June and October. It has 45 km (28 miles) of dry powder slopes and has accommodations for 2,000 people. Charter flights bring skiers from Mendoza to the

nearby town of **Malargüe** , where buses take them the rest of the way. The city of Malargüe, located on the site of a mid-19th century fort, is a smallish oil town well known for its gaucho crafts. In the former Estancia La Orteguita at the entrance to the city is the **Museo Regional** (open daily 8am–8pm), a small museum with three rooms containing historical, archeological, and mineralogical exhibits. Around Malargüe there are many places to visit, including the lakes of La Niña Encantada and Llancanelo, the caves at Cavernas las Brujas, and the Bosque Petrificado (Petrified Forest).

Map on page 268

TIP

The area around Merlo has several quarries containing onyx, marble, and rose quartz; the town of La Toma, to the northeast of San Luis, specializes in green onyx. These stones can be purchased inexpensively locally.

San Luis and watersports

Although **San Luis** ⓫ does not really merit an extra trip, it lies on the road between Buenos Aires and Mendoza, so those going overland may want to rest here for a day or so. The town sits at the northwest corner of the pampas, and was a lonely frontier outpost; it retains a faintly colonial atmosphere, with some interesting buildings such as the restored 18th-century Convento de San Domingo, on Plaza Independencia. Recently, however, industrial promotion schemes offering tax breaks to companies investing in the province have created a significant industrial base in the area around the city.

Several resorts clustered around reservoirs in the San Luis province are popular with anglers and windsurfers. On Ruta 1, which leads to the Sierras de Córdoba, is the spa resort of **Merlo** ⓬. With a particularly sunny, dry, and mild microclimate, Merlo offers a range of hotels, holiday chalets, casinos, a river, and attractive surrounding country. It is this region's most popular tourist destination. The resort becomes especially crowded during Semana Santa (Holy Week) and the winter vacation period. While it has few buildings of great architectural or historical interest, the town offers a well-developed tourist infrastructure, with activities such as horseback riding, trekking, climbing, and hang-gliding all available locally.

BELOW: pre-Columbian milling stone, Talampaya National Park.

San Juan

The city of **San Juan** ⓭, capital of the province of the same name, is 177 km (106 miles) north of Mendoza along RN40. An earthquake on January 15, 1944 leveled the town, and it has been completely rebuilt since then. It was Juan Perón's theatrical and highly successful efforts to raise funds for the devastated town that first brought him to national prominence, and which incidentally first brought him into contact with the actress Eva Duarte, later to become his second wife and famous as Evita Perón. Unfortunately, the town's architecture is on the whole very modern and not especially attractive.

San Juan is a major center of wine production, although the bulk of its production is of the table variety rather than fine wine; in general the quality of its wines is lower than that of Mendoza or Salta. However, the city is most famous for being the birthplace of Domingo Faustino Sarmiento (1811–88), the noted historian and educator who was president of the republic from 1868 to 1874. His former home, on the corner of Avenida San Martín and Sarmiento is the site of the **Museo Histórico Sarmiento** (open

Tues–Fri 9am–1pm and 3–8pm), which has nine rooms around two patios, containing various items of furniture and personal effects. There is also the **Museo de Ciencias Naturales** (open Mon–Fri, 9.30am–1.30pm), which is near the Parque de Mayo, close to the intersection of 25 de Mayo and España. Besides the usual natural history exhibits, this museum also has an important collection of fossils from the Parque Natural Provincial Ischigualasto – better known as Valle de la Luna *(see page 281)* – which date from 200 million years ago.

On the other side of the city center, to the east, on the corner of Avenida General Rawson and General Paz, is the **Museo Histórico Provincial** (open Tues–Sun 9am–1pm), which houses a large collection, primarily of 18th- and 19th-century crafts and artwork, weapons, silver, furniture, and clothing. Located in the former warehouses of the General Belgrano railroad is the Mercado Artesanal Tradicional (traditional artisans' market; open Mon–Fri 8am–9pm), specializing in weaving and other rural crafts.

Climbing and rafting

To the west of San Juan is the Sierra de Tontal, with peaks of around 4,000 meters (13,120 ft), which involve less strenuous climbs than those of the Mendoza peaks. You can inquire at the local tourist office about the possibility of white-water rafting on the area's rivers *(see also Travel Tips, page 358)*. Some 30 km (18½ miles) away to the west lies the Embalse de Ullum (dam and reservoir) on the Río San Juan, in a pleasantly contrasting green setting. The dam has a hydroelectric plant and the reservoir is used for various water sports.

BELOW: roadside shrine to La Difunta Correa.

About 60 km (37 miles) to the east of San Juan, on RN20, is the small village of **Vallecito**  and the shrine to La Difunta Correa, one of the most

THE TRUCKDRIVERS' SHRINE

In 1841, in the course of the civil wars between federalists and unitarians, Deolinda Correa was forced to leave San Juan after the death of her husband, and to make the trek north toward La Rioja through the desert with her infant son. Deolinda was later found dead in the desert, although the baby was found to be alive and still able to nurse from his dead mother's breast.

Many years later, at the end of the 19th century, herdsmen stumbled across Deolinda's grave while they were searching for their cattle lost in a storm. They prayed for her assistance in recovering their herd and were astonished when the next morning they found them on a nearby hill. The herdsmen built a crude chapel by Deolinda's grave to show their gratitude and soon the story spread, attracting hopeful pilgrims.

Thus was born the shrine to Deolinda Correa, to whom miracles are popularly attributed, although she has not been canonised by the Catholic Church. A chapel has been erected on the spot, to the east of San Juan, and La Difunta (The Deceased) Correa has become the patron of road travelers and truck drivers, with visitors to the shrine leaving a bottle of water at her grave. At Easter and Christmas it is not uncommon for 200,000 pilgrims to visit the tomb.

visited religious sites in the whole of South America *(see box, page 280)*.

About 250 km (155 miles) to the northeast of Vallecito, along RN141 and Ruta 510, is the Valle Fértil, where the town of **San Agustín de Valle Fértil** ⓯ lies in the middle of a desert oasis surrounded by vineyards and citrus groves, which are irrigated by the adjacent San Agustín reservoir.

Map on page 268

Valle de la Luna

San Agustín del Valle Fértil is the gateway to the **Parque Natural Provincial Ischigualasto** ⓰ (including the World Heritage Site of Valle de la Luna), about 75 km (47 miles) to the southeast. This extensive park covers a 62,000-hectare (153,000-acre) area, which includes the Parque Provincial Talampaya in La Rioja, set in a large natural depression where constant erosion by wind and water through millennia has sculpted a series of sandstone formations of strange shapes and an abundance of colors. Beyond its beauty, the Valle de la Luna has great geological and paleontological significance. In prehistoric times (even before the birth of the Andes) this area was covered by an immense lake, surrounded, during the Triassic period, by rich fauna and flora. A 2-meter (6-ft) long reptile, the Dicinodonte, was one of the most typical inhabitants of the area. Sixty-three different species of fossilized animals have been found here.

The small town of **Barreal** ⓱ lies 94 km (58 miles) to the west of San Juan, amid spectacular scenery. The drive there takes some three hours, via Ruta 12, along a difficult mountain road. Barreal lies at 1,650 meters (5,410 ft) above sea level, on the banks of the Río Los Patos and flanked by birch trees. It is the region's main tourist center, with trekking and other outdoor activities

Precariously balanced rock formation in the Valle de la Luna.

BELOW: the Valle de la Luna.

TIP

If you are visiting La Unión, try *patero*, the local white wine, a homemade variety, produced in the traditional way, crushing the grapes underfoot.

organized locally. North of Barreal, on Ruta 412, is the Calingasta Valley, reached after passing through the Cerros Pintados ("Painted Hills"), which show a spectacular array of white, green, and red coloration. The town of **Calingasta** ⓲, in the middle of the valley at the joining of four rivers, is an important center for local fruit cultivation, primarily apples and tomatoes, and in the past gold, silver, and copper were mined and smelted in the area.

San Guillermo Wildlife Reserve

Some 200 km (120 miles) to the north of Calingasta is the small town of **Angualasto** ⓳, located in a grape- and wheat-growing oasis between two mountain ranges. The town's **Museo Arqueológico Municipal Luis Benedetti** (open Tues–Sun, 8am–1pm and 3–7pm) houses a 400-year-old mummy, as well as other archeological exhibits. The town is close to the **Reserva Provincial y de la Biosfera San Guillermo**, devoted to the preservation of regional fauna, primarily vicuñas and guanacos. The park lies at over 3,000 meters (9,840 ft) above sea level and is accessible only by 4x4 vehicles. For much of the year, the area is extremely cold and wet, and is best visited in the summer. Information on access and guides can be obtained from the tourist office in Angualasto.

About 150 km (93 miles) further north, via San José de Jachal on RN40, brings you to the arid province of La Rioja, also a wine-producing province, although on a lesser scale than Mendoza and San Juan. La Rioja is primarily famous as the birthplace of the 19th-century federalist caudillo Facundo Quiroga and of late 20th-century president Carlos Menem.

BELOW: Cerro Aconcagua (6962 meters/22,840 ft), the highest peak in the Americas.

The provincial capital, **La Rioja** ⓴ is a small city situated in the desert, whose principal architectural interest lies in the church of **Santo Domingo**,

the oldest convent in Argentina. Dating from 1623, it is also the only colonial building left in this city. Located in an Italian-style 19th-century mansion two blocks from the main plaza is an important artisans' market (open Tues–Sun) offering crafts in leather, wood, silver, and ceramics, as well as woven textiles. The city also has a **Museo Folklórico** (open Tues–Sun 9am–noon and 4pm to 8pm), one block away from the artisans' market along Pelagio Luna, with fascinating exhibits of pre- and post-colonial life in the province, as well as a room devoted to provincial mythology. About 130 km (81 miles) northwest of La Rioja, in a valley between the Los Colorados and Sañogasta mountain ranges, is **Chilecito** ㉑, the second-largest city in the province and the center of its wine industry (controlled by the Menem family). A cable car leads from a station in the south of the city to the former La Mejicana copper mine. Between 1904 and 1929 the cable car linked the copper refinery with the railroad, although both the mine and the railroad have long since ceased to operate.

Map on page 268

Condors are often spotted soaring on the thermals around this region's highest mountain valleys.

Canyons and condors

The modern town of **Villa Unión** ㉒ lies at the entrance to the Vinchina Valley, parallel to that of Chilecito, and separated by the Sañogasta mountain range. It is reached by the road through the dramatic Cuesta de Miranda pass, and is a popular base for visiting some interesting sites in the vicinity.

Some 65 km (40 miles) to the north of Villa Unión is the small town of **Villa San José de Vinchina**, which has been inhabited since pre-Columbian times. It has an old water mill and dotted around the area are six unusual flattened mounds, painted with multicolored, 10-pointed stars which are thought to have been used as ritual sites. One of the stars can be seen just outside the town, across the Río Vinchina.

BELOW: a scenic road through the Cuyo country.

Also worth a visit is **Jagüe**, a tiny hamlet 37 km (23 miles) to the north of Vinchina, cradled at the foot of the giant **Volcán Bonete** (5,943 meters/19,500 ft), on the old mule track that connects the green meadows on the Argentina side with the Chilean mining towns in the southern Atacama Desert.

The main destination from Villa Unión though, and a suitably dramatic conclusion to this tour of the Cuyo, is the **Parque Nacional Talampaya** ㉓, a 270,000-hectare (667,000-acre) area 65 km (40 miles) to the southeast, which has some of the most spectacular scenery in Argentina. The park is set in an impressive gorge with cliffs towering to more than 145 meters (480 ft), and is full of amazing rock shapes carved by centuries of wind. The area was occupied by the Diaguita culture, which left behind innumerable rock paintings and engravings that can still be seen on some rock faces, offering a fascinating archeological contrast to the impressive geological formations of the canyon. A wide variety of animals, including foxes, hares, pumas, and guanacos, also inhabit the park, and look out for condors soaring high above the gorge, whose nests are perched on the cliffs. Although private vehicles are not allowed within the park, there are guides with their own vehicles who run excursions. ❏

BODEGA HOPPING IN THE CUYO

With enormous industrial plants and friendly, family-based enterprises, Mendoza has vineyards galore, and tastings are positively encouraged

There are more than 1,290 vineyards in the Mendoza region, which produce 80 percent of the country's wines, Many of them offer tours and the chance to sample and buy wine. Local agencies organize excursions to many of the vineyards, some of which are listed here:

Bodegas López, Carril Ozamis 375, Maipú, tel: 0261-497 2406 Guided tours, Mon–Fri 9am–5pm.

Museo del Vino Bodega La Rural, Montecaseros 2625, Coquimbito, tel: 0261-497 2013. Includes a museum, open Mon–Fri 9.30am–5pm.

Bodega Trapiche, Mitre and Nueva Mayorga, Coquimbito, tel: 0261-520 7210. Guided tours, Mon–Fri 10am–4.30pm.

Museo Nacional del Vino y Antigua Bodega La Giol, Carril Ozamis 914, Maipú, tel: 0261-497 6777. Guided tours daily, Sat am only, Sun pm only.

Bodega Chandón, Km 29, Agrelo, tel: 0261-490 9968. Guided tours daily.

Bodega Catena Zapata, J. Cobos s/n, Agrelo, tel: 0261-490 0214. Visits best arranged in advance, see www.catenawines.com.

▷ **DIVINE ORIGINS**
Argentina's first wine producers were 16th-century Jesuit missionaries, who planted the vines to make communion wine.

△ **STUNNING BACKDROP**
The foothills of the Andes overlook Mendoza's vineyards, providing a spectacular setting and a crucial supply of fresh mountain water.

▷ **DRINKING HABITS**
Argentina is the world's fifth-largest wine producer. Its export market is growing, but most wine is kept for domestic consumption.

◁ **WINE WORSHIP**
the distinctive Catena Zapata bodega was designed to resemble a Mayan temple and produces excellent wines grown from French grapes.

△ **PEST CONTROL**
Rose bushes planted next to the vines are prone to pests and diseases, giving early warning to protect the precious grape crop.

▽ **ANTIQUE ARTIFACTS**
Several bodegas in the Mendoza area have their own museum, displaying hand-operated machinery and tools used in the past.

▷ **GRAPE VARIETY**
Argentina's best wines are the reds, and the most widely planted grapes are the Italian Bonarda, as well as Malbec, Cabernet Sauvignon, and Pinot Noir varieties.

THE PICK OF THE BUNCH

The most popular destinations for bodega hoppers are the major, streamlined operations at Peñaflor (producers of Trapiche), and Chandón. The best time to visit is during the March harvest, when the roads are clogged by trucks spilling over with grapes. Visitors are taken on a standard tour through the areas where the various stages of production take place (English-speaking tour guides can also be arranged). Huge oak casks are set on rollers as an anti-seismic precaution.

One of the less-visited but more interesting bodegas is La Rural, with a small but fascinating museum. This winery, whose brand is San Felipe, retains a lot of charm, with its original pink adobe architecture.

Cuyo Vineyards

Panquehua
Espejo
El Plumerillo
Las Heras
Zanjón Bermejo
Pescara
Mendoza
Villa Nueva
Estancia Guaymallén
Rodeo de la Cruz
Godoy Cruz
Confin
Luzuriaga
General Gutiérrez
Gobernador Benegas
La Puntilla
Garrodilla
Bodega López
Bodega La Rural
Bodega Trapiche
Museo Nacional del Vino y Antigua Bodega La Giol
Maipú
Bodega Fabre Montmayou
Santiago
Luján de Cuyo
Bodega Catena Zapata
Bodega Chandón
Agrelo
Zanjón
San Luis
Pescara

0   2 km
0   2 miles

PATAGONIA

*At the very end of the South American subcontinent lies the land
that Magellan and his chronicler Pigafetta, while grounded on a
desolate coast during the winter of 1520, named Patagonia*

Map
on page
290

This wild and isolated terrain has figured prominently in the exotic fantasies of many armchair adventurers through the ages. From whale watching and out-of-the-way ranch stays to deep green lakes and the crashing icy waters of Tierra del Fuego, Patagonia inspires.

Even though this large triangle of land comprises roughly a third of Argentina, one is still surprised by the wide range of spectacles that are contained here, and there are three World Heritage sites in the region. It has some of the hemisphere's highest peaks, forests of strange primeval trees, several of the world's most noteworthy glaciers (although sadly these are retreating due to global warming) and fossil-rich coastal cliffs that were explored by Charles Darwin. The abundance of rare wildlife is astounding, and, for the athletic traveler, Patagonia has some of the most challenging skiing and mountain climbing to be found.

At the top of the wedge-shaped territory are the provinces of Neuquén and Río Negro, the former famed for its ancient *Araucaria araucana* (monkey-puzzle) forests and Mapuche reservations, and the latter for the alpine-style town of Bariloche in Parque Nacional Nahuel Huapi. Both provinces border on trout-rich Lago Nahuel Huapi, have their own ski resorts, and offer summer hiking, horseback riding, mountain climbing, and water sports.

Further south, Chubut flaunts the marine fauna of the Valdés Peninsula and an exotic cultural mix comprising the Mapuches and the customs of the Welsh communities of the Atlantic coast and the hinterland. Puerto Madryn's Golfo Nuevo is Argentina's scuba-diving capital and is home to the southern right whale during the winter and fall months. Santa Cruz, at the tip of the Patagonian wedge, is the country's second-largest and least-inhabited province. It harbors some of nature's most imposing glaciers, a large petrified forest that is 150 million years old, and numerous cave paintings more than 10,000 years old.

PRECEDING PAGES:
Cerro Norte and Río
Onelli.
LEFT: Perito
Moreno glacier.
BELOW: Argentine
Mapuche woman.

Bold explorers

Ferdinand Magellan, Pedro Sarmiento de Gamboa, Francis Drake, and Thomas Cavendish are just a few of the many explorers who set foot on this land. Here, European law and customs gave way to the most violent passions: revolts, mutinies, banishments, and executions were common. In 1578, in the Port of San Julian (now the town of Puerto San Julian in Santa Cruz province), Sir Francis Drake used the same scaffold Magellan had used to hang his mutineers half a century before.

Sarmiento de Gamboa founded the first settlements in 1584, naming them Nombre de Jesus and Rey Felipe, on the Strait of Misfortunes. His first encounter with the native inhabitants should have sounded a

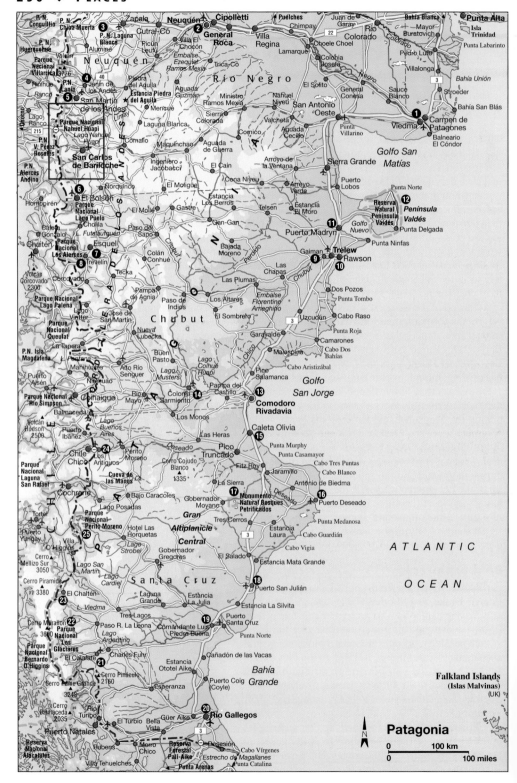

P.N.
Conguillío
P.N.
Chita Muerta
Zapala
Neuquén
Cipolletti
Puélches
Juan de
Garay
Río
Colorado
Bahía Blanca
Mayor
Buratovich
Punta Alta
Isla
Trinidad

Cutral-Co
General
Roca
Villa El
Chocón
Villa Regina
Villa Regina
Chimpay
Choele Choel
Colonia
Josefa
Lamarque
Pedro Luro
Villalonga
Punta Labarinto

P.N. Laguna
Blanca
Ricún
Leufú
Piedra
del Aguila
Aguada
Guzmán
Neuquén
Río Negro
El Solito
Negro
General
Conesa
Sauce
Blanco
Stroeder
Bahía Unión
3

P. N.
Huerquehue
Parque
Nacional
Villarrica
Volcán
Lanín
3776
P.N.
Lanín
Junín de
los Andes
Estancia Piedra
del Aguila
Ministro
Ramos Mexía
Nahuel
Niyeu
San Antonio
Oeste
Carmen de
Patagones
Viedma
Bahía San Blás

Rinihue
L. Ranco
San Martín
de los Andes
Limay
Menqué
Sierra
Colorada
Valcheta
Punta
Villarino
Balneario
El Cóndor

Lago
Ranco
P.N.
Nahuel Huapi
Lago Nahuel
Huapi
Comallo
Maquinchao
Aguada
de Guerra
Comicó
Aguada
Cecilio
Golfo San
Matías
Osorno
215
Parque Nacional
Nahuel Huapi

P.N.
V. Pérez
Rosales
San Carlos
de Bariloche
Ingeniero
Jacobacci
El Caín
Arroyo de
la Ventana
Sierra Grande

P.N.
Alerces
Andino
Norquinco
Cona Niyeu
Puerto
Lobos
Punta Norte

El Bolsón
Estancia
Los Berros
Gastre
Telsen
Estancía
El Moro
Reserva
Natural
Península
Valdés
Península
Valdés
Punta Delgada

Hornopirén
Parque
Nacional
Lago Puelo
El Molle
Gan-Gan
Golfo
Nuevo
Puerto Madryn
Punta Ninfas

Caleta
Gonzalo
L. Futalaufquen
Cholila
Paso del
Sapo
Bajada
Moreno
Gaiman
Trelew
Rawson

Chaitén
Parque
Nacional
Los Alerces
Esquel
Colán
Conhué
Las
Chapas
Chubut

Trevelín
Tecka
Las Plumas
Dos Pozos
Punta Tombo

Volcán
Corcovado
2300
Corcovado
Pampa
de Agnia
Paso de
Indios
Los Altares
El Sombrero
Embalse
Florentino
Ameghino
Uzcudún
Cabo Raso

Parque Nacional
Lago Palena
Lago
Vintter
José de
San Martín
Chubut
Garayalde
Punta Roja
Camarones
Cabo Dos
Bahías

P.N. Isla
Magdalena
La Tapera
Nueva
Lubecka
Chico
Malaspina
Cabo Aristízabal

Puerto
Aysén
Mañihuales
Ñirihuao
Alto Río
Senguer
Buen
Pasto
Lago
Colhué
Huapi
Pico
Salamanca
Golfo
San Jorge

Parque Nacional
Río Simpson
Coihaique
Lago
Musters
Pampa del
Castillo
Colonia
Sarmiento

Balmaceda
Lago
Buenos
Aires
Río
Mayo
Los Monos
Comodoro
Rivadavia

Volcán
Hudson
2500
Puerto
Ibáñez
Las Heras
Caleta Olivia
Punta Murphy

Chile
Chico
Los
Antiguos
Perito
Moreno
Cerro Cojudo
Blanco
1335
Pico
Truncado
Fitz Roy
Jaramillo
Punta Casamayor
Cabo Tres Puntas
Cabo Blanco

Parque
Nacional
Laguna
San Rafael
Cueva de
las Manos
La Sierra
Antonio de Biedma

Cochrane
Bajo Caracoles
Gobernador
Moyano
Monumento
Natural Bosques
Petrificados
Deseado
Puerto Deseado

Tortel
Puerto
Yungay
O'Higgins
Parque
Nacional
Perito Moreno
Lago Posadas
Hotel Las
Horquetas
Gran
Altiplanicie
Central
Tres Cerros
Estancia
Laura
Punta Medanosa
Cabo Guardián

Cerro
Mellizo Sur
3050
Cerro Piramide
3380
Lago San
Martín
Lago
Strobel
Gobernador
Gregores
El Salado
Estancia Mata Grande
Cabo Vigía

Parque
Nacional
Bernardo
O'Higgins
El Chaltén
L. Viedma
Santa Cruz
Laguna
Grande
Estancia
La Julia
Puerto San Julián
Estancia La Silvita

Cerro Murallón
3600
Parque
Nacional
Los
Glaciares
Paso R. La Leona
Lago
Argentino
Tres Lagos
Comandante Luis
Piedra Buena
Puerto
Santa Cruz
Punta Norte

El Calafate
Charles Fuhr
Estancia
Ototel Aike
Cañadón de las Vacas
Bahía
Grande

Cerro Pinaculo
2160
Esperanza
Puerto Coig
(Coyle)

Cerro Prime Grande
3249
Río
Turbio
El Turbio
Güer Aike
Río Gallegos

Cerro
Balmaceda
2035
Puerto Natales
Rubens
Morro
Chico
Bella
Vista
Posesión
Cabo Vírgenes

Reserva
Nacional
Alacalufes
Reserva
Forestal
Pali-Aike
Villa Tehuelches
Punta Arenas
Estrecho de Magallanes
Cabo Catalina

ATLANTIC

OCEAN

Falkland Islands
(Islas Malvinas)
(UK)

Patagonia

0   100 km

0   100 miles

warning: "Ten naked indians approached us and pronounced words of welcome in an unknown language. The Chief, trying to prove their friendship, took a long arrow and swallowed it till it almost disappeared down his throat; when he slowly took it out, it was covered in blood." Two years later, Thomas Cavendish, the English privateer captain, found the survivors of this expedition wandering on the deserted coast, and after spending four days there, gave it the desolate name of Port Famine.

Stretching westward from the white cliffs on the coast lie the vast plains and mesas that remained unexplored for centuries. The Jesuits were among the few who, driven by the spell of the "lost city of the Caesars," dared to take a look at the endless plateau. They came from Chile, across the Andes, and never ventured far from the mountains. In 1670, they founded a mission in a remote place, on the shores of Lago Nahuel Huapi. It didn't last long. The indigenous community had a premonition that they would be doomed if the Spanish found their secret trails across the Andes, and so murdered most of the missionaries.

*The origin of the name Patagonia, according to some historians, comes from the name given to the natives because of their big feet (*pata *is Spanish for an animal's foot, -*gón *is a common affix for "big").*

The desert conquest

The early inhabitants of this land were, from the start, part of the exotic spell that attracted the first settlers, but soon became an obstacle to their purposes. They had been there long before the white man arrived and they stood their ground. The bravest were the Mapuches, a nomadic tribe who lived on both sides of the Andes in the northern part of Patagonia. For 300 years they led a violent lifestyle on the plains by stealing and plundering the larger estancias (ranches) of the rich pampas, herding the cattle over the Andes and selling them to the Spaniards on the Chilean side.

BELOW: beautiful Magellanic fuchsia.

STIRRING PATAGONIAN PROSE

Nobody has ever expressed more precisely than British naturalist Charles Darwin the emotions that remote Patagonia stirs in a visitor. Darwin, back in England after sailing five years on the *Beagle*, wrote, "In calling up images of the past, I find that the plains of Patagonia frequently cross before my eyes; yet these plains are pronounced by all wretched and useless… Why then… have these arid wastes taken so firm a hold on my memory?"

Since Darwin's time, Patagonia has attracted a steady stream of foreign writers. In the 19th century, Argentine-born William Henry Hudson wrote *Idle Days in Patagonia*, a poetic narrative of his youth spent discovering the flora and fauna of the region.

But perhaps the best-known modern account of the place and its people is Bruce Chatwin's *In Patagonia*, which captures the essence of Patagonia through his meetings with local inhabitants encountered during his travels: "So next day, as we drove through the desert, I sleepily watched the rags of silver cloud spinning across the sky, and the sea of grey-green thornscrub lying off in sweeps and rising in terraces and the white dust streaming off the saltpans and, on the horizon, land and sky dissolving into an absence of color."

Mapuche jewelry, now produced primarily for the tourist industry.

In 1879, the Argentine Army, under General Roca, set out to conquer the land from the Amerindians. The campaign, which lasted until 1883, is known as the Conquest of the Desert. It put an end to years of Amerindian dominion in Patagonia and opened up a whole new territory to colonization. The natives vanished: some died in epic battles, others succumbed to new diseases, and others simply became cow hands on the huge estancias. Fragments of their world can still be found in the land, in the features of some of the people, in customs, and in religious rituals still performed on Amerindian reservations.

European settlement

When the Amerindian wars ended, colonization began. The large inland plateau, a dry expanse of shrubs and alkaline lagoons, was slowly occupied by people of very diverse origins: Spaniards, Italians, Scots, and English in the far south, Welsh in the Chubut Valley, Italians in the Río Negro Valley, Swiss and Germans in the Northern Lake District, and a few North Americans scattered throughout the country.

These people inherited the land and reproduced in the far south a situation similar to the American West. Ports and towns developed on the coast to ship the wool and import the goods needed by the settlers. Large wool-producing estancias were established on the plains. To the west, where the plains meet the Andes, several national parks were designated to protect the rich natural inheritance, to develop tourism, and to secure the national borders.

BELOW: Carmen de Patagones in the early 19th century.

The Patagonian towns grew fast. Coal mining, oilfields, agriculture, industry, large hydroelectrical projects, and tourism attracted people from all over the country and from Chile, transforming Patagonia into a modern industrial frontier

land. Some people came to start a quiet new life in the midst of mountains, forests, and lakes. In the Patagonian interior, descendants of the first sheep-breeding settlers and their ranch hands still ride over the enormous estancias.

Map on page 290

A few geographical facts

With defined geographical and political boundaries, Patagonia extends from the Río Colorado in the north, more than 2,000 km (1,200 miles) to Cabo de Hornos (Cape Horn) at the southernmost tip of the continent. It covers more than 1 million sq km (400,000 sq miles) and belongs to two neighboring countries, Chile and Argentina. The final agreement on this long, irregular, international border was not an easy matter to settle. Although the land was still unexplored, there were times when both countries were almost on the brink of war. Fortunately, it never reached that point, due to the common sense of both governments. In 1978, both countries agreed on the last stretch of undefined boundary, which concerned some small islands in the Beagle Channel. The Argentine part of Patagonia includes approximately 800,000 sq km (308,000 sq miles), and can easily be divided into three definite areas: the coast, the plateau, and the Andes.

The change of seasons

Seasons are well-defined in Patagonia. Considering the latitude, the average temperature is mild; winters are never as cold and summers never as warm as in similar latitudes in the northern hemisphere. The average temperature in Ushuaia is 6°C (43°F) and, in Bariloche, 8°C (46°F). Even so, the climate can turn quite rough on the desert plateau. There, the weather is more continental

The population density of Patagonia averages fewer than three inhabitants per sq km (less than one per sq mile), compared to more than 2,500 people per square km (more than 1,000 per sq mile) in Buenos Aires.

BELOW: horseback trekking above Lago Nahuel Huapi, near Bariloche.

TIP

There are only two main roads in Patagonia: RN40, which runs down the Andes, and RN3, which follows the coast. Many smaller roads link the coast to the mountains, but not many are paved, so you may have to choose between a smooth but longer journey or a quick but bumpy dirt road.

BELOW:
fall comes
to the plains.

than in the rest of the region. The ever-present companion is the wind, which blows hard all year round, from the mountains to the sea, making life here unbearable for many people.

In spring, the snow on the mountains begins to melt, alpine flowers bloom almost everywhere, and ranchers prepare for the hard work of tending sheep and shearing. Although tourism starts in late springtime, most people visit during the summer (December to March). During this period, all roads are fit for traffic, the airports are open and, normally, the hotels are booked solid.

The fall brings changes on the plateau. The poplars around the lonesome estancias turn to beautiful shades of yellow. The mountains, covered by deciduous beech trees, offer a panorama of reds and yellows, and the air slowly gets colder. At this time of the year, tourism thins out. Parque Nacional Los Glaciares *(see page 314)*, in the far south, closes down for the winter. While the wide plains sleep, the winter resorts on the mountains thrive. San Martín de los Andes, Bariloche, Esquel, and even Ushuaia attract thousands of skiers, including many from the northern hemisphere who take advantage of the reversal of seasons.

Northern Patagonia

The northern boundary of Patagonia is the **Río Colorado**. The steppe starts further north and extends through inland Patagonia and the coast, down to the Straits of Magellan. Near to the mouth of the Río Negro, which runs parallel to the south of the Colorado, are the twin towns of **Carmen de Patagones** and **Viedma ❶**, on opposite banks of the river. Carmen de Patagones is one of the oldest Spanish settlements in Patagonia, founded in 1779. The cobblestone streets and historic buildings provide a fitting introduction to the region.

Fertile fruit orchards

Nearby, you can see the caves used for shelter by the first settlers. Where the river meets the sea, there is a sea-lion colony similar to the many others along the coast. **Puerto San Antonio Este**, the port from where all the fruit production of the valley is shipped to foreign countries, lies 180 km (110 miles) to the west on the Golfo de San Martín, and nearby is **Las Grutas**, a popular seaside resort with extensive sandy beaches. The warm, clear waters here make it a popular destination for divers; game fishing and whale watching are also very popular.

The **Río Negro** flows through an oasis of intensive agriculture, which stretches for more than 400 km (250 miles). The valley itself is a narrow strip of fertile land, in sharp contrast to the desert surroundings that threaten to swallow it. Anyone interested in visiting agricultural areas specializing in growing fruit (mainly apples, pears, and grapes), should not miss this place. Fruit farms, juice factories, and packing establishments give the area a thriving appearance.

Traveling inland along the Río Negro, past cultivated strips of land that alternate with steppe, you arrive at a string of cities: **Neuquén ❷**, Cipoletti, General Roca, and Villa Regina, the latter some 540 km (330 miles) from the coast. These are the region's most important cities, forming a rare ribbon of urbanization, interspersed with fruit orchards. The main road here is heavily used, but traffic thins out markedly beyond Villa Regina.

The northern Lake District

Going west from Neuquén to the Andes, you come to the northern limit of the Patagonian Lake District, an enormous area of beautiful lakes and spectacular

Map on page 290

The black-necked swan, a common sight in Patagonia's Lake District.

BELOW: winter comes to the mountains.

mountain peaks, which stretches 1,500 km (900 miles) from Lago Aluminé in the north to Parque Nacional Los Glaciares in the south. One can divide this region into two sections, the northern and southern Lake Districts. The zone that lies in between is sparsely populated and traveling is a challenge to be taken on only by the most adventurous.

January and July are the most popular months for visitors, reflecting the vacations in Buenos Aires. However, apart from May and June, which tend to be rainy months, the area has its attractions in all seasons. There are many tours available to local landmarks and abundant opportunities for hiking, climbing, fishing, and horseback riding in summer, or skiing and snowboarding in winter.

The northern Lake District covers the area from Lago Aluminé southward to Lago Amutui Quimei. It encompasses a 500-km (300-mile) stretch of lakes, forests, and mountains divided into four national parks. From north to south is the Parque Nacional Lanín and the nearby towns of San Martín de los Andes and Junín de los Andes; Parque Nacional Nahuel Huapi and the alpine-style resort of Bariloche; Parque Nacional Lago Puelo and the village of El Bolsón; and, farthest south, Parque Nacional Los Alerces with the town of Esquel. This region connects to the so-called Lake District in Chile.

Entering the Lake District from the north, the first place of interest you'll reach is the **Parque Nacional Laguna Blanca ❸**. The park lies just to the southwest of Zapala, which is about 185 km (115 miles) west of Neuquén on RN22. It includes a large lake, and is home to hundreds of interesting bird species: the prime attractions are the black-necked swans, which gather in flocks of up to 2,000 birds. Flamingos are also part of the scenery, and the surround-

ing hills give shelter to large groups of eagles, peregrine falcons, and other birds of prey. There is a visitor's center at the park, and a campsite. There are infrequent buses to the park from the nearest town, Zapala, 35 km (22 miles) away, which has an information office.

Traveling southwest from Neuquén along RN237, after about 76 km (47 miles) you'll come to the huge Embalse E. Ramos Mejía. This reservoir is an impressive sight, created by building a dam across the Río Limay, and is now one of the biggest hydroelectric plants in the country.

Monkey puzzles and trout

The area around Lago Aluminé is well known for its Amerindian reservations where you can find handicrafts such as ponchos and carpets. This area is also home to one of the most peculiar-looking trees in the world, the *Araucaria araucana* or monkey puzzle. This prehistoric tree, which grows at considerable altitudes, still has a primeval look to it. Its fruit, the *piñón*, which can be boiled and eaten, was a treat for the indigenous peoples on their way across the Andean trails.

Parque Nacional Lanín, near the town of San Martín de los Andes, covers 3,920 sq km (1,508 sq miles) and gets its name from the imposing Lanín volcano, on the border with Chile. The volcano soars to 3,776 meters (12,388 ft), far above the height of the surrounding peaks.

The national park is noted for its fine fishing; the fishing season is from mid-November through mid-April. The rivers and streams around the small town of **Junín de los Andes ❹** are famed for their abundance and variety of trout. Fly-casters come from around the world to fish for the brook, brown, fontinalis, and steelhead. The best catch on record is a 12-kg (27-lb) brown trout – the average weight for this fish is 4–5 kg (9–11 lbs). Although Junín has several good restaurants and hotels, most anglers prefer the fishermen's lodges located in the park.

Parque Nacional Lanín is also well known for hunting. Wild boar and red and fallow deer are the main prey in the fall rutting season. The national park takes bids for hunting rights over most of the hunting grounds, and local farm owners make their own agreements with hunters. For information, contact the tourist office in San Martín de los Andes.

Guided tours, by bus or boat, depart from **San Martín de los Andes ❺**, a fashionable, exclusive town at the eastern end of Lago Lacar. Fishing and hunting, and mountain climbing guides are available, as well as car rentals, a good range of accommodations and two interesting Mapuche museums. Also recommended is a trip to lakes Huechulafquen and Paimun and the majestic Lanín volcano, fringed by a forest of *Araucaria* or monkey puzzle trees.

Cerro Chapelco, at 2,441 meters (8,000 ft) and 20 minutes or so by car from San Martín, is one of the country's most important winter-sports centers. The ski season here runs from mid-June to mid-October.

Three roads link San Martín de los Andes with Bariloche. The middle (shortest, but unpaved) road runs across the Paso del Córdoba through narrow

TIP

A Pase Verde allows entry to four national parks at a reduced rate, available from national park offices.

BELOW: a good day's catch.

Wily Patagonian fox (zorro patagónico).

valleys where the scenery is beautiful, especially in the fall when the slopes turn to rich shades of gold and deep red. This road reaches the paved highway at Confluencia. From here, if you turn back inland, you come to the **Estancia La Primavera**, with its trout farm. To the dismay of locals who used to fish here, it is now private property, belonging to US media tycoon Ted Turner. Returning to the paved road to Bariloche, you follow Río Limay through the Valle Encantado, a valley of bizarre rock formations, also skirting the Rincón Grande, a ring of steep escarpments formed by river erosion, creating a striking natural amphitheater.

The third road from San Martín is the famed **Ruta de los Siete Lagos** (Route of the Seven Lakes). This road, of which about half is paved, takes you past beautiful lakes and forests and approaches Bariloche from the northern shore of Lago Nahuel Huapi. In summer, all-day tours make the trip from Bariloche to San Martín, combining the Paso del Córdoba and the Ruta de los Siete Lagos. Another good way of traveling the route is by mountain bike; these can be easily hired in San Martín de los Andes.

Switzerland in Argentina

San Carlos de Bariloche **, in the middle of **Parque Nacional Nahuel Huapi, is the real center of the northern Lake District. Buses, trains, and planes arrive daily from all over the country and from Chile, across the Paso Puyehue.

Founded in 1902, Bariloche, as it is commonly called, has a very strong Central European influence; most of the first settlers were of Swiss, German, or northern Italian origin. These people gave the city its alpine atmosphere, with Swiss-style chalets, fondue restaurants, and chocolates. However, something

BELOW:
gauchos on the
Patagonian steppe.

tells you that you are not in Europe; boats are seldom seen on the huge Lago Nahuel Huapi, the roads are swallowed in the wilderness as soon as they leave the city, and at night there are no lights on the opposite shore of the lake.

Map on page 301

The town has grown rapidly in recent decades, spreading along the foot of **Cerro Otto**. This long ridge offers a good introductory walk, or take a cable-car ride to the top, where there are splendid views of the town, the lake, and the surrounding park, as well as a revolving cafe. There are also pleasant woodland walks descending the far side of the ridge to Arelauquen and the quiet Lago Gutiérrez.

The best way to begin your tour of Bariloche is by visiting the **Museo de la Patagonia** (open Tues–Fri 10am–12.30pm and 2–7pm; Mon and Sat 10am–1pm) in the Civic Center. This building and the Hotel Llao Llao were designed by architect Ezequiel Bustillo in his own interpretation of traditional alpine style, and they give Bariloche a distinctive architectural personality. The museum has displays on the geological origins of the region and of local wildlife. It also has a stunning collection of indigenous artifacts, which chronicle the demise of local tribes.

Regional buys

Chocolates, jams, ceramics, and sweaters are among the most important local products. The large chocolate industry has remained in the hands of Italian families and visiting some of the downtown factories is worthwhile. So is a visit to the ceramics factory, where you can watch the artisans at work. Sweaters are for sale everywhere, as are locally produced jewelry and handicrafts.

Bariloche has many accommodations, ranging from cozy inns to luxury hotels.

BELOW: Cerro Lanín.

CROSSING THE ANDES

While you are in the northern Lake District there are various options for crossing over to Chile. From Bariloche, if you want to reach Puerto Montt on the Pacific coast, try the old route first used by the Jesuits across the lakes. This day-long journey combines short bus rides with leisurely boat crossings of lakes Nahuel Huapi, Frías, Todos los Santos, and Llanquihue, through marvelous settings of forests and snowcapped volcanoes.

While the lake crossing has the advantage of escaping normal traffic, the road through the Puyehue Pass, northwest of Bariloche, gives views of Lago Correntoso and Lago Espejo. Over the border, the Parque Nacional Puyehue offers the opportunity to sample thermal springs and mud baths, or to explore the temperate rainforest.

Further north, via San Martín de los Andes, is the little-used Hua-Hum Pass. A small car ferry carries you the length of Lago Pirihueico with its steep-forested sides and glimpses of the Choshuenco volcano, and at the far end a road continues into the village of Choshuenco.

More northerly still, beyond Junín de los Andes, is Paso Tromen. This is much higher and sometimes closed in winter, but affords wonderful views of the Lanín volcano and the native *Araucaria* (monkey-puzzle) forests.

The local cuisine reflects the area's large population of settlers from Germany and Italy, with specialties such as fondue, trout, venison, and wild boar.

Lakes, forests, and mountains

There are some excellent excursions to choose from in the Bariloche area: 17 km (11 miles) southwest is the **Villa Cerro Catedral** ❸, one of Argentina's largest and most important ski centers, also with fine walking trails on the mountainside and around Lago Gutiérrez. The base of the ski lifts is at 1,050 meters (3,465 ft) above sea level, and a cable car and chair lifts take you up to a height of 2,010 meters (6,633 ft). The view from the slopes is absolutely superb. The ski runs range in difficulty from novice to expert, and cover more than 25 km (15 miles), and there are full facilities. The ski season runs from the end of June to September. Snowboarding, bungee jumping, and paragliding are also possible.

Another 10 km (6 miles) further south is **Villa Mascardi** ❹, a small tourist resort on the shore of Lago Mascardi. Picturesque boat cruises are available from here across the turquoise waters of the lake toward Monte Tronador, the highest peak in the national park, at 3,478 meters (11,411 ft). The mountain can also be visited via a long and winding scenic drive. Between lakes Gutiérrez and Mascardi lies the watershed of rivers draining into the Atlantic and the Pacific oceans. Past Pampa Linda, where there is one hostel, and approaching the mountain, you pass the Black Glacier, so-called because of all the muddy debris churned up onto the surface of the glacier. Another route from Lago Mascardi goes to lakes Fonck and Hess, both popular fishing spots, with campsites. En route, you pass the lovely Cascada Los Alerces, which cascades for some 20 meters (66 ft) over drenched, mossy rocks. A number of

"It is not the imagination, it is that nature in these desolate scenes, for a reason to be guessed at by and by, moves us more deeply than in others."

— W. H. HUDSON
(*Anglo-Argentine naturalist*, 1841–1922)

BELOW: San Martín de los Andes.

these routes operate one-way systems allowing only ascent or descent within certain times, in order to regulate peak season tourist traffic, so you'd be advised to check the details at the Bariloche tourist office if traveling independently by road.

Llao Llao Peninsula

One of the most popular half-day excursions from Bariloche is the so-called Circuito Chico, or small circuit. This takes you westward along the shore of the lake and up to the Punto Panorámico, with its breathtaking views over the water toward Chile. It is a rare building that could blend into, even enhance, such a magnificent landscape, but the **Hotel Llao Llao ⓓ** at the base of the Península Llao Llao, is equal to the challenge. The enormous, alpine-style hotel was built in 1939, and in 1995 was the setting for a summit meeting of presidents of the Americas, including Cuba's Fidel Castro.

One of Bariloche's tempting chocolate shops.

Continuing the circuit, farther round the lake is **Bahía López**, a tranquil inlet where it is often possible to see condors circling the huge bulk of Cerro López overshadowing the bay. There is a well-defined path leading up this mountain as far as the mountain refuge, with a more rugged track thereafter up to the summit ridge. On the road back to Bariloche you will pass the Cerro Campanario chairlift at Km 17. Although much lower than lifts at Cerro Otto or Catedral, the views are unrivaled.

At the far end of Lago Nahuel Huapi, en route to Chile, **Puerto Blest ⓔ** is host to much through traffic. Few stay, however, so outside these brief flurries of traffic it is a place of exceptional peace and beauty. There is a small hotel, a pleasant walking trail to the Cascada Los Cantares, and a warden to give

BELOW: Bariloche's Civic Center.

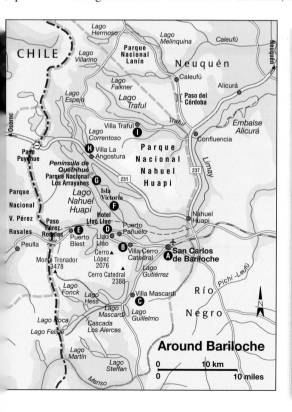

Around Bariloche

directions for more demanding walks. You can visit Puerto Blest and Isla Victoria by catamaran excursions across Lago Nahuel Huapi from Puerto Pañuelo.

Bambi's forest

Isla Victoria ⓕ, on Lago Nahuel Huapi, is renowned for its *arrayanes*, rare trees related to myrtles, found only in this area and in the Parque Nacional Los Alerces *(see page 304)*. The story goes that a visiting group of Walt Disney's advisors were so impressed by the white and cinnamon-colored trees here that they used them as the basis for the scenery in the 1942 film *Bambi*. Most visitors to the island come in groups on the catamaran excursions, but you require only a little ingenuity to discover the beauties of the island away from the crowds.

Extending from the northern shore of the lake is the Península de Quetrihue. containing the **Parque Nacional Los Arrayanes ⓖ**, dedicated to protecting the rare *arrayán* trees, some of which are 300 years old and 28 meters (92 ft) high. Boat excursions to Isla Victoria often stop at Quetrihue, allowing time to walk in the park. You can also reach the Península de Quetrihue from **Villa La Angostura ⓗ**, an increasingly busy chic resort at the far end of the lake. There is a good selection of hotels, campsites, and other amenities in the vicinity, which has been developed to cater to the tourist overflow of the nearby skiing center of Cerro Bayo.

Another popular excursion heads east from Bariloche, then north through the Valle Encantado, until turning off at Confluencia for **Villa Traful ⓘ**. The small town is famous for the excellent salmon fishing in Lago Traful, as well as for some inspiring hiking and horseback riding in the surrounding countryside. The road continues through the town, climbing to a commanding viewpoint

BELOW:
above the clouds
at Cerro Catedral.

high above Lago Traful and takes a scenic route back through Villa la Angostura. This circuit, predictably described as the Circuito Grande (long circuit), covers some 240 km (149 miles) and is offered as a full-day excursion from Bariloche. Most travel agencies in Bariloche offer a variety of bus and boat excursions visiting the above-mentioned sites, but if you fancy something a little more energetic to tap this area's vast potential for outdoor pursuits, visit the Club Andino, the city's specialist mountaineering organization *(see page 358)*.

Maps on pages 290 and 301

Hippie refuge

El Bolsón ❻ is a small town 130 km (80 miles) south of Bariloche, situated in a narrow valley with its own microclimate. Beer hops and all sorts of berries are grown on small farms. Hippies favored El Bolsón in the 1960s, and today many lead peaceful lives on farms perched in the mountains. Some 20 km (12½ miles) south of El Bolsón, and bordering Chile, is the serene **Parque Nacional Lago Puelo** (237 sq km/92 sq miles), established in 1937 as an annex to nearby Parque Nacional Los Alerces. Another angler's paradise, the park has mountains covered with ancient forests of deciduous beech trees and cypresses and more than 100 species of birds. Basic camping facilities are available by the lakeshore, with some marked trails.

Handicrafts market at El Bolsón.

The gringo outlaws

Further south, on the road to Esquel, you come across the beautiful **Cholila Valley**, a little-known area where in early summer the fields are carpeted in blue by wild lupins. This was the place chosen by Butch Cassidy and the Sundance Kid, the US outlaws made famous by George Hill's 1969 movie

BELOW: Hotel Llao Llao, on Lago Nahuel Huapi.

starring Paul Newman and Robert Redford. Butch and Sundance sheltered temporarily in Cholila, while they were on the run from Pinkerton's agents. A letter sent by them to Matilda Davis in Utah, dated August 10, 1902, was posted at Cholila. After their famous hold-up of the Río Gallegos Bank in 1905, they were again on the run, until they were finally killed in Bolivia. Other members of the gang who stayed on in this region were ambushed and killed, years later, by the Argentine constabulary.

From Cholila, the road going south splits in two. RN40 turns slightly to the east, through the large Estancia Leleque, alongside the narrow-gauge railroad, until it reaches Esquel. The other route to Esquel takes you right into **Parque Nacional Los Alerces**. This park covers 2,630 sq km (1,012 sq miles) and is less spoiled by towns and people than other parks are in this region. Summer visitors to the park stay at campsites and fishermen's lodges around **Lago Futalaufquen**. One tour you should not miss is the all-day boat excursion, which leaves in the summer from Puerto Chucao to Lago Menéndez, the largest lake in the national park. There are outstanding views of **Cerro Torrecillas** (2,200 meters/7,260 ft) and its glaciers, and be sure to see the huge *Fitzroya* trees (related to the American redwood), some of which are over 2,000 years old.

Many sheep farms in Patagonia (see box on page 306) are being bought out by large multinational enterprises, who buy the majority of their raw wool for processing abroad. Italian clothing magnate Luciano Benetton bought seven sheep farms in the region, totaling 20,000 hectares (50,000 acres).

The Old Patagonian Express

As you get closer to Trevelín and Esquel you begin to leave behind the northern Lake District. This area is strongly influenced by Welsh culture, as a sizeable community of Welsh people settled here in 1888 after a long trek from the Atlantic coast along the Chubut Valley *(see page 308)*.

Traveling 167 km (104 miles) south of El Bolsón on RN40 and RN258 brings you to **Esquel ❼**, an offshoot of the Welsh Chubut colony. The town, with 32,000 inhabitants, lies to the east of the Andes, on the border of the Patagonian desert. In its remote location, on the edge of the desert, Esquel has the feel of a town in the old American West. You are as likely to see people riding on horseback here as in cars. Sometimes the rider will be a gaucho dandy, all dressed up with broad-brimmed hat, kerchief, and *bombachas* (baggy pleated pants). Several times a year, principally in January, a rural fair is held in Esquel. People come from miles around to trade livestock and agricultural supplies. In town, several stores *(talabarterías)* are well-stocked with riding tackle and ranch equipment. Ornate stirrups and hand-tooled saddles sit next to braided, rawhide ropes, and cast-iron cookware. This was once goose-hunting country, but the rare local species have since become protected.

BELOW: Cascada Los Césares, in the northern Lake District.

Esquel's railway station is the most southerly point of the Argentine rail network. The narrow-gauge railway (0.75 meters/2.48 ft), used to provide a regular service between Esquel and Ingeniero Jacobacci to the north. The train – La Trochita – was made famous abroad by US author Paul Theroux, in his book *The Old Patagonian Express*. These days it runs only a partial and intermittent schedule largely for the benefit of tourists. Nevertheless, if you happen to arrive at the right time, there is no better way to get acquainted with Patagonia and its people than by a trip on this quaint little train, which is pulled by an old-fashioned steam locomotive. For serious railway buffs, there are workshops open to visitors in El Maitén, providing a further glimpse of the romantic past.

In winter, Esquel turns into a ski resort, with **La Hoya Ski Center** only 15 km (10 miles) away. Compared with Bariloche and Villa Cerro Catedral, this ski area is considerably smaller and cozier but a range of rental facilities is available.

Trevelín ❽, 23 km (14 miles) southwest of Esquel, is a small village, also of Welsh origin. Its name in Welsh means "town of the mill." The old mill has been converted into a museum, the Museo Molino Viejo (open daily 11am–9pm), which houses all sorts of implements that belonged to the first Welsh settlers, together with old photographs and a Welsh Bible. As in all the Welsh communities of Patagonia, you can enjoy a typical tea with Welsh cookies and cakes in several cafes in Esquel.

The "Beautiful Valley" of Chubut

Between the Atlantic coast and Esquel lies the **Chubut Valley**. Only the lower valley, covering an area of 50 sq km (19 sq miles) is irrigated, while the rest is parched. The Welsh used this valley, which they called **Cwm Hyfrwd** (Beautiful Valley), to reach the Esquel/Trevelín area. Halfway down the valley, the river cuts through the plateau, forming an impressive canyon with red and white ravines named the Valle de los Altares and the Valle de los Mártires (Altars and Martyrs valleys). The latter refers to an ambush set by the Amerindians in 1884, in which a group of young Welshmen was wiped out. The lone survivor, John Evans, managed to escape, thanks to his horse, Malacara, which leapt over the steep ravine. The graves of these unfortunate people can be seen alongside the

Map on page 290

La Trochita, *the Old Patagonian Express, one of the oldest steam trains still in operation in South America.*

BELOW: tea time in Gaiman.

road. Before coming to the lower valley, you will reach the **Dique Embalse Florentino Ameghino** and its artificial lake. The dam and the reservoir are nestled in a narrow rocky gorge, forming an impressive sight.

Sea lions at Punta Tombo

The lower Chubut Valley was the site of the first settlement established by the Welsh. The towns of Dolavon, Gaiman, Trelew, and Rawson developed here, and today they are surrounded by intensively cultivated lands.

Gaiman ❾ has an interesting museum similar to the one in Trevelín, the **Museo Histórico Regional** (open Mon–Fri 4–8pm), housed in the old train station, with a gift shop. The town is famous for its Welsh teas, which are offered by four leading *casas de té* (teahouses) in somber rooms crowded with evocative memorabilia of the first settlers. An *eisteddfod* – Welsh Arts Festival – which features singing and reciting, is held here every August. The river meets the sea close to **Rawson ❿**, the provincial capital city. Coming back in the afternoon from an excursion to Punta Tombo, drive by the small fishermen's port at Rawson to watch the men as they unload their day's catch to see lazy sea lions grab whatever falls overboard.

Trelew is the most important city in the lower valley, and its airport is the gateway for visitors to the wildlife-rich Península Valdés area. Due to a program to promote industry in the 1980s, the population swelled here to 100,000. Its Welsh ambiance has faded and, apart from a leafy central square, it is not a particularly attractive city. One point of interest is a paleontological museum marking the important dinosaur remains that have been found in Patagonia. The **Museo Paleontológico Egidio Feruglio** (open daily Sept–Mar 9am–8pm,

BELOW: an itinerant sheep shearer plying his trade.

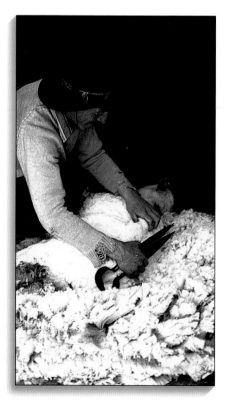

THE BIG SHEEP BOOM

The first governor of Santa Cruz, Carlos Moyano, could find no one to settle in the desolate south of Patagonia. In desperation, he invited young couples from the Malvinas/Falklands to try their hand "on the coast," and the first sheep farmers were English and Scottish shepherds. They were soon followed by people from many other nations, mainly in central Europe, who remained behind after the 1890s gold rush. The sheep rearing proved hugely successful, and, by the 1920s, Argentinian wool commanded record prices on the world market.

The sheep in southern Patagonia are mainly Scottish corriedale, although some merinos have been brought from Australia, and two hardy new breeds have been developed for the region. Farm work intensifies from October to April, with lamb marking, shearing, dipping, and moving the animals to the summer camps. In the fall they are moved back to the winter camps and the wool around the eyes is shorn.

Shearing is usually done by a *comparsa*, a group of professionals who travel from farm to farm, moving south with the season. However, each farm has its own shepherds and *peones* (unskilled workmen) who stay year round, tending fences and animals.

Apr–Aug 10am–6pm), on Avenida Fontana 140, contains fossil remains of dinosaurs such as carnotosaurus, the only known meat-eating dinosaur with horns, and the 65-million-year-old eggs of titanosaurus.

The Valdés Peninsula

Puerto Madryn ⓫ is the gateway for visitors to the Península Valdés and Punta Tombo. It is a spruce seaside town with extensive sands and flamingos in the bay. The **Museo Oceanográfico y de Ciencias Naturales** (open Mon–Fri 9am–1pm and 3–7pm), on the corner of Domecq and García Menéndez, is worth a visit for its collections of coastal and marine flora and fauna.

Don't miss the magnificent **EcoCentro**, Julio Verne 3784 (open Tues–Sun 10am–7pm). where local marine life is fascinatingly explained in various interactive displays and exhibits.

Punta Tombo, 165 km (102 miles) south of Madryn (108 km/67 miles of which is dirt road), has the largest colony of Magellanic penguins in the world. The penguins arrive in September and stay until March. In this colony you can literally walk among thousands of these comical birds as they come and go along well-defined "penguin highways" that link their nests with the sea across the tourist path, and see them fish near the coast for their meals.

The **Península Valdés ⓬** is one of the most important wildlife reserves in Argentina and was designated a World Heritage site in 1999. It is the breeding ground for southern right whales, elephant seals, and sea lions, and the nesting site for thousands of shore birds, including pelicans, cormorants, and oyster-catchers. Guanacos, rheas, and maras can all be spotted with sharp eyes. There is an interpretive center and museum at the entrance to the peninsula itself,

One of Gaiman's Welsh-built solid-brick houses, dating from the late 1800s.

BELOW: Cerro Guanaco, towering over the Río Negro.

The Welsh in Patagonia

Patagonia is partly pampas, largely desert and unrelentingly windblown, with only small areas of fertile soil and little discovered mineral wealth. Why would anyone leave the lush valleys and green hills of Wales to settle in such a place? The Welsh came, between 1865 and 1914, partly to escape conditions in Wales which they deemed culturally oppressive, partly because of the promise – later discovered to be exaggerated – of exciting economic opportunities, and largely to be able to pursue their religious traditions in their own language.

The disruptions of the 19th-century Industrial Revolution uprooted many Welsh agricultural workers: the cost of delivering produce to market became exorbitant because of turnpike fees, grazing land was enclosed, and landless laborers were exploited. Increasing domination of public life by arrogant English officials further upset the Welsh. Thus alienated in his own land, the Welshman left.

Equally powerful was the effect on the Welsh people of the religious revivals of the period, which precipitated a pious religionism that continued beyond World War I. For many, the worldliness of modern life made impossible the quiet spirituality of earlier times, and they saw their escape in distant, unpopulated areas of the world then opening up. Some had already tried Canada and the United States and were frustrated by the tides of other European nationalities which threatened the purity of their communities. They responded when Argentina offered cheap land to immigrants who would settle and develop its vast spaces before an aggressive Chile pre-empted them. From the United States and from Wales they came in small ships on hazardous voyages to Puerto Madryn, and settled in the Chubut Valley.

Although the hardships of those gritty pioneers are more than a century behind their descendants, the pioneer tradition is proudly remembered. Some remain in agriculture, many are in trade and commerce. Only a dwindling number of the older generation still speaks Welsh, but descendants will proudly show you their chapels and cemeteries (very similar to those in Wales), take you for Welsh tea in one of the area's many teahouses, and reminisce about their forebears and the difficulties they overcame. They speak of the devastating floods of the Chubut which almost demolished the community at the turn of the 20th century, the scouts who went on indigenous trails to the Andean foothills to settle in the Cwm Hyfrwd (the Beautiful Valley), the loneliness of the prairies in the long cold winters, the incessant winds, and the lack of capital which made all undertakings a matter of backbreaking labor.

Unfortunately, the old ways are being discarded in our modern technological era. The Welsh language will not long be spoken in Patagonia. But traditions are still upheld, and descendants of the Patagonian Welsh still hold eisteddfods to compete in song and verse. They revere the tradition of the chapel even when they do not attend, and they take enormous pride in their links with Wales. ❑

LEFT: a Welsh farmer proud of his crop.

Map on page 290

which is a large wasteland, with the lowest point on the South American continent, 40 meters (132 ft) below sea level. Some 40,000 elephant seals are found along a 200-km (125-mile) stretch of coastline, the outer edge of the Valdés Peninsula – the only such colony accessible by land outside Antarctica. Most of the beach is protected but tourists have a chance to observe the wildlife from specially constructed viewing hides at **Punta Norte** and **Caleta Valdés**, where two reserves have been established. About 10,000 elephant-seal pups are born each year from late August to early November.

Whale watching

Puerto Pirámides, 95 km (59 miles) from Puerto Madryn, was once a major center for whaling and trading in seal skins. In the 19th century there were more than 700 whalers operating in these waters. An international protection treaty was signed in 1935, and since then the whale population has recovered slowly, now standing at about 2,000. The whales come to breed near these shores around July and stay until mid-December. Whale watching is concentrated on mother and calf pairs and is organized by a few authorized, experienced boat owners from Puerto Pirámides *(see page 359)*. On shore, you can observe the sea lions and cormorant colonies from a viewing platform at the foot of the pyramid-shaped cliff that gives this location its name.

There are a couple of hotels and a shore-side campsite where you can wake to the sound of whales blowing in the bay. It is an ideal center for exploring the peninsula's other wildlife sites, too, although if you hire a vehicle, beware of the tricky driving conditions. On the small side road out of the peninsula stands a monument dedicated to the first Spanish settlement here, which only lasted

Years ago, huge quantities of salt were extracted from salt pits on the Península Valdés, and shipped out from Puerto Madryn.

LEFT: a Welsh Bible in the chapel.
BELOW: a Welsh gravestone.

A preserved tree trunk in the Bosque Petrificado José Ormachea.

from 1774 to 1810, when the settlers were forced to flee from the native warriors. Here too, is a sea-bird reserve, the **Isla de los Pájaros**.

Oil country

Some 440 km (270 miles) down the coast south of Trelew is Patagonia's major city, **Comodoro Rivadavia** ⓭, with a population exceeding 160,000. Its airport has daily flights connecting the Patagonian cities and Buenos Aires.

In 1907, while a desperate search for drinking water was underway, oil was discovered here. Since then, this has become one of the most important oil-producing regions in the country, and the vast landscape is strewn with "nodding donkey" oil pumps. There is an interesting petroleum museum (Museo Nacional del Petroleo; San Lorenzo 250; open Mon–Fri 9am–6pm), which traces the history of the industry in Argentina. The town witnessed the immigration of Boers from the Transvaal and the Orange State in South Africa, who left their homeland in search of a new place to live after the Boer War. The first arrivals landed in 1903, under the leadership of Conrad Visser and Martin Venter. Although some returned to South Africa, there are still many of their descendants living in the region. Today, Comodoro Rivadavia is a typical Patagonian city, with flat roofs, tall buildings, fisheries, textile factories, and the ever-present Patagonian wind.

Colonia Sarmiento ⓮, 190 km (118 miles) west of Comodoro Rivadavia, lies in a fertile valley flanked by two huge lakes, Lagos Musters and Colhué Huapi, which attract black-necked swans. Heading south from the valley for 30 km (19 miles), you reach the **Bosque Petrificado José Ormachea**, which has remains that are more than a million years old. This forest tells us much about the geological past of this land, which a long time ago was covered in trees.

BELOW: wildlife in action at the Península Valdés.

Santa Cruz

The province of **Santa Cruz** is the second largest in Argentina but with the smallest population per square kilometer. Before becoming president, Néstor Kirchner was governor here. Most of Santa Cruz is dry grassland or semidesert, with high *mesetas* (plateaux) interspersed with protected valleys and covered with large sheep estancias.

RN3, nearly all of which is paved, is the province's main coastal road. It follows the shoreline of Golfo San Jorge south to the oil town of **Caleta Olivia** ⓯, with its huge central statue of an oil worker, then climbs inland. After 86 km (53 miles), RN281 branches off RN3 for 126 km (78 miles) to the coastal port of **Puerto Deseado** ⓰, named after the *Desire*, flagship of the 16th-century English global navigator, Thomas Cavendish.

Virtually unknown for many years, Puerto Deseado is the home base for a number of ships which fish in the western South Atlantic. It is beginning to develop as a tourist center, particularly for its rich coastal wildlife. There are sea-lion colonies at Cabo Blanco to the north, and Isla Pingüino to the south of the bay, where you might see yellow-crested penguins and the unusual Guanay cormorant, and where spectacular black and white Commerson's dolphins play with boats sailing in the estuary just outside the town.

Back on RN3, the next important stop is a pristine natural wonder, the **Monumento Natural Bosques Petrificados 🇹**, just 80 km (50 miles) to the west of the highway. This enormous petrified forest occupies over 15,000 hectares (247,000 acres). At the edges of canyons and mesas, the rock-hard trunks of 150 million-year-old monkey-puzzle trees stick out of the ground. Some trunks are 30 meters (100 ft) long and a meter (a yard) thick – among the largest in the world. There are no overnight facilities at the park, and it closes at sundown, but there is a campsite with a store at La Paloma, 20 km (12 miles) from the park headquarters.

Map on page 290

Explorers' traces

About 250 km (155 miles) further south on RN3 is the picturesque port of **Puerto San Julián 🇹**, also awakening to tourism, with several hotels and a small museum. Both Magellan (in 1520) and Drake (in 1578) spent the winter here and hanged mutineers on the eastern shore. Nothing remains there except a small plaque. Not far to the south of San Julián is the little town of **Comandante Luis Piedra Buena 🇹**, on the Río Santa Cruz, which was followed upstream by FitzRoy, Moreno, and other early explorers. Its main attraction is the tiny shack on Isla Pavón, occupied in 1859 by Piedra Buena, an Argentine naval hero. The island, on the river, is linked to the town by road bridge.

About 29 km (18 miles) downstream lies the sleepy town of **Puerto Santa Cruz**, with its port, Punta Quilla, which is the base for ships that service the offshore oil rigs.

BELOW: oil pumps in the Patagonian south.

Gateway to national parks

The capital of the province is **Río Gallegos ⓴**, some 180 km (112 miles) south of Puerto Santa Cruz. It is a sprawling city of 100,000 on the south bank of the eponymous river, which has the third-highest tides in the world, at 16 meters (53 ft). At low tide, ships are left high and dry on mud flats. It is perhaps one of the most austere places in Argentina, but it has some historic appeal if you're interested in industrial heritage. There are several museums and signs designate historical spots. The enormous Swift meat-packing plant has been abandoned, but the train yards, with several old engines, still receive coal from the Río Turbio, on the opposite side of the province.

The town's main function for tourism however, is for visitors heading inland to the lovely scenic areas of El Calafate on Lago Argentino, the Parque Nacional Los Glaciares, and to Punta Arenas and the Parque Nacional Torres del Paine in Chile.

Moving southwest of Río Gallegos, RN3 enters Chile near a series of rims of long-extinct volcanoes. One of these, Laguna Azul, is a geological reserve, 3 km (1½ miles) off the main highway near the border post.

Penguins and dolphins

Some 11 km (6 miles) south of Río Gallegos, Ruta 1 branches southeast off RN3, over open plains to **Cabo Vírgenes** (129 km/80 miles from Río Gallegos) and Punta Dungeness (on the border with Chile) at the northeast mouth of the Strait of Magellan. Here you can see Argentina's second-largest penguin colony, home to some 300,000 birds; visit the lighthouse; and perhaps watch dolphins just offshore. Near the cliffs are the meagre remains of Ciudad Nombre de Jesús,

BELOW: the empty coastline of Santa Cruz.

founded by the Spanish explorer Pedro Sarmiento de Gamboa in 1584. The road to Cabo Virgenes passes a couple of sheep farms: Estancia Cóndor, one of the larger estancias in the area, which is now owned by the Benetton famil; a few kilometers beyond that is Estancia Monte Dinero, which has a separate guesthouse for visitors and which also offers wildlife trips to the penguin colony at Cabo Virgenes (tel: 02966-426 900).

Map on page 290

Westward on Ruta Nacional 40

Western Santa Cruz province is spectacular but desolate. The main route through it is on **RN40** – the longest road in the country, snaking its way up through the Northwest as far as the Bolivian border – and not a road to be taken lightly. Those who have traveled it from top to bottom are full of admiration for the rugged beauty of the country and are proud they have survived it. RN40 is not even accurately detailed on most maps, including those of the prestigious Instituto Geográfico Militar. The best one is the ACA (Automóvil Club Argentino) map of the province of Santa Cruz. In winter, some parts of the road may be inaccessible.

Southern RN40 is a difficult gravel road – rocky and dusty when dry, muddy when wet. Places marked on the map may consist of just one shack or may not exist at all. You must carry extra fuel and/or go out of your way at several places to refill. Sometimes small towns, or even larger ones run out of gasoline and you may have to wait several days until a fuel truck comes along. In southwestern Patagonia there are gas stations only at Perito Moreno, Bajo Caracoles, Tres Lagos, El Calafate, and Río Turbio.

If you take any secondary roads, remember that there is no fuel available.

BELOW: the José Ormachea Petrified Forest Reserve.

You also need to carry spare tires, some food, and probably even your bed. There are few places to buy food or even a soft drink outside the larger towns. El Calafate is the main town of the southern Lake District, 313 km (194 miles) from Río Gallegos. Halfway there is Esperanza, a truck stop with a gas station and road-side snack bar; nearby is Estancia Chali-Aike, which takes paying guests. Most of the drive is past ranches over the *meseta central*, coming to a high lookout at Cuesta de Miguez, where the whole of Lake Argentino, the mountains and glaciers beyond, and even Mount Fitz Roy can be seen.

El Calafate ㉑, a town of about 10,000, nestles at the base of cliffs on the south shore of beautiful **Lago Argentino**, one of Argentina's largest lakes. An airport constructed in 2000 receives direct flights from Buenos Aires and this is the jumping-off point for the surrounding area, particularly to the Parque Nacional Los Glaciares. On the eastern shore of Lago Argentino, at the edge of town, is Laguna Nimez, a small bird reserve (open daily 9am–9pm), which is home to a variety of ducks, geese, flamingos, and elegant black-necked swans. Walking around the lake from here is tricky however, as the ground is boggy and crisscrossed with wide streams. Accommodations range from campsites and a youth hostel to elegant hotels. There are several tourist agencies and a number of good restaurants. Large tour groups do the circuit – Buenos Aires, Puerto Madryn, El Calafate, Ushuaia, Buenos Aires – every week.

The Hotel Los Alamos, one of the best hotels in El Calafate and a typical example of the locally popular Alpine-style architecture.

BELOW: El Calafate, on the shores of Lago Argentino.

Parque Nacional Los Glaciares

Traveling 51 km (32 miles) west of El Calafate, along the south shore of the Península Magallanes, brings you to the **Parque Nacional Los Glaciares ㉒**, one of the most spectacular parks in Argentina. The southern Patagonian icecap,

which is about 400 km (250 miles) long, spills over into innumerable glaciers *(ventisqueros)*, which end on high cliffs or wend their way down to fjords. Just beyond the Península Magallanes, you can cross Brazo Rico in a boat for a guided climb on the World Heritage Site of the glacier of **Ventisquero Perito Moreno**. A few kilometers on, the road ends at the *pasarelas*, a series of walkways and terraces down a steep cliff, which faces the glacier head on. It's a magnificent sight, especially on a sunny day. Visitors line up along the walkways, cameras at the ready like paparazzi at the Oscar awards ceremony, waiting for a chunk of glacier to calve off into the water with a resounding thunderous crack.

The Perito Moreno glacier advances across the narrow stretch of water in front of it until it cuts off Brazo Rico and Brazo Sur from the rest of Lago Argentino. Pressure slowly builds up behind the glacial wall until, about every three to four years, the wall collapses dramatically and the cycle begins again. The glacier has not advanced since 1988, however, leading scientists to question whether global warming is to blame: 90 percent of the world's glaciers are retreating. Old water levels can be seen around these lakes. Hiking too near the glacial front is prohibited because of the danger from waves caused by falling ice.

Upsala Glacier

The second major trip from El Calafate is a visit to the **Ventisquero Upsala**, at the far northwest end of Lago Argentino. Boats leave every morning from Punta Bandera, 40 km (25 miles) west of El Calafate. In early spring, they cannot get near Upsala because of the large field of icebergs, so may visit Spegazzini and other glaciers instead. Some trips stop for a short walk through the forest to Onelli glacier. On the way back, stop at Estancia Alice, on the road to El Calafate. *Asados* (barbecues) and tea are available here, and shearing demonstrations are held in season. You may also see black-necked swans and other birds.

It is only a short distance across the Sierra Los Baguales from Parque Nacional Los Glaciares, Argentina, to Parque Nacional Torres del Paine, in Chile. From some spots near El Calafate, the Paine mountains can be seen. But there is no road through. Instead, you must backtrack to Puerto El Cerrito (at least that section is paved) and then take RN40 again west and south to enter Chile either at Cancha Carrera or further south at Río Turbio. You can also fly back to Río Gallegos and fly on to Punta Arenas, in Chile, from where it is still a seven-hour drive north to the Paine National Park.

Some 230 km (143 miles) south of El Calafate, **Río Turbio** is a coal-mining and oil town little visited by tourists although it does have an airport and a small skiing center nearby. From here, RN40 makes a winding loop across the bottom of the province, then heads east to meet RN3 just west of Río Gallegos.

Monte Fitz Roy

Returning north, up RN40 from El Calafate, at the far northern end of the Parque Nacional Los Glaciares

Map on page 290

A shop in El Calafate selling handmade chocolates – a local specialty.

BELOW: the Perito Moreno Glacier.

Map on page 290

are some of the most impressive peaks in the Andes, including Cerro Torre (3,128 meters/10,263 ft) and Monte Fitz Roy (3,406 meters/11,175 ft). In good weather Fitz Roy can be seen from El Calafate. The sheer granite peaks attract climbers from all over the world, who describe their experiences in the register at the northern entrance to the park.

The best base for visiting this part of the national park is the village of **El Chaltén ㉓**, some 90 km (56 miles) west, off RN40, above the western end of **Lago Viedma**. The village – whose name means "blue mountain," the Amerindian name for Fitz Roy – nestles in a hidden bowl at the foot of the mountain, with its glacier coming down off the Southern Patagonian Ice Field. The once tiny village has expanded rapidly in recent years due to its ever-growing popularity with visiting trekkers and mountain climbers. It has a national park information office, food and souvenir stores, and a gas station. There is a range of accommodations available including holiday bungalows, hostels, and basic campsites. In summer, there are two daily buses from El Calafate, 219 km (136 miles) to the south.

Continuing north on RN40, at Tres Lagos, Ruta 31 leads northwest to **Lago San Martín** (called Lago O'Higgins in Chile). Estancia La Maipú is situated on the south shore, offering accommodations, horseback riding, and trekking.

About 560 km (348 miles) north of El Chaltén, the northwesternmost town in Santa Cruz province is **Perito Moreno**, a dusty place with little to offer. From here however, a paved road leads 57 km (35 miles) west to the small town of **Los Antiguos ㉔**, on the shore of Lago Buenos Aires. Small farms here produce milk, honey, fruit, and vegetables; the town has a couple of hotels and a campsite. Three km (1½ miles) to the west, you can cross the Chilean border to the town of Chile Chico and other scenic areas near the Río Baker.

BELOW: Lago Espejo in the northern Lake District.
RIGHT: Monte Fitz Roy at sunrise.

Cave paintings

South of Perito Moreno is the **Cueva de las Manos** (Cave of the Hands), a national historical monument and World Heritage Site located in a beautiful canyon 56 km (35 miles) off RN40 from just north of Bajo Caracoles. Pre-Columbian cave paintings are found all over Santa Cruz, but those at Cueva de las Manos are the finest. The walls here are covered by paintings of hands and animals, principally guanacos (relatives of the llama), which are thought to be anything between 3,000 and 10,000 years old. Numerous lakes straddle the Argentine–Chilean border in this region. RN40 lies well to the east of the mountains. Any excursions to the lakes to the west, such as Lago Ghio, Pueyrredón, Belgrano, and San Martín, must be made along side roads; there are no circuits – you must go in and out on the same road. The road to Lago Pueyrredón leaves from Bajo Caracoles.

Parque Nacional Perito Moreno ㉕ (not to be confused with the town of the same name) is the next major stop, 72 km (45 miles) to the west of RN40. In the distance is Monte San Lorenzo, the highest peak in Santa Cruz at 3,706 meters (12,150 ft). Within the park are lakes Belgrano and Burmeister. Near the latter is the Casa de Piedra, a strange rock formation with ancient paintings. ❑

SAFARI TO THE SOUTHERN STEPPE

In the vast and lonely expanses of Patagonia, people are far outnumbered by the region's wild inhabitants, ranging from condors to cougars

From its harsh interior to its strikingly beautiful coast, Patagonia is tailor-made for wildlife watching. Grey foxes are a common sight almost everywhere, and the open steppe is home to Patagonian hares or maras, to rheas (relatives of the ostrich), and to the elusive puma or cougar. Patches of marshy ground are good places to watch southern lapwings – probably Patagonia's noisiest birds – while to the west, the foothills of the Andes offer a good chance to spot condors as they soar high overhead in search of food. However, for most visitors, Patagonia's biggest attraction is its coastal wildlife, and the best time to see it is during the southern spring and summer, when penguins, seals, and whales all gather along the shore to breed.

WHALE WATCHING

Like seals and penguins, Patagonia's whales are animals of fixed habits, breeding at the same sites year after year. The Península Valdés is one of the most famous of them all, hosting over 10 percent of the world's southern right whale population for three or four months each year. With so many of these huge, docile mammals crowded into the peninsula's bays, the result is a wildlife spectacle not to be missed, and whale-watching boat trips can be organized locally.

▷ **UNDERGROUND OWL**
In a bleak, treeless landscape, burrowing owls raise their young under-ground. These birds feed by night and day, often on insects.

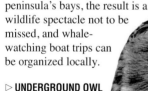

▷ **PENINSULA VALDES**
Despite its barren landscape, this peninsula in northern Patagonia is one of the country's richest sites for shore birds and sea mammals.

△ **RAPID EXIT**
With its strange bouncing run, the Patagonian hare or mara can speed along at 45 km/h (28 mph). True hares – from Europe – are also common here.

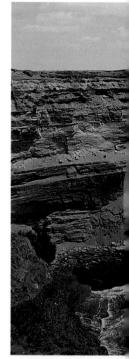

△ **SOCIAL BIRDS**
Huge rookeries of Magellanic penguins can be seen on the Península Valdés and the adjacent coastline.

▷ **TOP CAT**
Puma has one of the biggest ranges of any cat – Patagonia to western Canada.

WHERE TO SPOT THE WILDLIFE

Wildlife tourism is still relatively new in Patagonia, but there are numerous companies in Trelew and Puerto Madryn that can arrange tours to Península Valdés and whale-watching boat trips. Be aware also that the distances involved here can be very large: with day trips especially, you may find that you spend a lot of time on the move.

The penguin breeding season runs from about October to March, with the down-covered chicks hatching from late November onwards. The biggest colony – and the most visited one by far – is at Punta Tombo. The colony at Cabo dos Bahías, further down the coast, is more time-consuming to reach, but offers the added attraction of other kinds of wildlife, including rheas and numerous guanacos.

On the Península Valdés, the whale-watching season extends from June to December – roughly from early winter to early summer. To make the most of this spectacular area it's worth staying here for several days.

◁ **ON THE ALERT**
Patagonian foxes are hunted mainly for their fur, but they still skillfully manage to survive in large numbers.

△ **SLIM PICKINGS**
A condor picks over a carcass high up in the Andes. These carrion-eating birds can be seen all the way down the Andes to the far south of Patagonia.

◁ **BLACK-NECKED SWANS**
These distinctive birds live mainly in freshwater lakes and marshes, although they occasionally feed on the coast.

TIERRA DEL FUEGO

Map on page 326

Wild and windswept, the uttermost south has been the ultimate challenge to travelers and explorers since the early days of global navigation and discovery

Tierra del Fuego, the Land of Fire, lies at the southern tip of the South American continent. Beyond is only the icy mass of Antarctica. You really feel that you have reached the end of the earth here, in a wild, mysterious land. The very name evokes feelings of distance, fear of the elements, isolation, and loneliness. But the feeling of isolation can be an invigorating one, allied with a spirit of adventure.

In the days of sail, many people – the early merchants, explorers, and scientists – were able to claim that they had rounded Cape Horn. Some were shipwrecked there, but few stayed to settle. With the opening of the Panama Canal in 1914, fewer ships took the southernmost route. By then, Europeans had settled parts of Tierra del Fuego, but it was difficult for tourists to reach.

Transport links to Tierra del Fuego have improved considerably since then and it has become a popular destination for the discerning traveler. And although all the above images can be true enough, most visitors are pleasantly surprised by the uttermost south. The best months to visit are October to April, before the southern winter closes in.

PRECEDING PAGES: Fuegian king crab rivals Alaska's in size and taste. **LEFT:** Isla de los Estados. **BELOW:** figurehead in Ushuaia.

Geography and climate

About 9,000 years ago, the waters of the Strait of Magellan broke through the tip of the continent, isolating Tierra del Fuego from Patagonia. Technically, Tierra del Fuego includes all the land south of the Strait of Magellan and north of the Drake Passage, although only one island, the Isla Grande, is actually called Tierra del Fuego. Locally, the Isla Grande is known simply as "La Isla." It is surrounded, to the south and west, by a maze of mountainous islands, islets, channels, and fjords, most of them uninhabited and many unexplored.

The Fuegian Archipelago is within the Subantarctic Zone. Its cool climate is dominated by the prevailing southwesterly winds which sweep in off the South Pacific and waters further south. These often gale-force winds can occur throughout the year but are strongest from the end of August to March (spring and summer).

The Andes, curving from northwest to east across the archipelago, ensure high rain over the western and southern islands, leaving less moisture for the northeastern plains. Temperatures along the Beagle Channel range from a record high of 30°C (86°F) in summer to a record low of about -14°C (7°F) in winter. Temperatures in the plains region are more extreme, but all of Tierra del Fuego lives in a perpetual "cool spring."

Exploration and settlement

Humans arrived on the archipelago in two ways. The earliest record is an 11,800-year-old site in northern

Tierra del Fuego occupied by nomadic hunters – people who, near the end of the last ice age, crossed the Magellanic land bridge before waters broke through it. In southern Tierra del Fuego, the oldest adaptation to a marine environment is a 6,000-year-old site at Tunel on the Beagle Channel, developed by canoe peoples. On the arrival of the Europeans, four cultural groups populated the area: the Ona (Selk'nam) and Haush were the guanaco-hunters of the plains, while the Yahgans (Yámana) and Alaculuf were the spear-hunting canoe natives of the islands and channels. Eliminated mainly by white man's diseases, less than five pure members remain of the first three groups, although there are many people of mixed race.

The European exploration of Tierra del Fuego – first by Magellan in 1520, then by pirates, explorers, collectors, scientists, sealers and whalers, missionaries, seekers of gold, and merchants – is among the most fascinating in the world. Many tourists visit Tierra del Fuego because of childhood memories of stories of Drake, Cook, and Darwin, or the arduous, careful surveys of Fitzroy and King. In his book, *Uttermost Part of the Earth* (1946), E. Lucas Bridges tells how his father, Thomas Bridges, began the Anglican Mission in Ushuaia (1869), explored unknown areas, worked with and taught the Yahgans, and finally settled the first farm. The missionaries were followed by a coastguards' station, gold miners, sheep farmers, small merchants, oil workers, and all those needed to make up a modern town. In one century, Tierra del Fuego went from a land of near-naked natives to a major tourist destination for cruise liners and yachtsmen.

Across the strait

Politically, Tierra del Fuego is split between Chile (to the west and south) and Argentina (north and east). The Argentine section is part of the Provincia

Map of Tierra del Fuego, marking the southern limit of Ruta Nacional 3.

BELOW: back from the barber's.

Map on page 326

de Tierra del Fuego, Antártida e Islas del Atlántico Sur, with its capital in the town of Ushuaia. The rough triangle that is Argentina's part of the Isla Grande covers some 21,340 sq km (8,300 sq miles).

Visitors arrive by several means. Aerolíneas Argentinas, LADE, and smaller airlines provide daily flights from Buenos Aires and other areas. Tourist ships visit Ushuaia briefly as part of longer cruises between Río de Janeiro, Buenos Aires, and the west coast of South America. Ushuaia, like Punta Arenas in Chile, is a jumping-off point for a number of ships to Antarctica.

Visitors coming by land must cross the Strait of Magellan by ferry, either at the First Narrows (a 20–30-minute crossing) or between Punta Arenas and Porvenir (a 2–3-hour crossing) in Chile. There are no regular bus routes between Río Gallegos and Río Grande (charter services may be available), but there are two routes between Río Grande and Ushuaia.

Flora and fauna

Plant and animal life in this subantarctic climate is less varied in species than in warmer regions. Only six kinds of tree are found; the dominant three are species of *Nothofagus* or southern beech. Several kinds of shrubs produce beautiful flowers or edible berries. The most famous is the calafate *(Berberis buxifolia)*; legend says you will come back again if you brave its long thorns to eat the delicious, seedy berries. Most wildflowers are small but well worth searching for. Flowering plants and ferns total about 500 species, but some 150 of these have been introduced or naturalized.

Native land animals are few: the guanaco, Fuegian fox (or Andean wolf), bats, tucu-tucu, and mice. An abundance of introduced animals, such as beaver,

BELOW:
a sheep farm
near Río Grande.

muskrats, rabbits, and Patagonian foxes thrive here. About 200 species of birds are resident or visit. Surprisingly, this cool climate is also home to parrots (the *Austral conure*), flamingos, and hummingbirds. The sea is highly productive in algae, with the result that 27 species of whale visit the archipelago.

Escaping the northern winter

Many visitors find the northern plains of Tierra del Fuego rather barren, but there is much to do and see. Those arriving by road must enter from Chile at **Bahía San Sebastián ❶**, where there is border control, a small *hostería* (reservations with the Argentine Automobile Club, ACA), a restaurant, and a gas station. Enormous mud flats, periodically covered by 11-meter (36-ft) tides, extend along the west of the bay. This is an important feeding area for thousands of small birds which escape the northern hemisphere winter here; the entire coast is part of the Hemispheric Shorebird Reserve network.

Gold, fossils, and sheep

This is sheep-farming and oil country, where wells dot the grasslands and rolling hills. The western Strait of Magellan, in Chile, is peppered with oil platforms. Oil supply roads run in all directions, while sheep, cattle, guanacos, and wild geese graze among them. In winter, guanacos can be seen along any of the secondary roads. The best way to see them in summer is to drive north along the bay from the San Sebastián border post.

A 45-minute drive will take you to the base of the stony, super-barren **Península El Páramo**, but family groups of guanacos can be seen on the salt flats long before that. The Páramo was once the main site of the gold rush

An Ona man, from E. Lucas Bridges' The Uttermost Part of the Earth *(1946), the classic portrayal of the Amerindians of Tierra del Fuego.*

BELOW: signpost in Ushuaia.

(1886–98). The Romanian-born adventurer, Julius Popper, set up his mining operation here and became immensely rich. Today, nothing remains of his buildings, dredges, or cemetery.

Cliffs along the coast near Cabo Espíritu Santo and the roads near San Sebastián yield both marine and forest fossils while sandstone hills farther south are littered with fossilized shells and crabs. The plains may look yellow or brown and appear to have little life, but this is Tierra del Fuego's best sheep land. If you stop to look and listen, you will discover many birds. A short walk will reveal hidden wildflowers.

Before the days of oil, sheep farming was the main industry of northern Fuegia. Thousands of sheep, mainly Corriedale, covered the plains. The larger farms produced (and still do) world-class, prize-winning pedigree sheep.

Further south down RN3 is the **Escuela Agrotécnica Salesiana**, which functions on the site of the Salesian Mission to the Onas, established in 1893. It is now a national monument. The original church and several other buildings have been restored; there is a small museum of artifacts and mounted birds.

Río Grande

Founded as recently as 1921, the town of **Río Grande ❷** (population 40,000) is the center of the sheep and oil region, as well as the home of a number of companies producing television sets, radios, synthetics, and other products – the result of a special 1972 law designed to bring development and more residents to this far reach of the republic.

Río Grande sprawls over the flat northern coast of the river. The wide, wind-blown streets overlook the waters of the South Atlantic. The Río Grande has silted up, allowing for little shipping. The town was an important center during the 1982 Falklands/Malvinas conflict, and has several monuments to those killed.

Río Grande has a cultural center, a number of video clubs, but no movie theater. The municipal **Museo de Ciencias Naturales e Historia** (open daily, weekends pm only), on Calle Elcano near the sea, is well worth a visit.

This is Tierra del Fuego's fishing center. Trout (rainbow, brook, and brown) and salmon were introduced in the 1930s, and reach record sizes. Until recently fishing was open in all areas, permission being needed only to cross estancia land. Now access to this land can be gained only with guides and there is a charge. The Río Grande is ideal for sea-run brown trout. Best fishing times are January to March and upmarket estancias are the ideal choice as a fishing base.

West of Río Grande lies **Estancia María Behety**, a picturesque village with an enormous shearing shed (room for 40 shearers), which is reported to be the world's largest.

Forest and mountain

Roads heading west and southwest from Río Grande branch off into the mountains, and cover steep hills, plains, forest, *vegas* (damp meadows), and estancias. This is a fascinating area to explore, if you have time. *Kau-tapen* ("fishing-house" in Ona) on Estancia La

Map on page 326

TIP

A popular site for keen fossil hunters is Cabo Domingo, up the coast just to the north of Río Grande, and near to the Salesian Mission Museum.

BELOW: a glacial valley along the Beagle Channel.

Homesteads in Tierra del Fuego are sparsely scattered, with neighbors few and far between.

Retranca is an exclusive fishing lodge. To the south, **Lago Yehuin**, favored for camping and horseback riding, and the Río Claro to the west are good fishing areas being developed for tourism.

The eastern point of Tierra del Fuego is a mostly unused wilderness of forest, swamp, and mountain and can be reached only on foot, horseback, or helicopter.

South of Río Grande

Driving to Ushuaia along RN3 is an education in ecology, for one goes from the flat sea coast through hilly, grassy plains and *vegas*, from low bush land on to scrubby deciduous forest (*ñire* or "low beech"); then, turning inland, the road climbs to healthier deciduous forest (*lenga* or "high beech"); up the mountain slopes nearly to the tree line, and then down on the south side of the mountains to thick forest interspersed with evergreen beech *(coihue* or *guindo)* and valleys filled with sphagnum swamps.

The small town of **Tolhuin** ❸ lies just north of the 100-km (60-mile) long Lago Fagnano, in the heart of the island. The word Tolhuin is the Ona name for a nearby heart-shaped hill. Take the back road out of town to the beach on Lago Fagnano, a popular site with fishing facilities and a place for barbecues. RN3 then turns inland past burnt-over forest and sawmills to wind up the mountains at **Paso Garibaldi**. Although sawmills here were once prosperous, pine imported from Chile is cheaper and generally used for construction. In the valley just north of the pass lies the tranquil Lago Escondido. Be sure to stop at the lookout on Paso Garibaldi to look north over Lago Escondido and Lago Fagnano. This windswept spot attracts many local birds, and you can walk along the rocky lakeshore for a short distance, past beavers' dams and small farmsteads.

BELOW: headed for the shearer.

WHAT'S IN A NAME?

The story goes that Tierra del Fuego (Land of Fire) got its name from early European explorers, who, when passing by on ships en route to riches further west, could see the landscape dotted with the campfires of the islands' original inhabitants.

This theory was expanded upon by Lucas Bridges (1874–1949), the son of an English missionary who spent his life in Tierra del Fuego and who wrote an account of frontier life among the Amerindians, *The Uttermost Part of the Earth*: "If a distant sail appeared, or anything else occurred to startle those who had remained at home, they [the Yahgan] would send out a signal to those away fishing by piling green branches or shrubs on the wigwam fire. At the sight of the black signal smoke the fishers would hurry back home. The early explorers of that archipelago would see these countless columns of smoke rising at short intervals for miles along the coast."

Perhaps the final word on the matter can be found in Bruce Chatwin's *In Patagonia*: "The fires were the camp fires of the Fuegian Indians. In one version Magellan saw smoke only and called it Tierra del Humo, the Land of Smoke, but Charles V said there was no smoke without fire and changed the name."

The Beagle Channel

South of the pass, the road curves downward to Rancho Hambre and the Tierra Mayor Valley. RN3 runs westward through this valley and then southward through that of the Río Olivia to the Canal Beagle (Beagle Channel) and Ushuaia. At Bahía Brown the beach is lined with Yahgan shell middens, the circular heaps of discarded mussel shells that once surrounded their low shelters.

In the hills above the Canal Beagle lies **Estancia Harberton ④**, the oldest farm in Argentine Tierra del Fuego, founded by the Reverend Thomas Bridges in 1886. Open to the public from October to April (9am–7pm), the farm offers a guided walking tour of the property, which includes Tierra del Fuego's oldest nature reserve: a small wood with native trees. There are also some Yahgan kitchen middens and a model wigwam. Visitors can have tea in the original farmhouse by the bay. You can also visit Harberton by catamaran from Ushuaia (daily in summer), but traveling this way the stay at the farm is short. The area around Harberton is ideal for bird-watching, with the opportunity to see steamer ducks, cormorants, oystercatchers, and perhaps an eagle or condor.

Back on RN3, the **Valle Tierra Mayor** is a winter-sports center in a picturesque setting between the Sorondo and Alvear mountain ranges. It has several lodges for cross-country skiing, snowmobiles, and dog sleds in winter.

West of the Tierra Mayor valley lies the Valle Carbajal, between high mountains with views toward Chile. The road follows the Río Olivia along the west side of the beautiful **Monte Olivia**, where peat is harvested from swamps in the valley for sale in Buenos Aires. At last, the **Canal Beagle** appears in the distance.

At the mouth of the Río Olivia a rustic hiking trail follows the coast eastward to Estancia Túnel and eventually all the way to Harberton and points east. On the west shore of the river is the local government fish hatchery.

RN3 turns westward on a new paved road above the city of Ushuaia, or you can follow the older gravel road along the coast.

Bright lights

The city of **Ushuaia ⑤** (population about 60,000) sits in a picturesque bowl on the southern side of the mountains, overlooking Bahía Ushuaia, the Canal Beagle, and Navarino and Hoste islands (both in Chile) to the south. To the east rise the peaks of the spectacular, pointed Monte Olivia and the Cinco Hermanos (Five Brothers). Ushuaia is the home of a large naval base, government offices, and stores for imported goods. It is a base for one or two farms, sawmills, a crab fishery, and a growing offshore fishing industry.

A simple triangular monument near the airfield marks the site of the **Anglican Mission** (1869–1907). Thomas and Mary Bridges (1870) and John and Clara Lawrence (1873) became the archipelago's first non-indigenous permanent residents. The official founding of the town was the establishment of a sub-prefecture (coastguard) in 1884.

Ushuaia's prison (1902–47) is now within the naval base. The octopus-shaped jail is open to the public and contains a small naval museum, the **Museo Marítimo y Presidio de Ushuaia** (open daily 9am–8pm), which includes fascinating miniature scenes from the

BELOW: the firebrush *(notro)* blossom, a commonly seen blaze of color on the hillsides.

Map on page 326

Plaque in Ushuaia commemorating the War of the Malvinas (Falkland Islands) in 1982.

BELOW: a testimony to the force of the wind in Tierra del Fuego.

earliest days of the discovery, exploration, and settlement of Tierra del Fuego.

Houses with decorative cornices built by prisoners are still scattered in the older part of town. A train once took inmates to fell trees in the outlying forests along the same route plied by the diminutive steam-powered Ferrocarril Austral Fueguino trains (Tren del Fin del Mundo), that today treat tourists to a 2½-hour excursion through Tierra del Fuego National Park.

A walk through the town's steep streets reveals a strange variety of architecture. The early wooden houses covered with corrugated iron (to help prevent fires) with their prisoner-produced gingerbread decorations have a somewhat Russian flavor. They are intermingled with modern concrete structures, imported Swedish prefabs, and hundreds of small, wooden shanties.

Ushuaia is much more geared to the tourist than Río Grande. There are a number of hotels and budget hostels, including two large ones on the mountain behind the town. The tourist office (open daily) on Avenida San Martín 674 provides information and brochures and has branches at the airport and port.

The restaurants of Ushuaia feature *róbalo* (mullet) and *centolla* (southern king crab) from the Canal Beagle. For those who prefer meat, *asado* (lamb, mutton, or beef roasted over an open fire) is another specialty.

Stores in Ushuaia pay only half the import duty that is charged in the rest of the country, and so focus on imported items (sweaters, jackets, and china from Europe; cigarettes, whisky, and radios). There is little to buy that is native to Tierra del Fuego.

The **Museo del Fin del Mundo** (open Mon–Sat, pm winter; daily in summer), on the corner of Maipú and Rivadavia, has information on the indigenous Yamana people, explorers' and missionaries' artifacts, and an attractive collec-

tion of (stuffed) local birds. Active historical research, especially of the eastern tip of the island, Península Mitre, is carried out from here. The **Museo Mundo Yamana** on Rivadavia 56 (open daily 10am–8pm) tells the story of the Yamana people who were wiped out by Europeans.

Tierra del Fuego National Park

A winding road climbs behind the town to the slopes of the **Montes Martial**, past two large hotels to a chair lift which goes up to the valley at the foot of the small, hanging Martial Glacier. In winter the lift takes you to ski slopes; in summer, the glacial hollow at the top of the lift is an ideal place to hike and see Andean flowers, such as the chocolate-scented *Nassauvia*, or even the rare mountain seed snipe.

A 20-minute drive west of Ushuaia brings you to the **Parque Nacional Tierra del Fuego ❻**, Argentina's first coastal national park. Near the park entrance, a road drops down to the channel at Ensenada, with native trees and Yahgan shell middens. To the north, the Río Pipo, with low falls, winds into the mountains. Further west, you catch a view of the Murray Narrows to the south, the narrow channel between islas Navarino and Hoste through which came Master Murray of the *Beagle*. Further on is Lago Roca, a large lake hemmed by mountains, shared by Argentina and Chile. The park is ideal for birding, hiking, camping, and kayaking. The best time of year to visit is late April, when the fall brings out the colors of the trees.

Cruising the southern seas

Daily, three-hour excursions on the Beagle Channel aboard large catamarans visit the islands off Bahía Ushuaia to see colonies of sea lions, southern fur seals, cormorants, gulls, and terns. Longer trips go westward to Lapataia or eastward on the channel to see the Magellan penguins on Isla Yecapasela (Martillo) and visit Estancia Harberton.

Several yachts based in Ushuaia's harbor offer a charter service to the Fuegian Channels, Cape Horn, Isla de los Estados, and Antarctica. The northwest arm of the Canal Beagle with its spectacular glaciers is only several hours by boat west of Ushuaia. It is possible to get there from Ushuaia on board the Chilean chartered yacht, the *Terra Australis,* or on one of the larger tourist cruise ships.

Large tourist cruise ships make the circuit of southern South America in summer (usually November to March). They leave from Río de Janeiro or Buenos Aires, visit Ushuaia and Punta Arenas, and go up through the Chilean channels to Puerto Montt or Valparaíso. There are usually only 4 to 6 hours in each port.

Cruise ships also visit Antarctica, part of whose territory is claimed by Argentina, Chile, and Great Britain. Regular sailings depart from Ushuaia or from Punta Arenas in Chile during the tourist season, which runs from late November to late February.

The Antarctic cruises last from 7 to 15 days, at least two of which are spent crossing the Drake Passage. Most are intensive learning experiences – naturalists and guest lecturers giving talks aboard and guided walks ashore.* Many ships offer a full gourmet menu and accommodations tend toward the luxurious. ❏

Map on page 326

TIP

When it comes to nightlife, Ushuaia is no threat to Buenos Aires, but every year the Fuegian capital holds an all-night party on June 21, the longest night of the year, and an ice sculpture contest each August.

BELOW: crab traps and fishing boats by the shores of the Beagle Channel.

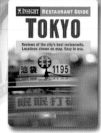

TRAVEL TIPS

TRANSPORTATION

ACCOMMODATIONS

EATING OUT

ACTIVITIES

A – Z

LANGUAGE

T RANSPORTATION

GETTING THERE
AND GETTING AROUND

from bordering countries (see
Domestic Air Travel, page 338).

GETTING THERE

By Air

All international flights arrive at
Ezeiza International Airport (EZE),
35 km (22 miles) from the center of
Buenos Aires.
   Avoid the floods of taxi drivers who
greet arrivals at the airport and buy a
ticket from one of the remise (private
car) stands in the foyer. A cheaper
option is to take the airport bus run
by the Manuel Tienda León company
(offices on Carlos Pellegrini 509.
Tel: (011) 4314 3636,
www.tiendaleon.com). Tickets for this
comfortable service can be bought
at the airport. It runs hourly, takes
around 1 hour depending on traffic,
and drops you off in Plaza San
Martín. From here, most hotels are
a short taxi ride away.
   Another airport, **Aeroparque Jorge
Newbery**, is located within the city
and is used mostly for domestic
travel as well as for travel to and

International Airlines

The following airlines operate
international flights to Buenos
Aires:
British Airways www.ba.com
Air France www.airfrance.com
Lufthansa www.lufthansa.com
KLM www.klm.com
Iberia www.iberia.com
United Airlines www.unitedairlines.com
Aerolíneas Argentinas
www.aerolineas.com.ar
Lan www.lan.com
Air Canada www.aircanada.com
South African Airways www.flysaa.com
Qantas Airlines www.qantas.com.au

Flights from Europe

There are flights to Buenos Aires
from London, Barcelona, Madrid,
Frankfurt, Paris, Amsterdam, Milan,
Rome, and Zurich with European and
North and South American carriers.
Aerolíneas Argentinas flies direct
from Madrid, Barcelona, and Rome.

Flights from the US

Aerolíneas Argentinas and other
major North and South American
airlines fly from Dallas, New Orleans,
Atlanta, Los Angeles, San Francisco,
New York, Washington, and Chicago.

Flights from Canada

From Canada, the cheapest option is
to go via the US. Alternatively, Air
Canada and LAN fly direct to Buenos
Aires from Toronto and Montreal.

Flights from South Africa

There are only a few flights to
Argentina from South Africa and most
go via the US. You can fly with South
African Airways from Johannesburg
via New York. Malaysia Airways also
flies twice a week from Kuala Lumpur
to Buenos Aires via Johannesburg.

Flights from Australasia

Qantas Airlines and Aerolíneas
Argentinas fly to Buenos Aires from
Sydney, via Auckland, several times
a week.

By Sea

There are only a few cruise ships that
come to Buenos Aires. Most of these
originate in Brazil or Europe. The
better-known cruises are with the
Linea C Company, on their ships
Eugenio and Enrico. These operate

from December to March.
   Another cruise ship, the Pegasus,
from the **Epirotiki Line**, also operates
from December to April. **Antartur
Lines** has cruises from Ushuaia to
the Antarctic and Tierra del Fuego.
These only operate in January.
   The US-operated **Kapitan
Dranitsyn** also cruises around the
Antarctic region and South Atlantic
islands, with various packages on
offer from November to March.
Contact: **Quark Expeditions**, 1019
Boston Post Road, Darien, CT
06820, USA. Tel: (0203) 656 0499;
toll-free: (800) 356 5699; fax:
(0203) 655 6623;
www.quarkexpeditions.com
   Australis (www.australis.com) has a
new cruise ship, Mare Australis,
which explores Patagonia and Tierra
del Fuego on 3-, 4-, or 7-night
journeys with a program of activities
between October and April.
   For more details contact a local
travel agent or contact the tourist
office in Argentina by fax on (5411)
4313 6834 or e-mail: info@turismo.gov.ar.

Overland

Most tourists do not arrive by land.
However, for the adventurous type,
this can be accomplished by bus or
automobile. Bus services are
available from Chile, Bolivia,
Paraguay, Uruguay, and Brazil. Large
air-conditioned buses are available
for long-distance overland travel. Bus
tickets do not usually have seat
numbers, so it is worth getting on the
bus in good time to make sure you
have a seat. Also be warned that air
conditioning is often very powerful,
so take a warm sweater, even during
the summer months.
   All international train services to
and from Argentina have ceased.

Tren de la Costa

Inaugurated in 1891 but only re-opened after 30 years' closure in 1995, this coastal train runs from Olivos to Tigre in the suburbs of Buenos Aires. Trains leave every 15 minutes, there are 11 stops, and the full journey takes under 30 minutes. Tel: (011) 4732 6000, www.trendelacosta.com.ar.

GETTING AROUND

Public transport in Argentina varies substantially. In Buenos Aires it is very efficient with regular and cheap buses and subways, but towns and cities outside of the capital generally have a poor public-transport system. There is no national train service, but comfortable long-distance buses cover a wide network of destinations.

Buses

City Transport

Buses *(colectivos)* are a good and speedy way to get around Buenos Aires. The grid system of roads makes planning a journey relatively simple. There are 140 bus lines which cover most of the city. During the day *colectivos* come very frequently. They also run all night, when they are required to come at least every 30 minutes.

A *colectivo* fare costs between 70–80 cents. You must carry change as notes are not accepted. You may find it useful to purchase a pocket-size *Guia "T"* for a few pesos from a *kiosco* (newsstand) when you arrive in Buenos Aires. This contains detailed maps of the city and all the bus routes.

In most cities, there is a bus service that links the airport to the city center. In addition, some airlines run a minibus service that is coordinated with flight schedules.

Long-distance Buses

The network of long-distance buses throughout Argentina is efficient, cheap, and comfortable. Distances involved often mean an overnight journey, but the well-paved roads should not hinder sleep and *coche camas*, or bed buses, are extremely comfortable. *Común* buses are cheaper and more basic than the higher-standard *diferencial*.

Buses for destinations throughout the country leave from the Retiro bus station in Buenos Aires. Dozens of bus companies are located within the

ABOVE: king of the road: traveling through Patagonia by bus.

terminal and are grouped together by destination. Two of the largest – **Andesmar**, tel: (0261) 425 9401, www.andesmar.com, and **Chevallier**, tel: (011) 4016 7000, www.nuevachevallier.com – operate buses to destinations throughout Argentina. Numerous smaller companies serve specific regions, as well as destinations in neighboring countries.

There is an information office on the 1st floor (tel: (011) 4314 2323). Left-luggage lockers are available for a few pesos with payment by tokens on sale at kiosks in the station. The nearest subway station is Retiro on Linea C, and the entrance is in the nearby Retiro train station.

Trains

With the exception of a few tourist services, passenger services around the country are virtually non-existent since the government privatized the network in 1994. Trains do run to the suburbs of Buenos Aires, however. There are four main train terminals in the city:
Retiro, tel: (011) 4311 8074. For services to Delta Tigre, Capilla del Señor, and Bartolomé Mitre.
Constitución, tel: (011) 4304 0028. For local trains.
Federico Lacroze, tel: (011) 4553 5213. For excursions on a Scottish 1888 Neilson steam engine.
Once, tel: (011) 4861 0043. For travel around Buenos Aires province. The journey from Olivos to Tigre along the coast provides excellent views of the River Plate *(see Tren de la Costa, above)*.

Subway

The Buenos Aires subway system, better known as the Subte, is

usually the fastest and definitely the cheapest way to get around the sprawling city. The rides are quick, taking no more than 25 minutes, and the waiting time is about 3–5 minutes. There are five subway lines in Buenos Aires: A, B, C, D, and E. The Subte is open from 5am–1pm, except on Sundays when it is open from 8am–10pm. Tickets for travel can be bought from the *boletería* (ticket office) located in the station and cost 80 cents for one journey.

Private Transport

Remises

Remises are private automobiles, with a driver, that can be rented by the hour, excursion, day, or any other time period. Telephone numbers for *remise* firms can be found in the

Taxis

Taxis are widely used by *porteños* and are often a cheap way to get around, particularly outside the rush hour and if you are sharing the fare with traveling companions. Taxis can be easily recognized (black with a yellow roof), and in Buenos Aires are readily available 24 hours a day. The meter registers a number that will correspond to the amount of the fare appearing on a list. These must be shown to the passenger by law. A small tip is usually given.

Radio taxis are ordered by telephone or waved down in the street. *Remise* is a similar service but the cars are unmarked and the fare is calculated according to the distance traveled *(see Remises, above)*.

telephone directory or at hotel information desks.

AAA Limousine, Viamonte 1620 piso 4. Tel: (011) 4371 9107.

Plaza de Mayo, Azopardo 523. Tel: (011) 4331 4705.

Driving

Due to its size and geographical diversity, Argentina is a great place for road trips and you may find yourself at a loss without a car should you wish to visit more remote areas, such as parts of Salta, the Northeast, Patagonia, and Tierra del Fuego. It is best to share some of the driving with others as distances are very long and arduous.

Road safety (or lack of it) is a big problem in Argentina. There are many dangerous roads and careless, hazardous drivers. Although this shouldn't put you off, you should drive extra safely.

Approximately 30 percent of roads in the country are paved. The rest are *ripio* (dirt roads with loose gravel) which can be challenging, especially it wet conditions. 60 km (37 miles) per hour is the maximum speed for cars driving on *ripio*. Paved roads are sometimes covered with potholes which you should watch out for.

Buenos Aires is very congested, making driving extremely time-consuming, and *porteños* have little discipline on the roads, a cause of frequent accidents. Seat belts should be worn at all times whilst driving, as you can be fined for not wearing one, although this is a law that many Argentines take little notice of. The law also requires that you always carry full car documentation and your driver's license with you.

If you plan to do a lot of driving,

BELOW: congestion on Avenida Callao.

Domestic Airlines

Aerolíneas Argentinas Perú 2, Buenos Aires, tel: (011) 4320 2000, (Mon–Fri 9am–7pm) www.aerolineas.com.ar. Argentina's national airline flies internationally and domestically.

LADE Perú 710, Buenos Aires, tel: (011) 5129 9000, (Mon–Fri 9.30am–5.30pm) www.lade.com.ar. Flies mostly to destinations in Patagonia.

LAN Cerrito 866, Buenos Aires, tel: (0810) 9999 526, (Mon–Fri 9am–6pm) www.lan.com. Flies to Córdoba, Rosario, and Salta.

Pluna Florida 1, Buenos Aires, tel: (011) 4342 4420, (Mon–Fri 9am–6pm) www.pluna.com.uy. Uruguay's national carrier. Offers flights to Uruguay.

you may want to consider a monthly membership with the **Automovil Club Argentino (ACA)**. This has a useful emergency breakdown towing and repair service. You can join in Buenos Aires at Santa Fe 887 (Mon–Fri 9am–7pm), tel: (011) 4311 5341; at the head office on Av. de Libertador 1850 (Mon–Fri 10am–6pm), tel: (011) 4802 6061; or at any ACA service station.

Rutas de la Argentina are national and town maps provided free by tourist offices. **YPF**, the state oil company, also produces good road maps, available from gas stations.

Some main roads have private tolls, which charge around US$5 for every 100 km (62 miles). This fee also covers you for emergency towing. Gas stations are infrequent in remote areas so it is best to top up wherever possible.

Parking

Car theft is more common in Buenos Aires than in the rest of the country. Make sure you park your car in well-lit and busy parts of the city where possible. Often in the tourist areas of the capital, street children will offer to guard your car for 50 cents. Outside busy bars or restaurants there is usually a man who will guard your car for a peso. Finding parking space in the street is not normally a problem, although there are parking lots in the center of Buenos Aires for those wanting to play it safe.

Car Rental

You can rent a car at the airport upon arrival, but it is better to book from home, especially during the high season. You must be over 21 (although some places require you to

be over 25) and hold an international driver's license to rent a car in Argentina. You will usually be asked to leave your credit card details as a deposit. The following better-known car-rental agencies have offices in Buenos Aires:

Avis, Cerrito 1257, tel: (011) 4326 5542.

Budget, Santa Fe 869, tel: (011) 4311 9870.

Hertz, Dr R. Rojas 451, tel: (011) 4312 1317.

Serra Lima, Av. Cordoba 3121, tel: (011) 4961 5276.

Domestic Air Travel

Traveling by air in a country as big as Argentina is a good way to get from one region to the other, saving time on some long and, frankly, mind-numbing journeys. **Jorge Newbery Airport** or **El Aeroparque** is Buenos Aires' airport for national traffic and is located 10 minutes' drive from the city center at Avenida Costanera Rafael Obilgado, between La Pampa and Sarmiento, Costanera Norte. When traveling to or from the airport it is best to take a taxi, which will cost around US$15.

It is no longer possible to purchase a coupon-system air pass to fly within Argentina. Domestic air travel is now done by purchasing individual flights. **Aerolíneas Argentinas**, offers a *Visit Argentina* air pass which has specific prices for each destination.

Ferries

Traveling by ferry to Uruguay is a good excursion away from the hustle and bustle of Buenos Aires. The most popular destinations are the historic port of Colonia del Sacramento, Montevideo, or the beaches of Punte del Este. **Buquebus** operates fast and slow ferries to Colonia and Montevideo, with bus connections to other destinations along the Uruguayan coast. Find them at Av. Córdoba 879 or Terminal Dársena Norte, Av. Antártida Argentina 821. Tel: (011) 4316 6500, www.buquebus.com.

The journey across the murky waters of the River Plate costs around US$35 for the slick 45-minute catamaran ride or US$20 for the 3-hour trip by traditional ferry, not including Uruguayan port taxes. Should you wish to stay over in Colonia, a good hotel is the **Hotel Beltrán**. Tel: (+598) 52 21030/ 22955; www.colonianet.com/hbeltran. It has pretty, leafy terraces and rooms start at US$40 a night.

A CCOMMODATIONS

HOTELS, YOUTH HOSTELS, BED & BREAKFAST

Choosing a Hotel

Since the collapse of the peso, the cost of accommodations has dropped dramatically throughout the country. Like most destinations in the world, prices are considerably higher in the capital. In addition to hotels, there are also *hosterías*, *hospedajes*, and *pensiones*, all of which offer more basic but usually clean rooms at cheaper prices. Many of these places are found near bus and train stations which, although they may be noisy, are convenient if you're traveling overland. It is worth asking for a room at the back *(en el interior)* if the hotel is on a particularly busy street.

Outside the cities, there are numerous estancias (ranches) – a popular choice for those wishing to sample rural life and gaucho culture.

During the hot summer months, the beach resorts along the Atlantic coast are besieged by millions of *porteños*. In **Pinamar**, **Villa Gesell**, and **Mar de la Plata** the huge hotel complexes are fully booked and discos and bars everywhere are packed until sunrise. In winter, however, these holiday resorts become ghost towns. Quiet, undeveloped beaches are only to be found further south near **Bahía Blanca**. **Mar del Sur**, below Miramar, is a peaceful haven with 40 km (25 miles) of sandy beach.

The following is a selection of recommended places. Because of the recent tourist boom in Argentina, it is advisable to book in advance, especially during the summer months (December through March).

Accommodations have been arranged by region, matching the order of the same regions covered in the Places section of this book.

ACCOMMODATIONS LISTINGS

BUENOS AIRES

Alvear Palace Hotel
Av. Alvear 1891
Tel: (011) 4808 2100
Fax: (011) 4804 9246
www.alvearpalace.com
BA's most elegant hotel in the city's most chic neighborhood – Recoleta. French decor, several restaurants, tearoom, boutiques, health club, and business center. **$$$$**

Caesar Park
Posadas 1232
Tel: (011) 4819 1100
Fax: (011) 4819 1121
www.caesar-park.com
Modern, large luxury hotel in the Recoleta. Lobby piano bar, three restaurants including elegant buffet, health club with swimming pool.

Popular with business set. **$$$$**
Claridge Hotel
Tucumán 535
Tel: (011) 4314 7700
Fax: (011) 4314 8022
www.claridge-hotel.com
Very British, old-fashioned, centrally located. Health club with swimming pool, penthouse suites with gardens, pleasant bar. **$$$$**

Faena Hotel and Universe
Martha Salotti 445, Dique 2, Madero Este, Puerto Madero
Tel: (011) 4010 9000
www.faenahotelanduniverse.com
This swish new landmark has modestly been given the title "hotel and universe" as it claims to cater to your every need.

Includes boutiques, bars, swimming pool, restaurants, and cabaret. The kitsch decor alone makes it worth a visit. Aparthotels are available for longer stays. **$$$$**
Four Seasons Hotel
Posadas 1086/88
Tel: (011) 4321 1200
Fax: (011) 4321 1201
www.fourseasons.com
Near the French Embassy and the Recoleta, large modern hotel in French style, with garden restaurant, lounge, health club, and outdoor pool. Popular with business people and visiting rock stars. **$$$$**
Gran Hotel Colón
Carlos Pellegrini 507

Tel: (011) 4320 3500
Fax: (011) 4320 3507/3516
www.colon-hotel.com.ar
Across from Teatro Colón on 9 de Julio. Modern but cozy, luxury suites available with patios. Rooftop outdoor pool, restaurant. **$$$$**
Hotel Inter-Continental
Moreno 809
Tel: (011) 4340 7100
Fax: (011) 4340 7199
www.intercontinental.com
Four blocks from Plaza de Mayo in Monserrat, modern 19-story hotel, with restaurant/bar, health club, and indoor pool. Popular with business people. **$$$$**
Hotel Panamericano
Carlos Pellegrini 551

Tel: (011) 4348 5000
Fax: (011) 4348 5250
www.panamericanobuenosaires.com
Located in the shadow of the Obelisco. Modern 18-floor twin towers, plus health club with rooftop pool. Popular for conferences; excellent restaurant. **$$$$**

Marriott Plaza Hotel
Florida 1005
Tel: (011) 4318 3000
Fax: (011) 4318 3008
www.marriottplaza.com.ar
Elegant hotel on Plaza San Martín, favorite with visiting heads of state and royalty. Famous restaurant Plaza Grill, health club, outdoor pool. Central but quiet location, very comfortable, and excellent service. **$$$$**

Sheraton Buenos Aires
San Martín 1225
Tel: (011) 4318 9000
Fax: (011) 4318 9346
www.sheraton.com/buenosaires
Located in Retiro, 24-story high-rise towers commanding magnificent view of the river and port area. Rooftop bar, international restaurants, tennis courts, and swimming pool; favorite with the business set. **$$$$**

Sheraton Libertador Hotel
Av. Córdoba 690
Tel: (011) 4322 8800
Fax: (011) 4322 9703
www.sheraton.com/libertador
In the heart of the microcenter, bar and swimming pool on the top floor. Restaurant. Popular with business visitors and tourists. **$$$$**

Carsson
Viamonte 650
Tel: (011) 4322 3601
Faded elegance conveniently located in the center of the city. **$$$**

Bisonte Palace
Marcelo T. de Alvear 910
Esq. Suipacha
Tel: (011) 4328 4751
Fax: (011) 4328 6476
www.hotelesbisonte.com
Two branches under the same ownership. Pleasant and modern hotel with a bar and conference rooms available. Highly recommended. **$$$**

Five Cool Rooms
Honduras 4742, between Armenia and Malabia, Palermo Viejo
Tel: (011) 5235 5555
www.fivebuenosaires.com
Super stylish and minimalist. A good place to escape the stress of the city; some rooms come with superb balconies and jacuzzis. **$$$**

Hotel Crillon
Santa Fe 796
Tel: (011) 4310 2000
Fax: (011) 4310 2020
French-style antique building which has been refurbished; very modern inside, with many services for the business traveler, including 24-hour room service. Located on Plaza San Martín. **$$$**

Hotel Phoenix
San Martín 780
Tel: (011) 4312 4845
Fax: (011) 4311 2846
Faded old-world charm, fabulous large rooms, friendly staff, all in a central location. **$$$**

Hotel Plaza Francia
E. Schiaffino 2189
Tel/Fax: (011) 4804 9631/37
www.hotelplazafrancia.com
Classic brick-colored building, located in the Recoleta, near the Museo Nacional de Bellas Artes. Quiet, with a good breakfast served in your room if desired; highly recommended. **$$$**

Lafayette Hotel
Reconquista 546
Tel: (011) 9393 9081
Fax: (011) 9393 9192
www.lafayettehotel.com.ar
Conveniently located in microcentro and recently remodeled with English-style decor, restaurant, and room service. **$$$**

Lancaster Hotel
Córdoba 405
Tel: (011) 4312 4061
Fax: (011) 4311 3021
Very European, fancy lobby, pretty sunlit rooms, nice bar/cafe. **$$$**

Park Plaza Kempinski Hotel
Parera 183
Tel: (011) 6777 0200
www.parkplazahotels.com
On a quiet side street in the Recoleta; elegant classic European style, with

eight floors – each one dedicated to a famous painter. **$$$**

Posado Palermo
Salguero 1655, between Soler and Paraguay, Palermo
Tel: (011) 4826 8792
www.posadapalermo.com.ar
Rustic-feel retreat in the city. Located in a 19th-century "chorizo" house built by Italian immigrants. **$$$**

Gran Hotel Hispano
Av. de Mayo 861
Tel/Fax: (011) 4345 2020
www.hhispano.com.ar
One block from Plaza de Mayo and close to San Telmo, a renovated antique building, popular with European budget travelers. **$$**

Hotel Arenales
Arenales 2580, Palermo
Tel: (011) 4824 1760
www.hotelarenales.com.ar
Comfortable, simple rooms, good service, located in Barrio Norte. **$$**

Hotel Embajador
Carlos Pellegrini 1185
Tel/Fax: (011) 4326 5302/5311
www.embajadorhotel.com.ar
Good location at Av. 9 de Julio and Santa Fe, with modern, large rooms and a cafe. **$$**

Hotel Impala
Libertad 1215
Tel/Fax: (011) 4816 0430
www.hotelimpala.com.ar
Two blocks from Santa Fe shopping street and very near to Recoleta, this is modern, basic accommodation, with a cafe. **$$**

Uruguay
Tacuari 83
Tel: (011) 4334 2788
Simple, inexpensive, and clean. **$$**

Waldorf Hotel
Paraguay 450
Tel: (011) 4312 2071
Fax: (011) 4312 2079
www.waldorf-hotel.com.ar
Close to Florida and Santa Fe shopping streets. Modern and comfortable, with a bar; larger rooms and suites. **$$**

Orly Hotel
Paraguay 474
Tel: (011) 4312 5344
Basic rooms, but a good location. **$–$$**

APARTHOTELS

For longer visits to the capital, a good alternative is an aparthotel or suite hotel which give you the services of a hotel with the convenience of a furnished apartment, including a kitchenette. Prices per night range from US$150 for a studio to US$450 for a three-room apartment.

Feir's Park All-Suites Hotel
Esmeralda 1366
Tel: (011) 4327 1900
Fax: (011) 4327 1935
www.feirspark.com.ar
One block from Libertador in elegant neighborhood, with room service, pool, health club, business center; option of connecting suites.

Plaza San Martín Suites
Suipacha 1092
Tel: (011) 4328 4740
Fax: (011) 4328 9385
www.plazasanmartin.com.ar
Newly built, with a health club and room service.

Dazzler Suites Arroyo
Suipacha 1359
Tel: (011) 4325 8200
www.dazzlersuites.com
Situated in an upscale neighborhood near Libertador and Av. 9 de Julio, with good service, a health club and outdoor pool, patio, garden, and garage facilities.

Torre Cristóforo Colombo Suites
Oro 2747
Tel: (011) 4777 9622
Fax: (011) 4778 4944
www.torrecc.com.ar
In Palermo, two blocks from US Embassy. A modern tower, with rooftop bar, restaurant, health club, and outdoor pool. High standard of service.

Ulises Recoleta
Ayacucho 2016
Tel: (011) 4804 4571
Fax: (011) 4806 0838
www.ulisesrecoleta.com.ar
Across from the Alvear Palace in Recoleta, this classic European-style building has only 25 apartments (including a Penthouse suite). Antique furnishings and a welcoming atmosphere.

MAR Y SIERRAS

Mar del Plata

Gran Hotel Continental
Córdoba 1929
Tel: (0223) 492 1300
www.hotelcontinentalmdq.com.ar
Mid-range hotel;
recommended. **$$$**

Gran Hotel Provincial
Blvd Marítimo 2500
Tel: (0223) 491 5949
Fax: (0223) 491 5894
Traditional "grand hotel"
with a large number of
rooms and a very good
restaurant. **$$$**

Hotel Bisonte
Belgrano 2609
Tel: (0223) 495 6060
One block south of the
cathedral; recommended.
$$$

Compostela
Belgrano 2561
Tel: (0223) 495 2796/493 2925
www.mardelcomercial.com.ar/
compostela
55 basic rooms with cable
TV. **$$**

Gran Hotel Dorá
Buenos Aires 1841
Tel/Fax: (0223) 491 0033
Close to the casino, two
blocks from the beach. **$$**

San Jorge
Alsina 2353
Tel: (0223) 451 3895
Inexpensive mid-range
hotel. **$**

Villa Gesell

Hotel Bahia
Av. 1, between Paseos 108 and 109
Tel: (02255) 462 838
Fax: (02255) 460 838

www.hotelbahia-gesell.com.ar
Modern 11-story block
located on the beach with
full spa facilities. **$$$**

Hotel Gran Internacional
Av. 1 and Paseo 103
Tel/Fax: (02255) 468 672
www.hotelgraninternational.com
Beach-side location. **$$$**

Pinamar

Hotel Ivamar
Progreso 49 and El Mar
Tel: (02254) 480 654
Pleasant hotel on the
beach front. **$$$**

Hotel Las Araucarias
Bunge 1411
Tel: (02254) 480 812
Close to the beach and the
center of town. A well-kept
hotel with a pool. **$$$**

Mar Azul

Puerto de Palos
Calle 35 and Mar del Plata
Tel: (02255) 470 311
www.puertodepalos.rtu.com.ar
The best-value
accommodations in the
area. Clean and well-run
cabin complex set in the
woods, 7 km (4 miles) from
Villa Gesell, with pool. **$$$**

Mar de las Pampas

Miradores del Bosque
JA Roca and Hudson
Tel: (02255) 452 147
www.miradoresdelbosque.com
Luxurious seaside
apartments for 2–6 people.
Complex includes spa. **$$$$**

ABOVE: seafront accommodations at Mar del Plata.

Rincón del Duende
Virazon and Cuyo
Tel: (02255) 479 866
www.rincondelduende.com
Cabins situated a few
meters from the beach,
with swimming pool and
one of the best restaurants
in the area. **$$$$**

Cariló

Cariló Village
Carpintero and Divisadero
Tel: (02254) 470 244
www.carilovillage.com
Bungalows scattered
throughout the forest, with
a spa. **$$$$**

Hotel Marcín
Laurel and El Mar

Tel: (02254) 570 888
www.hotelmarcin.com.ar
Beach-front hotel with two
swimming pools. Rooms
come with an ocean or
forest view. **$$$$**

Tandil

Plaza Hotel
Gral. Pinto 438
Tel: (02293) 427 160/80/89
www.plazahoteldetandil.com.ar
Comfortable hotel situated
in the heart of Tandil. **$$**

Rocas Descanso
Paraje El Centinela
Tel: (02293) 15 632 180
A small, cozy option just
outside the center with a
garden and pool. **$**

CENTRAL SIERRAS

La Cumbre

Gran Hotel La Cumbre
Posadas s/n
Tel: (03548) 451 550
www.granhotellacumbre.com.ar
Alpine-style, traditional
family hotel with panoramic
views. **$$$**

Posada los Cedros
Av. Argentina 837
Tel: (03548) 451 028
www.posadaloscedros.com
Situated in the heart of the
golfing district, this
pleasant complex offers a
range of sporting activities

as well as high-quality
rooms. **$$$**

Río Ceballos

Hostería del Molino
Peru 281
Tel: (0251) 452 197
Friendly, clean, basic union-
run hotel situated right on
the river; excellent home
cooking. **$**

Alta Gracia

Hostal Hispania
Vélez Sarsfield 57

Tel: (03547) 426 555
Lovely place with large,
pleasant rooms. **$$**

Córdoba

Hotel Windsor
Buenos Aires 214
Tel: (0351) 422 4012
Great hotel with a rooftop
pool as well as sauna and
fitness facilities. **$$**

Hotel Felipe
San Jerónimo 279
Tel: (0351) 425 5500
www.hotelfelipe.com.ar
Centrally located near Plaza

San Martín. **$$**

Gran Hotel Dorá
Entre Ríos 70
Tel: (0351) 421 2031
www.hoteldora.com
A top-end option in the
heart of Córdoba city.
$$$

PRICE CATEGORIES

Prices are all for a double
room:

$$$$	US$100 plus
$$$	US$50–100
$$	US$30–50
$	US$30 or under

THE NORTHEAST

Rosario

Hotel Plaza Real
Santa Fe 1632
Tel/fax: (0341) 440 8800
Central location, 4-star
facilities. $$$
Urquiza Apart Hotel
Urquiza 1491
Tel: (0341) 449 4900
www.apart-urquiza.com.ar
Good suites at decent
prices. $$

San Ignacio

La Doka
Alberdi 518
Tel: (03752) 470 131
A family-run place that
offers clean rooms and
self-catering facilities. $
Hotel San Ignacio
Sarmiento 823
Tel: (0598) 470 422
Basic rooms, situated
close to the Jesuit ruins.
$

Puerto Iguazú

**Sheraton Internacional
Iguazú Resort**
Parque Nacional Iguazú
Tel: (03757) 491 800
Fax: (03757) 491 848
www.sheraton.com/iguazu
Ugly building housing
5-star facilities inside the
national park, with tennis
courts, pool, and great
views. $$$

ABOVE: a stunning backdrop for the pool at the Sheraton Internacional Iguazú Resort.

Las Orquídeas
RN12, Km 5
Tel: (03757) 420 472/420 195
www.orquideashotel.com
Comfortable and
inexpensive with
restaurant, in a great
location outside Iguazú. $

Colonia Carlos Pellegrini

Posada de la Laguna
Reserva Provincial de Iberá
Tel/Fax: (03773) 499 413
www.posadadelalaguna.com
Very comfortable rooms,

tranquil setting, with pool
and great home cooking.
Well situated for the Iberá
wetlands, with the lagoon
only meters away. Boat and
birding trips organized with
knowledgeable guides. Full
board only. $$$
Hostería Nandereta,
Reserva Provincial de Iberá
Tel: (03773) 499 411
www.nandereta.com
A comfortable lodge in the
heart of the Iberá wetlands
region. Air-conditioned
rooms with private
bathroom. Bar, restaurant,

video and games room.
Boat safaris and many
other activities organized.
Full board only. $$

El Soberbio

Posada la Bonita
RN14, between El Soberbio and
Saltos del Moconá
Tel: (03755) 15 492 178
www.posadalabonita.com.ar
About 30 km (18 miles)
from El Soberbio, this is
the best place in the area.
Beautiful rustic cabins in
the heart of the jungle. $$

THE NORTHWEST

Catamarca

Hotel Leo III
Sarmiento 727
Tel: (03833) 432 080
One of the best hotels
in town, with restaurant.
$$$
Hotel Ancasti
Sarmiento 520
Tel: (03833) 430 617
Very traditional,
comfortable, friendly, and
low-key. Recommended.
$$
Hotel Suma Huasi
Sarmiento 541
Tel: (03833) 435 699/5801
Economical, but rooms
near lounge can be noisy.
$

Tucumán

Grand Hotel
Av. Soldat 380
Tel: (0381) 450 2250
Five-star hotel in Tucumán.
Comfortable and central,
with all facilities. $$$
Hotel Ruinas de Quilmes
Amaichá del Valle, near Tucumán
Tel: (03892) 421 075
Beautiful and extremely
comfortable hotel at the
ruins of the former Quilmes
civilization and decorated in
similar style. Very highly
recommended and well
worth the detour. $$$
Hotel Garden
Crisóstomo Alvarez 627
Tel: (0381) 431 1246

Clean, comfortable, and
reasonably priced. $

Cachí

El Molino de Cachí
4 km from Cachí
Tel: (03868) 491 094
This is a sumptuous
rural retreat complete with
pool and a small vineyard.
$$$
Hostal El Cortijo
Av. del ACA s/n
Tel: (03868) 491 034
Small old colonial
farmhouse. Contains
rooms facing onto a
pleasant courtyard and
views of Nevado de Cachí.
$$$

Salta

Hotel Salta
Buenos Aires 1
Tel/Fax: (0387) 431 0740
www.hotelsalta.com
Traditional hotel with
wooden balconies and all
amenities, situated in the
main square. $$$
Portezuelo
Av. del Turista 1
Tel: (0387) 431 0104
www.portezuelohotel.com
Hotel in the hills with two
pools and all facilities. $$$
Provincial Plaza Hotel
Caseros 786
Tel: (0387) 432 2000
www.provincialplaza.com.ar
Huge rooms, and a pool.

$$$
Solar de la Plaza
JM Leguizamon 669
Tel: (0387) 431 5111
www.hoteldelaplaza.com.ar
Gorgeous hotel in the center of town, with balcony rooms over Plaza Güemes.

$$$
Hotel Las Lajitas
RP 5 and RP 30, Las Lajitas
Tel: (0387) 749 4131
Modern and good value. $
Hotel Regidor
Buenos Aires 8
Tel: (0387) 431 1305
Good value and good facilities. Comfortable. $

Cafayate

Vieja Posada
Salta 70, Cafayate
Tel: (03874) 422 251
www.viejaposada.com.ar
Relaxed hotel with a

selection of likeable rooms and an enchanting vine-covered courtyard. The owners also rent bikes. $

Jujuy

Hotel Termas de Reyes
Termas de Reyes
Tel: (0388) 492 2522
Fax: (0388) 424 2424
www.termasdereyes.com
Located about 19 km (12 miles) from the city, this hotel offers thermal baths in all rooms, good facilities, and heated pool.
$$$$
Jujuy Palace Hotel
Belgrano 1060
Tel: (0388) 423 0433
One of the few quality hotels in the city. Centrally located with restaurant and gym facilities. $$

Posada del Sol
Los Ceibos and Pucara, Libertador General San Martín
Tel: (0388) 642 4900
www.posadadelsoljujuy.com.ar
The best accommodations to be found close to Parque Nacional Caliegua. With pool and experienced staff able to help organize excursions. $$

Purmamarca

Hotel Manatial del Silencio
RN52, Km 3.5
Tel: (0388) 490 8080
www.hotelmanantial.com.ar
Set in the shadow of the stunning Montaña de los Siete Colores this hotel could be paradise. Large swimming pool and excellent restaurant. $$$

Tilcara

La Posada del Luz
Ambrosetti, esq. Alverro
Tel: (0388) 495 5017
www.posadadelluz.com.ar
This luxury hotel will provide a peaceful break, with great services and a large pool. $$$
Villar del Ala
Padilla 1000
Tel: (0388) 495 5100
Intimate pleasant hotel, with good restaurant. Good base for exploring local countryside. Local excursions organized. $$$

La Quiaca

Hotel de Turismo
Republica Arabe Siria and San Martín
Tel: (03885) 422 243
Clean and welcoming. $

THE CUYO

Mendoza

Reina Victoria Suites and Towers
San Juan 1127
Tel/Fax: (0261) 425 9800
www.reinavictoriasuites.com.ar
Luxury aparthotel in the center of town, with pool, solarium, health club, and cafe. Comfortable air-conditioned rooms. $$$
Hotel Aconcagua
San Lorenzo 545
Tel: (0261) 520 0500
Fax: (0261) 420 2083
www.hotelaconcagua.com
A few blocks from the main shopping area with very modern architecture, swimming pool, and air-conditioned rooms. $$
Hotel San Martín
Espejo 435
Tel: (0261) 438 0677
Recommended. $$
Hotel Imperial
Las Heras 88
Tel: (0261) 423 4671
Very basic, but a bargain. $

Potrerillos

Gran Hotel Potrerillos
RN7, Km 50
Tel: (02624) 482 130
Large estancia-style hotel in extensive grounds

overlooking the town. Rooms and apartments, with restaurant, bar, pool, tennis court, and other sports facilities. $$$$
Casas de la Montaña
Valle del Sol
Tel/fax: (02624) 481 035
www.casadelamontana.com
Comfortable family cabins in beautiful countryside 1 hour from Mendoza. Well situated for walking, horseback riding, and white-water rafting. $$$

Horcones

Hostería Puente del Inca
RN7, near Los Penitentes
Tel: (0361) 438 0480
Fax: 4380 477
www.puentedelinca.idoneos.com
Secluded inn 2,700 meters (8,900 ft) above sea level, with views of the Aconcagua massif. $$

Luján de Cuyo

Hotel Termas Cacheuta
RN7, Km 37, Cacheuta
Tel: (02624) 490 153
Surrounded by mountains, this is an excellent place for relaxing. Good restaurant. Massage and spa facilities available. $$$

San Luis

Hotel Aiello
Av. Presidente Illia 431
Tel: (02652) 425 609
Simple hotel with a pool; good value. $$
Huarpes Hotel
Belgrano 1568
Tel: (02652) 425 597
huarpeshotel@poraire.net
Another economical option where the basic rooms are pleasant enough to spend a night or two. $

San Juan

Hotel Alkazar
Laprida 82 Este
Tel: (0264) 421 4965
The city's only 5-star lodging; reasonably priced and fully equipped with spa and sauna. $$
Viñas del Sol
Ruta 20 and Gral. Roca
Tel: (0264) 425 3921
The the perfect spot for a luxury break; excellent restaurant and comfortable rooms. $$

San Agustín de Valle Fértil

Hostería y Cabañas Valle Fertil
Rivadavia s/n

Tel: (02646) 642 0015
www.alkazarhotel.com.ar/vallefertil
A sweet hotel with great views. Good value. $$
Cabañas Chuncay
Rivadavia, between Alem and Catamarca
Tel: (02646) 421 3180
www.chuncay.com.ar
Self catering cabins for 3–8 people, with a small swimming pool. $

La Rioja

La Plaza
San Nicolás de Bari 502
Tel: (03822) 425 215
www.plazahotel-larioja.com.ar
Elegant hotel with nice rooms, a smart cafe, and a rooftop pool. $$$
Naindo Park
San Nicolás de Bari 475
Tel: (03822) 470 700
www.naindoparkhotel.com
Five-star hotel with bar, restaurant, health club, and business center. $$$

PRICE CATEGORIES

Prices are all for a double room:

$$$$	US$100 plus
$$$	US$50–100
$$	US$30–50
$	US$30 or under

PATAGONIA

Bariloche

Dazzler Hotel
Av. San Martín 441
Tel: (02944) 456 900
www.dazzlerhotel.com
Centrally located, this slick hotel offers lake views and business facilities. **$$$$**

Design Suites
Av. Bustillo, Km 2.5
Tel: (011) 4814 8700
www.designsuites.com
Located just outside the city, this place is worth the journey. Beautifully furnished and designed with heated swimming pool, restaurant, and spa; a great place to escape the action in Bariloche. **$$$$**

La Cascada Hotel
Av. Bustillo, Km 6
Tel: (02944) 441 088/046/023
www.lacascada.com
En route to the skiing area Cerro Catedral, 11 km (6 miles) away, and set on the shores of Lago Nahuel Huapi. Rooms overlook the lake and mountains or the forest and waterfall. Indoor pool, sauna, and gym. **$$$$**

Llao Llao Hotel and Resort
Av. Bustillo, Km 25
Tel: (02944) 448 530
Fax: (02944) 445 781
www.llaollao.com
One of the best-located hotels in Argentina, approximately 29 km (18 miles) from Bariloche on the shores of Lago Nahuel Huapí, with its own marina and golf course. **$$$$**

Edelweiss Hotel
Av. San Martín 202
Tel: (02944) 445 500
Fax: (02944) 4032 0151
www.edelweiss.com.ar
Large hotel with 100 rooms. Sauna, heated pool, fitness rooms, and a good restaurant. Combines tradition with modernity. **$$$**

Hostería El Retorno
RN258
Tel: (02944) 467 333
www.hosteriaelretorno.com
On Lago Guttierez, about 10 km (6 miles) from Bariloche. Peaceful and attractive. **$$**

Hotel Tronador
RN237, Km 19
Tel: (02944) 441 062/490 550
www.hoteltronador.com
Family-run hotel in a beautiful secluded setting on the shores of Lago Mascardi. **$$**

Premier
Rolando 263
Tel: (02944) 426 168
www.premierhotel.com.ar
In the center of town and considerably cheaper than much of the competition. A clean and pleasant budget option. **$**

Villa la Angostura

Hotel Correntoso
RP 231
Tel: (02944) 1561 9728/29
www.correntoso.com
Recently refurbished, this hotel originally opened in 1922. One of the more luxurious on offer, it combines good hospitality with an up-to-date activities program. **$$$$**

Hostería La Posada
Villa La Angostura
Tel/Fax: (02944) 494 450/368
In its own secluded bay on the opposite side of the lake to Bariloche. **$$$**

San Martín de los Andes

Cerro Abanico
RN234, Km 4.5
Tel: (02972) 423 723
This small hotel, built into the side of a mountain, is delightful. It contains eight rooms (each painted a different color) which face onto the lake. **$$$$**

Patagonia Plaza Hotel
Av. San Martín and Rivadavia
Tel: (02972) 422 280
www.patagoniaplazahotel.com.ar
Centrally located, this is probably the most modern and upmarket hotel in the city. **$$$$**

El Bolson

Cabañas La Montaña
Villa Turismo
Tel: (02944) 492 776
www.montana.com.ar
A good place for those wanting a self-sufficient option, cabins come with a *parilla* to cook barbecues, DVD players, and access to a film library, as well as a shared swimming pool. **$**

Hotel Cordillera
Av. San Martín 3220
Tel: (02944) 492 235
E-mail: cordillera hotel@elbolsón.com
The only 3-star option in town. Pleasant rooms and good views. **$**

Esquel

Hostería Cumbres Blancas
Av. Ameghino 1683
Tel: (02945) 455 100
www.cpatagonia.com/esq/cblancas
Great views of the peak, a good restaurant, and a sauna, at a reasonable price. **$$**

Hostería El Trebol
Cholila, near Esquel
Tel/Fax: (02945) 498 055
Family-run hostel, with home produce and cooking. Hunting and fishing trips can be arranged with the proprietor. **$**

Hostería La Tour D'Argent
San Martín 1063
Tel: (02945) 454 612
www.cpatagonia.com/esq/latour
Located in the center of town, this cute little hotel has small but comfy rooms that are decently priced. **$**

El Calafate

Hostal del Glaciar Libertador
Av. del Libertador
Tel: (02902) 491 792

BELOW: Hostería El Retorno, set within picturesque grounds on the edge of Lago Gutierrez.

www.glaciar.com
Smart, clean, and decently priced Swiss-style hostel. **$$$**
Posada Los Alamos
Moyano and Bustillo
Tel: (02902) 491 144
www.posadalosalamos.com
Very comfortable Alpine-style lodge with sports facilities, putting course, shop, bar, and excellent restaurant. **$$**
La Loma
Julia A. Roca 849
Tel: (02902) 491 016
www.lalomahotel.com
Inexpensive and cozy. **$**

El Chaltén

Hostería El Pilar
RP 23, Km 17
Tel: (02902) 493 002
A cute and comfy lodging, this is the best place for a good view of Fitz Roy. Owned by Marcelo Pagani who has attempted to climb Fitz Roy several

times. Closed April–Sept. **$$$$**
Posada Poincenot
Av. San Martín 615
Tel: (02962) 493 022
One of the cheaper options in the area; good rooms, a lively shared living room, and fun bar. **$**

Parque Nacional los Glaciares

Helsingfors Lodge
Lago Viedma
Tel: (02902) 420 719
www.helsingfors.com.ar
Luxury hotel within the national park itself. Excellent food and service. **$$$$**
Los Notros
Glaciar Perito Moreno
Tel: (01148) 143 934
www.losnotros.com
Overlooking Perito Moreno glacier with stunning views in the heart of the national park. Very comfortable. Half-board only. **$$$**

Puerto Madryn

Hotel Peninsula Valdés
Av. Julio Roca 155
Tel: (02965) 471 292
Four-star seafront hotel within walking distance of the town center. Good restaurant and business center. **$$$$**
Hostería Solar de Costa
Blvd Brown 2057
Tel: (02965) 458 822
www.solardelacosta.com
Decent rooms overlooking the ocean; great value for money. **$**

Peninsula Valdés

Franca Hostería
Primera Bajada, Puerto Pirámides
Tel: (02965) 495 006
A pleasant hotel situated on the seafront. **$$**
Hostería The Paradise
Av. Julio Roca s/n, Puerto Pirámides
Tel: (02965) 495 003
www.hosteriaparadise.com.ar

Cozy hotel with a good restaurant. **$$**

Gaiman

Hostería Gwesty Plas y Coed
Irigoyen 314
Tel: (15) 697 069
A welcoming little bed and breakfast establishment. **$**

Puerto Deseado

Las Nubes: Cabañas y Quincho
Florentino Ameghino 1351
Tel: (15) 621 0278
Email: lasnubes@viadeseado.com.ar
Las Nubes offers well-equipped cabins set in gorgeous surroundings. **$$**
Los Acantilados
España 1611
Tel: (0297) 487 2167
acantour@pdeseado.com.ar
Medium-size hotel with sea views and a lovely cafe where you can enjoy an afternoon tea. **$**

TIERRA DEL FUEGO

Río Grande

Atlantida
Av. Belgrano 582
Tel: (02964) 431 914/431 917
Fax: (02964) 431 915
Modern and functional building, but a popular place to stay; probably the best hotel in town. **$$$**
Posada de los Sauces
El Cano 839
Tel/Fax: (02964) 432 895/430 868
www.posadadelossauces.com.ar
Comfortable hotel near the seafront, with a decent restaurant and bar. Recommended. **$$$**

Tolhuín

Hostería Kaiken
RN3, Km 2942
Lago Fagnano
Tel/Fax: (02901) 492 372
www.hosteriakaiken.com.ar
Comfortable hostel a few kilometers south of Tolhuín, with a beautiful outlook on the shore of Lake Fagnano. With rooms and cabins for up to five people, plus restaurant and *confitería*. **$$**

Ushuaia

Las Hayas Resort Hotel
Camino Glaciar Martial, Km 3
Tel: (02901) 430 710
Fax: (02901) 430 719
www.lashayashotel.com
Located on a hill outside Ushuaia, with impressive views. Spa and pool. Runs a minibus service to the city. **$$$$**
Hotel del Glaciar
Camino Glaciar Martial, Km 3.5
Tel: (02901) 430 640
Fax: (02901) 430 636
Reservations: (011) 4893 1346
www.hoteldelglaciar.com
Fantastic views and good service. Outside Ushuaia, but recommended. **$$$**
Cabo de Hornos
San Martín 899
Tel: (02901) 422 187/430 677
Fax: (02901) 422 313
Pleasant and popular, with restaurant **$$**
Hostal del Bosque Apart Hotel
Magallanes 709
Tel: (02901) 421 723/430 777
www.hostaldelbosque.com.ar
Pleasant hotel rooms with kitchens in city center. **$$**

Hostal Malvinas
Deloqui 615
Tel: (02901) 422 626
www.hostalmalvinas.net
Clean, comfortable, and quiet. Breakfast buffet. **$$**
Hostería Petrel
Lago Escondido, 60 km (37 miles) from Ushuaia on RN3
Tel: (02901) 433 569
Very pleasant hostel situated on the shores of the "hidden lake." Good service and a warm atmosphere. Breakfast included. Camping facilities are also available. **$$**
Hotel Tolkeyen
Del Tolkeyen 2145
Tel: (02901) 445 315/6/7
Excellent hotel outside town with fantastic views and very good service. **$$**
Hotel Ushuaia
Lasserre 933
Tel/Fax: (02901) 430 671/ 423 051/431 134/424 217
Modern, large, and pleasant hotel offering good service. Situated ten blocks from the center. **$$**

Hostería Mustapic
Piedrabuena 230
Tel: (02901) 421 718
Old, simple, and one of the city's few inexpensive hotels. **$**
Hotel Cesar
San Martín 753
Tel: (02901) 421 460/432 721
www.hotelcesarhostal.com.ar
Centrally located, with good service. Homey and friendly. **$**
Refugio del Mochilero
25 de Mayo 241
Tel: (02901) 436 129
Fax: (02901) 431 190
Another popular backpackers' hostel, with kitchen facilities, laundry, and internet access. **$**
Residencial Fernandez
Onachaga 72
Tel: (02901) 421 192
Small hostel. Highly recommended. **$**

PRICE CATEGORIES

Prices are all for a double room:
$$$$	US$100 plus
$$$	US$50–100
$$	US$30–50
$	US$30 or under

ESTANCIAS

For a comprehensive list of estancias in Argentina, see www.estanciasargentinas.com.ar

Around Buenos Aires

Estancia los dos Hermanos
RP 193, Km 10.5 Escalada, Zárate
Tel: (011) 4765 4320. **$$$**
www.estancialosdoshermanos.com
Situated 1 hour's drive from the city center. Specializes in horseback riding expeditions and offers good rooms and dining. **$$$**

Estancia Acelain
54 km (33½ miles) North of Tandil
Tel: (02293) 4322 2784
Luxurious rooms in Spanish-style mansion, set in beautiful grounds, offering horseback riding, polo, boating, hunting, and fishing. Full-board only. **$$$**

Estancia la Montaña
50 km (31 miles) south of Tandil, near the Río Quequen Chico
Tel: (02293) 4342 8417
Californian-style ranch, offering a wide range of outdoor activities: horseback riding, polo, wildlife photo safaris.
Full-board only. **$$$**

Estancia El Carmen de Sierra
RP 91, Arrecifes, near San Antonio de Areco
Tel: (03664) 641 083
Offers horseback riding and a swimming pool. **$$$**

Estancia Los Patricios
RP 41, near San Antonio de Areco
Tel: (02326) 453 823
www.lospatricios.com.ar
Beautiful ivy-covered estancia with horseback riding, golf, swimming pool, local music and folk dancing, and barbecues in a barn. **$$$**

Northeast

Estancia Santa Cecilia
RN12, 30 km (18 miles) from Posadas
Tel: (03752) 493 018
www.santacecilia.com.ar
Situated in the middle of the jungle, this is a working estancia that offers excursions to its visitors and luxury stays. **$$$**

ABOVE: experience a taste of gaucho life by staying on one of Argentina's many estancias.

Estancia San Gará
25 km (14 miles) from Ituzaingó
Tel: (0786) 420 550; Buenos Aires tel: (0358) 464 6193 or (03786) 1561 6245
Offers guided tours of the Iberá wetlands as well as horseback riding and local wildlife trips. Full-board only. **$$$**

Central Sierras

Estancia los Portreros
Near Río Ceballos
Tel: (03548) 452 121
www.ride-americas.com
Offers everything you would want from a visit to an estancia. Demand is high so advance booking is required. **$$$**

Patagonia

Peuma Hue
Via RN258, near Bariloche
Tel: (02944) 501 030
www.peuma-hue.com
Luxurious estancia offering kayaking, horseback riding, golf, and tennis. An organic vegetable garden and delicious home cooking means you'll eat well. **$$$**

Estancia Huechahue
RP 234, near Junin de los Andes
Tel: (02972) 491 303
E-mail: jane@satlink.com
A picturesque place, 30 km (18 miles) outside of Junin de los Andes. Closed Apr–Nov. **$$$**

Estancia La Elvira
Peninsula Valdés
Tel: (02965) 474 248
www.laelvira.com.ar
This estancia has eight rooms offering the utmost in comfort and relaxation. **$$$**

Estancia La Oriental
Parque Nacional Perito Moreno
www.estanciasdesantacruz.com
Offers lots of activities and lodging for up to 25 people. **$$$**

Estancia Telken
RN40, near Perito Moreno
Tel: (02963) 432 079
www.estanciasdesantacruz.com
Stunning place en route to the Cave of Painted Hands. Closed May–Aug. **$$$**

YOUTH HOSTELS

Hostelling International Argentina, tel: (011) 4511 8712, fax: (011) 4312 0089, www.hostels.org.ar, runs youth hostels from Salta in the north to Ushuaia in the far south:

Buenos Aires: Milhouse Hostel, Hipólito Yrigoyen 959.
Tel: (011) 4345 9604.
www.milhousehostel.com

Salta: Backpackers, Buenos Aires 930. Tel/fax: (0387) 4235 910. www.backpackerssalta.com

Tilcara: Malka, San Martín, 400 m/yards from the square.
Tel: (0388) 495 5197.
www.malkahostel.com.ar

Villa Paranacito: Top Malo, RP 46, Km 18.2, near Zárate. Tel: (03446) 495 255.

Mendoza: Campo Base, Av. Mitre 946. Tel: (0261) 429 0707.
www.hostelcampobase.com.ar
Hostal Internacional Mendoza, España 343. Tel/Fax: (0261) 424 0018. www.hostelmendoza.net

San Rafael: Tierrasoles Hostel, Alsina 245. Tel: (02627) 433 449. www.tierrasoles.com.ar

Bariloche: Marcopolo Inn, Salta 422. Tel: (02944) 400 105.
www.marcopoloinn.com.ar

El Bolsón: El Pueblito, Barrio Luján, 1 km (⅔ mile) from RN258. Tel: (02944) 493 560.
E-mail: elpueblito@elbolson.com

Puerto Madryn: El Gualicho Hostel, Marcos A. Zar 480.
Tel: (02965) 454 163.
www.elgualicho.com.ar

Esquel: Casa del Pueblo Hostel, San Martín 661.
Tel: (02945) 450 581.
www.epaadventure.com.ar/albergue.htm
Lago Verde Hostel, Volta 1081.
Tel: (03945) 452 251.
E-mail: lagoverd@hostels.org.ar

El Chaltén: Albergue Patagonia, Av. San Martín 493. Tel/fax: (02962) 493 019.
www.elchalten.com/patagonia
Rancho Grande, Av. San Martín 724. Tel/fax: (02962) 493 005.

El Calafate: Hostel del Glaciar Pioneros, Los Pioneros 251.
Tel: (02902) 491 243.
www.glaciar.com/pioneros.asp

Ushuaia: Torre al Sur, Gobernador Paz 1437. Tel: (02901) 430 745. www.torrealsur.com.ar

E ATING OUT

RECOMMENDED RESTAURANTS & CAFES

What to Eat

Argentina is well known for its beef and *asados* (barbecues), but in the past decade or so, the country has undergone something of a culinary revolution. Imaginative fusions, smart sushi restaurants, and exotic, authentic cuisines from around the world can be found, particularly in Buenos Aires.

Despite the array of international foods on offer, there is still a lot to be said for traditional Argentine cuisine *(see pages 129–131)* and there are many regional specialties.

Options for vegetarians have improved considerably in recent years with many menus offering vegetarian dishes. Vegetarian restaurants can also be found in major cities.

Where to Eat

Dining out is a favorite pastime in Argentina, but the menu is not the only attraction. Restaurants are a place to socialize, to see and be seen, and to share a bottle of wine until the small hours.

There are many excellent restaurants in the major cities – in Buenos Aires particularly, it is possible to eat out every day of the year and still not savor all that the city's restaurants have to offer. A complete listing of all restaurants in the city would be impossible, but a good gourmet guide is the *Guide to Good Eating in Buenos Aires*, published by the *The Buenos Aires Herald* newspaper.

Restaurants in Argentina open for lunch at noon, though it is customary to have lunch between 2pm and 4pm. For dinner they open at around 8pm, although Argentines rarely dine before 9pm, with restaurants really coming alive between 10pm and 11pm. At the weekends, restaurants stay busy well after midnight. Many restaurants close on Monday.

RESTAURANT AND CAFE LISTINGS

BUENOS AIRES

Regional Argentine

Aires de Patagonia
Alicia M. de Justo 1798
Tel: (011) 4315 2151
Modern Patagonian cuisine featuring game, fish, and fine wines. **$$$**

Indian

Katmandu
Córdoba 3547
Tel: (011) 4963 3250
Up-market, authentic restaurant. **$$$**

French

Au Bec Fin
Vicente Lopez 1825
Tel: (011) 4807 3765
www.aubecfin.com.ar
Classic French cooking in a splendid restored mansion; a Buenos Aires institution. Dinner only. Reservations recommended. **$$$**

International

El Aljibe
Hotel Sheraton, San Martín 1225
Tel: (011) 4318 9329
Exciting menu featuring beef and an eclectic range of dishes. **$$$**
Te Mataré Ramirez
Primera Junta 702, San Isidro
Tel: (011) 4747 8618
An excellent, original, and international assortment of dishes. Ideal for either a romantic evening or a business dinner. Specializes in dishes with alleged aphrodisiac qualities. **$$–$$$**
Baez
Baez 240
Tel: (011) 4777 1313
Argentine, Mediterranean, and Japanese cuisine in sleek surroundings. **$$**
Roof
Costa Rica 4001
Tel: (011) 4867 5888
Bright and airy. Well-prepared international and vegetarian dishes. **$$**
Soul Café
Baez 248
Tel: (011) 4778 3115
Trendy bar and restaurant, with music. **$$**

Italian and Mediterranean

(See also Pizzerias, below)
Bice
Av. Alicia Moreau de Justo 192
Tel: (011) 4315 6216
The original Bice restaurant is in Milan, with ten more around the world, including this one in Puerto Madero. Upmarket Italian eatery, with modern twists on traditional pasta. **$$**
Los Inmortales
Paraná 1209
Tel: (011) 4811 2222
Trendy and lively restaurant

ABOVE: Abril Bistró in San Telmo, just one of Buenos Aires' many stylish eateries.

El Globo
H. Yrigoyen 1199
Tel: (011) 4381 3926
One block from Avenida de Mayo, near Congreso. Try their paella or *puchero* (seafood stew). **$$**

Tasca Tancat
Paraguay 645
Tel: (011) 4312 5442
Long, antique wooden bar which specializes in Spanish-style *tapas*. Closed at weekends. **$**

Scandinavian

Olsen
Gorriti 5870
Tel: (011) 4776 7677
Smart Scandinavian restaurant with a justly popular Sunday brunch.
$–$$

overlooking a beautiful plaza, with unusual fresh and imported Italian pastas, gourmet pizzas, and specialty salads. **$$**

Rodizio
Puerto Madero, Costanera
Tel: (0810) 999 7634
Charcoal-grilled steaks, fresh pasta, and a welcome drink on arrival. There is also a good buffet. **$$**

Teatriz
Riobamba 1220
Tel: (011) 4811 1915
Casual, warm atmosphere with a touch of elegance. Mediterranean menu with interesting pasta, chicken, and fish dishes, and wonderful desserts. **$$**

Mexican

Cielito Lindo
El Salvador 4999, Palermo Viejo
Tel: (011) 4832 8054
Fairly good, but expensive, Mexican food. **$$$**

Parrillas (Steakhouses)

El Mirasol
Av. Alicia Moreau de Justo 202
Tel: (011) 4326 7322
www.el-mirasol.com.ar
Large upscale *parrilla* in Puerto Madero, with an elegant atmosphere. Reservations recommended. **$$$**

Río Alba
Cerviño 4499

Tel: (011) 4773 5748
Popular restaurant famous for brochettes, grilled fish, and enormous filet mignon steaks. **$$$**

Chiquilín
Montevideo 321
Tel: (011) 4373 5163
Specializes in Italian pasta and *asado* (roasts). **$$**

Des Nivel
Defensa 855 and Estados Unidos
Highly popular spit-and-sawdust *parrilla* in San Telmo which serves mouth-watering steaks in a relaxed environment. **$$**

El Palacio de la Papa Frita
Lavalle 735
Tel: (011) 4393 5849
Popular place serving typical meat dishes and excellent soufflé potatoes. **$$**

La Chacra
Av. Córdoba 941
Tel: (011) 4322 1409
Typical *parrillada* (barbecue) restaurant with meat roasting in the window for pedestrians to drool over. Huge portions. **$$**

La Estancia
Lavalle 941
Tel: (011) 4326 0330
Fun, classic *asado* restaurant in the heart of La City. **$$**

Munich Recoleta
R.M. Ortíz 1879
Tel: (011) 4804 3981
Popular for nearly 40 years for its lively atmosphere and great steak. Reservations not accepted. **$$**

Pizzerias

Morelia
Baez 260
Tel: (011) 4772 0329
Delicious, crisp pizzas and a lively atmosphere. **$–$$**

El Cuartito
Talcahuano 937
Tel: (011) 4816 1758
The closest BA comes to a sports bar, with clippings and photos covering the walls, soccer on the television, delicious pizzas, and cold beer. **$**

Los Inmortales
Corrientes 1369, tel: (011) 4373 5305; Lavalle 746, tel: (011) 4322 5493; Callao 1165, tel: (011) 4815 7551
Small chain of BA pizzerias where the decor is dedicated to the life and times of tango stars and the pizza is consistently good. Try the classic Napolitana, covered with tomatoes and garlic. **$**

Spanish

Pedemonte
Av. de Mayo 682
Tel: (011) 4331 1676
Traditional *porteño* restaurant with early 20th-century decor; a favorite with BA politicians. The menu features Spanish cuisine, pasta dishes, and grilled beef. Also hosts tango shows. Reservations recommended. **$$$**

Vegetarian

Los Sabios
Corrientes 3733
Tel: (011) 4864 4407
Vegetarian Chinese food. **$$**

Tulasi
Marcelo T. de Alvear 628
Local 30
Tel: (011) 4311 0972
Located off leafy Plaza San Martín, this cafe is a good, inexpensive lunch place, offering a selection of Indian food. **$**

Yin Yang
Paraguay 858, tel: (011) 4703 1546; Echeverría 2444, tel: (011) 4783 1546
Two outlets run by the same owner. A delicious respite from Argentine beef, featuring fresh salads, soups, home-made wheat bread, brown rice, stir-fried vegetables, and other meatless treats. **$**

POPULAR EATERIES

Some of the best-value restaurants in Buenos Aires are those that serve a mixture of local and international dishes, but which are most popular for the lively ambiance provided by their regular clientele.

El Trapiche
Paraguay 5099

Tel: (011) 4772 7343
Typical neighborhood restaurant in Palermo, with cured hams, tins of olive oil, and bottles of wine decking the walls and ceiling. Great steaks, home-made pastas, and seafood. **$$**

Restaurant Dora
L.N. Além 1016
Tel: (011) 4311 2891
An upscale version of a popular eatery, with rave reviews on the enormous steaks and simple seafood dishes; a downtown "don't miss." **$$**

Bárbaro
Tres Sargentos 415
Tel: (011) 4311 6856
Literally a BA landmark – an old-world version of the hole-in-the-wall bar. A great place for a simple midday meal, or music, beer, and bar food in the evening. **$**

La Casa de Esteban de Luca
Defensa and Carlos Calvo
Tel: (011) 4361 4338
In the heart of San Telmo, the restored colonial-era home of the Argentine "poet of the revolution." A popular place for Sunday lunch after the San Telmo fair. **$**

Pippo
Montevideo 341
Tel: (011) 4372 1293
No frills, but great atmosphere and unbeatable prices. Try a *bife de chorizo* (T-bone steak), or a bowl of *vermicclli mixto* (pasta with pesto and bolognese sauce). **$**

Rodi Bar
Vicente Lopez 1900
Tel: (011) 4801 5230
Cozy, neighborhood restaurant nestled among the famous gourmets of the Recoleta, featuring simple home-made food. **$**

CONFITERÍAS

These traditional cafes are famous as lively neighborhood meeting places, offering not only good snacks and drinks, sometimes 24 hours a day, but also an eclectic mix of live music, poetry, and highbrow intellectual debate (*see Cafe Life, page 164.*)

Café La Paz
Corrientes 1599
Popular with students and intellectuals. Recently

modernized, with a salad bar. Open until late. **$$**

Café Tortoni
Av. de Mayo 829
Tel: (011) 4342 4328
Built in 1848, with billiards, live jazz, poetry readings, and decaying grandeur. **$$**

Florida Garden
Florida and Paraguay
Tel: (011) 4312 7902
Traditional *confitería* and journalists' meeting place, serving a good range of sandwiches, cakes, and other snacks. **$$**

Confitería Ideal
Suipacha 384
Tel: (011) 5265 8069
Stylish meeting point for the elderly, with polished marble floor and columns now in decline. Live music on Sunday evenings. **$$**

La Biela
Av. Quintana 600
Tel: (011) 4804 0449
www.labiela.com
At the heart of Recoleta. Attractive location opposite the Recoleta Cemetery, with outside tables. **$$**

La Giralda
Corrientes 1449
Delicious hot chocolate and *churros* (donuts) in a small, old-fashioned, wood-paneled cafe. **$$**

HELADERÍAS

The huge number of Italian descendants living in Buenos Aires must have inherited the secrets of a perfect ice-cream as the city is full of delicious *heladerías* (ice-cream parlors). During the summer these parlors become meeting places for the young and old who sit late into the night sampling the flavors on offer. Two of the most popular *heladerías* are *Freddo* and *Persicco* who have outlets throughout the city and are open til late. In both places the *dulce de leche* flavored ice-cream is irresistible.

Freddo
Vicente López 2008, Recoleta
Tel: (0800) 3337 3336
www.freddo.com
One of many branches in the capital serving exquisite ice-cream.

Persicco
Corner of J.Salguero and Cabello, Palermo
Tel: (0810) 333 7377
www.persicco.com
Popular *heladería* with branches throughout Buenos Aires province.

MAR Y SIERRAS

Mar del Plata

There are literally hundreds of restaurants here. Most are acceptable, and seafood is likely to be fresh almost anywhere.

Tío Curzio
Blvd Maritimo 2657 and Colón
Tel: (0223) 451 3115
Enjoy delicious seafood overlooking the beach. **$$$**

Ambos Mundos
Rivadavía 2644
Tel: (0223) 495 0450
Spanish and Argentine cooking. **$$**

Taberna Baska
Martinez de Hoz, near 12 de Octubre
Tel: (0223) 480 0209
Fresh seafood. Spanish cuisine. **$$**

1930
Avellaneda 2657

Popular place serving tasty traditional dishes. **$**

Stella Maris
Corner of Alsina and Alberti, two blocks from bus terminal
Tel: (0223) 451 5183
Serves an outstanding *cazuela de mariscos* (seafood stew) and other fresh seafood. Highly recommended. **$**

Villa Gesell

Cantina Caprese
Buenos Aires, between Alameda 206 and 208
Good Italian cuisine. **$$–$$$**

La Jirafa Azul
Av. 3, between Buenos Aires and Paseo 102
An informal restaurant and bar serving pasta and other simple dishes. **$**

Pinamar

El Viejo Lobo
Av. del Mar and Bunge
Tel: (02254) 483 218
One of the oldest seafood restaurants in town, with a very good wine selection. **$**

Green Mango
Quinana 56
Tel: (02254) 407 990
An elegant and tasty seafood restaurant. **$**

Mar de las Pampas

Amorinda Tutto Pasta
Corner of Av. Cerchunoff and Lucero
Tel: (02255) 479 759
A tasty and popular pasta restaurant located in a small village near Villa Gesell. **$**

Cariló

Acqua & Farina
Cerezo, corner of Boyero, Galería Cariló
Tel: (02254) 570 278
A good selection of seafood and a friendly atmosphere. **$$$**

Jalisco
Av. Divisadero 1510
Tel: (02254) 571 717
A good option, serving a variety of Argentine dishes. **$$$**

PRICE CATEGORIES

Categories are based on the cost of a meal for two people, with a bottle of house wine:

$$$ US$40 or more
$$ US$20–40
$ US$20 or less

TRANSPORTATION

ACCOMMODATIONS

EATING OUT

ACTIVITIES

A – Z

LANGUAGE

CENTRAL SIERRAS

Córdoba

There are many self-service restaurants in the city center. Popular with students, they sell a variety of dishes by weight, most of which are good and cheap, especially for the set lunch menu. Otherwise, you could try the following:
Betos
Blvd. San Juan 450
Tel: (0351) 421 2022

Established restaurant that is well known for serving the best meat dishes in the city. Part of a small chain with several branches in and around Córdoba city. **$$$**
La Mamma
Figueroa Alcorta 272
Tel: (0351) 421 2212
Traditional Italian restaurant serving good meat and pasta dishes. **$$**

Rancho Grande
Rafael Nunez 4142
Tel: (0351) 481 1529
International cooking, including lots of beef dishes. One of the oldest and most traditional restaurants in Córdoba. **$$**

Río Ceballos

Confitería Nueva Vienesa
Av. San Martín 5285

Popular cafe serving an impressive and delicious range of pastries, cakes, and tarts. **$$**

La Cumbre

Restauranté Tomás
25 de Mayo 463
Tel: (03548) 452 840
A friendly restaurant serving good traditional Argentine food and international dishes. **$**

THE NORTHEAST

Rosario

There are a number of good restaurants in Rosario offering an attractive view of the river, including the following:
La Cangreja
Av. Lisandro de la Torre and El Río
Tel: (0341) 471 3860

Serves very good and fresh seafood. **$$$**
Rich
San Juan 1031
Tel: (0341) 440 8657
Up-market restaurant serving Italian and Argentine cuisine. **$$$**
Señor Arenero
Costanera 2568

Tel: (0341) 454 2155
Another long-standing Rosario restaurant. **$$**

Posadas

La Querencia
Bolívar 322
Tel: (03752) 437 117
A traditional *parrilla*

serving good meat dishes. **$$**

Puerto Iguazú

El Tío Querido
Bompland 110
Tel: (03757) 420 151
Decent, reasonably priced *parrilla*. **$**

THE NORTHWEST

Catamarca

Sociedad Española
Virgen del Valle 725
Tel: (03833) 431 896/7
International, Spanish, and Argentine cuisine, specializing in *parrillada* and seafood. **$$**
Trattoria Montecarlo
República 548
Excellent pasta and meat dishes, located on the plaza. Recommended.
$–$$
Hotel Casino Catamarca
Pasaje Cesar Carmen s/n
Tel: (03833) 430891/432928
Restaurant located in one of Catamarca's most popular hotels. International menu and good service. Also hosts dinner shows. **$**

Tucumán

La Leñita
25 de Mayo 377
Tel: (0381) 422 9196
An attractive family-run restaurant, specializing in *parrillada* meats.
$$–$$$

Carlos V
25 de Mayo 330
Tel: (0381) 431 1666
Located inside Carlos V Hotel. International cooking, especially Spanish and Italian. **$$**

Salta

Boliche Balderrama
Av. San Martín 1126
Tel: (0387) 421 1542
Traditional restaurant, with regional dishes and folklore show. **$$–$$$**
Hotel Portezuelo
Av. Turística 1
Tel: (0387) 431 0104
Fairly standard Argentine beef and pasta menu. Worth a visit for its location on a hill with a beautiful view of the city.
$$–$$$
Peña Gauchos de Güemes
Av. Uruguay 750
Tel: (0387) 421 7007
Restaurant offering folklore shows. Food is average and the atmosphere is very touristy, but the show is worth seeing. **$$–$$$**

La Estrella Oriental
San Juan 137
Middle Eastern cooking – a tasty alternative to steaks or pasta. **$$**
Santana
Mendoza 208
Tel: (0387) 432 0941
Good Argentine food, including regional specialties. **$$**

Jujuy

The two best restaurants in Jujuy are located in the **Hotel Jujuy Palace** (Belgrano 1060, tel: 0388-423 0433) and the **Gran Hotel Panorama** (Belgrano 1295, tel: 0388-423 2533); both of which are moderate/expensive. **Hotel Alto La Viña**, located a few kilometers out of town on Ruta 56 (tel: 0388-142 6588), serves reasonable lunches, with spectacular views. The city-center pedestrian street, **Belgrano**, has many bars and *confiterías*, all reasonable and moderately priced.

Madre Tierra Restaurante Naturista
Belgrano 619
Tel: (0388) 422 9578
Excellent and inexpensive vegetarian cooking. A great lunchtime venue. **$**

Cafayate

La Casona de Luis
Almagro 87
Tel: (03868) 421 249
Restaurant serving good regional cooking. Situated in a colonial building, which is also a hotel. **$$**
El Comedor Criollo
Güemes 254
Tel: (03868) 421 140
Traditional restaurant with local specialties, such as kid. **$–$$**
La Carreta de Don Olegario
Güemes 2
Tel: (03868) 421 004
Restaurant located on the central plaza serving regional cooking, including meat dishes, *locro* (meat and corn stew) and other local specialties. Sometimes hosts folkloric shows in the evenings. **$**

THE CUYO

Mendoza

La Marchigiana
Patricias Mendocinas 1550
International cuisine;
top-level service. **$$$**
La Nuova Pizza
Av. Sarmiento 785, Mendoza
Tel: (0261) 423 0751
Bright and lively pizza parlor
with air conditioning. **$$**
Trevi
Las Heras 70
Tel: (0261) 423 3195
Italian food, including good
home-made pastas and
meat dishes. **$$**
Class
Paseo Sarmiento and Av. San
Martín, Mendoza

Good, inexpensive set
meals and beer by the jug.
Pleasant outside tables, or
air conditioning inside. **$**
Dali
Espejo and 9 de Julio
Friendly restaurant serving
good food of the standard
variety – beef, *milanesas*
(schnitzel), and pasta. **$**

San Luis

La Pulpería del Arriero
9 de Julio 753
Tel: (02652) 432 446
A good place for traditional
Argentine dishes. **$**
Mojito's Resto Bar
Illía 365

Lively place which serves
drinks and food. **$**

San Juan

Club Sirio Libanés
Entre Rios 33 Sur
Tel: (0264) 422 3841
For those wanting a change
from the Argentine *asados*,
this is a great Lebanese
option. **$**
El Portal
Laprida 82 Este
Tel: (0264) 421 4965
This restaurant is part of
the Hotel Alkazar. The
restaurant serves a
selection of traditional
Argentine dishes. **$**

La Rioja

L'Stanza
Dorrego 220
Tel: (03822) 435 214
A great restaurant serving
home-made Italian food.
$$
La Querencia
Perón 1200
Tel: (03822) 435 214
A good option, serving
traditional Argentine food.
$$
La Vieja Casona
Rivadavia 427
Tel: (03822) 425 996
Probably the best *parrilla* in
town, although the decor is
on the tacky side. **$$**

PATAGONIA

Bariloche

Casita Suiza
Quaglia 342, Bariloche
Tel: (02944) 423 775/426 111
www.casitasuiza.com
Traditional Swiss-style
restaurant, with a wide
range of dishes, including
raclette, fondue, and rosti.
$$$
Kandahar
20 de Febrero 698
Tel: (02944) 424 702
www.kandahar.com.ar
Delightful ambiance and
imaginative menu featuring

Patagonian specialties
such as trout and lamb
dishes. **$$–$$$**
Cervecería Blest
Av. Bustillo, Km 11.6
Tel: (02944) 461 026
Situated out of town on the
road to Llao Llao, this bar
is attached to the area's
only brewery, serving tasty
snacks. **$$**
La Marmite
Mitre 329
Tel: (02944) 423 685
A popular coffee house
and restaurant right in the
heart of town. **$$**

Villa La Angostura

Las Balsas
Bahia las Balsas
Tel: (02944) 494 308
Slightly outside of the
center but worth the trip,
offers an exciting and
scrumptious menu. **$$$**
Tinto Bistro
Nahuel Huapi 34
Tel: (02944) 292 924
Although expensive, this is
one of the best options in
the area, serving a
selection of Spanish and
Oriental foods. **$$$**

Delfina
Puerto Manzano
Tel: (02944) 494 813
A great place, which
serves traditional
Argentine recipes in the
rooms of an ancient
house. **$**
Rincón Suizo
Av. Arrayanes 44
Tel: (02944) 292 248
Despite the slight
tackiness of the interior,
thc food is an intriguing
mix of Central European,
Swiss, and Argentine
cuisine. **$**

San Martín de los Andes

Restaurant Caleuche
RN234, km 78
Tel: (02972) 428 154
Probably the best place on
offer. Serves delicious
Patagonian food and has
great lake views. **$$$**
La Reserva
Belgrano 940
Tel: (02972) 428 734
Tasty food and a good
atmosphere. Specializes in

BELOW: feasting on giant steaks and fine wines at a *parrilla* in Bariloche.

TRANSPORTATION

ACCOMMODATIONS

EATING OUT

ACTIVITIES

A – Z

LANGUAGE

dishes cooked in a clay oven. **$**

La Tasca
Mariano Moreno 886
Tel: (02972) 428 663
Very lively tapas-style restaurant. **$**

El Bolsón

Cerro Lindo
Av. San Martín 2524
Tel: (02944) 492 899
Laid back place serving mainly pizza and pasta. Live jazz on Sunday evenings. **$**

La Calabaza
Av. San Martín 2518
Tel: (02944) 492 910
A good option for vegetarians serving mostly meat-free, fresh food. **$**

La Casona de Odile
Barrio Luján, Ruta 30, Subida los Maitenes
Tel: (02944) 492 753
www.montana.com.ar
This restaurant forms part of Casona de Odile lodge. The setting is beautiful and the food is delicious and fresh. Not to be missed if you are in the area. **$**

Esquel

Parrilla de María
Rivadavia 1024
Tel: (02945) 452 503
Despite the slightly dodgy decor this is a great place

for a good Argentine *parrilla*. **$**

Pizzería Fitz Roya
Rivadavia 1048
Tel: (02945) 450 512
Good, classic pizza. **$**

Vascongada
9 de Julio 675
Tel: (02945) 452 229
An interesting selection of delicious food. **$**

El Calafate

El Rancho Pizza Bar
Moyano and 9 de Julio
Tel: (02902) 491 644
Serves good pizza and classic Argentine dishes. **$**

La Tablita
Coronel Rosales 24
Tel: (02902) 491 065
Busy and casual *parrilla* frequented by locals and tourists alike. **$**

Punto de Encuentro
Los Pioneros 251
Tel: (02902) 491 243
Part of the Hostal del Glaciar. This is a popular restaurant worth a visit. **$**

Pura Vida
Av. del Libertador 1876
Tel: (02902) 493 356
No-frills option that serves good, hearty food. **$**

El Chaltén

Ruca Mahuida
Lionnel Terray 104
Tel: (02962) 493 018

Classy establishment, serving good traditional Argentine and European cuisine. **$$**

Club Británico
Roca 935
Tel: (02966) 425 223
Good-value meals and a friendly bar. **$**

Las Lengas
Av. Güemes
Tel: (02962) 493 044
Family-run restaurant offering a tasty selection of home-cooked meals. **$**

Malbec
Antonio Rojo and Cabo García
Tel: (02962) 493 195
Sophisticated and stylish; serves particularly good steaks. **$**

Patagonicus
Av. Güemes
Tel: (02962) 403 025
Popular pizzeria. **$**

Puerto Madryn

Cantina el Náutico
Av. Julio A Roca 790
Tel: (02965) 471 404
A friendly place serving *parrilla* and fresh fish. **$**

Estela
Roque Sáenz Peña 27
Tel: (02965) 451 573
Go for the excellent *parrillada*. **$**

La Vaca y el Pollito
Av. Storni 49
Tel: (02965) 458 486
The name (the cow and the

little chicken) says it all. Serves classic Argentine meat dishes. **$**

Mediterranean
Blvd. Brown 1040
Tel: (02965) 458 145
Good selection of Argentine and European foods. **$**

Nativo Sur
Blvd. Brown 2000
Tel: (02965) 457 403
Probably the best-known seafood restaurant in town. Its seafront location makes it ideal for a romantic evening. **$**

Taska Beltza
9 de Julio 345
Tel: (02965) 474 003
The seafood is fresh and the price is right. Recommended. **$**

Puerto Pirámides

The Paradise
Av. las Ballenas, 2nd bajada al mar
Tel: (02965) 495 003
Part of the hotel of the same name; a very good restaurant serving local seafood and lamb dishes. **$**

Perito Moreno

Rotisería Chee's
25 de Mayo 1896
Tel: (02963) 432 842
A good place to grab a quick bite. The *empanadas* (meat or vegetable patties) are especially good. **$**

TIERRA DEL FUEGO

Río Grande

Atlántida
Belgrano 582
Tel: (02964) 431 915
In the elegant Hotel Atlántida, with international cuisine and good seafood. **$$$**

El Comedor de May
Elcano 839
Tel: (02964) 430 868/432 895
www.posadadelossauces.com.ar
The best eating place in town, in the hotel Posada de los Sauces, with tasty meat and seafood dishes, and a reliable wine list. **$$$**

Rotisería CAI
Av. Perito Moreno s/n
A popular local place, serving good meat dishes. **$**

Tolhuín

La Posada de los Ramirez
Av. Shelknam 411
Tel: (02901) 492 128
Friendly, small restaurant. **$$**

Restaurante Hostería Kaiken
Cabecera Lago Fagnano. RN3
Tel: (02901) 492 208
Extremely nice restaurant belonging to the hostel 120 km (75 miles) south of Río Grande. Good food, excellent views. **$$**

Ushuaia

Kaupé
Roca 470
Tel: (02901) 422 704
www.kaupe.com.ar
Small restaurant with

excellent seafood and lovely view of bay. The best in town so booking is advised. **$$$**

Tia Elvira
Maipu 349
Tel: (02901) 424 725
Excellent food – particularly good seafood and German-style dishes; very popular. **$$$**

Barcito Ideal
San Martín 393
Tel: (02901) 437 860
Beautiful old house in the town center. Good atmosphere and reasonable food. **$$**

Club Náutico
Maipú and Belgrano
Tel: (02901) 430 415/424 330
Very nice restaurant in the Yacht Club on the seafront. **$$**

Opíparo
Maipú 1255
Tel: (02901) 434 022
Beautiful old house in front of the Yacht Club. Specializes in pizza and pasta, which are excellent. **$$**

Volver
Av. Maipú 37
Tel: (02901) 423 977
Cozy restaurant in a converted early 20th-century home. **$$**

El Turco
San Martin 1440
Tel: (02901) 424 711
The most popular place in town with the locals. Excellent food, including pizza, pasta, and meat and fish dishes, with friendly atmosphere. Strongly recommended. **$**

ACTIVITIES

FESTIVALS, THE ARTS, NIGHTLIFE, SHOPPING AND SPECTATOR SPORTS

Calendar of Festivals and Events

The following are just some of the festivals and events that take place in Argentina. Dates vary each year so check with provincial tourist offices *(see page 365)* for details.

January

Festival Internacional de Tango, La Falda, Córdoba province. Tango aficionados from all over the world come to this tango festival.
Festival Nacional del Folklore, Cosquín, Córdoba province. Annual folk festival which draws crowds from all over the country with a line-up of top artists from South American and European countries.

February

Carnaval. Argentina's carnival takes place mainly in the capital and in Gualeguaychú and Corrientes in the Northeast. There is also a colorful Shrove Tuesday procession in Salta.
Festival del Viñador, Villa Unión, La Rioja province. Wine merchants' festival.
Fiesta Nacional de la Chaya, La Rioja. Folk festival which takes its inspiration from pre-Columbian Diaguita legend.
Festival de Tango, Buenos Aires. Concerts, tango shows, and classes in venues throughout the city.

March

Exposición de Caballos Criollos, Predio Ferial, Rosario. Exhibition showcasing Argentina's finest horses.
Festival Internacional de Cine, Mar del Plata. Prestigious international film festival.
Festival de la Vendimia, Mendoza. Grape harvest festival culminating in an extravaganza of lights, music, and dancing in an amphitheater set in the Andean foothills.

April

Festival Internacional de Cine Independiente, Buenos Aires. Independent film festival which is helping new talent gain recognition.

May

Arte BA, Buenos Aires. Contemporary art fair hosted by galleries throughout the city.

June

Día de Muerte de Carlos Gardel. June 24 marks the death of Argentina's favorite tango hero. A week of events culminates in a pilgrimage to his tomb in the Cementerio de la Chacarita, in Buenos Aires.

July

Fiesta de San Francisco Solano, Santiago del Estero. Folk music and dance in the home of the *gato* and *chacarera* (24 July).
Festival Nacional del Poncho, San Fernanda del Valle de Catamarca, Catamarca province. Four wild days of traditional celebrations.
Fiesta del Chocolate Alpino, Villa General Belgrano, Córdoba province. Confectioners demonstrate the art of chocolate-making.

September

Fiesta Nacional del Inmigrante, Misiones. Festival celebrating the cultural diversity of this province.

October

Semana Musical, Llao Llao, Río Negro. Held in the beautiful Llao Llao Hotel, this festival brings classical music to the Andes.
Oktoberfest, Villa General Belgrano, Córdoba province. German-style beer festival.

November

Día de la Tradicíon. A celebration of traditional culture with gaucho displays of horsemanship and enormous *asados* throughout Argentina. The largest festival takes place in San Antonio de Areco.

December

Día del Tango. In homage to Carlos Gardel, the day of his birth (December 11) has been christened "day of the tango." Various tango events take place around the capital.
Campeonato Abiero Argentino de Polo, Campo Argentino de Polo, Palermo, Buenos Aires. Spring polo season championship.

BELOW: carnival time in Corrientes.

THE ARTS

Art Galleries

Art is greatly appreciated in Argentina, with a traditionally strong influence from France, where many artists go to study. Buenos Aires is the dominant force of the country's artistic output, but some provincial capitals, such as Resistencia in the Northeast, are also important centers. There are several museums of art in Buenos Aires *(see pages 145–184)*, but smaller galleries can also be found as you walk around the city. Some well-known ones are: **British Arts Center**, Suipacha 1333. **Centro Cultural Recoleta**, Junín 1930. Tel: (011) 4803 1041. **Galería Praxis**, Arenales 1311. **Galería Palatina**, Arroyo 821. **Colección Alvear de Zurbarán**, Av. Alvear 1658. A small collection of modern art (mostly Argentine artists) which changes monthly.

If you have the time to browse, take the side streets and you might run into some exquisite old houses containing interesting exhibits.

Theaters

The **Teatro Colón** is Buenos Aires' opera house, probably the best-known theater in all Latin America. Tickets for operas, ballets, and classical concerts are available from the box office on Calle Libertad 621. Tel: (011) 4378 7344; www.teatrocolon.org.ar. Many of the world's top performers are acquainted with this magnificent theater. The building is Italian Renaissance style with French and Greek influence. It holds up to 3,000 people, with standing room for 500. The acoustics are considered to be nearly perfect. The Colón also has a magnificent museum, where all of the theater's history and its mementos are stored. For a guided tour, call (011) 4378 7132 to make an appointment.

State-funded, innovative **Teatro San Martín**, Av. Corrientes 1550, tel: (0800) 333 5254, www.teatrosanmartin.com.ar, offers a variety of plays and musicals. Check the local newspapers for performances.

What's On

Various national newspapers provide listings of events in the capital and other major cities. The best are included in the *Buenos Aires Herald* and *La Nacion*.

Cultural Life

The Argentine people are extremely culture-oriented. European trends are watched carefully, but Argentines maintain their own traditions. Most cities, particularly those with a university, offer a lively round of cultural activities, centered around the local museums, galleries, theaters, bookstores, and libraries.

NIGHTLIFE

Buenos Aires is often labeled the city that never sleeps and this is probably true of most of the country's urban areas. Argentines are creatures of the night and city centers tend to be busy until very late. To get a real taste of the nightlife, be prepared to begin at 2am and party until the early hours. Buenos Aires has an internationally renowned club scene that attracts DJs from all over the world.

Cabarets and live bands are also very popular and can be found in many cities. Again, shows do not begin until after midnight. Cafes and ice-cream parlors are also open late. During the summer months, it is customary to see groups of elderly women gossiping at ice-cream parlors late into the night.

The big cities of the interior, such as Córdoba, Mendoza, Bariloche, and Salta, also have a lively nightlife. The theater shows are not as varied as in the capital, but a little bit of everything is available.

Bars and Nightclubs

Buenos Aires

El Codo, Guardia Vieja 4085. Tel: (011) 4862 1381. Very cozy; thirty-something creative crowd. Soul-funk music. Long-established. **El Dorado**, Hipólito Yrigoyen 947. Tel: (011) 4334 2155. For drinking, dining, and dancing. **El Living**, M. T. de Alvear 1540. Tel: (011) 4811 4730. Popular with the trendy set. **La Morocha**, Dorrego 3307. Tel: (011) 4773 3888. In an old railway station, beautifully done up. Jet-set crowd with lots of posing. Separate room for rock 'n' roll. **Ozono**, Uruguay 142. Tel: (011) 4373 2666. Nice mixed crowd. Quiet bar upstairs, dancing downstairs. **Bahrein**, Lavalle 345 and Reconquista. Tel: (011) 4771 5751. Popular night spot spread over several floors, plus a restaurant. **Mint**, Av. Costanera Rafael Obligado and Sarmiento. Tel: (011) 4771 5870. One of the more extravagant options.

Getting Tickets

For tango shows, cinema, concerts, and theater performances you can usually buy tickets at the *boletería* (box office) of the venue. For very popular performances it is advisable to book by phone through **Ticketek**, tel: (011) 5327 7200, www.ticketek.com.ar, or **Ticketmaster**, tel: (011) 4321 9700. Credit cards accepted and booking fees apply. You can sometimes purchase discounted tickets (30–50 percent off) to theater shows, musicals, cinema, and concerts at: **Cartelera Baires**, Unit 24, Av. Corrientes 1382, Tribunales, tel: (011) 4372 5319; **Cartelera Lavalle**, Lavalle 742, Microcentro, tel: (011) 4322 1559, www.123info.com.ar; or **Unica Cartelera**, Unit 27, Lavalle 835, Microcentro, tel: (011) 4370 5319, www.unica-cartelera.com.ar.

A terrace provides the perfect spot for cooling down. **Millón**, Paraná 1048, between Marcelo T. de Alvear and Santa Fe. (011) 4815 9925. Capacious bar in a stately town mansion. Cutting-edge interior design and a gorgeous garden. Well worth braving the crowds. **Bar Seddón**, Defensa 695 and Chile. Tel: (011) 4342 3700. Cozy, traditional Buenos Aires bar. Busy at weekends when live bands play.

La Plata

El Ayuntamiento, Av. 1, between 47 and 48, La Plata. Live music on Fridays; popular with students. **Bar Esquina San Juan**, Calle 55 and 7. Chilled-out late-night bar with a friendly atmosphere and crowd.

Mar del Plata

32 Sur, La Rioja 2042. Busy and lively bar situated in the center. **Azúcar**, Av. Constitución 4478. Relaxed place which plays salsa and merengue. **Vitti**, San Martín 2299. A good place to relax after a day on the beach. Open all year round.

Villa Gesell

Bacará, Av. 3 and Paseo 106. A good place to grab a beer and a snack. **L'Brique**, Av. 3, between Buenos Aires and Paseo 102. A good place for a dance; attracts a young crowd. **Chauen**, Paseo 104, between Av. 3 and 4. Lively little place that fills up at the weekend.

Córdoba

La Alameda, Obispo Trejo 170. Laid-back cafe/bar serving beers and

The Battle of the Sexes in Traditional Dance

Argentina's music and dance traditions have been greatly influenced by colonization over the centuries. Most folk dances are based on the orchestrated couple dances of the Spanish courts and Parisian ballrooms. However, native influence in music is prevalent in the north of the country, which benefits from the Andean influences of Chile, Bolivia, and Peru. In the mountainous regions of Jujuy and Salta many ancient dances still exist in their most colorful, intricate, and bold forms. Archived in the choreography and arrangement of these ancient dances are the memories and rituals of highly sophisticated pre-Columbian civilizations.

The Zamacueca, originally from Peru, developed into two dances: the **zamba**, which moves to a slowed melancholic rhythm, and the more light-hearted **cueca** (or Chilena). The *cueca*, the **bailecitos**, and the **carnavalitos** employ the use of indigenous instruments such as the *charango* (an Andean mandolin), small drums, and the shrill sound of the *zampoña* flutes. Clad in rich orange cloth and sporting black bowler-style hats, men and women perform the complex repertoire of group reels known as the *carnavalito*. In short, scurrying

steps spurred on by *bombo* drumbeats, panpipe bursts, and energetic *charango* chords, they follow the commands of a cane-wielding caller.

Most folk dances enact a form of role-play – the battle of the sexes. The female and male dancers play out a dual of evasion and seduction, flirtation and rebuttal, full of sudden dramatic movements and equally emotional responses.

The gaucho is a romantic figure in Argentine folklore, as wild and intractable as the landscape itself. Dances and music that are particular to gaucho culture are the **chacarera**, the **gato**, and the **escondido**. Unlike the dances of the north, these forms descended from old colonial and modern European culture and are known as "creole" dance. They reflect the harshness and joy of life on the open plains.

Both the *chacarera* and the *gato* resonate with the repetitive beat of large drums and employ guitar and accordion accompaniments and a soloist storyteller. The rhythm of both may often be uplifting and infectious; but the lyrical content of the *chacarera* centers on themes of pain and misery – a favorite of the gauchos who were always keen to play heavily on melancholic

moments – while the lyrics of the *gato* celebrate the joys of life, dance, and drink.

The *escondido* is a particularly entertaining dance to watch as man and woman act out a pantomime of hide and seek (the name of the dance means "the hidden or lost one"). The woman hides by crouching down on one knee, shielding her eyes, while the man-protector struts around in spurred boots, snapping his fingers in the air as he mimics a frantic search for her.

The arrival of salon dances such as the polka and waltz in the mid-19th century centered upon couples who embraced (some light relief from the preceding warfare). By the 1920s many of the older creole dances were exiled to the northwest regions where they found new homes such as Santiago del Estero, which adopted the *chacarera* and the *gato*.

Salta is one of the best places in the country to hear folk music, with several restaurants and *peñas* (folk clubs) putting on live shows. Among the recommended places are: **Boliche Balderrama**, San Martín 1126; **Gauchos de Güemes**, Uruguay 750; and **Manolo**, San Martín 1296. The city also hosts an annual festival in mid-June with folk music and gaucho parades.

traditional Argentine snacks.
Jazz Beat, Arenal. Lively bar that plays jazz music.
La Boca, Calle Alfaros. Popular trendy bar with live music and DJs.
Piccadilly, Av. Hipólito Yrigoyen 464. British-style pub.

Bariloche

Cúbico, Elfein 47. Tel: (02944) 522 260. Live DJs and an extended list of cocktails. Closed Mon.
Grisu, J.M. Rosas 574. Tel: (02944) 422 269. One of Bariloche's main nightclubs with different styles of music playing on each floor.
Genux, J.M. Rosas 412. Tel: (02944) 524 020. Capacious nightclub which caters to school-leavers and tourists.
South Bar, Pasaje Juramento 30. Cozy bar frequented by both locals and tourists.

Rosario

Bar del Mar, Balcarce and Tucumán. Chilled-out and friendly bar.
Mob, Jujuy 2239. Tel: (0341) 430 1652. Popular *restobar*.
Soho Club, Salta and Alvear. Tel: (0341) 430 7421. Decent bar that also serves food.

Salta

Bar 22, Balcarce 717. Tel: (0387) 422 2656. One of the more popular bars in the city. A good place to have a social drink.
Casino, Mitre 331. A fun bar popular with locals.
Takos Pub, Av. Reyes Catolicos 1677. Social hub with reasonably priced drinks.

Mendoza

Apeteco, J. Barraquero and San Juan. Lively bar with a good selection of beverages.
Banana Rana, San Martín 45. Good place for dancing; music varies.
Liverpool, San Martín and Rivadavia. British-style pub.
Soul Café, San Juan 456. Tel: (0261) 425 7489. Tasty food and soulful music.

Movies

Going to the movies is popular throughout Argentina. Recent national and international films are shown, usually in English with Spanish subtitles. Listings appear in local papers. In central Buenos Aires,

many movie theaters can be found in Lavalle and Corrientes.

Tango Venues

Good tango shows can be found almost everywhere, but the best are in Buenos Aires. Visit www.argentinatango.com or www.buenosairestango.com for up-to-date information.
Bar Sur, Estados Unidos 299. Tel: (011) 4362 6086. Intimate venue that also runs classes.
El Viejo Almacén, Balcarce/Av. Independencia 300. Tel: (011) 4307 7388, www.viejoalmacen.com. Traditional venue with impressive performances.
Michelangelo, Balcarce 433. Tel: (011) 4342 7007. Mixed repertoire of tango and folk music and dance, in an atmospheric former monastery.
La Ventana, Balcarce 431. Tel: (011) 4331 0217. Atmospheric venue with good food and excellent shows, featuring both tango and folk music from around South America. Inclusive show and meal, with pick up and drop off from your hotel.
Señor Tango, Vieytes 1653, Barracas. Tel: (011) 4303 0231,

ABOVE: hunting for a bargain at the San Telmo Fair.

www.senortango.com.ar. The grandest tango venue in the country, with a capacity of 1,500.
La Catedral, Sarmineto 4006 and Medrano. A cool place to dance tango. Also offers classes.
Centro Cultural Torquato Tasso, Defensa 1575, San Telmo. Tel: (011)

"Shoppings"

American-style shopping malls, known simply as "shoppings," began appearing in Buenos Aires in the late 1980s. The shops they contain are mostly chains, with some luxury outlets. Many of the larger malls have food courts, movie theaters, and other facilities.
Mercado de Abasto, Av. Corrientes 3247, Balvanera. A shopping mall housed in an historic building, with restaurants, movie theaters, and an ice-skating rink.
Galerías Pacífico, Florida 787, San Nicolas. Renovated mall containing popular clothes stores, such as Vitamina, Chocolate, and Sol Porteño.
Patio Bullrich, Posadas 1245, Recoleta. Another mall in an historic building, with all facilities and games for children.
Alto Palermo, Av. Santa Fe 3253, between Colonel Diaz and Bulnes. One of the oldest malls in the city; all the popular Argentine designers have stores here.
Paseo Alcorta, Salguero and Figueroa Alcorta. An immense shopping mall complete with a food mall and large movie theater.
Solar de la Abadía, Acre 940. A smaller mall which attracts families and young people, with a movie theater.

4307 6506. Shows and classes in the area where tango was born.
Club Gricel, La Rioja 1180. Tel: (011) 4957 7157. Popular *milonga* venue, particularly on a Friday night.
La Marshall, Maipú 444, Plaza Bohemia, e-mail: lamarshallmilonga@yahoo.com.ar. Particularly popular with gay and lesbian lovers of tango.
Confitería Ideal, Suipacha 384. Tel: (011) 4605 8234. One of the most traditional places to dance tango in the city. Dancing takes place at weekends.
Parakultural, Scalabrini Ortiz 1331, Palermo. Tel: (011) 4342 4794/ 4832 6753. Shows held weekly.
Peña de Tango Alma de Bohemio, Neochea 948, Boca. Tel: (011) 4307 0114. Dancing on Saturdays from 10pm. The place to dance tango in La Boca.
La Viruta, Armenia 1366. Tel: (011) 4774 6357, www.lavirutatango.com. A great place where people of all ages come to dance. Also has shows.

SHOPPING

Since the devaluation of the peso in 2001, Argentina has been a very affordable place for foreigners to shop, offering a wide variety of well-produced goods. In addition, the government has introduced a tax-refund scheme for foreign tourists on any Argentine-made product purchased for over US$70 from an outlet with a "Global Refund" sticker in its window. You will need to obtain an invoice and appropriate form at the time of purchase. These should be presented at customs when leaving the country. The *puesto de*

pago will then reimburse 10–16 percent of the 21 percent sales tax.

Where to Shop
Clothes

The best shopping districts in the country are in Buenos Aires, namely Florida, Avenida Sante Fe, and the maze of boutiques in Palermo Viejo. Florida is a long pedestrianized road full of well-known stores such as Benetton, Gucci, and Stefanel.

Palermo Viejo is a wonderful place to spend an afternoon strolling through its labyrinthine streets dotted with boutiques and small designer stores. Many established Argentine designers have outlets here, such as Jazmín Chebar and Maria Cher.

The exclusive part of town is located in Recoleta along Avenida Alvear, Avenida Quintana, Ayacucho, and down the nearby side-streets. Alternatively, you could make a trip to one of the many shopping malls *(see "Shoppings", left)*.

Galería Bond Street (Santa Fe 85) has a range of second-hand clothes. Here, young Argentine designers try their hand at selling their own ranges, and you will find some interesting garments on show.

Supermarkets

For food, the main supermarkets are **Disco**, **Norte**, and **Coto**, all of which have branches in towns and cities throughout the country.

Bookstores

Avenida Corrientes is full of bookstores, including the sumptuous **El Ateneo Gran Splendid**, the largest bookstore in South America.

A first-class travel bookstore, with a wide range of both Spanish and English books and maps, is **Patagonia & Tierra del Fuego Travel Shop**, at Viamonte 500, off Florida.

Souvenirs

There are several souvenir stores clustered on Paraguay as it crosses Florida selling items such as silver photo frames, maté holders, ponchos, and leather goods.

Antiques

The best-known area of Buenos Aires for antiques is San Telmo. It's one of the most historic barrios (neighborhoods) of the city. Every Sunday the San Telmo Fair takes place in Plaza Dorrego. The plaza is surrounded by stalls which sell quite an array of objects, from new to old, ordinary to odd, and which can be very cheap or outrageously expensive. Only the trained eye can

find the bargains among the many imitations. Around the plaza, there are many reputable antiques stores. Prices are high, but some beautiful pieces can still be found. Auction houses are very popular and there are good buys. Some of these are:
Roldán y Cia, R. Peña 1673.
Naon y Cia, Guido 1785.
Banco de la Ciudad, Esmeralda 660.

Small antiques shops are located throughout the city and the prices are negotiable. There are a number of these shops along Avenida Rivadavia, around the 4000 block. As these stores are not known to many, the prices and the attention are good.

Also, along Avenida Libertador, toward Martínez and the San Isidro area, are a number of shops with some very worthwhile pieces; it just takes time and a little knowledge.

La Baulera, on Av. Monroe 2753, has quite a different assortment of collectibles, and the owners will try to help find that unique piece.

Jewelers
Koltai Joyeria, Esmeralda 616. Antique quality jewelry.
Ricciardi, Florida 1001.
Antoniazzi-Chiappe, Av. Alvear 1895.
Stern Jewellers, Sheraton Hotel.
Lovasi Joyeria, Rodriguez Peña 419.

Leather Goods
Coalpe México 3325. Handbags.
Colicuer Tte. Gral. Perón 1615, 1st floor. Handbags.
Maximilian Klein Humberto Primo 3435. Handbags.
Viel Viel 1550. Handbags and shoes.
La Mia Scarpa Thames 1617. Custom-made shoes.
Belt Factory Fco. Acuña de Figueroa 454. Belts and other leather goods.
Le Fauve Sarandí 1226.Latest leather fashions and competitive prices with personal attention.

Regional Handicrafts
Artesanías Argentina, Montevideo 1386. Handicrafts.
Tuyunti, Florida 971.
Cardon, Av. Santa Fe 1287 – a talabartería selling gaucho gear, leather, and silverware.

Artisan fairs take place at the weekends in different parts of the city. Some of these are:
Plaza Francia, near the Recoleta area on Sunday.
Plaza Manuel Belgrano, Juramento 2200 on Sunday.
Plaza Mitre, San Isidro, on Sunday.
Puerto de los Frutos, Tigre, every Saturday and Sunday.

Artisan fairs also take place in other parts of the country, including Mendoza, Bariloche, and El Bolson.

Latin Beats
Far from merely assimilating rock music from the USA and Europe, popular Argentine music has always been a home-grown product. The 1980s and 1990s created a uniquely Argentine genre known simply as Rock Nacional Argentino (National Argentine Rock).

Fito Paez, Charly Garcia, and León Gieco are celebrated artists from this period which was defined by a type of rock that had strong roots in national affairs. They built on the nueva canción (new song) movement of the 1960s, when artists such as Mercedes Sosa and Atahualpa Yupanqui used folk songs to denounce social injustice – to the annoyance of the military regime and at great risk to themselves. National Argentine Rockers continued to represent the voice of protest, infuriating the establishment with songs which questioned the whereabouts of the desaparecidos (disappeared) and criticized the government. These artists have become megastars in their homeland and their music is still widely listened to.

In recent years, Rock Nacional has given way to electro-rock and fusion music. One of the most notable successes has been Gotan Project who have made their distinct tango-fusion music well known throughout the world. Yet they are an exception: tango hasn't been re-embraced by the mainstream. Instead popular music is nowadays characterized by electro-rock bands who shy away from any talk of politics and protests and are more concerned with getting their audience on their feet and dancing. The most popular of these bands are Miranda and Los Látigos whose catchy beats and lyrics have gained them a large following throughout Latin America.

SPORTS

Outdoor Activities
The size and diversity of Argentina means that it is a great place to participate in outdoor activities. The Argentine Andes offer some of the best mountain climbing and skiing in the world, while idyllic horseback riding is not to be missed at one of the country's many working estancias. The following is a breakdown of some of the activities available.

Fishing
There are many places in Argentina to enjoy fishing, both along the Atlantic coast and in the lakes scattered throughout the country. The north is home to two species with the highest sports value, trout and dorado, which can be caught at the **Parque Nacional Baritú**, Salta province, where the rivers are ideal for fly-fishing. In mid-October the Fiesta Internacional de Pesca del Dorado is held in the village of Paso de la Patria which attracts fishing enthusiasts from all over the world.

Equipment can be hired at **La Casa del Pescador**, San Martín 1690, Salta, tel: (0387) 422 4634, and at **Todo Pesca**, Av. Paraguay 1261, Salta.

The spectacular mountains of Patagonia provide a stunning backdrop for visiting anglers and this area includes some of the best locations for trout fishing in the world. The most popular destinations are San Martín de los Andes, Bariloche, and Junín de los Andes. The trout-fishing season runs from November to April. Equipment can be hired from:
San Martín Orvies, Villegas 835, San Martín de los Andes, tel: (02972) 425 892, e-mail: smorvis@mandes.com.ar. Also organizes fly-fishing trips.
Fly Master's, Gaviotas 464, Bariloche. Tel: (02944) 462 101.
Patagonia Fly Fishing, Laura Vicuña 135, Junin de los Andes. Tel/Fax: (02972) 491538.

Laguna Chascomús is about 125 km (78 miles) south of Buenos Aires and is accessible by car or train. The lagoon has brackish water, and the main catches are pejerrey (a type of catfish) and a very aggressive fish called the tararira. Equipment can be rented at the local fishing club, the **Club de Pesca y Naútica**, which has a boardwalk on the lagoon, at the end of Avenida Lastra.

The chain of coastal resorts stretching from San Clemente del Tuyo south to Necochea are also popular destinations for fishing, with most local clubs offering equipment for hire and sea-fishing trips. The following operators run regular excursions and have boats for hire:
Turimar, Mar del Plata. Tel: (023) 484 1450. Boat excursions and fishing trips, daily in summer.
Daniel Rodriguez, Mar del Tuyú. Tel: (0246) 421 508. Fishing trips by arrangement.

Eco-organization

The Fundación Vida Silvestre Argentina (Argentine Wildlife Foundation) manages some of the country's protected areas of special environmental importance. It is a useful source of information about these areas, and their facilities for visitors. Open Mon–Fri 10am–6pm. Defensa 251, Buenos Aires. Tel/Fax: (011) 4331 3631/ 4343 4086; www.vidasilvestre.org.ar.

Casa de Pesca La Trucha, Esq. Calle 10 and Calle 59, Necochea. Tel: (0262) 428 601. Fishing cruises, daily in summer.
El Pique, Av. Los Talas del Tuyú and Calle 72, San Clemente del Tuyú. Tel: (0252) 421 601. Fishing trips by arrangement.

Fishing permits are required and can be purchased at fishing equipment stores and national park offices. For more information on fly-fishing in Argentina contact the **Asociación Argentina de Pesca con Mosca**, Lerma 452, Buenos Aires, tel: (011) 4773 0821, e-mail: aapm@cvtci.com.ar.

Horseback Riding

There are great horseback riding expeditions on offer throughout the country, although the best are in the Pampas and Patagonia. The flat terrain of the pampas is ideal and there are many estancias just a couple of hours' drive from Buenos Aires, some of which have rooms and offer inclusive packages *(see page 346 for details of estancias throughout the country.)*

Horseback riding in Patagonia is a very different experience owing to the mountainous terrain and makes a wonderful way to explore the region. There are numerous travel agencies in Bariloche that can organize excursions. **Ariane Patagonia** based near Bariloche, tel: (02944) 523 488, www.arianepatagonia.com.ar, offers packages which include horses, equipment hire, and accommodations.

Hiking

Argentina's varied and beautiful landscape makes it a superb place for hiking. It is still possible to find areas where you can trek for days without meeting another soul. The best treks are often found in the national parks. Visit www.parquesnacionales.gov.ar.

One of the principal trekking destinations is the mountainous area of **Parque Nacional Nahuel Huapi**, near Bariloche. This area of

breathtaking scenery is also one of the most accessible national parks, with clear trails and wonderful mountain refuges.

Many people also head for the region around **El Chaltén**, further south, to discover the immense granite mountain Fitz Roy and the Perito Moreno glacier. This is a popular destination among travelers, and campsites often fill up during high season (Dec–Feb).

In the north the best destinations are **Jujuy** and **Salta**. Salta offers a good range of hikes, from high mountain valleys to cloud-forest trails, and even a national park full of cacti (Parque Nacional de los Cardones.)

Hiking trails can be hard to follow so make sure you always have a good map to hand. Always carry enough drinking water with you and take warm clothing as temperatures can fall drastically at night. Wind-proof jackets are essential for mountainous routes. Always inform a park ranger of your plans when entering a national park; it is also important to report your safe arrival at your destination so that they don't send out a search party.

Climbing

Argentina's Andes offer great variety for climbers, from some of the world's tallest peaks to some of its toughest, and from volcanoes and granite to shale summits. The climbing season is Nov–Mar, although the best time to go is Dec–Feb.

Argentina offers a plethora of peaks to climb, the most famous being Aconcagua which at 6,962 meters (22,840 ft) is the highest in South America and should only be braved by experts.

There are more accessible peaks in the area of Parque Nacional Nahuel Huapi. **Cerro Catedral** (2,405 meters/7,890 ft) and **Monte Tronador** (3,478 meters/11,411 ft) are good options. Both have refuges at the summit where it is possible to stay the night. Further south, Fitz Roy and Cerro Torre offer some of the most technically difficult climbs on the planet.

Travel agencies that specialize in climbing and trekking include:
Ascensiones y Trekking, Reconquista 702, Godoy Cruz, Mendoza. Tel: (061) 424 4292. Organizes treks and climbing expeditions.
Andes Patagónicos, Mitre 125, Bariloche. Tel: (02944) 431 777, www.andespatagonicos.com. Organizes treks, excursions, and accommodations.

Infinito Sur, Bariloche, tel: (02944) 15 639 624, www.infinito-sur.com. Arranges trekking expeditions.
Andes Cross, Bariloche, tel: (02944) 467 502, www.andescross.com. Organizes trips to and across the Andes.

Adventure Sports

The Cuyo is rapidly becoming one of the country's main adventure tourism centers, with a whole range of "white-knuckle" activities on offer, including white-water rafting, mountain biking, and snowboarding. Travel agencies specializing in these activities include:
Betancourt Rafting, Lavalle 35, Independencia Loc. 8, Mendoza, tel: (0261) 429 9665, www.betancourt.com.ar.
Exploring Turismo Aventura, Av. H Yrigoyen 284, San Rafael, tel: (0627) 436 439.

A wide range of adventure sports are also on offer in Bariloche in Patagonia. There are many agencies in the town that specialize in these activities, but one of the best places to visit for advice is **Club Andino Bariloche**, 20 de Febrero, Bariloche, tel: (02944) 422 266, www.clubandino.org.

In the Northwest, the Río Hondo Reservoir in the province of Santiago del Estero, 63 km (39 miles) north of the city of the same name, offers a wide range of water sports organized by the **Club Naútico**, whose clubhouse is on the shore of the reservoir.

Salta Rafting is located in a spectacular region, at the heart of Juramento River gorge known as Peñas Blancas, within a short distance from the majestic Cabra Corral Dam. They organize an array of adventure sports including rafting, abseiling, and paragliding. They can be reached at their base – RP 47, Km 34, Cabra Corral, tel: (0387) 401 0301, or in the city of Salta, Buenos Aires 88, Of. 13, tel: (0387) 401 0301/421 4114, www.saltarafting.com.

Saltur S.A., Caseros 485, Salta, tel: (0387) 421 2012, e-mail: saltursalta@arnet.com.ar, also organizes a wide range of adventure sports. They are well established and have English-speaking members of staff who can help you plan your trip.

Skiing

Argentina's ski resorts are thriving as more tourists travel from within Latin America and further afield to sample the deep south's snow. The ski season is rather short: the best time to go is between late July and August, although you can try it in June and September. Snowfall varies from year to year, but you often find excellent powdery snow and sunny skies. The facilities in the main

ABOVE: the churning rapids on the Rio Mendoza make for some of the best whitewater rafting in Argentina.

resorts are very good and rental gear and ski passes are much cheaper than in Europe. The most prestigious and well-known resort is **Las Leñas**, in the province of Mendoza. It offers the most challenging skiing and the best infrastructure. For more information, visit: www.laslenasvacations.com.

Chapelco, near San Martín de los Andes, offers cross-country options as well as great downhill skiing, plus impressive views of Lanín. San Martín de los Andes is also a very picturesque place to stay when covered in snow. For more information, visit: www.chapelco.com.ar.

The oldest established resorts in the country are those near Bariloche, **Cerro Catedral** and **Cerro Otto**, which offer wonderful panoramas of the Nahuel Huapi region. For information, see www.bariloche.ski.com. There are a number of smaller resorts located throughout the southern provinces, including one in Tierra del Fuego and another near Esquel which is good for beginners. For up-to-date information on resorts, booking trips, and weather conditions visit: www.andesweb.com.

Birdwatching

Due to the variety of Argentina's wildlife there is an array of birds to see the length and breadth of the country. Birdwatching is one of the big outdoor attractions in the **Sierra de Córdoba**, with a wide range of species commonly seen. Condors are

often spotted around the aptly named El Cóndor, to the south of Córdoba. The **Club Andino**, Deán Funes 2100, Córdoba, tel: (0351) 480 5126, www.clubandinocordoba.com.ar, runs birdwatching tours.

Parque Nacional Iguazú is home to 400 different bird species and birdwatching trails can be arranged through the national park. Enquire at the visitor's center in the park.

The Atlantic Patagonian region is also a great place to watch for marine birds. At the **Península Valdés**, Puerto Pirámides, and Punta Loma localities it is possible to spot black-necked swans, upland geese, penguins, and more. The main tourist agencies know how to guide visitors to special circuits in order to get the best sights. **Sur Turismo**, Julio A. Roca, Puerto Madryn, tel: (0965) 434 550, is a good one to start with.

Safaris

The geographical diversity of Argentina means that is has a lot to offer in terms of flora and fauna, and there are a range of wildlife safaris available. **Patagonia** has the lion's share of the country's most spectacular scenery. Bariloche, on the shore of Lago Nahuel Huapi, in the heart of the Parque Nacional Nahuel Huapi, is a starting point for many safaris. In town you will find many specialist agencies organizing safaris but the best place to visit first

for advice is **Club Andino Bariloche**, 20 de Febrero, Bariloche, tel: (02944) 422 266, www.clubandino.org.

Península Valdés is probably Argentina's best-known wildlife center, particularly for its huge colonies of sea lions, penguins, and whales. Many of the main safari agencies operate from Puerto Pirámides, a small town near Puerto Madryn. The following agencies offer a range of wildlife safaris, including whale-watching boat trips:

Moby Dick, Primera Bajada al Mar, Puerto Pirámides, tel: (02965) 495 114/495 014.

Peke Sosa, Segunda Bajada al Mar, Puerto Pirámides, tel: (02965) 495 010, www.pekesosa.com.ar.

In Misiones, the best place to view flora and fauna is the **Parque Nacional Iguazú**. Here you will find numerous mammals and an immeasurable number of insects, making this eco-system one of the richest natural environments in the country. For information on organized safaris, ask at the visitor's center in the national park.

Cycling

It is possible to rent bikes throughout the country, although the terrain varies considerably from the flat pampas to the mountainous Andes. Here is a selection of bike hire agencies:

Bike Tours, Florida 868, Piso 14, tel: (011) 4311 5199, Buenos Aires.

Stay in Buenos Aires, Buenos Aires, tel: (011) 4361 9239, www.stayinbuenosaires.com.
Mountain Bike Hire, Señor Rodríguez, Calle Uriburu 1488, Tandil, tel: (0293) 428 669.
Tolhuín Aventuras, Cerro Jeujepen 466, Tolhuín, tel: (066) 966 569.

Spectator Sports

To claim that "sport is life" in Argentina is not an exaggeration; it is certainly a very big deal. Not only are the majority of the population obsessed with soccer, but the country also has very strong contenders in polo, basketball, and tennis.

Soccer

This is by far the most popular spectator sport in Argentina. Local teams attract a following of almost religious devotion and rivalry between fans can be fierce. The country's top teams are in Buenos Aires, including the world-famous Boca Juniors and River Plate. Boca Juniors stadium, La Bombonera, is in the heart of La Boca, close to the tourist street El Caminito. River Plate's stadium, known as the Monumental or La Gallinera, is in the more affluent area of Palermo. Matches are usually played on Wednesdays and Sundays, but the schedule varies at different times of the year.

If you are planning to visit a domestic match while in Argentina, be aware that the matches can get very rowdy. It is best to sit towards the back of the stadium to avoid getting caught up in the surge towards the front of the stands that follows a goal.
Boca Juniors, Brandsen 805, tel: (011) 4362 2050/4700.
River Plate Av. Figueroa Alcorta 7597, tel: (011) 4789 1200.

Pato

Pato is a combination of polo and basketball in which two four-member teams riding on horses fight for possession of the ball and score by throwing it through a vertically positioned ring. After 48 minutes playing time, the team that has scored the most goals is the winner. The word *pato* means "duck" and the game, which dates to the 17th century, was originally played using a duck inside a bag. Fortunately, the duck was later replaced with a leather ball with six handles and in 1953 it was declared Argentina's national game by Juan Perón. You can catch this uniquely Argentine sport live, as it is often played on the estancias around Buenos Aires. **Hípico y de**

Pato Barracas al Sur, tel: (011) 4222 7070, has games, public exhibitions, and riding displays.

Polo

Argentine polo horses are prized around the world for their agility and speed, and many European polo teams come to Argentina to enhance their skills. The three most important polo tournaments in the world are played here: the Argentinean Open, the Hurlingham Open, and the Tortugas Open. The best place to see polo in Buenos Aires is at the Palermo polo field on Avenida del Libertador and Dorrego. Tickets can be purchased at the box office in the grounds.

For more information about matches, tournaments, and schools, visit the **Asociación Argentina de Polo**, Arévalo 3065, tel: (011) 4777 6444, www.aapolo.com.

Horse Racing

The two main tracks in Buenos Aires are the **Jockey Club**, on the corner of Avenida Márquez and Avenida Centenario in San Isidrio, and the **Hipódromo Palermo**, on Avenida del Libertador, between Dorrego and Olleros, in Palermo. Races are held about four times a week, in the afternoons and evenings. To find out more visit www.palermo.com. Smaller tracks are located in most of the major Argentine cities.

Motor Racing

Motor racing has been very popular in Argentina for years and (now deceased) Juan Manuel Fangio, a five-time Formula One champion of

the 1950s, is virtually a folk hero. It is a source of great sorrow to many Argentines that financial problems have prohibited holding a Formula One championship race here in recent years.

The nearest thing to grand-prix racing in Argentina is the South American Formula Three series which holds half a dozen races every year in various parts of the country. Stock-car racing is also very popular for which there are races all over the country every weekend, as well as several annual championships. Visit www.tc2000.com.ar for more details.

Yearly motor-rally events are held as part of the world championship series, usually in August or September in the province of Córdoba.

Rugby

Argentina is among the world's top-ten rugby nations, and during the season from April to November matches attract large crowds. Argentina's national squad, The Pumas, play in the Vélez Sársfiled stadium, in the Liniers neighborhood of Buenos Aires. Visit www.uar.com for more information on Argentine rugby.

Basketball

Basketball has become increasingly popular in Argentina due to its successful national team which won an Olympic gold in 2004. Unusually, the sport is more popular in the provinces of Argentina than in Buenos Aires, and it is in the provinces where the most powerful clubs are based. Information on upcoming games can be found at www.latinbasket.com.

BELOW: the Argentine national basketball team have inspired a generation.

A – Z

A HANDY SUMMARY OF PRACTICAL INFORMATION, ARRANGED ALPHABETICALLY

Admission Charges

Admission to galleries and museums in Argentina costs around US$1.50, with a discounted price of US$1 offered to concessions (students and pensioners). Children usually get free admission. Galleries and museums are legally required to be free of charge at least one day a week; that day varies from museum to museum so you may want to plan your visits accordingly.

Budgeting for your Trip

The following prices should be taken as an approximate guide.
Airport Transfer: an authorized taxi or *remise* from Ezeiza airport into the center of Buenos Aires: US$12–15. Manuel Tienda León bus service from Ezeiza into the center of Buenos Aires: US$8.
Car Hire: (international company) Vauxhall Corsa: US$20 per day. 4x4 pick-up: US$35 per day (prices include insurance, mechanical assistance, and value added tax).

Petrol: US60–80 cents per liter.
Taxis: taxis in Argentina are inexpensive though you may be taken on a "scenic route" if you speak English. Stick to metered taxis which start at about US60 cents. A small tip is expected.
Accommodations: Prices vary throughout the country and according to quality. The north of Argentina offers by far the cheapest accommodations in the country – around US$25 per night for a 3-star double room. In Buenos Aires and the south, accommodations are more expensive and a similar room will set you back US$30.
Food: Most restaurants are very reasonably priced. A three-course meal, including wine, at an up-market establishment will cost around US$30 for two people.
Airport Departure Tax: US$18.

Business Hours

From Monday to Friday, the business hours are 9am–7pm, and the banking hours 10am–3pm. In most of the country outside Buenos Aires, the stores open 9am–1pm and 4pm–7pm, almost invariably closing for the siesta, although local hours can vary somewhat.

Climate

Argentina, the world's eighth-largest country, extends from the deserts of Salta in the north to the glaciers of Patagonia in the south. Most of the country lies in the temperate zone of the Southern Hemisphere.

The Northeast is humid and subtropical. The Northwest is tropical but has a mild winter. The Pampas are temperate. The south has colder temperatures and rain most of the year. The rainfall varies in the humid Pampa (which comprises the province of Buenos Aires, and some of the Córdoba and La Pampa provinces) from 99 cm (39 inches) in the eastern parts to about 51 cm (20 inches) in the areas near the Andes.

Summer months in Buenos Aires are indeed very hot and the majority of the people leave soon after

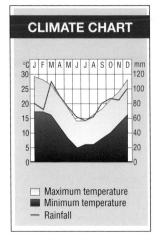

CLIMATE CHART

°C J F M A M J J A S O N D mm
30 — 120
25 — 100
20 — 80
15 — 60
10 — 40
5 — 20
0 — 0

☐ Maximum temperature
■ Minimum temperature
— Rainfall

Christmas for the beaches and mountain resorts. The city is almost empty during the months of January and February, when the heat and humidity can be overpowering.

Winter is generally pleasant, although July and August have very cold patches. Torrential rain is also common at this time, but is usually short-lived.

Crime and Safety

Argentina has been suffering a rise in crime since the economic crash in 2001, especially in larger cities. This has led to increased incidents of kidnappings and armed robbery. Although cases of violent crime are unlikely to affect tourists, it is best to follow certain precautionary measures. It is not advisable to walk the streets after dark, particularly alone. Keep expensive jewelry, electrical equipment, and expensive watches out of sight when walking around large cities, especially in Buenos Aires. Do not take unofficial taxis – always use *remises* or cars that are part of a taxi firm and have a sign reading "Radio Taxi" *(see page 337)*.

To report a crime, go to the Comisaría del Turista, Av. Corrientes 436, tel: (0800) 999 5000, open 24 hours, where English speaking staff are on hand.

Electricity

220V/50hz is the standard current throughout the country. Argentina uses the European round two-pin plug and the Australian slanted plugs. Travelers from the UK and US will need to bring an adapter with them.

Alternatively, go to the police station in the area where the incident occurred.

Customs Regulations

Citizens of Western Europe, the US, Canada, South Africa, Australia, and New Zealand do not need a visa for tourist trips of up to 90 days. A valid passport is required and a landing card must be filled in on arrival. On entering Argentina you will also be given a customs declaration form. Should you wish to extend your trip past the 90-day limit, you could try leaving the country and returning to get a fresh stamp. This usually works, but is frowned upon if done regularly, and the provision of a stamp is at the discretion of the border guards. When leaving the country you must obtain an exit stamp. Visas for work or study must be obtained prior to your trip from your consulate.

Travelers entering Argentina can bring personal effects, including clothes, jewelry, and professional equipment such as cameras and computers, without paying duty. In addition, 21 liters of alcohol, 400 cigarettes, and 50 cigars can be brought into the country duty-free.

E mbassies and Consulates

Foreign Embassies in Buenos Aires

Australian Embassy
Villanueva 1400. Tel: (011) 4779 3500, fax: (011) 4779 3581, www.argentina.embassy.gov.au.

British Embassy
Luis Agote 2412, Recoleta. Tel: (011) 4808 2200, fax: (011) 4808 2274, www.fco.gov.uk.

Canadian Embassy
Tagle 2828. Tel: (011) 4808 1000, fax: (011) 4808 1111, www.dfait-maeci.gc.ca/argentina.

Embassy of New Zealand
Carlos Pellegrini 1427, 5th Floor. Tel: (011) 4328 0747, fax: (011) 4328 0757, www.nzembassy.com.

Irish Embassy
Av. del Libertador 1068, 6th Floor. Tel: (011) 4787 0801, fax: (011) 4787 0802, www.irlanda.org.ar.

US Embassy
Av. Colombia 4300, Palermo. Tel: (011) 5777 4533, fax: (011) 5777 4240, http://buenosaires.usembassy.gov.

Argentine Embassies and Consulates Abroad

Australia
Embassy: John McEwen House, Level 2, 7 National Circuit, Barton, ACT

Emergencies

Police 101
Medical 107
Fire 100

2600. Tel: (02) 6273 9111, fax: (02) 6273 0500, www.argentina.org.au.
Consulate: 44 Market Street, Floor 20, Sydney, NSW. Tel: (02) 9262 2993, fax: (02) 9262 3998.

Canada
Embassy: 81 Metcalfe Street, Suite 700, Ottawa, Ontario, K1P 6K7. Tel: (0613) 236 2351, fax: (0613) 235 2659, www.argentina-canada.net.
Consulate: 2000 Peel Street, 7th floor, suite 710, Montreal, Quebec H3A 2W5. Tel: (0514) 842 6582, fax: (0514) 842 5797.

Ireland
Embassy: 15 Ailesbury Drive, Ballsbridge, Dublin. Tel: (01) 269 1546, fax: (01) 260 0404, e-mail: embassyofargentina@eircom.net.

New Zealand
Embassy: Level 14, 142 Lambton Quay, PO Box 5430, Wellington. Tel: (04) 472 8330, fax: (04) 472 8331, www.arg.org.nz.

UK
Embassy: 65 Brook Street, London W1Y 1YE. Tel: (020) 7318 1300, fax: (020) 7318 1301, www.argentine-embassy-uk.org.
Consulate: 27 Three Kings Yard, London W1Y 1FL. Tel: (020) 7318 1340, fax: (020) 7318 1349.

US
Embassy: 1600 New Hampshire Avenue, NW, Washington DC 20009. Tel: (202) 238 6400, fax: (202) 332 3171
Consulate: 12 West 56th Street, New York, NY 10019. Tel: (212) 603 0400, e-mail: consular@embassyofargentina.us.

G ay and Lesbian Travelers

Argentina is rightly considered one of the most gay-friendly countries in South America. Buenos Aires has become a major global destination for gay and lesbian visitors in recent years. The city offers many services and activities directed towards gay and lesbian travelers, including themed circuits of the city and increasingly popular gay tango and *milonga* nights.

Buenos Aires recently became the first city in South America to grant gay and lesbian couples the right to a civil partnership union allowing them to have the same legal rights as heterosexual couples. Although the capital is generally accepting of homosexuality and signs of affection in public, the rest of the country does lag behind a bit and prejudice may be more prevalent in smaller towns and the countryside. For a gay guide to Argentina, visit www.guiag.com or www.thegayguide.com.ar.

H ealth and Medical Care

Medical Services

Health care is generally good and many hospitals have trained personnel who have studied in Argentina and abroad. There are excellent specialists in most medical fields, who make it a point to attend international medical congresses and inform themselves of recent advances in medical science.

Medical equipment is very costly, but all efforts are coordinated in order to maximize benefits. In some sections of the country, the hospitals may not have up-to-date equipment, but what is available is adequate for an emergency situation.

A visit to a doctor will cost upwards of US$20 and cash payment is often expected.

Pharmacies

Most pharmaceutical drugs can be purchased over the counter without a prescription. There is usually a pharmacist on duty. If you are prescribed any form of injection, the pharmacist offers this service. All over the country, pharmacies rotate a 24-hour service. A listing of the ones on duty and nearest to you appears in the local newspaper as "Farmacias de Turno."

The pharmacist can also recommend remedies for common ailments, such as flu, stomach disorders, and headaches.

Hospitals in Buenos Aires

British Hospital, Perdriel 74. Tel: (011) 4309 6400.
German Hospital, Pueyrredón 1640. Tel: (011) 4827 7000.
Dental Hospital, Pueyrredon 940. Tel: (011) 4805 5521.
Eye Hospital Santa Lucía, San Juan 2021. Tel: (011) 4941 5555.

I nternet

The Internet can be used throughout the country. Connections are particularly good in cities and rates in Buenos Aires are the cheapest at only a few pesos an hour. Outlets come and go, but there are some big chains and internet cafes where you can sip coffee and listen to music as you surf, as well as connections at larger airports and railway stations.

ABOVE: surfing the net in Buenos Aires.

M edia

The local papers are La Nación, Clarín, Ambito Financiero, La Razón, and Página 12 (all in Spanish). National and international news in English is provided by the Buenos Aires Herald, which also has useful "what's on" listings for the city. There are newspaper and magazine stands on almost every city-center street corner, where foreign papers and magazines can also be found.

There are five television stations and cable TV is widely available. Many of the programs are bought in from the US and Europe and clumsily dubbed into Spanish. A few are in English with Spanish subtitles.

There are numerous radio stations, ranging from rock to tango. Radio Horizonte 93.5 FM offers a good selection of the latest international music.

Money

Since the peso was devalued in January 2002, prices have fallen in dollar terms. At the time of writing, the peso was trading at around 3.05 to the dollar, although economic uncertainty is likely to force the exchange rate even lower. Although inflation has picked up again, Argentina is still remarkably cheap for foreign tourists.

Dollars in small denominations are widely accepted, and there are casas de cambio (bureaux de change) in the center of Buenos Aires around Plaza San Martín and Lavalle. American Express at Arenales 707 (near Plaza San Martín) changes currency and traveler's checks.

P hotography

Photographic film is not cheap in Argentina. Standard film of all brands is easy enough to get hold of, but black-and-white and fast film, especially slide film, is hard to come by. Developing is expensive throughout the country and few places develop black-and-white and slide film. Take care about where you take photographs. Sensitive border areas and all military installations, including many civilian airports, are no-go areas for cameras – keep a look out for signs. Photographic equipment is very expensive in Argentina, even in the duty-free zones.

Postal Services

Offices of Correo Argentino, the national post office, are located in all major towns and cities. The main post office in Buenos Aires is located on Sarmiento 189, and operates Monday to Friday 9am–7.30pm. Stamps are often available at hotels.

Public Holidays

The summer vacation season, when internal transportation and hotels are heavily booked, runs from January through March. The middle two weeks of July are the school winter vacation, which is also very busy.

Government agencies and banks close on public holidays (see box, opposite). With the exception of Christmas, New Year's Day, May 25, July 9, and December 8, holidays are observed on the closest Monday to allow for long weekends.

In addition to national holidays, there are many provincial festivals

Public Holidays

New Year's Day: January 1
Good Friday: Variable
Labor Day: May 1
Commemoration of First
Government: May 25
Malvinas Day: June 10
Flag Day: June 20
Declaration of Independence:
  July 9
Death of San Martín: August 17
Columbus Day: October 12
Día de la Tradición November 10
Annunciation Day: December 8
Christmas Day: December 25

around the country, which are celebrated with local folklore customs, music, and dancing. (*See Calendar of Festivals and Events, page 353.*)

R eligious Services

Like the rest of South America, Argentina is a predominantly Roman Catholic country. The country's main cathedral is the **Catedral Metropolitana**, Rivadavia and San Martín, Mon–Fri 8am–7pm; Sat 9am–12.30pm and 5–7.30pm; Sun 9–2pm and 4–7.30pm.

Argentina is home to the largest Jewish community in South America. Much of Jewish life in Buenos Aires centers around the Once district, where there are several synagogues, including **Yesod Hadat** (Lavalle 2449), which was founded in 1932.

Once also has a Jewish cultural center, which hosts concerts and lectures, and a high school, located at Sarmiento 2233. Argentina's oldest synagogue, **Congregacion Israelita de la Republica Argentina** (Libertad 733) houses a small Jewish museum, which has a good collection of photographs and Jewish ritual objects.

Buenos Aires is home to the largest mosque in Latin America, donated by the late King Fahd of Saudi Arabia and situated within the **Centro Cultural Rey Fahd** (Av. Bullrich 55 and Cervio, tel: 011-4899 1144, www.ccislamicoreyfahd.org). The center also houses a school, a library, and a meeting place for Muslims.

S tudent Travelers

Student travelers obtaining an ISIC card before departure may be entitled to discounts on museums, hostel accommodations, and bus travel.

Argentina's student travel agency, ASATEJ *(see Tour Operators and Travel Agents, opposite)* has up-to-date information about flights, coach fares, tours, and discounts on its website, www.asatej.com.

T elecommunications

Since the telecommunications service was privatized in 1989, it has been split between Telecom and Telefónica Argentina. Prices have fluctuated and, although they are

becoming more competitive, telephone calls from Argentina are still among the most expensive in the world. However, the service is becoming much more efficient and the line quality is high.

International and national calls can be made from *locutorios*, or "call shops," throughout the country.

Local calls can be made from the blue phone booths in the street. Phones accept coins or phone cards, which can be bought from *kioscos* (newsstands).

There are three mobile phone companies in Argentina. Movistar, Personal, and CTI; which all charge around the same. The cheapest way to use a mobile if coming from abroad is to bring a handset with you and buy a SIM card once in Argentina. These cost around US$14 and can be purchased at mobile phone stores in cities around the country.

Dialing Codes

COUNTRY CODE (if dialing Argentina from abroad): 54

REGIONAL CODES
Don't dial the area code if calling the same area you are in. If calling from abroad, drop the initial 0.

Bahía Blanca	0291
Bariloche	02944
Buenos Aires	011
Comodoro Rivadavia	0297
Córdoba	0351
Corrientes	03783
El Bolsón	02944
El Calafate	02902
El Chaltén	02962
Esquel	02945
Jujuy	0388
La Plata	0221
La Rioja	03822
Mar del Plata	0223
Mendoza	0261
Merlo	02656
Neuquén	0299
Posadas	03752
Puerto Iguazú	03757
Resistencia	03722
Río Gallegos	02966
Río Grande	02964
Rosario	0341
Salta	0387
San Fernando	03833
San Juan	0264
San Luis	02652
San Martín de los Andes	02972
Santa Fe	0342
Santiago del Estero	0385
Trevelín	02945
Tucumán	0381
Ushuaia	02901
Viedma	02920
Villa Gesell	02255

BELOW: kiosks are a handy source of anything from phone cards to camera film.

INTERNATIONAL CODES

Dial 00, and then the country code, followed by the number.

Australia	61
Bolivia	591
Brazil	55
Canada	1
Chile	56
France	33
Germany	49
Ireland, Republic of	353
New Zealand	64
UK	44
Uruguay	598
USA	1

Time Zone

Argentina stays at -3 GMT all year round.

Tipping

A ten percent tip is usual in restaurants. Those in more touristy areas may add this to the bill in the form of a service charge. Taxi drivers also expect a small tip.

Toilets

Apart from the odd exception in the center of Buenos Aires, public toilets are a rarity. Toilets in shopping malls are the best place to head for as they are often spotless. Bars and cafes will usually let you use their toilet facilities, although it is best to bring your own toilet paper as this is often absent. In airports and bus stations there is usually an attendant who keeps the toilets clean for a small fee of around one peso per person. In small towns and rural areas toilet paper is often disposed of in a waste-paper basket (rather than flushed).

Toilets are referred to as *baños* and men should follow the signs that read *hombres*, *caballeros*, *señores*, or *varones* and women *mujeres*, *damas*, or *señoras*.

Tour Operators and Travel Agents

Argentina

Swan Turismo, Cerrito 822, 5th, 6th, and 9th floors, Buenos Aires. Tel: (011) 4129 7926, www.swanturismo.com.ar. Long-established and high-quality specialist travel agency that organizes trips to a variety of destinations throughout the country. **Eurotur**, Viamonte 486, Buenos Aires. Tel: (011) 4312 6077/8, www.eurotur.com. Tours, transportation, and accommodations throughout Argentina for individuals and groups.

Provincial Tourist Offices

Each province in Argentina has its own tourist office in Buenos Aires where experts on the area can answer questions about your trip and provide you with relevant reading materials.
Buenos Aires: Av. Callao 237. Tel: (011) 4371 3587. Mon–Fri 9am–3pm.
Catamarca: Av. Córdoba 2080. Tel: (011) 4374 6891. Mon–Fri 9am–4pm.
Chaco: Av. Callao 322. Tel: (011) 4372 5209. Mon–Fri 10am–4pm.
Chubut: Sarmiento 1172. Tel: (011) 4382 8126. Mon–Fri 10am–4pm.
Córdoba: Av. Callao 232. Tel: (011) 4373 4277. Mon–Fri 10am–5pm.
Corrientes: San Martín 333, 4th Floor. Tel: (011) 4394 0859. Mon–Fri 10am–4pm.
Entre Ríos: Suipacha 844. Tel: (011) 4328 9327. Mon–Fri 10am–4pm.
Formosa: H. Yrigoyen 1429. Tel: (011) 4383 0721. Feb–Mar Mon–Fri 9am–3pm; closes at 1pm during the rest of the year.
Jujuy: Av. Santa Fe 967. Tel: (011) 4393 6096. Mon–Fri 10am–4pm.
La Pampa: Suipacha 246. Tel: (011) 4326 0511.

Mon–Fri 10am–4pm.
La Rioja: Callao 745. Tel: (011) 4815 1929. Mon–Fri 10am–4pm.
Mendoza: Av. Callao 445. Tel: (011) 4371 0835. Mon–Fri 10am–4pm.
Misiones: Santa Fe 989. Tel: (011) 4393 1211. Mon–Fri 10am–5pm.
Neuquén: Pte Perón 687, 1st Floor. Tel: (011) 4326 6812. Mon–Fri 10am–4pm.
Río Negro: Tucumán 1916. Tel: (011) 4371 7273. Mon–Fri 10am–4pm.
Salta: Av. Roque Saènz Pena 933. Tel: (011) 4326 2456. Mon–Fri 10am–5pm.
San Juan: Sarmiento 1251. Tel: (011) 4382 9241. Mon–Fri 10am–6pm.
Santa Cruz: Suipacha 1120. Tel: (011) 4325 3098. Mon–Fri 10am–4pm.
Santa Fe: Montevideo 373, 2nd Floor. Tel: (011) 4375 4635. Mon–Fri 10am–3.30pm.
Santiago del Estero: Florida 274. Tel: (011) 4322 1389. Mon–Fri 10am–6pm.
Tierra del Fuego: Santa Fe 919. Tel: (011) 4322 8855. Mon–Fri 10am–4pm.
Tucumán: Suipacha 140. Tel: (011) 4322 0564. Mon–Fri 10am–3pm.

English spoken; highly professional and recommended.
Eves Turismo, Tucumán 702, Buenos Aires. Tel: (011) 4393 6151, fax: (011) 4393 6411, www.eves.com. Helpful and efficient staff can advise you on travel both within Argentina and abroad.
Kallpa Tours, Roque Saenz Peña 811, 1st Floor, Office 3, Buenos Aires. Tel: (011) 4394 1860. Fax: (011) 4326 2500. www.kallpatour.com. Specializes in wine and cultural tours, trekking, and horseback riding.
ASATEJ, Florida 835, Floor 3, Office 320, Buenos Aires. Tel: (011) 4511 8700, www.asatej.com. One of the largest agencies, primarily aimed at students, but there's no age limit. Bright and cheerful office with noticeboard brimming with items for sale, travel news, and messages from travelers seeking companions.
Cosmopolitan Viajes, Av. 23 1515, Miramar. Tel: (02291) 420 571, www.cosmopolitanviajes.com.ar. Organizes trips to popular destinations in Argentina and neighboring countries.
Yaten, Av. Gregorio Ibáñez 150, Local 4, Cmte. Luis Piedra Buena, Santa Cruz, www.yaten.com.ar. Specializes in fishing trips.

Puna Expeditions, Agustín Usandivaras 230, 4400 Salta. Tel: (0387) 434 1875, www.punaexpeditions.com.ar. Local agency specializing in adventure tours and trekking trips in and around Salta.
Optar Tours, Contact Fernando Grajales at Mendoza Hostería, Puente del Inca, Mendoza. Tel: (02614) 380 480. Arranges eight-day trips to the foot of Aconcagua.
Rumbo Sur Excursiones, San Martín 350, Ushuaia. Tel: (02901) 422 275, www.rumbosur.com.ar. Runs catamaran trips to Isla de los Lobos, local penguin colonies, and Harberton.
Tolkeyen Servicios Marítimos, Muelle Turístico de Puerto de Ushuaia, Ushuaia. Tel: (09011) 433 080. Boat excursions to Isla de los Lobos and penguin colonies.

Australia

Adventure Associates, Level 7, 12–14 O'Connell Street, Sydney NSW 2000. Tel: (02) 8916 3000, www.adventureassociates.com. Established specialist tour operator, offering tailored trips to numerous destinations in Argentina.

TRANSPORTATION
ACCOMMODATIONS
EATING OUT
ACTIVITIES
A – Z
LANGUAGE

ABOVE: keeping cool in the sunshine.

UK

Journey Latin America, 12–13 Heathfield Terrace, London W4 4JE. Tel: (020) 8747 8315, www.journeylatinamerica.co.uk. Long-established company offering non-escorted trips throughout Latin America.

Dragoman Overland, Camp Green, Debenham, Stowmarket Suffolk. IP14 6LA. Tel: (01728) 861 133, www.dragoman.co.uk. Specializes in South American overland trips.

Jagged Globe, The Foundry Studios, 45 Mowbray Street, Sheffield, S3 8EN. Tel: (0845) 345 8848, www.jaggedglobe.co.uk. Specializes in climbing expeditions, including trips to Argentina and other South American countries.

Del Plata Travel, Quilley Brook, Pethybridge, Devon TQ13 9TG. Tel: (0800) 587 1381, www.delplata.co.uk. Special-interest travel agency which organizes tango, horseback riding, golf, and estancia trips.

US

Wilderness Travel, 1102 Ninth Street, Berkeley, CA 94710 Tel: 1 800 368 2794, www.wildernesstravel.com Organizes trips throughout Argentina and Chile, including walking trips through Patagonia.

Anglatin, 4800 SW Meadows Road, Suite 300 Lake Oswego, OR 97035, Tel: (503) 534 3720, www.anglatin.com Specialized travel agency offering trips to destinations throughout Latin America.

Quark Expeditions, 1019 Post Road, Darien, CT 06820. Tel: (0203) 656 0499, www.quarkexpeditions.com. A wide range of fully inclusive cruises

from Ushuaia to Antartica and the South Atlantic Islands.

Tourist Information Offices

Secretaría de Turismo de la Nación, Av. Santa Fe 883, Ground Floor, Buenos Aires. Mon–Fri 9am–5pm. Tel: (011) 4312 2232, www.turismo.gov.ar. The Argentine state tourist board.
Administración de Parques Nacionales
Av. Santa Fe 690, Buenos Aires. Mon–Fri 10am–5pm. Tel: (011) 4311 0303, www.parquesnacionales.gov.ar. Provides information on Argentina's many national parks.

Weights and Measures

The metric system is used to calculate distances and weights.

What to Wear

Many Argentines complain about the heat and humidity during the summer months (Nov–Mar), so you'll be most comfortable in light cotton clothing. Argentines are famous for their elegance and style so you may feel out of place and get the odd evil stare if you do not make an effort to dress elegantly, especially when out for dinner in a hotel or restaurant.

In winter (June–Sept) Argentina does get rather cold and rainy. Warm clothing is recommended. If visiting the glaciers in the south, prepare for extreme cold weather. Layers and waterproof jackets are essential.

During the summer, the north of the country is one of the hottest parts of Latin America, so it is advisable to take plenty of sun cream with you and to wear a brimmed hat to stay cool.

Laundry services are usually readily available, especially since many people do not own washing machines. Self-service places are unheard of: you leave your laundry and collect it when it has been cleaned. Laverap is a nationwide laundry chain which is very dependable. Some of them also do dry cleaning. Laundry is either charged by weight or itemized; either way going outside of your hotel will be more economical.

Wheelchair Access

Efforts have been made to make buildings more accessible to wheelchair users, such as the recent introduction of ramps in larger cities, but many pavements are still in a bad condition. Very few of the *colectivos* (buses) are *super-bajo*

(ultra low), and the Subte is almost impossible to access. Outside of the cities, finding facilities for the disabled is a hit-and-miss affair. Major tourist attractions like Iguazú Falls have made some notable improvements, such as the introduction of new ramps and catwalks, making the vast majority of the falls area accessible to disabled travelers.

A few companies specialize in transport and trips for disabled passengers. **QRV Transportes Especiales**, tel: (011) 4306 6635, run adapted minibuses for wheelchair users, equipped with microphones and guides. A standard journey within the capital costs around US$6. The hostel associations, **Red Argentina de Albergues Juveniles**, Florida 835, 3rd floor, Buenos Aires, and the **Asociación Argentina de Albergues de la Juventud**, Talchahuano 214, 2nd floor, Buenos Aires, can provide information on access.

Women Travelers

Women travelers shouldn't experience any problems in Argentina, although they are likely to receive plenty of male attention. While some may find this attention annoying, it is unlikely to ever be aggressive. The *piropo*, a flattering comment made in the street, traditionally made by a man to a woman, has now become something of a national custom. This is often little more than a whistle, although the more poetic may declare their undying love for you whilst passing you in the street.

L ANGUAGE

UNDERSTANDING THE LANGUAGE

General

Of the many versions of Spanish in South America, the Argentine version is amongst the most difficult to understand. However, it is much better to know a little Spanish when you arrive. English might be spoken at major hotels and by quite a few Argentines in Buenos Aires, but don't count on it outside of the capital.

Pronunciation and Grammar Tips

Argentines tend to use a local vocabulary with little resemblance to classical Spanish, while the local accent imposes a soft "j" sound on the "ll" and "y" and most people speak very rapidly without enunciating clearly. At the same time, when using the second person familiar, Argentines use the form "vos" instead of the more common "tú." (Note also that in Latin American Spanish the plural form of you is "ustedes" rather than "vosotros," as used in Spain.) The verb form used with "vos" places the accent on the last, rather than the penultimate syllable (for example, "¿que hacÉs?" instead of "¿quÉ hAces?" – what are you doing?). Television newsreaders are the only exception, although here too the Italianate accent also prevails.

Language Schools

Argentina is not the ideal place to learn Spanish, because of the linguistic idiosyncracies explained above. (The place which is best value for classes, as well as best for understanding, is probably Quito, Ecuador if you are considering further travel in South America.)

Language schools, apart from advertised private tuition (see the *Buenos Aires Herald*, especially on Sunday), include the ILEE and CEDIC, both of which also offer accommodations. These and other main private language schools, including Berlitz, offer tailor-made individual courses. Berlitz also offers phrasebooks and audio CDs that are worthwhile for beginners. Some well-known language schools in Buenos Aires are:

Berlitz Language Centers
Av. de Mayo 847
Tel: (011) 4342 0202
www.berlitz.com
CEDIC
Reconquista 715, 11th Floor/"E"
Av. de Mayo 847
Tel: (011) 4312 1016
www.cedic.com.ar
ILEE
Av. Callao 339, 3rd Floor
Tel/Fax: (011) 4782 7173
www.argentinailee.com

It is not essential for foreign speakers to use the correct form of address, i.e. formal or informal, or even the correct masculine or feminine conjugations, as long as you can make yourself understood. Many travelers learn Spanish to the "present tense" stage and manage very well on this alone. However, in order to be well received in Argentina, there are a few things worth remembering. Upon meeting someone, whether they be a taxi driver or a long-lost uncle, you always use the greeting, *Buendía* (Good morning) or *Buenas tardes* (Good afternoon/evening). It is then appropriate to wait for the response before continuing your conversation. A woman is addressed as Señora, a girl or young woman as Señorita, and a man as Señor.

Basics

Yes *Sí*
No *No*
Thank you *Gracias*
You're welcome *De nada/Por nada*
Okay *Está bien*
Please *Por favor*
Excuse me (to get attention) *¡Perdón!/¡Por favor!*
Excuse me (to get through a crowd) *¡Permiso!*
Excuse me (sorry) *Perdóneme*
Wait a minute! *¡Un momento!*
Please help me (formal) *Por favor, ayúdame*
Certainly *¡Claro!/¡Claro que sí!/¡Por cierto!*
Can I help you? (formal) *¿Puedo ayudarle?*
Can you show me...? *¿Puede mostrarme...?*
I'm lost *Estoy perdido(a)*
I'm sorry *Lo siento*
I don't know *No sé*
I don't understand *No entiendo*
Do you speak English/French/German? (formal) *¿Habla inglés/francés/alemán?*
Could you speak more slowly, please? *¿Puede hablar más despacio, por favor?*
Could you repeat that, please? *¿Puede repetirlo, por favor?*
here/there *aquí (place where), acá (motion to)/allí, allá, ahí (near you)*
What? *¿Qué?/¿Cómo?*
When? *¿Cuándo?*
Why? *¿Por qué?*
Where? *¿Dónde?*
Who? *¿Quién(es)?*
How? *¿Cómo?*
Which? *¿Cuál?*
How much/how many? *¿Cuánto?/¿Cuántos?*
Do you have...? *¿Hay...?*
How long? *¿Cuanto tiempo?*

TRANSPORTATION · ACCOMMODATIONS · EATING OUT · ACTIVITIES · A – Z · LANGUAGE

Big, bigger *Grande, más grande*
Small, smaller
Chico, mas chico
I want.../I would like.../I need...
Quiero.../Quisiera.../Necesito...
**Where is the lavatory
(men's/women's)?**
*¿Dónde está el baño
(de caballeros/de damas)?*
Which way is it to...?
¿Como se va a...?

Greetings

Hello! *¡Hola!*
Hello *Buenos días*
Good afternoon/night
Buenas tardes/noches
Goodbye/see you later
Chau/¡Adios!/Hasta luego
My name is... *Me llamo...*
What is your name? (formal)
¿Cómo se llama usted?
Mr/Miss/Mrs
Señor/Señorita/Señora
Pleased to meet you
¡Encantado(a)!/Mucho gusto
**I am English/American/Canadian/
Irish/Scottish/Australian**
*Soy inglés(a)/norteamericano(a)/
canadiense/irlandés(a)/
escocés(a)/australiano(a)*
Do you speak English? (formal)
¿Habla inglés?
How are you? (formal/informal)
¿Cómo está? ¿Qué tal?
Fine, thanks *Muy bien, gracias*
See you later *Hasta luego*
Take care (informal) *¡Cuídate!*

Telephone Calls

The area code *El código de área*
Where can I buy telephone cards?
*¿Dónde puedo comprar tarjetas
telefónicas?*
**May I use your telephone to make
a local call?** *¿Puedo usar su teléfono
para hacer una llamada local?*
Of course you may *¡Claro!*
Hello (on the phone) *¡Hola!*
May I speak to...? *¿Puedo hablar
con... (name), por favor?*
Sorry, he/she isn't in
Lo siento, no se encuentra
Can he/she call you back?
¿Puede devolver la llamada?
Yes, he/she can reach me at...
*Sí, él/ella puede llamarme a
[number]*
I'll try again later
Voy a intentar más tarde
Can I leave a message?
¿Puedo dejar un mensaje?
Please tell him/her I called
Por favor avisarle que llamé
Hold on *Un momento, por favor*
Can you speak up, please?
*¿Puede hablar más fuerte,
por favor?*

In the Hotel

Do you have a vacant room?
¿Tiene una habitación disponible?
I have a reservation
Tengo una reserva
I'd like... *Quisiera...*
**a single/double (with double bed)/
a room with twin beds**
*una habitación individual
(sencilla)/una habitación
matrimonial/una habitación doble*
for one night/two nights
por una noche/dos noches
**ground floor/first floor/top floor
room** *una habitación en la planta
baja/en el primer piso/ en el
último piso*
with a sea view *con vista al mar*
**Does the room have a private
bathroom or shared bathroom?**
*¿Tiene la habitación baño privado
o baño compartido?*
Does it have hot water?
¿Tiene agua caliente?
**Could you show me another room,
please?** *¿Puede mostrarme otra
habitación, por favor?*
Is it a quiet room?
¿Es una habitación tranquila?
**What time do you close (lock)
the doors?**
¿A qué hora se cierran las puertas?
I would like to change rooms
Quisiera cambiar la habitación
**This room is too noisy/hot/cold/
small** *Esta habitación es demasiado
ruidosa/caliente/fría/pequeña*
How much is it?
¿Cuánto cuesta?/¿Cuánto sale?
**Does the price include tax/
breakfast/meals/drinks?**
*¿El precio incluye el impuesto/
desayuno/comidas/bebidas?*
**Do you accept credit cards/
traveler's checks/dollars?**
*¿Se aceptan tarjetas de crédito/
cheques de viajeros/dólares?*
**What time is breakfast/
lunch/dinner?** *¿A qué hora es el
desayuno/almuerzo/la cena?*
Please wake me at...
Favor despertarme a...
Come in! *¡Pase!, ¡Adelante!*
I'd like to pay the bill now, please
*Quisiera cancelar la cuenta ahora,
por favor*

bath/bathroom *el baño*
dining room *el comedor*
elevator/lift *el ascensor*
key *la llave*
push/pull *empuje/tire*
safety deposit box *la caja de
seguridad*
soap *el jabón*
shampoo *el champú*
shower *la ducha*
toilet paper *el papel higiénico*
towel *la toalla*

In the Restaurant

I'd like to book a table *Quisiera
reservar una mesa, por favor*
Do you have a table for...?
¿Tiene una mesa para...?
I have a reservation
Tengo una reserva
breakfast/lunch/dinner
desayuno/almuerzo/cena
I'm a vegetarian *Soy vegetariano(a)*
Is there a vegetarian dish?
¿Hay un plato vegetariano?
May we have the menu? *¿Puede
traernos la carta (or el menú)?*
wine list *la carta de vinos*
What would you recommend?
¿Qué recomienda?
home-made *casero(a)*
fixed-price menu *el menú fijo*
special of the day
plato del día/sugerencia del chef
The meal was very good
La comida fue muy buena
waiter *mozo*
main course *segundo/plato
principal*
What would you like to drink?
¿Qué quiere tomar?
coffee... *un café*
with milk *con leche*
strong *fuerte*
small/large *pequeño/grande*
without sugar *sin azúcar*
tea... *té*
with lemon/milk *con limón/leche*
herbal tea *té de manzanilla*
hot chocolate *chocolate caliente*
fresh orange juice
jugo de naranja natural
orangeade *naranjada*
soft drink *gaseosa*
mineral water (still/carbonated)
agua mineral (sin gas/con gas)
with/without ice *con/sin hielo*
cover charge *precio del cubierto*
minimum consumption
consumo mínimo
a bottle/half a bottle
una botella/media botella
a glass of red/white/rosé wine *una
copa de vino tinto/rosado/blanco*
beer *una cerveza*
Is service included?
¿Incluye el servicio?
I need a receipt, please
Necesito un recibo, por favor
Keep the change
Está bien/Quédese con el vuelto
Cheers! *¡Salud!*

Entremeses/Primer Plato
(First Course)

sopa/crema *soup/cream soup*
sopa de ajo *garlic soup*
sopa de cebolla *onion soup*
ensalada mixta *mixed salad*
ensalada de palta con tomate
avocado and tomato salad
pan con ajo *garlic bread*

La Carne (Meat)

crudo raw
jugoso(a) rare
término medio medium rare
a punto medium
bien hecho well done
a la brasa/a la parrilla charcoal grilled
a la plancha grilled
al horno baked
ahumado(a) smoked
alas wings
albóndigas meat balls
asado(a)/horneado(a) roasted
aves poultry
cerdo/chancho/puerco pork
chivito goat
chorizo Spanish-style sausage
chuleta chop
conejo rabbit
cordero lamb
costillas ribs
empanizado(a) breaded
frito(a) fried
guisado(a) stewed
hamburguesa hamburger
hígado de res beef liver
jamón ham
lengua tongue
lomito tenderloin
milanesa breaded and fried thin cut of meat
morcilla blood sausage
muslo thigh
pato duck
pavo turkey
pechuga breast
pernil leg of pork
piernas legs
pollo chicken
rebozado(a) batter fried
riñones kidneys
salchichas/panchos sausages or hot dogs
ternera veal
chicharrón de pollo chicken cut up in small pieces and deep fried

Pescado/Mariscos (Fish/Seafood)

almejas clams
anchoa anchovy
atún tuna
bacalao cod
calamares squid
camarones shrimp
cangrejo crab
centolla kingcrab
langosta lobster
langostinos prawns
lenguado sole or flounder
mariscos shellfish
mejillones mussels
mero grouper, sea bass
ostras oysters
pulpo octopus
salmón salmon
sardinas sardines
trucha trout
vieiras scallops

Vegetales (Vegetables)

ajo garlic
alcaucil artichoke
arvejas peas
batata sweet potato
berenjena eggplant/aubergine
brócoli broccoli
calabaza pumpkin or yellow squash
cebolla onion
chauchas green beans
choclo corn (on the cob)
coliflor cauliflower
espárrago asparagus
espinaca spinach
hongos, champiñones mushrooms
lechuga lettuce
papa potato
pepino cucumber
pimentón green (bell) pepper
porotos Lima beans
puerro leeks
remolacha beets/beetroot
repollo cabbage
zanahorias carrots
zapallo yellow squash
zapallito green squash
zapallito largo zucchini/courgette

Frutas (Fruit)

banana banana
palta avocado
plátano green banana
cereza cherry
ciruela plum
dátil date
durazno peach
frambuesa raspberry
frutilla strawberry
guayaba guava
higo fig
papaya papaya
lima lime
limón lemon
mandarina tangerine
manzana apple
melón cantelope/melon
mora blackberry
naranja orange
parchita passion fruit
sandía watermelon
pera pear
piña pineapple
pomelo grapefruit
uvas grapes

Miscellaneous

arroz rice
azúcar sugar
empanada savory turnover
fideos spaghetti
huevos (revueltos/fritos/hervidos) eggs (scrambled/fried/boiled)
ice cream helado
manteca butter
margarina margarine
mermelada jam
mostaza mustard
pan bread
pan integral wholewheat bread
pan tostado/tostadas toast

pimienta negra black pepper
queso cheese
sal salt
salsa picante spicy sauce
sandwich sandwich
panceta bacon
tortilla omelet

Tourist Attractions/ Terms

aguas termales hot springs
artesanía handicrafts
campamento campsite
capilla chapel
castillo/fuerte fort
catedral cathedral
cerro hill
cervecería beer hall/pub
club nocturno nightclub
comunidad indígena indigenous community
convento convent
disco/discoteca boliche
galería gallery
glaciar glacier
iglesia church
isla island
jardín botánico botanical garden
laguna lagoon
lago lake
mar sea
mercado market
mirador viewpoint
montaña mountain
monumento monument
Océano Atlántico Atlantic Ocean
oficina de turismo tourist office
parque infantil playground
parque park
pico (mountain) peak
pileta swimming pool
playa beach
plaza town square
postál postcard
puente bridge
quebrada stream
río river
ruinas ruins
teleférico cable car
torre tower
zona colonial colonial zone
zoológico zoo

Road Signs

autopista freeway
bajada/subida peligrosa dangerous downgrade/ incline
calle sin salida dead-end street
calle flechada/de una sola mano one-way street
carril derecho right lane
carril izquierdo left lane
carretera highway, road
gomería tire repair shop
cede el paso yield/give way
circunvalación by-pass road/ ringroad

conserve su derecha
keep to the right
conserve su carril
do not change lanes
cruce de ferrocarril (sin señal)
railway crossing (without signal)
despacio *slow*
desvío *detour*
distribuidor *freeway interchange*
doble vía *two-way traffic*
Enciende luces en el túnel
Turn on lights in the tunnel
encrucijada *crossroads*
entrada prohibida *no entry*
estacionamiento *parking lot*
fuera de servicio *not in service*
hundimiento *sunken road*
intercomunal *interconnecting freeway between two close towns*
no estacione/prohibido estacionar
no parking
no gire en U *no U-turn*
no hay paso, vía cerrada
road blocked
sin salida *no exit*
no pare *no stopping here*
no toque la bocina *no horn honking*
¡ojo! *watch out!*
pare *stop*
paso de ganado *cattle crossing*
paso de peatones *pedestrian crossing*
peaje *toll booth*
peligro *danger*
pendiente fuerte, curva fuerte *steep hill, sharp curve*
rotonda *traffic circle/roundabout*
lomo de burro, reductor de velocidad, obstáculos en la vía, muros en la vía, policia acostada
speed bump(s)
resbaladizo al humedecerse
slippery when wet
ruta *highway*
salida *exit*
semáforo *traffic light*
sólo tránsito local *local traffic only*
tome precauciones *caution*
un solo carril *single lane*
velocidad controlada
speed controlled or restricted

vía en reparación/en recuperación
road under repair
zona de construcción
construction zone
zona de derrumbes *landslide zone*
zona de niebla (neblina) *fog zone*
zona de remolque *tow zone*
zona escolar *school zone*
zona militar *military zone*

Driving

Where can I rent a car?
¿Dónde puedo alquiler un coche?
Is mileage included?
¿Está incluido el kilometraje?
comprehensive insurance
seguros comprensivos
spare tire/jack/emergency triangle *goma de repuesto/ gato/triángulo de emergencia*
Where is the registration document?
¿Dónde está el carnet de circulación?
Does the car have an alarm?
¿El coche tiene alarma?
a road map/a city map
un mapa vial/plano de la ciudad
How do I get to...?
¿Cómo se llega a...?
Turn right/left *Cruzar (or girar, doblar) hacia la derecha/izquierda*
at the next corner/street
en la próxima esquina/calle
Go straight ahead *Siga derecho*
You are on the wrong road
Esta no es la calle
Please show me where I am on the map *Por favor, indíqueme dónde estoy en el mapa*
Where can I find...?
¿Dónde hay...?
Where is the nearest...?
¿Dónde está el/la... más cerca?
How long does it take to get there? *¿Cuánto tiempo lleva para llegar?*
driver's license
licencia de conducir/manejar
service/gasoline station *estación de servicio*

My car won't start
Mi coche no arranca
My car is overheating
Mi coche está recalentando
My car has broken down
Mi coche se rompió/no anda
tow truck *una grúa*
Where can I find a car repair shop?
¿Dónde hay un taller mecánico?
Can you check the...?
¿Puede revisar/chequear...?
There's something wrong with the... *Hay un problema con...*
oil/water/air *aceite/agua/aire*
brake fluid/light bulb *líquido de frenos/bombita*
trunk/hood/door/window
maletín/capó/puerta/ventana

Traveling

airline *línea aérea*
airport *aeropuerto*
arrivals/departures
llegadas/salidas
bus stop
parada (de colectivo/micro)
boat dock for small boats/large boats *embarcadero/muelle*
bus terminal *terminal de pasajeros*
bus *colectivo* (urban), *micro* (long distance)
car *coche/automóvil*
car rental *alquiler de coche*
connection *conexión*
ferry *ferry*
first class/second class
primera clase/segunda clase, clase de turista
flight *vuelo*
luggage, bag(s) *equipaje, valija(s)*
Next stop please (for buses)
La próxima parada, por favor
one-way ticket *boleto de ida*
platform *el andén*
round-trip, return ticket
boleto de ida y vuelta
sailboat, yacht *velero, yate*
ship *barco*
subway *Metro/subterráneo/Subte*
taxi *taxi*

Conversion Tables

LENGTH		WEIGHT		VOLUME	
Inches	**Centimeters**	**Pounds**	**Kilograms**	**US Pints**	**Liters**
1	2.54	1	0.45	1	0.47
2	5.08	2	0.90	2	0.95
3	7.62	3	1.36	3	1.42
6	15.24	4	1.81	4	1.89
9	22.86	5	2.27		
		6	2.72	**US Gallons**	**Liters**
Feet	**Centimeters**	7	3.18	1	3.78
1	30.48	8	3.63	2	7.57
2	60.96	9	4.08	3	11.36
3	91.44	10	4.53	5	18.93
6	182.88	20	9.07	10	37.85
9	274.32	50	22.68	20	75.71
12	365.76	100	45.36	50	189.27

Terms for Directions

a la derecha *on the right*
a la izquierda *on the left*
abajo *under*
adelante de *in front of*
al lado de *beside*
alrededor de *around*
arriba/abajo *above/below*
atrás de *behind*
avenida (Av) *avenue*
calle *street*
cerca de *near*
cruce con/con
at the junction of (two streets)
cruce hacia la izquierda/la
derecha *turn to the left/right*
derecho *straight ahead*
edificio (Edif) *building*
en frente de/frente de/frente a
in front of
en *in, on, at*
en la parte de atrás
in the rear area (as in behind
a building)
encima de *on top of*
entre *between*
esquina (Esq) *corner*
PH – penthouse/PB – planta baja/
PA – planta alta/mezanina/sótano
penthouse/ground floor/upper floor
(of two)/mezzanine/basement
residencia (Res) *small pension*
transversal(es) *crossroad(s)*
una cuadra *a block*

Airport or Travel Agency

customs and immigration
aduana y migraciones
travel/tour agency *agencia de*
viajes/de turismo
ticket *boleto pasaje*
I would like to purchase a ticket
for... *Quisiera comprar un boleto*
(pasaje) para...
When is the next/last flight/
departure for...? *¿Cuándo es el*
próximo/último vuelo/para...?
What time does the
plane/bus/boat/ferry
[leave/return?] *¿A qué hora*
[sale/regresa] el avión/el autobús/
la lancha/el ferry?
What time do I have to be at the
airport? *¿A qué hora tengo que*
estar en el aeropuerto?
Is the tax included?
¿Se incluye el impuesto?
What is included in the price?
¿Qué está incluido en el precio?
departure tax
el impuesto de salida
I would like a seat in first class/
business class/tourist class
Quisiera un asiento en primera
clase/ejecutivo/clase de turista
lost-luggage office
oficina de reclamos
on time *a tiempo*

late *atrasado*
I need to change my ticket
Necesito cambiar mi boleto
How long is the flight?
¿Cuánto tiempo dura el vuelo?
Is this seat taken?
¿Está ocupado este asiento?
Which is the stop closest to...?
¿Cuál es la parada más cerca de...?
Could you please advise me when
we reach/the stop for...?
¿Por favor, puede avisarme
cuando llegamos a/a la parada
para...?
Is this the stop for...?
¿Es ésta la parada para...?

Emergencies

Help! *¡Socorro! ¡Auxilio!*
Stop! *¡Pare!*
Watch out! *¡Cuidado! ¡Ojo!*
I've had an accident *He tenido un*
accidente/Sufrí un accidente
Call a doctor *Llame a un médico*
Call an ambulance
Llame una ambulancia
Call the... *Llame a...*
...police
la policía (for minor accidents)
...transit police *la policía de tránsito*
(for traffic accidents)
the fire brigade *los bomberos*
This is an emergency, where is a
telephone? *Esto es una emergencia.*
¿Dónde hay un teléfono?
Where is the nearest hospital?
¿Dónde queda el hospital más
cercano?
I want to report an assault/
a robbery
Quisiera reportar un asalto/
un robo
Thank you very much for your
help *Muchísimas gracias por*
su ayuda

Health

shift duty pharmacy
farmacia de turno
hospital/clinic *hospital/clínica*
I need a doctor/dentist *Necesito un*
médico/dentista (odontólogo)
I don't feel well *Me siento mal*
I am sick *Estoy enfermo(a)*
It hurts here *Duele aquí*
I have a headache/stomachache/
cramps *Tengo dolor de cabeza/de*
estómago/de vientre
I feel dizzy *Me siento mareado(a)*
Do you have (something for)...?
¿Tiene (algo para)...?
a cold/flu *resfrío/gripe*
diarrhea *diarrea*
constipation *estreñimiento*
fever *fiebre*
aspirin *aspirina*
heartburn *acidez*
insect/mosquito bites
picaduras de insectos/mosquitos

Shopping

What time do you open/close?
¿A qué hora abre/cierra?
Open/closed *Abierto/cerrado*
I'd like... *Quisiera...*
I'm just looking *Sólo estoy*
mirando, gracias
How much does it cost?
¿Cuánto cuesta/sale?
It doesn't fit *No queda bien*
Do you have it in another color?
¿Tiene en otro color?
Do you have it in another size?
¿Tiene en otro talle/número
(clothing)/tamaño (objects)?
smaller/larger
más chico/más grande
It's too expensive
Es demasiado caro
Do you have something less
expensive?
¿Tiene algo más económico?
Where do I pay for it?
¿Dónde está la caja?
Would you like anything else?
¿Quiere algo más?
A little more/less
Un poco más/menos
That's enough/no more
Está bien/nada más

Shops and Services

antiques shop *antigüedades*
bakery *panadería*
bank *banco*
barber shop
peluquería para hombres
bookstore *librería*
butcher shop *carnicería*
cake shop *pastelería*
currency exchange bureau
casa de cambio
delicatessen *delicatessen*
department store *tienda por*
departamentos
fish shop *pescadería*
florist *florista*
fruit shop *frutería*
hairdressers, beauty salon
peluquería, salón de belleza
hardware store *ferretería*
shopping center, centro comercial
mall, shopping
jewelers *joyería*
laundromat *lavadero*
library *biblioteca*
liquor store *licorería*
market *mercado*
newsstand *kiosco*
post office *correos*
shoe repair shop/shoe store
zapatero/zapatería
small grocery store *almacén*
small shop *tienda*
stationers *papelería*
supermarket *supermercado,*
autoservicio
toy store *juguetería*
vegetable shop *verdulería*

Colors

light/dark *claro/oscuro*
red *rojo/colorado*
yellow *amarillo*
blue *azul*
brown *marrón*
black *negro*
white *blanco*
cream *color crema*
beige *beige*
green *verde*
wine *bordó*
gray *gris*
orange *naranja*
pink *rosa*
purple *púrpura*
silver *plateado*
gold *dorado*

Numbers

1 *uno*
2 *dos*
3 *tres*
4 *cuatro*
5 *cinco*
6 *seis*
7 *siete*
8 *ocho*
9 *nueve*
10 *diez*
11 *once*
12 *doce*
13 *trece*
14 *catorce*
15 *quince*
16 *dieciséis*
17 *diecisiete*
18 *dieciocho*
19 *diecinueve*
20 *veinte*
21 *veintiuno*
21 *veintidos*
25 *veinticinco*
30 *treinta*
40 *cuarenta*
50 *cincuenta*
60 *sesenta*
70 *setenta*
80 *ochenta*
90 *noventa*
100 *cien*
101 *ciento uno*
102 *ciento dos*
200 *doscientos*
300 *trescientos*
400 *cuatrocientos*
500 *quinientos*
600 *seiscientos*
700 *setecientos*
800 *ochocientos*
900 *novecientos*

1,000 *mil*
2,000 *dos mil*
10,000 *diez mil*
100,000 *cien mil*
1,000,000 *un millón*
1,000,000,000 *mil millones*

NOTE: In Spanish, in numbers, commas are used where decimal points would be used in English and vice versa. For example, in English: $19.50 = in Spanish: $19,50; 1,000 m = 1.000 m; and 9.5% = 9,5%.

Days and Dates

morning *la mañana*
afternoon *la tarde*
late afternoon *la tardecita*
dusk *atardecer*
evening *la noche*
dawn *la madrugada*
sunrise *el amanecer*
sunset *la puesta del sol*
last night *anoche*
yesterday *ayer*
today *hoy*
tonight *esta noche*
tomorrow *mañana*
tomorrow morning *mañana por la mañana*
the day after tomorrow *pasado mañana*
now *ahora*
early *temprano*
late *tarde*
a minute *un minuto*
an hour *una hora*
half an hour *media hora*
a day *un día*
a week *una semana*
a month *un mes*
a year *un año*
weekday *día laboral*
weekend *fin de semana*
holiday *día feriado*

Months

January *enero*
February *febrero*
March *marzo*
April *abril*
May *mayo*
June *junio*
July *julio*
August *agosto*
September *septiembre*
October *octubre*
November *noviembre*
December *diciembre*

Days of the Week

Monday *lunes*
Tuesday *martes*
Wednesday *miércoles*
Thursday *jueves*
Friday *viernes*
Saturday *sábado*
Sunday *domingo*

Seasons

spring *primavera*
summer *verano*
fall, autumn *otoño*
winter *invierno*

Time

at nine o'clock *a las nueve*
at a quarter past ten *a las diez y cuarto*
at half past one/one thirty *a la una y media*
at a quarter to two *a las dos menos cuarto*
at midday/noon *a mediodía*
at midnight *a medianoche*
it is five past three *son las tres y cinco*
it is twenty five past seven *son las siete y veinticinco*
it is ten to eight *son las ocho menos diez*
in five minutes *en cinco minutos*
does it take long? *¿tarda mucho?*

NOTE: Times are usually followed by *de la mañana* (in the morning) or *de la tarde* (in the afternoon). Transport schedules are often given using the 24-hour clock.

Feedback

We do our best to ensure the information in our books is as accurate and up-to-date as possible. The books are updated on a regular basis, using local contacts, who painstakingly add, amend, and correct as required. However, some mistakes and omissions are inevitable and we are ultimately reliant on our readers to put us in the picture. We would welcome your feedback on any details related to your experiences using the book "on the road." Maybe we recommended a hotel that you liked (or another that you didn't), as well as interesting new attractions, or facts and figures you have found out about the country itself. The more details you can give us (particularly with regard to addresses, e-mails, and telephone numbers), the better. We will acknowledge all contributions, and we'll offer an Insight Guide to the best letters received.

Please write to us at:
Insight Guides
PO Box 7910
London SE1 1WE
United Kingdom
Or send e-mail to:
insight@apaguide.co.uk

FURTHER READING

History

Argentina: 1516–1987 by David Rock. Univ. of California Press, 1988. Good overview of Argentine history.
Buenos Aires: A Cultural and Literary Companion by Jason Wilson. Signal Books, 1999. A brilliant description of the history and cultural life of the Argentine capital.
Gauchos and the Vanishing Frontier by Richard W. Slatta. Univ. of Nebraska Press, 1992. Fascinating account of the cowboys who roamed the Pampas hundreds of years before the Wild West existed.
The Voyage of the Beagle by Charles Darwin. Penguin, 1989. Shortened journal of Darwin's five-year voyage around the world, covering natural history and civil war in Argentina. A classic.
The Real Odessa: Smuggling the Nazis to Perón's Argentina by Uki Goni. Granta, 2002.

Fiction

Labyrinths by Jorge Luis Borges. New Directions Pub., 1988. Short stories and other writings from one of the most original modern writers.
On Heroes and Tombs by Ernesto Sabato. David R. Godine, 1981. Complex and sad tale of a tormented love affair.
Kiss of the Spider Woman by Manuel Puig. Vintage books, 1991. Story of two men imprisoned under the dictatorship. Adapted into a film.
Blow-up and Other Stories by Julio Cortazar. Pantheon Modern Writers, 1987.
The Invention of Morel by Adolfo Bioy Casares. New York Review of Books Classics, 2003. 1940 novella of suspense and unlikely romance.

Travel Literature

Bad Times in Buenos Aires by Miranda France. Ecco, 1999. Personal and sometimes generalized overview of life in Buenos Aires through a foreigner's eyes.
Far Away and Long Ago; Birds of La Plata; Idle Days in Patagonia by W.H. Hudson. Everyman's Library, 1984.

Tales of the Pampas by W.H. Hudson. Creative Arts Book Co., 1979. Early classic novel.
In Patagonia by Bruce Chatwin. Picador, 1998. A combination of fact and fiction, beautifully written by one of the greatest travel writers.
Two Thousand Miles' Ride Through the Argentine Provinces by William MacCann. Ams Press. Reprint of 1853 historical account of the country and people.
Uttermost Part of the Earth: Indians of Tierra Del Fuego by E. Lucas Bridges. Dover pubs, 1988. A true story – a mix of biography and adventure.
The Drunken Forest by Gerald Durrell. Penguin, 1958. Searching for animals in Argentina's tropical north.

People

Santa Evita by Tomás Eloy Martínez. Vintage, 1997. A mix of fact and fiction about Argentina's most famous icon.
The Tango Singer by Tomás Eloy Martínez. Bloomsbury, 2006. The life and times of tango icon Carlos Gardel.
Hand of God: The Life of Diego Maradona by Jimmy Burns. Bloomsbury, 1996.
And Here the World Ends: The Life of an Argentinian Village by K.H. Ruggiero. Stanford Univ. Press, 1988.
Falkland People by Angela Wigglesworth. Paul and Co. Pub Consortium, 1992.

Arts and Crafts

Arts and Crafts of Argentina by A. Bassetti de Roca. 2001

Food and Wine

Argentina Cooks! by Shirley Lomax Brooks. Hippocrene Books, 2001. One of the few books covering Argentine cuisine, with recipes from the nine regions.
Wine Routes of Argentina by Alan Young. International Wine Academy, 1998. Guide to Argentine wines which follows an historical framework. Illustrated with detailed maps.

The Wines of Argentina, Chile, and Latin America by Christopher Fielden. Mitchell Beazley 2003.
Food and Drink in Argentina: A guide for Tourists and Residents by Dereck Foster and Richard Tripp. Aromas y Sabores, 2006.

Miscellaneous

Argentine Trout Fishing by William C. Leitch. Frank Amato Pubs, 1991. Detailed and entertaining, with color photographs.

Other Guides

Among nearly 200 companion books to this one are several guides highlighting destinations in this region. Titles include *Insight Guides* to *South America, Buenos Aires, Brazil, Rio de Janeiro, Peru, Chile, Ecuador & the Galápagos,* and *Venezuela,* and the *Berlitz Guide to Buenos Aires.*
Insight Guide: Amazon Wildlife vividly captures the flora and fauna of the world's greatest rainforest.

Films

Butch Cassidy and the Sundance Kid (Roy Hill, 1969). Starring Robert Redford and Paul Newman.
The Mission (Roland Joffe, 1986). Robert de Niro and Jeremy Irons as Jesuit priests in Argentina and Paraguay.
Evita (Alan Parker, 1997), starring Madonna.
Nine Queens (Fabián Bielinsky. 2000). Engaging thriller about two conmen on the streets of Buenos Aires.
The Motorcycle Diaries (Walter Salles, 2004) The story of how a young medical student sets out from Buenos Aires to discover Latin America: his name, Che Guevara.

ART & PHOTO CREDITS

*All photography by **EDUARDO GIL** except for the following:*

Jenny Acheson/Axiom 155
Peter Adams/Alamy back cover CL, spine, 366
Peter Adams/Jon Arnold Images back flap B, 185, 202
age fotostock/SuperStock 112/113, 271T
Arthur D'Arazien/SuperStock 346
Flora Bemporad 34/35, 36, 38, 39, 40, 41, 42/43, 44, 46, 47, 49, 50, 51, 53, 54, 55, 56, 57, 59, 60, 65, 77, 94, 146, 160, 170, 269, 292
Flora Bemporad/National Archives 58
Flora Bemporad/Witcomb Collection 147T
Don Boroughs 14, 62, 81, 83, 122, 125, 152T, 153T, 228, 302, 320/1
Brand X/SuperStock front flap B, 148L
Marcos Brindicci/Reuters/Corbis 163
Marcelo Brodsky/Focus back flap T, 154, 312
Roberto Bunge/PW 132/133, 238, 261, 267, 274, 276
Gustavo Calligaris/Focus 198T
Laurie Campbell/NHPA 281T, 295T, 298T
Marcelo Canevari 95
Anthony Cassidy/JAI/Corbis 126/127
Maria Cassinelli/Focus 196, 297
Roberto Cinti/PW 12/13, 18, 19, 21, 22, 23, 109, 242, 247, 250, 253, 254, 291, 294, 309L&R, 310, 314, 325
Chris Coe/Axiom 262
Tim Cuff/Alamy 6B
Jeff Curtes/Corbis 116
Pablo Corral V/Corbis 179
Pablo Rafael Cottescu 96, 114, 303, 311
Fridmar Damm/SIME/4Corners back cover TR, 149, 150
Keith Dannemiller/Corbis 363
Danita Delimont/Alamy 6T
DEPLiX/Alamy 123
Karl Eelmaa/Alamy 82
Chad Ehlers/Alamy 80
Keith Ellis 275T
Abbie Enoch/Travel Ink 93
Carlos Fadigati/Focus 97, 257, 264/265
Sindo Fariña/Focus 115
FoodPix/Alamy 351
Raymond Forbes/Superstock 344
David R. Frazier Photolibrary Inc/Alamy 197
Michel Friang/Alamy 8C
Su Garfinkle/Axiom 337
Glyn Genin 10/11
Carlos Goldin/Focus 308
Rae Goodall 322, 327, 328, 330
Thomas Goodall 329, 324, 325

Ximena Griscti/Alamy 356
Ximena Griscti/Superstock 338
Guacamole Films/OK Films/The Kobal Collection 183
Derek Hall 245, 251T, 279, 280
Robert Harding Picture Library/Alamy 353
Huw Hennessy 148T, 169T, 173T, 175, 180T, 181, 182T, 191T, 192, 192T, 193, 229, 236T, 237T, 238T, 270T, 274T, 278T, 310T, 312T, 313T
Jeremy Hoare/Alamy 147
Jeremy Hoare/Pictures Colour Library 27
Joseph Hooper 293
Dave G. Houser 4/5, 129, 164, 176, 178T, 182, 270, 330T
Max W. Hunn/SuperStock 202T
Intervision/Pictures Colour Library 171
Volkmar Janicke 33, 138, 246, 248, 251, 252, 315
Andre Jenny/Alamy 7B
Marcus Joly/Focus 233, 263
Christian Kapteyn/Alamy 173
Per Karlsson-BKWine.com/Alamy 7C, 130
Frederico B. Kirbus 105, 243
T. Kitchin & V. Hurst/NHPA 110
Frank Krahmer/zefa/Corbis 9T
Walter Kvaternik/Naturpress 304
Adrian Lascom/Alamy 166
Eric Lawrie 296, 299
Eduardo Lerke/Focus 61, 119, 194/195, 204T
Michael Lewis/Corbis 348, 359
Craig Lovell/Corbis 317
Luis Martin/Focus 32
G. Miles 245T, 248T, 249, 254T, 257T, 258, 259T, 260
Quique Kierszenbaum/Getty Images 72
Kimimasa Mayama/Reuters/Corbis 360
Michele Molinari/Alamy 9B
Kimball Morrison/South American Pictures 16/17, 273, 275, 277, 282, 305
Marion Morrison/South American Pictures 8T
Tony Morrison/South American Pictures 45, 108, 111, 169, 189, 214T, 364
Pablo Neidermayer/La Demasiada 7T
Arlette Neyens front flap T, 30, 78, 107, 144
Frank Nowikowski/South American Pictures 106, 178, 269T
Alex Ocampo/PW 37, 120/121, 153, 156T, 161, 172, 188, 208/209, 210, 212, 222, 223
Carlos A. Passera/PW 100/101, 102, 103, 104, 288, 306, 313, 331
Michael J. Pettypool 231
Susan Pierres 234, 235

Andrea Pistolesi/The Image Bank/Getty Images 184
Whit Richardson/Alamy 278
Gabriel Rojo/Nature Picture Library 239
Alfredo Sanchez/Focus 76, 226/227
Jorge Juan Schulte 24/25, 28, 31, 92, 240/241
Hugh Sitton/Zefa/Corbis 85
Eric Soder/NHPA 236
Hubert Stadler/Corbis 342
StockShot/Alamy 353
Keren Su/Corbis 8B
Homer Sykes/Alamy 9C
David Toase/Travel Ink 203
Topham Picturepoint 298, 307
Mireille Vautier 20, 26, 48, 73, 159T, 163T, 266, 281, 281T, 283, 286/287, 289, 324T, 326
Horacio Villalobos/Corbis 168
Westend61/Alamy 2/3
David Welna 159, 180
Martin Wendler/NHPA 237
Fulvio Zanettini/laif/Camera Press 162, 165

88/89: Jenny Acheson/Axiom 88BL; Chris Coe/Axiom 89CR; Pablo Corral Vega/Corbis 89BL; Eduardo Gil 88TL, 89TC, TR, CL; Bernhart Udo/Simephoto-4Corners Images 88CR; Horacio Villalobos/Corbis 88/89.
98/99: Chris Coe/Axiom 98CR; Abbie Enoch/Travel Ink 98/99TC, 98BR; Eduardo Gil 99TR, 99BR; Huw Hennessey 98TCR; Michael J Pettypool 98BL; Swerve/Alamy 99C; Mireille Vautier 98TL.
186/187: age footstock/Super-Stock 186CR; Eduardo Gil 186/187TC, 186TL, TR, BL, BR, 187TR, BL; Dave G. Houser 187CL, CR.
284/285: Bowman/Axiom 284CR; Andy Christodolo/Cephas 284/285TC; Chris Coe/Axiom 284TL, BR, 285TR, Huw Hennessey 284 BL, 285TCR, CL, BR.
318/319: Laurie Campbell/NHPA 319CR; Eduardo Gil 318TL, CR, BR, 319CL, BR; Derek Hall 318/319 TC; Tony Morrison/South American Pictures 319BL; Frank Nowikowski/South American Pictures 318TCR, BL, 319TR.

Book Production: Linton Donaldson
Cartographic Editor: Zoë Goodwin
Map Production: Colourmap Scanning Ltd
© 2007 Apa Publications GmbH & Co.
Verlag KG (Singapore branch)

INSIGHT GUIDES

The classic series that puts you in the picture

Alaska
Amazon Wildlife
American Southwest
Amsterdam
Argentina
Arizona & Grand Canyon
Asia's Best Hotels & Resorts
Asia, East
Asia, Southeast
Australia
Austria
Bahamas
Bali & Lombok
Baltic States
Bangkok
Barbados
Barcelona
Beijing
Belgium
Belize
Berlin
Bermuda
Boston
Brazil
Brittany
Bruges, Ghent & Antwerp
Brussels
Buenos Aires
Burgundy
Burma (Myanmar)
Cairo
California
California, Southern
Canada
Cape Town
Caribbean
Caribbean Cruises
Channel Islands
Chicago
Chile
China
Colorado
Continental Europe
Corsica
Costa Rica
Crete
Croatia
Cuba
Cyprus
Czech & Slovak Republic
Delhi, Jaipur & Agra
Denmark

Dominican Rep. & Haiti
Dublin
East African Wildlife
Eastern Europe
Ecuador
Edinburgh
Egypt
England
Finland
Florence
Florida
France
France, Southwest
French Riviera
Gambia & Senegal
Germany
Glasgow
Gran Canaria
Great Britain
Great Gardens of Britain
   & Ireland
Great Railway Journeys
   of Europe
Great River Cruises:
   Europe & the Nile
Greece
Greek Islands
Guatemala, Belize
   & Yucatán
Hawaii
Hong Kong
Hungary
Iceland
India
India, South
Indonesia
Ireland
Israel
Istanbul
Italy
Italy, Northern
Italy, Southern
Jamaica
Japan
Jerusalem
Jordan
Kenya
Korea
Laos & Cambodia
Las Vegas
Lisbon
London

Los Angeles
Madeira
Madrid
Malaysia
Mallorca & Ibiza
Malta
Mauritius Réunion
   & Seychelles
Mediterranean Cruises
Melbourne
Mexico
Miami
Montreal
Morocco
Moscow
Namibia
Nepal
Netherlands
New England
New Mexico
New Orleans
New York City
New York State
New Zealand
Nile
Normandy
North American &
   Alaskan Cruises
Norway
Oman & The UAE
Oxford
Pacific Northwest
Pakistan
Paris
Peru
Philadelphia
Philippines
Poland
Portugal
Prague
Provence
Puerto Rico
Rajasthan
Rio de Janeiro
Rome

Russia
St Petersburg
San Francisco
Sardinia
Scandinavia
Scotland
Seattle
Shanghai
Sicily
Singapore
South Africa
South America
Spain
Spain, Northern
Spain, Southern
Sri Lanka
Sweden
Switzerland
Sydney
Syria & Lebanon
Taipei
Taiwan
Tanzania & Zanzibar
Tenerife
Texas
Thailand
Tokyo
Toronto
Trinidad & Tobago
Tunisia
Turkey
Tuscany
Umbria
USA: The New South
USA: On The Road
USA: Western States
US National Parks: West
Utah
Venezuela
Venice
Vienna
Vietnam
Wales
Walt Disney World/Orlando
Washington, DC

 INSIGHT GUIDES

*The world's largest collection of
visual travel guides & maps*

INDEX

Numbers in italics refer to photographs

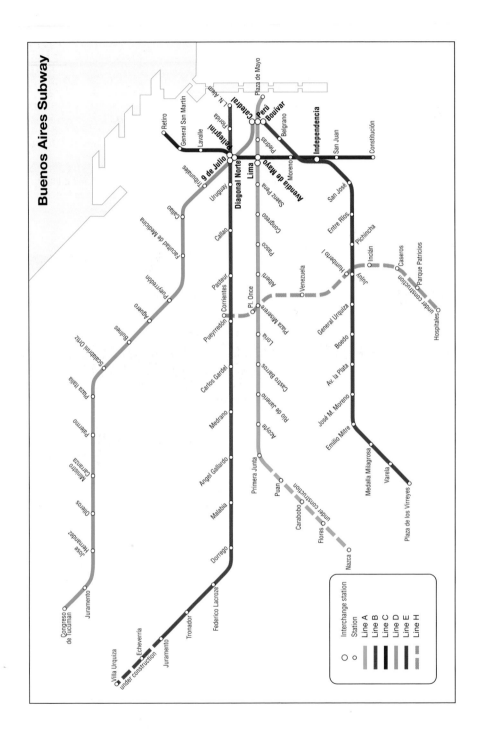

Buenos Aires Subway